STEEL PRODUCTION

STEEL PRODUCTION:
Processes, Products,
and Residuals

CLIFFORD S. RUSSELL
and WILLIAM J. VAUGHAN

PUBLISHED FOR RESOURCES FOR THE FUTURE
By The Johns Hopkins University Press
Baltimore and London

TD
8 99
S 7
R87

Jacket photo courtesy of American Iron and Steel Institute.

Library of Congress Catalog Card Number 75-36945

ISBN 0-8018-1824-9

Library of Congress Cataloging in Publication Data will be found on the last printed
page of this book.

CONTENTS

LIST OF TABLES

LIST OF FIGURES

PREFACE

This book represents the latest product from a series of RFF industry studies extending back into the middle 1960s. From the beginning, the underlying rationale for these studies has been the conviction that the public debate about industrial use of our common property resources (water and air, especially) would be sharpened by the provision both of specific facts and of improved analytical methodologies. To these general ends, the studies have been designed to display, in the context of the best available data from a particular industry, the workings of a methodology, usually one developed here at RFF. The methodologies range from careful delineation of the alternatives for changing water use or residuals discharge to the construction of linear programming models designed to allow simultaneous consideration of all the production opportunities and constraints relevant to the industrial decision maker.

The first book in this series, published in 1966, was a study of water use for cooling in steam electric generation done by Paul Cootner and George Löf (*Water Demand for Steam Electric Generation*). In those early days the stress was on water quantity problems and the industry studied was a fairly simple one from this point of view. That is, it seemed reasonable to assume that decisions about plant thermal efficiency would be made independently of cooling water considerations, and that if efforts to reduce water withdrawals subsequently seemed worthwhile, they would be handled using cooling ponds or towers which permit recirculation of cooling water. No attention was paid in this study to the ecological effects of the heated-water discharges from a once-through plant, to the chemical problems with cooling tower blowdown, or to any other residuals discharged from thermal-electric plants (for example, SO_2 and particulates).

Later studies in this series have reflected a shift in emphasis from water quantity to water quality and, in addition, a broadening of interest to include airborne and solid residuals problems. Thus, George Löf and Allen Kneese, in their study of beet sugar refining (*The Economics of Water Utilization in the Beet Sugar Industry*) concentrated on biological oxygen demand (BOD) discharges from this type of plant and on the costs implied by various discharge reduction techniques, including process changes and process water recirculation as well as the more familiar treatment and lagooning methods.

The next study to appear went even further. Blair Bower, George Löf, and W. M. Hearon, working on the very complex pulp and paper industry, looked at eleven residuals, five discharged to the atmosphere, four discharged to water courses, and two solids ["Residuals Management in the Pulp and Paper Industry," in *National Resources Journal*, vol. II (October 1971) pp. 605–623]. They initially dealt principally with the effects of changes in production processes and paper quality on the generation rates for these residuals per ton of finished paper. In later research, this team has gone on to bring in treatment alternatives and has recast their work in the form of an integer programming model (J. W. Sawyer, Jr., Blair Bower, and G. O. G. Löf, "Modeling Process Substitution in the Analysis of Liquid Residuals Management in a Paper Mill," presented at the TIMS/ORSA International Meeting, San Juan, Puerto Rico, October 1974).

Meanwhile, under the initial stimulus of a contract with the National Water Commission, and with the advice and encouragement of Blair Bower, Clifford Russell began the development of techniques for bringing residuals generation and control within the linear programming (or process analysis) framework which had been used so widely and successfully on the production side of industrial planning. These efforts were eventually reflected in Russell's book, *Residuals Management in Industry: A Case Study of Petroleum Refining* (1973). But even during the development phase it became clear to several of us in the Environmental Quality Program that the technique might be useful in the context of the regional residuals management modeling project in which we were then engaged. This was so because one of our most serious problems was the lack of data on discharges and on the cost of modifying discharges. And this type of model, constructed on the basis of such data as were available, promised to give us numbers which would at least be consistent, but which would certainly be the best publicly available basis for decisions.

Accordingly, in late 1970, we commissioned William J. Vaughan to begin construction of a linear programming model of integrated iron and steel production along the lines set out by Russell. The original intent was to produce a fairly rough model in a short time, but gradually it became obvious both that the problems were serious enough to make a quick study impossible and that there were significant opportunities here beyond the anticipated application to the Lower Delaware Valley Model. Thus, the project took on a life of its own, and the resulting model has gone through several stages of refinement, all with the patient encouragement of the former director of this program, Allen Kneese.

I believe that the results reported here have value not only as examples of a methodology, but in themselves as indicators of the costs and opportunities within the steel industry for residuals management and increased scrap recycling.

December 1975

> Walter O. Spofford, Jr.
> Head, Quality of the Environment Division
> Resources for the Future

ACKNOWLEDGMENTS

In the course of this study we have accumulated our share of debts to colleagues and friends, and to no one do we owe more than to Allen Kneese who, as Director of the Quality of the Environment Program at RFF, patiently supported the agonies of economists trying to educate themselves in the mysteries of metallurgy. Blair Bower, on whose pioneering ideas RFF's industrial models have been built, was also a continual source of encouragement and practical assistance. Vaughan's thesis advisor, Fr. Eugene Poirier of the Department of Economics, Georgetown University, served a valuable critical function and was wonderfully flexible in the face of several problems involved in creating a thesis out of such a large, cooperative study. Henry C. Bramer of Datagraphics, Inc. read the technical material in the first draft of the thesis and provided us with a critique which allowed us to refine the model for the next go around. We obtained helpful advice in the early stages from Jon Nelson, of Pennsylvania State University, and Charles Louis Trozzo, of the Institute for Defense Analysis.

A number of others have read various papers and chapter drafts and offered useful comment. We would especially like to thank James W. Sawyer and Walter O. Spofford, Jr., of RFF, and V. Kerry Smith, of the Department of Economics, State University of New York, Binghamton.

Initially, Elizabeth Mortland and later, for the bulk of the runs, Louanne Sawyer, provided the computer expertise that we lacked (especially facility with MPSX).

Our search for data and explanations took us to some exotic sources, and these were obtained for us by Mrs. Daphne Carter of the Brookings Library.

Every word of this book has been typed a painfully large number of times by Dee Stell, now retired from RFF; she has had the patience of Job with our several versions and innumerable changes. We also wish to thank Penelope Harpold and Ruth Haas for doing their best to make a readable volume from this mass of technical material. Finally, Sherrill Malloy helped us find the problems in the galley proofs.

C. S. R.
W. J. V.

Part I   OVERVIEW OF THE STEEL-MAKING SYSTEM AND THE MODEL

1

POLICY QUESTIONS AND METHODOLOGY

As this book goes to press, the United States is in the midst of a re-appraisal of the environmental decisions made in the last half-dozen years and embodied in some of the showpiece legislation of the environmental movement, such as the National Environmental Policy Act (NEPA)[1] and the 1972 amendments to the Federal Water Pollution Control Acts of 1965.[2] Some of this reappraisal has been informal and intensely public, punctuated by advertisements of interested parties, inflammatory statements from political leaders, and lawsuits filed by anxious guardians of the natural world. On the other hand, some of the reappraisal has been institutionalized, as in the National Academy of Sciences studies of auto pollution control regulations;[3] the ongoing cluster of academy studies of the entire decision-making process (concentrating on the use of scientific and technical information) within the Environmental Protection Agency (EPA);[4] and in the National Commission on Water Quality created by the 1972 amendments.

The public debate and the quieter, presumably more scholarly studies tend to focus on the costs, measured in different ways, of meeting the legislated environmental standards or complying with legislated

---

[1] The National Environmental Policy Act of 1969, 42 U.S.C. §4321 et seq., Public Law 91-190, 83 Stat. 852.

[2] Federal Water Pollution Control Amendments of 1972, 33 U.S.C. §1151 et seq., Public Law 92-500, 86 Stat. 816 (October 18, 1972).

[3] National Academy of Sciences–National Academy of Engineering, Air Quality and Automobile Emission Control: A Report by the Coordinating Committee on Air Quality Studies, prepared for the Committee on Public Works, U.S. Senate, ser. 93-24 (1974).

[4] These studies were initiated by the House Subcommittee on Agriculture, Environmental and Consumer Protection, of the House Appropriations Committee, in its report on fiscal year 1974 appropriations.

procedures. The measures of cost most widely estimated and quoted are:

1. The direct dollar cost that industries, government units, and private citizens will pay for control equipment, fuel switching, or lost production required or implied by particular laws. Thus, for example, the National Commission on Water Quality is spending a large fraction (19 percent) of its $15 million appropriation on technical, engineering studies to determine the cost to various industries of the treatment standards implied by the 1972 amendments.[5]

2. The short-term disruptive effects implied as the direct costs work themselves through the system: for example, unemployment, relative price changes, general price level increases.

3. The long-term effects on economic growth as determined by the traditional measures of aggregate economic welfare.

4. The increases (or decreases) in energy use per unit of output or, where appropriate, the effect on energy supply.

5. The implications for the use of any number of critical materials, the supply of which shifts because of the actions of various international cartels, or the vagaries of politics in developing countries.[6]

Unfortunately, the actual estimation of costs has not proved to be nearly so easy as the identification of the cost measures of greatest interest. A major reason for this has been the near monopoly on information concerning industrial costs held by industry itself. Data dealing with residuals generation and discharge have, until very re-

[5] For an excellent, brief description of the commission and its charge, see James A. Noone, "Environment Report: Water Study Panel Starts Slowly, May Miss Deadline," *National Journal Report* (October 5, 1974), pp. 1495–1499. The commission's study budgets for other cost categories (using their categories) are: economic impact, $1.4 million (9 percent); impact on GNP, $250,000 (less than 2 percent); aggregate costs, $150,000 (1 percent). Since the total study budget is about 77.5 percent of the $15 million appropriation, the specific cost studies really amount to about 40 percent of the planned research.

[6] The last two cost measures raise interesting, often frustrating issues for economists. On the one hand, if we really believe that market prices of energy have been held too low for decades in relation to the long-run cost problems implied by the depletion of nonrenewable resources, then it may be appropriate to consider energy use separately in our cost calculations, perhaps applying to it a shadow price reflecting long-run concerns. On the other hand, for many, the current concern with energy is simply an excuse for abandoning money prices entirely and adopting an energy theory of value and an energy numeraire for measuring costs. The frustration arises from attempts to distinguish between these two approaches in debate with environmentalists.

cently, been considered trade secrets.[7] This has allowed industry to control the debate by making its own claims about what it has spent on "pollution control" and to keep from the public knowledge of what residuals are actually being discharged. The tendency has been to take credit for every investment related to residuals, even though a particular action might very well have been taken in response to favorable market prices for, say, some recovered by-product. Further, industry has tended to exaggerate the anticipated costs of new policies, particularly in terms of the publicly sensitive issues of unemployment and growth effects.

But a second reason for our difficulties with cost estimation has to do with the complexity of the task, even given adequate data resources. For example, the level of residuals discharges from a particular plant in a particular industry, in the absence of government-imposed discharge limits or effluent charges, will vary with the relative prices of inputs, outputs, and by-products; with quality standards imposed on products; with available input qualities; and with the types of production processes in use. This raises a pair of symmetrical problems: The first problem lies in determining the cost of a policy that limits the discharge of residuals. This task is difficult because we cannot assume that reductions in discharge levels (and thus the cost of those reductions) can be attributed exclusively to the requirement for constraint. In some cases, part of the discharge reduction is attributable to forces, such as relative prices of by-products, which are exogenous to the constraint policy. The second problem lies in determining the effect of a given set of effluent charges. We cannot predict with any accuracy the level of effluent discharges resulting from the imposition of charges since, in fact, this level will continue to vary significantly with exogenous forces.

THE GOALS

This study has two complementary goals which grew out of our assessment of the difficulties and requirements just discussed. First, we

[7] This has changed largely because, in the case of water, the National Pollution Discharge Elimination System (NPDES) permit applications, with discharge information, have been made available to the public. Regarding air, data for the Air Quality Control Region inventories have been public for three or four years. Even now, however, discharge information can be kept confidential where disposal is not into public watercourses but is instead confined to private impoundments, even though seepage may eventually result in discharges to public waters.

aim to present a methodology for investigating the implications that alternative public policies, especially but not exclusively environmental policies, will have for industrial costs and resource use. Second, we produce some information, which we believe to be of value in its own right, about the environmental quality and resource use problems of the steel industry. The model structure, which we describe somewhat more fully below, was developed at Resources for the Future (RFF) in connection with a study of industrial water use funded by the National Water Commission.[8] It builds on the earlier conceptual work of Blair T. Bower,[9] and has since been applied to residuals management problems in petroleum refining.[10] We chose the steel industry for a second application of this model type primarily because a major regional modeling project at RFF was using the Delaware Estuary Region, which has five steel mills, as a case study area.[11]

We were impressed with the magnitude of the steel industry's residuals problems. For example, iron and steel production has been ranked fourth out of eighteen major industrial categories in its annual particulate emissions, which amounted to approximately 10 percent of the 1966 national total of particulate emissions. This is just slightly below fuel combustion; crushed stone, sand, and gravel; and operations related to agriculture.[12] In addition, approximately 33 percent of the volume of national industrial waste-water discharge emanates from the basic metals industrial category,[13] with gross water use in iron and

---

[8] C. W. Howe, C. S. Russell, R. A. Young, and W. J. Vaughan, "Water Use in Industry," in *Future Water Demands: The Impacts of Technological Change, Public Policies, and Changing Market Conditions on the Water Use Patterns of Selected Sectors of the United States Economy, 1970–1990.* Publication no. 197 877 (Springfield, Va.: NTIS, 1970), sect. II.

[9] See, for example, Bower, "Industrial Water Demands," in W. R. D. Sewell and B. T. Bower, eds., *Forecasting the Demands for Water* (Ottawa: Policy and Planning Branch, Department of Energy, Mines and Resources, 1968).

[10] C. S. Russell, *Residuals Management in Industry: A Case Study of Petroleum Refining* (Baltimore: Johns Hopkins University Press for Resources for the Future, 1973).

[11] The regional modeling framework developed at RFF was applied in the Delaware Estuary Region which contains five steel mills: U.S. Steel's Fairless works and Alan Wood Steel, both integrated from coke ovens through rolling and finishing; and Lukens Steel and two plants of the Phoenix Steel Company, all so-called cold-melt shops, that is, shops dependent on steel scrap and without iron-making capacity.

[12] A. E. Vandegrift and L. J. Shannon, *Particulate Pollutant System Study, Application Areas,* vol. 3: Report by the Midwest Research Institute for the U.S. Environmental Protection Agency, Air Pollution Control Office (Durham: U.S. Environmental Protection Agency, May 1, 1971), pp. 6–16, 91 Cong., 1 sess., *The Cost of Clean Air.* First Report of the Secretary of Health, Education and Welfare to the Congress of the United States in compliance with Public Law 90-148, the Air Quality Act of 1967, June 1969. Document No. 91-40, p. 25.

[13] Ross Nebolsine, "Today's Problems of Industrial Waste Water Pollution Abatement," *Natural Resources Lawyer,* vol. 1 (January 1968), p. 43.

steelmaking amounting to as much as 40,000 gallons per ton of finished steel.[14]

The steel industry's residuals problems are highly interconnected with its choice of raw materials—particularly its choice between hot iron (from blast furnaces using coke and ore) and steel scrap. This choice, in turn, depends primarily on the relative costs of the two inputs. Since steel scrap, particularly from junked cars, is a consumption residual with serious environmental amenity effects, pollution at the mill and dispersed, visual pollution are linked through the scrap–hot metal tradeoff. This connection seemed well worth further study.[15]

We also wish to address problems raised by studies appearing from the federal government purporting to establish a basis for effluent guidelines. In these studies, we were disturbed by:[16]

1. The faulty conceptual basis of many of the studies (for example, their frequent insistence on setting effluent standards by process unit and ignoring the possibility that the millwide totals could vary widely under this system).
2. Their relative inability to deal with changes in initial residuals loads and the costs of meeting effluent standards implied by changes in exogenous conditions.
3. The wide variation in reported costs per unit of output.

These problems are exactly the sort with which the linear programming method can deal effectively, so we believe that our study promises policy relevance as well as intellectual rewards.

We are not, of course, the first to propose a study of one facet or another of the steel industry from the outside. On the one hand, the patterns of technological change in the industry have fascinated economists, and any number have made efforts to explain, attack, or defend

[14] Henry C. Bramer, "Pollution Control in the Steel Industry," *Environmental Science and Technology*, vol. 5 (October 1971), pp. 1004–1008. In a personal communication, on July 18, 1973, Dr. Bramer reported a revised figure of 67,000 gallons of gross use per ton of finished steel.

[15] RFF has also supported research on the supply function for steel scrap based on junked auto bodies. See James W. Sawyer, Jr., *Automotive Scrap Recycling: Processes, Prices and Prospects* (Baltimore: Johns Hopkins University Press for Resources for the Future, 1974).

[16] See Cyrus William Rice Division, NUS Corporation, *Development Document for Effluent Limitations Guidelines and New Source Performance Standards.* Draft report prepared for the U.S. Environmental Protection Agency under contract no. 68-01-1507 (June 1973), for suggested guidelines made to EPA by a private consultant. For an estimate of the costs of water pollution abatement in the steel industry resulting from the guidelines, see A. T. Kearney Inc., *Economic Analysis of the Proposed Effluent Guidelines for the Integrated Iron and Steel Industry.* Report to the Office of Planning and Evaluation, U.S. Environmental Protection Agency under contract no. 68-01-1545 (February 1974).

the industry's actions in the past.[17] A separate set of research efforts has dealt with steel mill residuals problems, but this research has never been done in the context of a programming model, and more important, has never involved simultaneous consideration of process and input-mix changes. In addition, each study has focused on a single environmental medium (air or water) and often on a single residual as well.[18]

Thus, our specific goals in setting up the steel industry model were the following.

1. As far as possible, the model should include the major air- and waterborne residuals and solid wastes discharged from steel mills.
2. It should also reflect the available options for changing residual type and discharge medium.
3. It should allow us to explore the effect of energy cost on energy use and on residuals discharge, and conversely should show us how environmental policies and other exogenous factors affect energy use in steelmaking.
4. Similarly, the model ought to allow us to investigate steel scrap use in new steel production, both to find out how quantities and

---

[17] See, for example, W. Adams and J. B. Dirlam, "Big Steel, Invention and Innovation," *Quarterly Journal of Economics,* vol. 80 (May 1966), pp. 167–189; B. Gold, W. S. Pierce, and G. Rosegger, "Diffusion of Major Technological Innovations in U.S. Iron and Steel Manufacturing," *Journal of Industrial Economics,* vol. 18 (July 1970), pp. 218–241; P. T. Knight and G. S. Madalla, "International Diffusion of Technical Change—A Case Study of the Oxygen Steel-Making Process," *The Economic Journal,* vol. 77 (September 1967), pp. 531–558; and W. Reinfeld, "An Economic Analysis of Recent Technological Trends in the U.S. Steel Industry" (Ph.D. dissertation, Yale University, 1968).

Much of the best quantitative work on this question has been done by Professor Richard Day and his students at the University of Wisconsin. See Masatoshi A. Abe, "Dynamic Microeconomic Models of Production, Investment and Technological Change of the U.S. and Japanese Iron and Steel Industries" (Ph.D. dissertation, University of Wisconsin, 1970); Jon P. Nelson, "An Interregional Recursive Programming Model of the U.S. Iron and Steel Industry" (Ph.D. dissertation, University of Wisconsin, 1970); and Che S. Tsao and Richard H. Day, "A Process Analysis Model of the U.S. Iron and Steel Industry," *Management Science,* vol. 17 (June 1971), pp. B558–B608.

[18] Studies of the type which are concerned with steel mill discharges to a single medium include U.S. Department of the Interior, Federal Water Pollution Control Administration, *The Cost of Clean Water: vol. 3: Industrial Waste Profile, No. 1: Blast Furnaces and Steel Mills* (September 1967); Jean J. Schueneman, M. D. High, and W. E. Bye, *Air Pollution Aspects of the Iron and Steel Industry,* U.S. Department of Health, Education and Welfare, Public Health Service Publication no. 999-AP-1 (June 1963); and Thomas M. Barnes and H. W. Lownie, Jr., *A Cost Analysis of Air-Pollution Controls in the Integrated Iron and Steel Industry,* PB 184 576 (Springfield, Va.: NTIS, May 15, 1969).

For an example of a study which surveys the discharges from a number of steel mills without attempting to specify the relationships between discharges, technology, input quality and output quality, see James S. Cannon, *Environmental Steel* (New York: The Council on Economic Priorities, 1973).

qualities of scrap demanded respond to scrap prices, available technology, and other influences, and, on the other hand, to see how variations in scrap use affect residuals discharges and resource use (especially iron ore and coal).

5. The model should be set up to allow the representation of specific mill types, as differentiated by steel furnaces [that is, basic oxygen furnace (BOF), open hearth (OH), electric arc furnace (EA), and a duplex shop consisting of both BOF and EA capacity].

6. The model should include some version of the finishing section, which is a large source of residuals, but was commonly ignored in the studies available to us when we began.

A further aim is implied in the aforementioned link between this research project and the Delaware Estuary study also going on at RFF. That is, the steel mill model had to fit into the wider regional model, which contains air dispersion submodels operating on sulfur dioxide and particulate discharges, and an aquatic ecosystem submodel which takes as exogenous inputs, discharges of heat, biochemical oxygen demand (BOD), toxics, ammonia, and suspended solids.[19] The overall regional modeling framework is described in some detail elsewhere,[20] as is the method of using the individual plant models within that framework.[21]

METHODOLOGY

The methodological base for RFF's industry studies is an adaptation of the familiar linear programming problem:

$$\text{minimize } c'X$$

$$\text{subject to } AX \lessgtr b$$

$$\text{and } X \geq 0$$

[19] The toxic category represents here the sum of cyanide and phenol discharges, both of which are available from the steel mill model.

[20] C. S. Russell and W. O. Spofford, Jr., "A Quantitative Framework for Residuals Management Decisions," in A. V. Kneese and B. T. Bower, eds., *Environmental Quality Analysis: Theory and Method in the Social Sciences* (Baltimore: Johns Hopkins University Press for Resources for the Future, 1972), ch. 4; C. S. Russell, W. O. Spofford, and E. T. Haefele, "The Management of the Quality of the Environment," in *The Management of Water Quality and the Environment*, J. Rothenberg and Ian G. Heggie, eds. (London: Macmillan Press, 1974); and W. O. Spofford, C. S. Russell, and R. A. Kelly, "Operational Problems in Large-Scale Residuals Management Models," in *Economic Analysis of Environmental Problems*, Edwin S. Mills, ed. (New York: National Bureau of Economic Research, 1975).

[21] Russell, *Residuals Management*, pp. 181–185.

in which the constraint matrix, A, includes a number of continuity conditions (equality constraints with zero sums across each row).[22] These conditions are the mechanism for requiring that a residual generated in a particular production process (vector) is accounted for explicitly by treatment, some type of recycling, or by discharge to the environment. Continuity conditions are also used to ensure, for example, that all electricity used in the processes is actually generated at the on-site generating plant (or is purchased from the local utility if that possibility is allowed).

In order to reflect accurately the impact of changes in input mix and process type on residuals generation, it is necessary, in principle, to calculate a material and energy balance for each process and input alternative. Again in principle, the results of this calculation will appear in the actual vector representing that alternative. That is, within a single vector there will be explicit entries reflecting all material inputs and outputs and all energy inputs and outputs. The constraints in which these inputs and outputs appear may be continuity conditions, as discussed above, or they may be inequalities—as, for example, when a particular input is in limited supply. In practice it is possible to relax this requirement to the extent that specific inputs or outputs are not of interest in the context of the problem being studied. This, in turn, will depend largely on the spatial and temporal boundaries of the problem. For example, in the short to medium term (say, up to thirty or forty years) and for less-than-global regions (even entire nations), carbon dioxide discharges and heat rejection directly to the atmosphere are usually not considered problems.[23] Hence, in a model designed to explore steel production's contribution to short-term, local environmental problems, these two parts of the balances can be ignored.

Employing a cost-minimizing criterion allows us to deal with the residuals impacts of changing output mixes more easily than a profit-maximizing criterion does because in a linear model it is simpler to obtain realistic final product mixes by manipulating output constraints than by varying the structure of final product prices. Unemployment is not considered since we assume that a certain set of production levels must be met or exceeded.

There are, of course, many levels on which social scientists object to such a criterion. Some contend that firms maximize sales subject perhaps to a profit constraint. Others consider that "satisficing," or

[22] For a more detailed description of the nature of these constraints, see ibid., ch. 2.

[23] We emphasize that this is *not* to say that only short-term local problems should be studied or to imply that this methodology is only applicable to such problems. Our purpose in drawing the distinction is only to stress the flexibility of the formulation.

rule-of-thumb decision making under conditions of uncertainty and partial knowledge, is as far toward *homo economicus* as reality can carry us. We are inclined to believe that there *is* explanatory power in the cost-minimization assumption, at least at the plant level.

In this structure, a variety of indirect influences on residuals generation and discharge may be studied by manipulating values of the objective function, the right-hand side, or the matrix of coefficients itself. Thus, in the objective function any of the price or cost figures may, in principle, be altered and the effect observed, though in practice we may be interested only in the price of a key input (such as coal to a thermal electric generating plant), or of an actual or potential by-product (such as sulfur in the steel mill's coke oven gas). On the right-hand side, we may change input availabilities and output quantity and quality requirements. And, finally, we may reflect advances in production or residuals handling technology by changing coefficients within the A matrix itself. Such changes may take the form of introducing entire new columns to represent possible new processes.

All this is not to say, of course, that this methodology solves all our problems for us. For example, there is the matter of scale economies, which arises when capital or operating costs per unit vary inversely with the scale of the facility. On the practical level, there is no single correct unit price to attach to the activity vector for such a facility,[24] and the usual trick of approximating the nonlinear curve with piecewise linear segments will not work because the segments would not fill up in the correct order in the solution process. But on a more fundamental level, economies of scale make any problem involving a choice of capacity a difficult one because the response surface, corresponding to the falling marginal and average costs, will have multiple optima, so that even if we devise a trick to make the segments of a piecewise linear approximation fill up in correct order, we may not assume that we have solved the problem we set out to solve. Tests for multiple optima and a search technique for finding the best local optimum will, in general, be necessary.[25]

Our approach is to cost facilities which may or may not be part of the solution, such as treatment plants and by-product recovery units, on the basis of an assumed size. Generally, that size is taken to be the one which would handle the maximum daily volume of the gas or water stream in question under *bench mark* exogenous conditions. This has the virtue of simplicity, but it is certainly no solution to the

[24] That is, there is no single correct price until after the problem has been solved and the scale of the facility is known.

[25] For example, see R. Hesse, "A Heuristic Search Procedure for Estimating a Global Solution of Nonconvex Programming Problems," *Operations Research*, vol. 21, no. 6 (November–December 1973), pp. 1267–1280.

fundamental difficulty. Specifically, such an assumption, in a situation where economies of scale obtain, tends to be self-fulfilling. That is, assuming a large size implies low unit costs and increases the chance that, in fact, the optimal solution will include that unit at its maximum capacity and vice versa.

Similar effects are created whenever the marginal cost of obtaining some desired result falls as the amount obtained rises. Thus, in standard sewage treatment for removal of oxygen-demanding organics, the cost of BOD removal, when shown as a function of percentage removal achieved, follows an S-shaped curve, with falling marginal costs of additional removal over a significant range.[26] The determination of the appropriate treatment level is then subject to the same difficulties as is that of the proper size of a facility exhibiting economies of scale. It is possible to set up the constraint matrix entries for a standard treatment plant in such a way that the segments must be chosen in the proper order,[27] but the problem will still involve nonconvexity.[28]

A related problem arises in modeling the situation in which the decision must be made whether or not to install some residuals treatment equipment and, if it is installed, whether or not to operate it. One may again think of declining marginal cost: First, a very steep cost segment reflects the installation but not the operation of the equipment; then a flatter segment reflects operation costs (once installed) up to capacity; and finally, a vertical segment represents the impossibility of treating an amount greater than the equipment capacity (see figure 1.1).

ANTICIPATING SOME RESULTS

Some examples of specific questions addressed and answers obtained should provide a better understanding of the purposes of our study.

---

[26] See, for example, R. Frankel, *Economic Evaluation of Water Quality: An Engineering–Economic Model for Water Quality Management*, SERL report 65-3 (Berkeley: University of California at Berkeley, College of Engineering and School of Public Health, January 1965).

[27] See, for example, Russell and Spofford, "A Quantitative Framework"; and for a different approach, Daniel P. Loucks, *Stochastic Methods for Analyzing River Basin Systems*, Technical Report no. 16 (Ithaca: Cornell University Water Resources and Marine Sciences Center, August 1969).

[28] Where more than one residual is involved in a *single* process, removal efficiencies may be interdependent (for example, BOD and phenols removal in a standard biological treatment plant). This interdependence introduces cross-product terms into the problem and makes the linear model of doubtful value unless one can distinguish each concentration combination in a separate row and apply a separate treatment vector. If, however, interdependencies exist only *between* processes, the problem is potentially easier to solve.

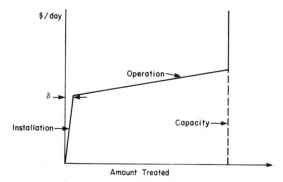

Figure 1.1. Cost of residuals treatment equipment where $\delta \to 0$. (From Clifford S. Russell, *Residuals Management in Industry: A Case Study of Petroleum Refining* (Baltimore: The Johns Hopkins University Press for Resources for the Future, 1973), p. 31.

These are given in the next several pages, with the caution, however, that this is *not* an "executive summary" of the sort so beloved in Washington. It is meant as an hors d'oeuvre, not a quick dinner.

Energy

Energy is currently very much in the limelight, and the "energy implications" of every governmental action are sought by those who must take responsibility for such actions. This estimable goal is, however, frequently unattainable because in this relatively new area of concern there simply is not enough knowledge to support realistic calculations. But because *some* answer must be given, a lack of knowledge is often concealed behind a facade of numbers. Consider, for example, the simple question, What are the relative energy-use intensities of the three production processes represented by the three major steel furnace types? One answer, provided to the National Commission on Water Quality, is that the electric arc route is "approximately seven times more energy efficient than the basic oxygen process."[29] Contrast this assertion with the results available from the model.

	OH	BOF	EA
Total energy use (10^6 Btu per ingot ton)	17.4	21.3	8.7

[29] This quotation is taken from a draft report on steel technology prepared for the commission. Since our intention here is only to illustrate a problem, not to criticize either the commission or a specific contractor, we refrain from giving a citation.

This analysis indicates that the EA is only about two and one-half times as energy efficient as the BOF and twice as efficient as the OH.

Another relevant question concerns the degree to which energy use will respond to increases in price. If, for example, the federal government were to impose a stiff tax on all forms of petroleum fuel, not just on gasoline, would the steel industry respond with meaningful decreases in energy use per ton of product? As we shall see later, the answer is probably not, for mills based on the BOF process, since such a shop is practically independent of purchased fuels. Nearly all its energy demands are met with the by-product gases from the coking units and blast furnaces, and since the quantities of these gases per ton of product are determined, within limits, by metallurgical considerations, there is little scope (or need) for reaction to oil price changes. On the other hand, the electric arc shop may be able to switch completely away from the use of residual oil in generating electricity, though it has very little flexibility in terms of its efficiency in applying the power at the furnace.[30]

Finally, at a shop based on open hearth technology and containing facilities for the production of hot iron (coking units and blast furnace), there is some flexibility in the choice of fuels—specifically, by-product fuels can be substituted for purchased oil—but there is again very little opportunity for reduction in total heat inputs. For this last case, the model indicates an arc elasticity of demand for purchased residual oil of 0.31 over the price range $0.12 to $0.78 per million Btu. Over the range $0.39 to $0.78 per million Btu the elasticity is considerably higher, 0.61.[31] But, as anticipated, this flexibility is obtained by more extensive use of by-product fuels—not by reduction in total heat input per ton of steel.

A third interesting question in the energy field concerns the role of anticipated technological change in altering the energy efficiency of steel production. One example dealt with in the model is the continuous caster, an alternative to the conventional system of ingot pouring, reheating, and rolling for the production of semifinished shapes.[32] Here the results are cheering for those concerned with the long-range energy outlook. Substitution of continuous for conventional casting saves about 13 percent of the total energy input per ton of steel prod-

[30] Fuel switching from oil to coal is not an option in our electric generating plant submodel.

[31] The price quoted here is for 2 percent sulfur-content residual oil. Lower sulfur-content oils (1.0 and 0.5 percent) are available in the model at correspondingly higher prices but are not chosen unless some limit or charge on sulfur dioxide emissions is imposed.

[32] See the descriptions of both routes in chapter 8.

uct. This decrease in energy use is accompanied by a roughly equivalent percentage decline in residuals discharges to both water and air.

Steel Scrap

Some environmentalists have been battling in the relatively esoteric field of materials use, aiming particularly at the incentives and disincentives for recycling postconsumer goods. A principal venue for this battle has been the legal challenge to the rate-making procedures of the Interstate Commerce Commission (ICC) raised by the group known as SCRAP.[33] The most important argument for our purposes is the one claiming that if railroad freight rates did not discriminate against steel scrap, significantly more scrap would be used. In the eyes of environmentalists, then, a reduction in rate discrimination would have the principal benefit of discouraging use of nonrenewable resources—especially coal and iron ore.

The first point we must make here is that there are many grades of scrap traded in markets and available to steelmakers. These are distinguished on several different bases, but, for us, the most important of these is the degree to which the steel is contaminated with other metallic elements (called "tramp alloy elements" or "tramps"). In the model, we represent the range of purchased-scrap qualities available to the steel mill by four grades, ranging from one consisting of compressed (bundled) auto hulks with relatively high tramp contamination, to one consisting principally of processing scrap from steel fabricating plants having very much lower tramp contamination. Notice that the lower-quality, auto-related scrap grades are connected to another environmental quality problem, that of the aesthetic costs of dispersed auto hulks and of auto scrap yards.

A second major point which can be made, and which we shall illustrate below using some results of model runs, is that because steel scrap is a substitute for hot iron in the production of new steel, its greater use implies smaller generation of waterborne residuals at steel mills. This effect results, of course, because decreased production of hot iron allows decreased use of the coking units, which are the major source of the organic and toxic water pollutants at the integrated mill. Thus, if lower scrap freight rates *will* encourage significantly greater use of scrap, they will not only save iron ore (and avoid attendant environmental disruption at the mine), but will tend to reduce the

---

[33] See *SCRAP* v. *United States*, 371 F. Supp. 1292 (D.D.C. 1974); and the *Draft Environmental Impact Statement, Ex Parte 270 (Sub. No. 5), Investigation of Railroad Freight Rate Structure—Iron Ores,* and *Ex Parte 270 (Sub. No. 6)—Scrap Iron and Steel*, ICC (April 1, 1974).

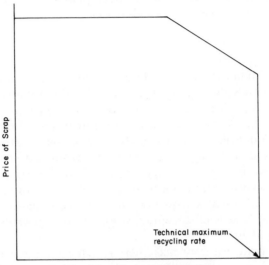

Figure 1.2.   Shape of demand curve for obsolete scrap.

overall water pollution problem attributable to the steel industry, and the visual pollution of dispersed auto hulks and auto graveyards.

What, then, does the model have to say about the fundamental contention that lower freight rates will affect scrap use? It suggests that, depending on where current demand and supply curves intersect in the several regional markets, a reduction in scrap price to steel mills through the reduction in freight rates may have virtually no effect on the use of such scrap in the short run.

An extended discussion in the final chapter indicates that the derived demand curves for purchased scrap have a peculiar shape—a shape which is most pronounced for the more heavily tramp-contaminated obsolete scraps. Thus, because of the tramp metallics which at present cannot be removed in the steel furnace, and because of the upper limits on allowable tramp content in the finished steels, there is, for any steel quality, quantity, and furnace type, a technological upper limit on the amount of such scrap that can be charged. On the other hand, the steel industry is very sensitive to increases in scrap price beyond some upper limit for each grade, depending primarily on the percentage of iron in the scrap and on the prices of other scraps. The net result of these two sensitivities is that the purchased scrap demand curves for a mill mimicking the overall industry by combining BOF and EA furnace capacity will have roughly the shape shown in figure 1.2. In the short run, then, the model would not lead us to expect any

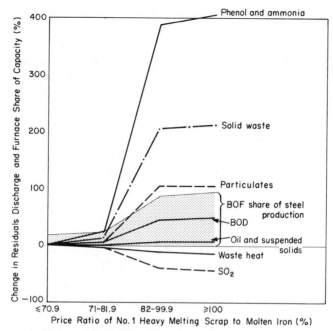

Figure 1.3. Effects of different anticipated scrap-to-hot iron price ratios on investment and residuals discharges (greenfield site).

immediate increase in the use of scrap as a result of reduction in freight rates.

The long run may be quite a different story, however, as we illustrate in figure 1.3, by showing how the expected relation between the price of purchased scrap and the marginal cost of hot iron would affect the investment choice between the EA furnace and the BOF.[34] The shaded area on figure 1.3 shows the proportion of a fixed output quantity which would be produced using the BOF at different expected scrap price- to hot metal-cost ratios, if the investment decision were to be made on the basis of each of those ratios. Thus, if in the future the price of scrap was expected to equal or exceed the marginal cost of hot iron, the company choosing its future plant type would opt for the BOF only. On the other hand, for expected ratios in the neighborhood of 75 percent, the investment decision would be tilted toward the EA furnace, with the BOF accounting for only about 20 percent of capacity.[35]

[34] The price of one important grade of scrap, no. 1 heavy melting, is used here as a proxy for the four purchased scrap prices, all of which are raised together in the model run used as a basis for this figure.

[35] Though this ratio has usually been less than one, at the peak of the scrap price surge, in April 1974, it went as high as about 1.5.

Notice also the dramatic evidence of the increase in water pollution problems attending the increased reliance on the BOF at the upper end of the scrap price scale. (There is a reduction in sulfur dioxide discharges attending the growth in BOF capacity relative to the EA. The size of this effect depends on the assumptions in the model about fuel oils available for use in electrical generation and might be greater or less as exogenous conditions dictate different fuel oil standards or availabilities.) Thus, over the long run, if changes in scrap freight rates can effect even a 10 percent reduction in scrap price at the steel mill, they may have a large effect on the makeup of the steel industry's capacity as well as on environmental problems in the vicinity of steel mills.

Cost of Pollution Control

As a final example of the type of question the model is capable of exploring, let us consider the costs of reducing residuals discharges from steel mills. This is, of course, directly relevant to the developing debate over the Water Pollution Control Amendments of 1972, to which we referred earlier. In particular, the amendments require the attainment of two levels of discharge reduction: one by 1977, and a second, more stringent level by 1983. These levels are defined in rather vague terms in the law, and it is not within the scope of this study to describe these definitions or discuss the legal problems inherent in them, but we can say that cost is one of the matters to be considered in passing from the definitions to operational effluent standards.

In this context, then, there is considerable interest in estimating the costs of very large percentage reductions in waterborne effluent discharges, a task the model is equipped to undertake for the various types of plants in the steel industry. Figure 1.4 shows the average cost, per ton of semifinished steel shapes, of various levels of reduction of all waterborne discharges from a BOF-based integrated mill.[36] In fact, the percentage reductions indicated are the minimums attained for each residual at that level. That is, because there are a few major waste-water streams and these contain several residuals which are reduced to different extents by the available treatment processes, the requirement of, say, 90 percent reduction in BOD discharge may result in a 95 percent reduction in phenol discharge. In fact, for the run discussed here, when a uniform reduction of 90 percent is required, we actually obtain 92 percent reduction for oil, over 98 percent reductions

---

[36] In chapter 12, we discuss in more detail the assumptions under which this result is obtained. For now, we simply note that the mill is not allowed to vaporize its coke unit effluent streams by using them to cool incandescent coke.

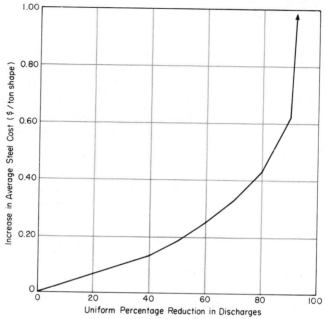

Figure 1.4. The cost of uniform reduction in watercourse discharges below the bench mark at the BOF plant.

for phenol and ammonia, and complete removal of dissolved hydrogen sulfide. Only BOD, cyanide, suspended solids, and heat discharges are actually at the 90 percent level.

With this in mind, we see that a uniform reduction of as much as 90 percent adds only about $0.62 to the cost of a ton of steel shapes, a cost increase of 0.9 percent. But the attainment of the maximum possible reductions across the board costs $3.33 per ton of shapes, an increase of about 4.6 percent. These percentage reductions range from 92.8 percent for cyanide to 100 percent for heat and are summarized below.

Residual	*Maximum Reduction (%)*
BOD	97.7
Oil	95.5
Phenol	99.4
Cyanide	92.8
Ammonia	98.7
Suspended solids	94.2
Hydrogen sulfide	99.7
Heat	100.0

It is difficult to say exactly how these correspond to the steel industry's effluent guidelines, but since those guidelines can be characterized as strict, it is probably not misleading to ask how our cost estimates compare with those coming out of EPA and the industry itself. The estimate, based on Cyrus Rice data, of the costs of compliance with the 1977 effluent standards, is $0.88 per ton of shapes, while industry data produce a figure of $5.04 per ton.[37] Thus, our figures for reductions in the range 90–100 percent fall in the same range as those developed by the parties to the debate, though we are inclined to suspect that the industry figure is inflated.

Now that we have indicated the kinds of policy questions the model is designed to address and suggested the nature of the answers obtained, in chapter 2 we shall describe the process structure of integrated steel mills and the corresponding mathematical structure of the model.

[37] See the summary given in A. T. Kearney, Inc., *Economic Analysis*, p. VI-3 and exhibit I-1. It is, of course, impossible to compare the methodologies used in our study with those employed to obtain the figures cited. Indeed, it is even difficult to follow the methodological descriptions provided in the basic documents summarized by Kearney.

2

AN OVERVIEW OF STEEL TECHNOLOGY

The steel production system is comprised of mining industries supplying raw material inputs of iron ore, coke, and limestone; the iron and steel industry itself; steel fabrication industries; and the steel scrap-processing industry which collects, separates, cleans, and grades discarded steel scrap for recycling to the steel-processing industry. In this investigation we concentrate on iron and steel production and treat the rest of the network as exogenous.

Although iron- and steelmaking is a highly complex subject, the major processing blocks in the technology matrix and the connections between blocks are not difficult to understand. A simple, schematic view is provided in figure 2.1, from which we can see that there are five major groups of activities: (1) coking, (2) sintering, (3) iron-making, (4) steelmaking, and (5) final rolling and finishing. Figure 2.1 also shows some of the residuals which emanate from each of these processing blocks. The specific residuals traced through the model are water-course discharges of five-day biochemical oxygen demand (BOD); dissolved phenols, ammonia, cyanide, and hydrogen sulfide; dissolved and suspended oil; suspended solids, and rejected heat; atmospheric discharges of sulfur dioxide, particulates, and vaporized oil, phenols, ammonia, and cyanide; and landfill discharge of solid waste. These are the residuals which leave the mill proper and affect the surrounding atmosphere and watercourses.

While our project does not deal with local environmental discharges—that is, those with impacts limited to the environs of the plant itself—these discharges do have serious implications for the occupational health of the steelworkers. This is especially true for coke oven workers, who are 2.5 times more likely to die from lung cancer than

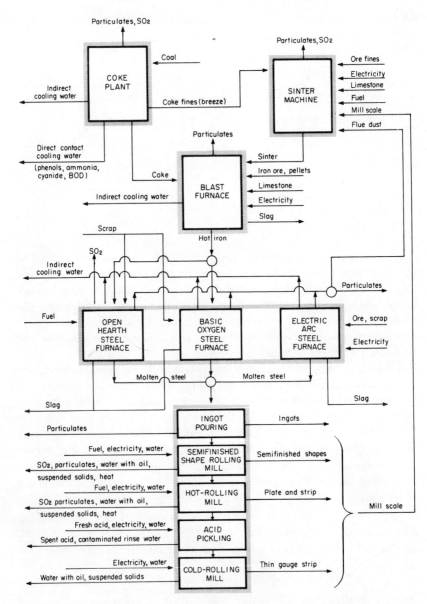

Figure 2.1.   A simplified schematic view of iron and steel production. A circle at a junction indicates a major choice point in this and subsequent charts.

are other steelworkers. Exposure to sulfuric acid fumes at the pickling baths, noise at the nail mill, lead in the galvanizing department, and carbon monoxide at the steel furnaces involves potential health risks and may consequently affect worker productivity.

The Labor Department's Occupational Safety and Health Administration and the Health, Education and Welfare Department's (HEW) National Institute of Occupational Safety and Health are responsible for promulgating worker health standards. However, the levels of local discharges are difficult to measure at present. The emissions involved are generally of the diffuse variety, such as those coming from around coke oven doors, from furnace seals, or from open-bath surfaces. Exposure to dangerous substances can be reduced by installing equipment to control process emissions, by introducing new technologies which reduce emissions, or by protecting workers directly by the use of respirators, ear muffs, or ear plugs. But eradication of such dangers depends primarily on the effectiveness of worker action, so that predictions of cost and degree of protection are problematic at best.[1]

The rest of this chapter is devoted to a brief description of the major process blocks. These are also discussed in more detail in chapters 3 through 8.

COKING

Coking involves heating coal in the absence of air, and results in the separation of some portion of the non-carbon constituents of the coal (volatile matter, water, and sulfur, which are carried off in a gas stream) from the product—coke—which is principally carbon (about 90 percent), the remainder being ash and sulfur. Coke is used as a fuel and source of carbon monoxide in the iron-making compartment (blast furnace), while the off gas from the coal is processed to remove salable by-products (light oil, sulfur, tar, phenol, ammonia).[2] The coke oven gas, net of these products, is used elsewhere in the mill as a fuel.

By-product coking is a complicated process which yields a number of complex organic waterborne residuals streams, as well as particulates, solid or semisolid residuals such as acid sludge and muck, and gaseous residuals such as sulfur dioxide and hydrogen sulfide. A number of recovery, treatment, and disposal options exist for the liquid

---

[1] See the series, "Workers in Peril," *Washington Post*, Jan. 2–5, 1975, for a comprehensive discussion on occupational ailments at steel plants.

[2] The actual level of by-product recovery depends on the cost of recovery, the market price of the by-product, and the absence or existence of residuals discharge limits on the residual from which the by-product can be manufactured.

streams. Phenol and ammonia may or may not be recovered as salable by-products from the liquid waste stream, depending on cost–price relationships. The liquor streams, either including or excluding phenols, ammonia, cyanides, and other compounds, can also be treated chemically or biologically, discharged directly to the watercourse, or evaporated in the water cooling of the incandescent coke (quenching). If quenching is practiced, the residuals in the water streams are vaporized and possibly oxidized, and become atmospheric discharges. The choice of routing options for these liquid streams (quenching, by-product recovery, biotreatment and/or chemical treatment) will be sensitive to both atmospheric and water-course discharge limits or charges on the residuals emitted. Similarly, the decision to remove hydrogen sulfide from the coke oven gas (and then to recover sulfur from it) will be sensitive to constraints or charges on sulfur dioxide emissions, because the gas can be burned throughout the plant with or without prior hydrogen sulfide removal.

The following options are included in our model:

1. Input options: high (1.2 percent) or low (0.6 percent) sulfur metallurgical coal.
2. By-product recovery options: ammonia recovery, phenol recovery, desulfurization of coke oven gas with subsequent sulfur recovery.
3. Treatment and disposal options: quenching of hot coke with treated or untreated coke plant waste-water streams, biological and/or activated carbon treatment of wastewaters, ammonia stripping and ammonia gas flaring.

SINTERING

Sintering is the process that agglomerates fine ore particles into a porous mass for charging to the blast furnace. This is accomplished by the application of heat from the combustion of coke mixed with an ore and flux (limestone) charge. Sintering was developed in order to make use of iron ore fines and recovered blast furnace flue dust, and its effect is to increase blast furnace efficiency by decreasing the weight of the blast furnace charge required to produce a ton of iron, principally through decreasing the dust loss, the coke requirement at the furnace, and the weight of flux required. On the other hand, sintering drives off into the atmosphere some impurities (especially sulfur) contained in the ore, and it poses a particulate emission problem because of the expense of collecting the gases from the moving bed of the sinter machine.

As we see, then, sintering can have both positive and negative environmental effects. It decreases the flue dust loss to the atmosphere experienced at the blast furnace and permits any flue dust recovered to be reused as an ore substitute, but causes some particulate losses of its own. It also drives off directly to the atmosphere sulfur from the ore charge which, in the absence of sintering, would be entrained in the furnace slag.

The options reflected in the sintering compartment of our model include the following.

1. Input options: high or low sulfur coke fines, four different ore qualities in terms of iron and sulfur contents, proportion of limestone added to sinter charge,[3] recovered flue dust and mill scale from elsewhere in the plant.
2. Treatment options: particulate removal devices and efficiencies.

IRONMAKING

In the blast furnace, molten iron is produced by the reduction of iron ore.[4] The ores and processed iron-bearing materials, such as sintered ore and sintered flue dust, are charged into the top of the furnace in combination with predetermined amounts of limestone and coke. At the bottom of the furnace, preheated air is blown into the charge to burn the coke in the descending mass. The gas from the burning of the coke (principally carbon monoxide) is responsible for most of the reduction as the stock of materials descends countercurrently to the flow of gases. The fusion of the acid part of the ores with the lime in the limestone and the other bases in the charge creates a slag which floats on the molten iron and is drawn periodically from the furnace. In this way, the iron in molten form is separated from the

[3] These input options are important because of the effect of sinters of differing basicity on blast furnace chemistry and input requirements. Certain high basicity or *self-fluxing* sinters, although improving blast furnace productivity, have an adverse effect on the removal efficiency of electrostatic gas cleaning equipment used for dust recovery at the sintering strand. Thus, there is a tradeoff between improved blast furnace performance and sulfur dioxide discharge across sinter types.

[4] Reduction and its opposite, oxidation, are chemical reactions, both of which are important in steel production. It is not worthwhile for us to go into the subtleties of definition which would satisfy the chemical engineer. Rather it will be sufficient for our purposes to say that oxidation involves the combination of an element or compound with oxygen (carbon and oxygen, for example, oxidize to give carbon monoxide) or an increase in the number of oxygen atoms in such a combination (carbon monoxide oxidizes to carbon dioxide). Reduction involves a decrease in the number of oxygen atoms in a compound or the separation of an element from the oxygen with which it is combined. (In iron manufacturing, elemental iron is separated by reduction from the oxygen with which it is combined in iron ore.)

nonmetallic part of the ore and from impurities such as sulfur and manganese.

Residuals from the process are mainly sulfur dioxide or hydrogen sulfide, which are driven off from the hot slag and particulates entrained in the top gas.[5] The generation of residuals will be affected by the input option chosen. For example, ungraded ores will generate more flue dust per ton of hot metal than graded ores or sinters. High sulfur input combinations will yield more slag and hence more sulfur dioxide discharge to the atmosphere per ton of hot metal than will low sulfur input combinations. Overall, the available options are as follows.

1. Input options: types of iron-bearing materials (ores, sinters, pellets), their size, iron and sulfur content, and high or low sulfur coke.

2. Treatment options: dust recovery equipment type and efficiency, extent to which entrained particulates are separated from washer water blowdown in a wet recovery system.

STEELMAKING

While the blast furnace is designed to reduce iron oxides and to separate the resulting iron from the large quantity of impurities in the ore, the making of steel from molten iron or scrap, or both, primarily involves removal of relatively small amounts of certain impurities from the metallic charge through oxidation. In particular, molten iron is saturated with carbon and contains undesirable amounts of silicon, manganese, phosphorus, and sulfur; these impurities are, with the exception of sulfur, oxidized, and the oxides are removed by solution in the furnace slag.

Another group of impurities is also important in steelmaking, but cannot, in general, be removed from the molten bath. These are the metallic elements, called tramps, which appear in steel scrap and, to a smaller extent, in molten iron. The most important of these are copper and tin, but the list also includes chromium, molybdenum, and nickel. They affect the workability of the steel, and upper limits on their

[5] Blast furnace gas is a useful in-plant fuel containing 75 to 90 Btu per cubic foot. Part of it is used in the blast furnace stoves, which heat the air injected into the bottom of the furnace. In order to keep the stoves from becoming clogged with dirt, gas cleaning is a necessary adjunct to the furnace operation, and some level of particulate removal will be undertaken even in the absence of environmental controls.

concentrations are part of the specifications of various grades of carbon steels. In alloy steels, these elements contribute to the desired properties (for example, hardness, resistance to corrosion), and the specifications may therefore include lower limits on their concentrations.

There are actually two different problems to be solved in constructing vectors for steel-making processes: refining and tramp dilution. We have simplified the task by assuming that the thermal and chemical requirements for refining are maintained, and we have concentrated our work on the tramp dilution problem. We consider three different grades of steel: (1) DQ—a high (drawing) quality carbon steel in which total tramp concentration is limited to 0.13 percent; (2) CQ—a medium (commercial) quality carbon steel with an upper limit on tramp concentrations of 0.21 percent; and (3) alloy—a representative alloy steel with a target level for total tramps of 1.76 percent. We allow the charging of hot metal from the blast furnace (except to the electric arc) along with a range of scraps, including home scraps (those produced in the finishing section) of the three steel qualities, and four purchased scraps, ranging from no. 1 factory bundles, with a total tramp element content of 0.175 percent, to no. 2 bundles (primarily compressed auto hulks), with a tramp content of 0.77 percent. The proportion of hot metal and total scrap in the charge is constrained to some extent by the furnace types, as we explain below, but within this constraint we determine charge proportions for eighteen combinations of steel output and scrap input. Total charge quantities are based on requirements for total elemental iron output, allowing for losses as flue dust and slag.

The Open Hearth Furnace

In the open hearth furnace (OH) a long, shallow charge bath of iron-bearing materials is heated by radiation from a flame. The fuel may be natural gas, coke oven gas, fuel oil, coal tar, or a combination of these. The choice of fuel will influence the sulfur dioxide generation per ton of steel produced. Oxygen may or may not be injected for combustion air enrichment and for removal of carbon from the steel. If oxygen injection is not practiced, most of the required refining oxygen will be provided by iron ore included in the charge.

The OH is the most flexible of the steel furnaces in its ability to handle different proportions of scrap and hot iron. The range covered in the model is from 70 percent hot iron and 30 percent scrap to 50 percent hot iron and 50 percent scrap, but the furnace can be used with 100 percent cold metal.

The Basic Oxygen Furnace

In the basic oxygen process, nearly pure oxygen is introduced from above the surface of a bath of molten iron contained in a basic-lined cylindrical furnace. The process is characterized by (1) use of oxygen as the sole refining agent, (2) dependence on molten iron and the oxidation reactions as the only sources of heat, implying a lower tolerance for cold metal, (3) achievement of rapid refining of the charge, and (4) generation of a large amount of red fume or dust.

The process is less flexible than the OH in its ability to use cold iron and scrap steel in the charge, due to the nature of its heat balance. The range of alternatives in the model is from 70 percent hot metal (molten iron) and 30 percent scrap to 90 percent hot metal and 10 percent iron ore.[6]

The Electric Arc Furnace

In the electric arc furnace (EA), electric power is the source of heat, with graphite electrodes positioned above the cold charge to produce an arc which melts the scrap. Refining is carried out by a combination of the heat developed by the electrical resistance of the molten metal and the heat radiated from the arc. Either oxygen injection or an ore charge may be used as the principal source of refining oxygen.

The EA is relatively inflexible in its ability to utilize molten iron in the charge. It is essentially a 100 percent cold metal user and this, in practice, means that it is essentially a 100 percent scrap user. Its economic advantage, or disadvantage, over the other furnaces is determined largely by the relative cost of fuels, scrap, and hot metal. The EA does not require supporting coke oven, sinter strand, and blast furnace facilities.

ROLLING AND FINISHING

In order to convert molten steel into a semifinished product, it must be solidified into a shape suitable for further processing. The traditional method has been to pour the metal into ingot molds, allowing the steel to cool and solidify. The ingots are subsequently removed from the mold, reheated, and rolled into semifinished shapes which are, in turn, converted into finished products by further hot and cold rolling, acid pickling (for surface cleaning), and galvanizing. All this

---

[6] Higher scrap use rates are possible in BOFs modified for scrap premelting using natural gas injection. This alternative is not included in our model.

involves considerable energy expenditure both in the reheating and the rolling activities. Consequently, the finishing section of the mill is an important source of combustion residuals (sulfur dioxide and particulates in the model) produced both directly and through the use of electricity generated in the plant. In addition, the rolling mills are sources of large volumes of wastewater containing suspended solids and dissolved and suspended oil. Finally, the acid pickling process produces a stream of spent acid, which is a liquid containing considerable residual acidity (too much to allow discharge to adjacent natural water bodies) as well as high concentrations of dissolved iron salts.

A new process, continuous casting, short-circuits the ingot stage of the finishing process, resulting in a considerable saving in energy and some reduction in the volume of mill wastewater.

Overall, the model may choose from among the following options at the finishing section.

1. Technology options: conventional or continuous casting (one or the other may be specified in advance, or the choice may be left to the solution).
2. Input options: sulfur content of fuels for reheating furnaces, sulfuric or hydrochloric pickling acid.
3. Treatment options: particulate removal devices and efficiencies, rolling mill waste-water recirculation and treatment methods (and hence efficiencies), spent acid and acid rinse water treatment and recovery alternatives.[7]

We have also provided a greatly simplified finishing module for use in runs involving changes in product mix by steel type. This module takes molten steel and converts it into semifinished shapes, in the process generating scale and home scrap in quantities roughly equivalent to those generated in the full finishing section. The options described for each process block are summarized in table 2.1.

SUMMARY OF OTHER TECHNICAL DETAILS

We have assumed a base set of production, by-product recovery, and treatment facilities which are in place and must be operated even in the absence of pollution control regulations. Other equipment is in place but may be left idle; and still other units constitute optional

---

[7] The output requirements by product type are set, as explained in chapter 7, and are not the subject of choice by the algorithm within a solution. These requirements may be changed between runs in order to explore the effect of product mix on residuals generation.

TABLE 2.1   *Alternatives in the Iron and Steel Model: Initial Conditions and Decision Variables*

	Coking	Sintering	Blast furnace	Steel shop	Finishing
Technology	No choices	No choices	No choices	*Furnace type*(I or D) 1. Basic Oxygen 2. Open Hearth 3. Electric Arc 4. BOF-EA combined	*Casting*(I or D) 1. Conventional 2. Continuous
Inputs	*Coal blend*(D) 1. High S (1.2%) 2. Low S (0.6%) *Underfiring fuel*(D) (various sulfur contents) 1. Blast furnace gas 2. Coke oven gas *Boiler fuel for steam and electricity production*(D) 1. Low S fuel oil 2. High S fuel oil 3. Medium S fuel oil 4. Natural gas	*Coke fines*(D) 1. High S 2. Low S *Ore*(D) 1. High Fe/low S 2. High Fe/high S 3. Low Fe/low S 4. Low Fe/high S *Other iron input*(D) 1. Flue dust 2. Mill scale *Limestone added*(D) 1. 5% raw mix 2. 10% raw mix 3. 15% raw mix	*Coke*(D) 1. High S 2. Low S *Charge type*[a] 1. Ore (run-of-mine or lump) 2. Sinter (high, medium, or low limestone) 3. Pellets	*Scrap-to-hot-metal ratio*(D) (for BOF, OH) *Scrap quality mix*(D) *Fuel in OH*(D) 1. Blast furnace gas 2. Coke oven gas 3. Natural gas 4. Fuel oil (various sulfur contents)	*Fuels in reheating furnaces*(D) 1. Natural gas 2. Coke oven gas 3. Low S fuel oil *Pickling acid*(D) 1. Hydrochloric 2. Sulfuric
Outputs	*Quantity of coke fines*(D) (by grinding) *Light oil*(D) 1. Refined 2. Unrefined 3. Fractionated	*Sinter Quality*(D) 1. Lime content 2. Iron content 3. Sulfur content	No choices	*Steel type mix*(I) 1. Carbon steel (drawing or commercial quality) 2. Alloy steel	*Output mix*(I) 1. Shapes 2. Strip (various thicknesses, hot or cold rolled, galvanized)
By-products(D)	1. Phenol 2. Ammonium sulfate 3. Elemental sulfur	None	1. Blast furnace gas	1. Steam from captured waste heat (at BOF and OH)	1. Road oil 2. Fuel oil (both from rolling mill emulsions)

Treatment and disposal(D)					
Water	1. Coke quenching 2. Biological treatment 3. Activated carbon treatment	No treatment	1. Wet system with sludge dewatering and sand filter	1. Wet system with sludge dewatering and sand filter	1. Scale and oil removal from mill wastewater 2. Spent acid neutralization and lagooning
Air	*Particulate removal at boiler plant*	*Particulate removal (various efficiencies)* 1. Wet system 2. Dry system	*Particulate removal* 1. Dry system	*Particulate removal (various efficiencies)* 1. Wet system 2. Dry system	No treatment
Land	1. Treatment sludge 2. Acid sludge 3. Forerunnings 4. Muck (to land)	1. Sludge 2. Recovered flue dust	1. Sludge 2. Recovered flue dust	1. Sludge 2. Recovered flue dust	1. Scale
Recirculation(D)	1. Cooling water 2. Forerunnings, acid sludge to boiler as fuel	1. Cooling water 2. Recovered flue dust to sinter	1. Cooling water 2. Recovered flue dust to sinter	1. Cooling water 2. Recovered flue dust to sinter	1. Cooling water 2. Mill scale to sinter 3. Spent acid 4. Rolling mill water
Residuals discharged(D)					
Water	1. Suspended solids 2. Heat 3. BOD 4. Oil 5. Phenols 6. NH₃ 7. Cyanide 8. Sulfide	1. Suspended solids 2. Heat	1. Suspended solids 2. Heat	1. Suspended solids 2. Heat	1. Suspended solids 2. Heat 3. BOD 4. Oil
Air	1. Particulates 2. SO₂	1. Particulates 2. SO₂	1. Particulates 2. SO₂	1. Particulates 2. SO₂	1. Particulates 2. SO₂
Land	1. Treatment sludge 2. Acid sludge 3. Muck 4. Forerunnings	1. Sludge 2. Recovered flue dust	1. Sludge 2. Slag 3. Recovered flue dust	1. Sludge 2. Slag 3. Recovered flue dust	1. Scale 2. Galvanized scrap

Note: (D) Decision variables—level determined as part of solution;   [a] Iron content of charge materials varies; see Table C.2, page 82.
(I) Initial conditions—chosen prior to solution.

investments which can be erected and operated in response to residuals discharge regulation or other influences. The former two categories of activities have been chosen to be representative of what appears to be standard industry practice. The objective function entries corresponding to these activities represent their variable costs of production, while the entries for the latter activities include both variable and discounted capital costs.

There is nothing eternal or even verifiably "right" about these bases. We do feel, however, that they represent a reasonable description of modern steel mill practice in the absence of strict environmental controls, but with some public pressure for elimination of the worst excesses of earlier periods. It is also worth setting out briefly certain other assumptions at this time.

1. We assume 1968 price levels for ore, coal, scrap, and other inputs. Other costs, most importantly capital charges for optional equipment, are also in 1968 dollars.
2. A typical annual production range of 0.8 to 1.2 million tons of semifinished shapes per plant.
3. A typical product mix, as described in chapter 6.
4. Required dust discharge control as summarized in chapter 7.
5. No required treatment of waterborne residuals discharges except at the finishing plant where hot- and cold-mill wastewaters must receive at least primary settling before discharge, and at the blast furnace, where gaswasher water must be clarified.

THE PLAN OF THE BOOK

The book is divided into two major sections: the first contains descriptions of the major processing blocks and discussions of the methods and sources used in constructing the relevant activities in the model; the second reports the results of running the model under different sets of exogenous conditions, including, among others, relative input prices, by-product prices, and residuals discharge limits. More specifically, the chapters in the first half run as follows: Chapter 3 deals with coking and related by-product and treatment activities;[8] chapter 4 is a description of sintering;[9] chapter 5 involves the blast furnace and ironmaking; and chapter 6 describes the steel furnaces and steelmaking; chapter 7 discusses the rolling and finishing section of the mill and the product mix; and, finally, chapter 8 details the nature of gas clean-

[8] Appendix A contains a description of the plant's steam- and electricity-generating facilities, and appendix B deals with the sulfur balance in the coking process.

[9] Appendix C shows our assumed ore and sinter characteristics.

ing equipment, both required and optional. In the second, or analytical, half of the book, we discuss in chapter 9 the bench mark solutions for different types of mills as defined by the steel furnace. Chapter 10 contains an analysis of how the residuals loads (and other features of the bench mark runs) are affected by changes in exogenous conditions such as input and by-product prices. In that chapter we also explore the demand for metallurgical coal (when allowance is made for sulfur content) and the supply function for by-product phenol and ammonium sulfate. We go on in chapter 11 to look at direct influences on residuals discharges, exploring marginal and total costs of achieving various levels of discharge reduction by residual and mill type. We further use the model to explore practical problems relevant to the choice between effluent charges and standards as instruments for attaining a desired level of ambient quality in a changing world. Finally, chapter 12 contains four other applications of the model to policy issues: investigation of the demand for steel scrap from auto hulks, exploration of the implications of EPA's effluent guidelines for steel mills, estimation of the cost of meeting strict air and water standards simultaneously, and prediction of the response of a particular steel mill to an actual set of effluent charges proposed by a state environmental management agency.

The material contained in chapters 3 through 8 will strike most economists as extremely tedious and as a long and annoying preamble to the discussion of the results and policy applications of the model in chapters 9 through 12. For readers of this persuasion—that is, those people without an interest in the methodology and calculations lying behind the activity matrix—we recommend skipping directly from here to chapter 9. The discussion in this chapter of the technology will provide enough background to understand 90 percent of the discussion of the final four chapters. A few arguments concerning a mill's reaction to some parameterization do depend on a more detailed knowledge of the processes involved. We have endeavored to refer the reader at these points to the pertinent pages of the descriptive chapters.

On the other hand, we feel there are two very persuasive reasons for including the detailed material in chapters 3 through 8. First, only by such an exposition can we provide a basis on which the solutions and policy implications can be judged. Second, the material in these chapters will be of interest in its own right to students of the industry, for it brings together data from a fairly wide range of sources, including some relatively unknown ones. This function may be of particular value in the context of an industry noted for its public reticence.

3

BY-PRODUCT COKING

It was during the industrial revolution that methods were developed which allowed iron smelting to be carried out using coal rather than wood as the ultimate source of the reducing agent, carbon monoxide. Just as wood had to be converted to charcoal before use in iron production, coal, which is a complex mixture of organic compounds, must be converted into coke, which is nearly pure elemental carbon, before it can be used in modern smelting (blast) furnaces. Historically, two technologies have been employed in the United States to effect this conversion: the beehive oven and the by-product (or slot) oven. The beehive process is now virtually extinct, and we shall not discuss it further. The by-product oven, on whose technology our activity matrix is based, is very much alive. It constitutes, in fact, one of the principal sources of pollution at an integrated steel mill.[1]

The by-product coking process involves the pyrolysis (heating) of coal in the absence of air for about 16 to 20 hours, depending on the design of the oven and the nature of the coal being coked. Simply described, pyrolysis is a process in which the coal bakes rather than burns. This results in the separation of some of the coal constituents (volatile matter, water, and sulfur) from the product, coke. These constituents are carried off in a gas stream, and it is from them that by-products are recov-

[1] The beehive process, from our point of view, was notable primarily for its tremendous air pollution potential, since the coal constituents driven off in coking were discharged to the atmosphere instead of being subject to at least partial recovery. New continuous coking processes are on the horizon. Their development has been stimulated by the desire to use cheaper coals (whose quality is too low for current practice) as a charge material. The proponents of these processes claim that the air pollution problems associated with them are not severe. Because their widespread commercial application is not expected before 1985, they too are ignored in our activity matrix.

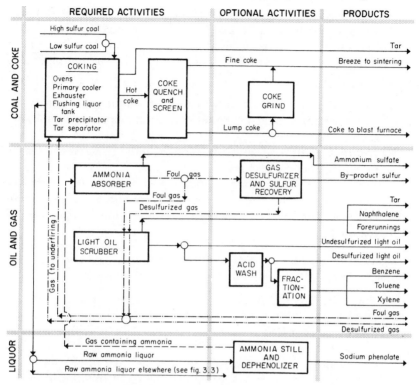

Figure 3.1. The coke and by-product system.

ered, as described below. Only about 10 percent of the coke consists of ash, sulfur, and nonvolatilized organic matter other than pure carbon.

The lump coke product from the ovens is used in the blast furnace after it has been cooled by direct application of water (quenched) and screened to a uniform size. Some small coke fines (breeze) are inevitably produced in the screening process, and these are mixed with iron ore fines and limestone at the sinter plant to form an agglomerate suitable for blast furnace charging. The off gas from the coke ovens, after being cooled by direct contact water sprays, is processed to remove such salable by-products as tar, naphthalene, ammonium sulfate, sulfur, and light oil. The coke oven gas, net of these products, is recycled for use as a fuel at the ovens or elsewhere in the mill.

Figure 3.1 is a schematic flow diagram of the intermediate output and by-product flows. The actual extent of by-product recovery depends, of course, upon the cost of recovery, the market price of the by-product, and the absence or existence of discharge limits on the residual from which the by-product can be manufactured.

We have constructed a module that reflects industry practice and provides for optional by-product treatment and recovery operations. We will discuss several required by-product recovery activities, all of which involve the coke oven gas stream. These activities and the equipment required are as follows.

1. Ammonia absorber. Removes ammonia from the gas stream.
2. Tar separator and tar precipitator. Separate tars from liquor and gas streams.
3. Light oil scrubber. Separates light oil, naphthalene, and some additional tar from the gas stream.
4. Light oil acid washer and fractionation equipment. Removes acids from recovered light oil and separates it into toluene, xylene, and benzene. This equipment must be installed, but its operation is optional.

In addition, we have included a number of recovery activities that are optional. These activities and the equipment used are as follows.

1. Ammonia still–dephenolizer. Recovers by-product ammonia and phenols from flushing liquor blowdown. This equipment may or may not be included as a required installation, but its operation is optional.
2. Coke crushing and grinding unit. Grinds coke to provide additional breeze for sintering operations. This and all following units are optional for both installation and operation.
3. Desulfurization unit. Removes hydrogen sulfide from coke oven gas.

Finally, the coking unit includes four major residuals treatment options. These are not shown in figure 3.1.

1. Ammonia stripper. Removes ammonia from flushing liquor blowdown.
2. Biological treatment facility. Converts water-soluble organic compounds into insoluble compounds by oxidation.
3. Carbon treatment facility. Adsorbs contaminants from wastewaters on activated carbon.
4. Cooling tower. Lowers the temperature of indirect cooling water prior to recirculation.

For several reasons, we have designed somewhat more treatment, recovery, and disposal flexibility into the vectors of the by-product coking module than into other parts of the model. In the first place, the module must deal with a complex process that yields a number of complex organic waterborne residuals, particulates, gaseous residuals such as sulfur dioxide, and the solid or semisolid acid sludge and muck that are generated in light oil recovery and upgrading. Second, the module must reflect the fact that by-product production and residuals treatment and disposal processes are intimately interconnected in coking. It must also reflect the fact that the particular combination of these operations chosen under differing sets of external conditions will greatly affect the mill's emissions of cyanide, phenol, and ammonia, and, in addition, will cause shifts in the content of waterborne and atmospheric discharges. Finally, the module must provide flexible alternatives for reducing direct discharge of highly concentrated coking streams into the watercourse. These liquors can have deleterious impacts on a lake or river because (1) their high oxygen demand burdens the self-purifying capacity of the watercourse, (2) their toxic nature may prove lethal to natural life and dangerous to humans, and (3) their undesirable tastes and odors may contaminate water withdrawn from the receiving watercourse for domestic supply.

In explaining the coke and coal by-product production process, we shall follow an outline which approximates the previously discussed structure of our coking module instead of using the product sequence approach often found in the literature. First, we discuss the required coke and by-product production processes and the choices available within this group. The second section deals with the by-product recovery activities whose installation and operation is optional. Then residuals removal from liquid streams by treatment will be accounted for. (In appendix A we describe the provisions in the model for the production of steam and electricity.)

BY-PRODUCT COKING

Coke Ovens and Required Processes

Let us first direct our attention to what we assume every coke plant must do: produce the intermediate outputs of coke and breeze and recover tar and ammonia from the volatilized stream for sale as by-product tar and ammonium sulfate. To represent compactly all of the processes involved, we collapse the separate process units (coke ovens, primary cooler, tar precipitators–separators, flushing liquor decanters, ammonia absorber and final coolers) into a single, summary vector.

Actual coking practice in the industry generally involves blending coals of different makeups with the aim of obtaining a product with desired physical and chemical properties. Rather than including as inputs to our model coals from many different seams and allowing the program to select an optimal blend under different sets of exogenous conditions, we have postulated two alternative bituminous blends which differ only in sulfur content.[2] Our high sulfur coal blend has a sulfur content of 1.2 percent; the low sulfur blend is 0.6 percent sulfur.[3] There is a separate summary vector for each of these coal blends.

In these vectors, the yields of the principal product, coke, and the various by-products have been determined by using rules of thumb reported in the literature. In general, yields have been assumed to be the same for both blends, except for a sulfur correction in certain cases. Specifically, based on inspection of a number of sources, we assume that one short ton of coal will yield 1,400 pounds of coke, 90 pounds of breeze, 89.3 pounds (10 gallons) of tar,[4] and about 356 pounds of gas. This gas is the principal source of by-products and has value within the mill as fuel. In order to prepare the gas for these further uses, it is cooled in two stages (figure 3.2): First, it is subjected to direct spraying with recirculating flushing liquor; and then it undergoes indirect cooling in a heat exchanger called the primary cooler.

Flushing liquor and the condensate from the gas side of the primary cooler are detained in a decanter, to separate out the tar, before being returned to the cooling sprays. About 30 gallons of flushing liquor per ton of coal are continuously withdrawn from the recirculating system for discharge, treatment, and/or recovery of phenols and ammonia at the dephenolizer and ammonia still.[5]

The ammonia remaining in the gas (plus the ammonia added to the gas stream from the ammonia still, if it is operated) is washed from the coke oven gas by direct contact with dilute sulfuric acid at the ammonia absorber, producing ammonium sulfate. The total amount of ammonia recoverable from 1 ton of coal with both the absorber and still in operation is approximately 5 pounds, which translates into 20 pounds of am-

[2] Trozzo included the coal-blending problem directly in the linear program he constructed to investigate blast furnace location problems. See Charles L. Trozzo, "The Technical Efficiency of Integrated Blast Furnace Capacity" (Ph.D. dissertation, Harvard University, 1966). Our approach represents a fairly severe simplification, but since we are principally concerned with sulfur in any event, it is doubtful that this simplification does real violence to the model's usefulness.

[3] The chemical composition of our high sulfur coking coal mixture is 60.8 percent fixed carbon, 6.4 percent ash, 1.2 percent sulfur, and 31.6 percent water and volatile matter. The low sulfur blend has 62.9 percent carbon, 4.6 percent ash, 0.6 percent sulfur and 31.9 percent water and volatile matter.

[4] Yields showing these values to be reasonable are reported by Harold E. McGannon, ed., The Making, Shaping and Treating of Steel, 8th ed. (Pittsburgh: United States Steel Corporation, 1964), pp. 73 and 99; Bureau of Mines, Minerals Yearbook, vols. 1 and 2; Metals, Minerals and Fuels; Watkins Cyclopedia of the Steel Industry, 12th ed. (Pittsburgh: Steel Publications Inc., 1969), p. 43.

[5] Phillip J. Wilson, Jr., and Joseph H. Wells, Coal, Coke and Coal Chemicals (New York: McGraw-Hill, 1950), p. 308.

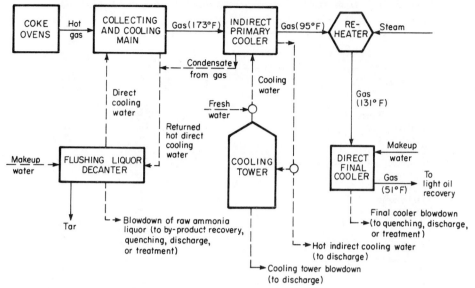

Figure 3.2. The coke oven gas cooling system.

monium sulfate. Of this total, 13.1 pounds are producible from 3.3 pounds of ammonia contained in the gas stream exclusive of the amount potentially available from the ammonia still.[6]

Process inputs. The essential coking processes require, in addition to coal, inputs of electricity and steam (see appendix A), cooling and process water, and sulfuric acid. The quantities of these, expressed per ton of coal coked, are summarized below. In addition, we show in this table the quantity of heat required.[7]

Input	Unit	Quantity
Electricity	kWh	37.8
Steam	lb.	8.3
Heat required for underfiring	10^6 Btu	2.0
Makeup process water	10^3 gal.	0.03
Sulfuric acid	lb.	13.1

[6] C. W. Fisher, "Coke and Gas," in C. Fred Gurnham, ed., *Industrial Wastewater Control*, Massachusetts Institute of Technology Chemical Technology Monograph Series, vol. 2 (New York: Academic Press, 1965), p. 220; and W. G. Cousins and A. B. Mindler, "Tertiary Treatment of Weak Ammonia Liquor," *Journal of the Water Pollution Control Federation*, vol. 44 (April 1972), p. 608.

[7] Bases for the figures used below are discussed in detail in W. J. Vaughan, "A Residuals Management Model of the Iron and Steel Industry: A Linear Programming Approach" (Ph.D. dissertation, Georgetown University, February 1975), pp. 64–65.

TABLE 3.1   *Base Prices of Inputs and Outputs in Coke and Coal By-product*
Production

Item	Unit	Price (1968 $/unit)
Inputs		
High sulfur metallurgical coal	short ton	10.25
Low sulfur metallurgical coal	short ton	10.62
Process water	10^3 gal.	0.015
Sulfuric acid (74% purity)	lb.	0.013
Lime	lb.	0.008
Caustic soda	lb.	0.040
Wash oil	lb.	0.015
Labor	hr.	5.000
Outputs		
High sulfur tar	gal.	0.099
Low sulfur tar	gal.	0.111
Ammonium sulfate	short ton	27.000
Phenol	lb.	0.090
High sulfur crude light oil	gal.	0.119
Low sulfur crude light oil	gal.	0.125
Acid-washed light oil	gal.	0.137
Naphthalene	lb.	0.060
Heavy solvents	gal.	0.160
Benzene	gal.	0.240
Toluene	gal.	0.220
Xylene	gal.	0.230
Sulfur	long ton	20.000

Note: For complete bibliographical information, see the Table References at the back of this book.
Sources: The principal sources of price information for coking inputs and outputs consulted in preparation of this table were U.S. Department of the Interior, Bureau of Mines, *Mineral Industry Surveys* (December 1969); U.S. Department of the Interior, Bureau of Mines, *1968 Minerals Yearbook;* W. L. Nelson, *Guide to Petroleum Refinery Operating Costs;* and *Chemical Pricing Patterns.*

Labor, of course, is also required in production, and our best information indicated that these essential activities involve a labor input of 0.36 man-hours per ton.[8] These inputs are all reflected in physical terms in the coking vectors and are provided to the overall model by purchase activities. The prices of these and other inputs as well as of by-products are summarized in table 3.1.

[8] Based on a *total* coke plant labor input of 0.41 man-hours per ton, calculated from the *Minerals Yearbook*, vol. 3, *Area Reports: Domestic, 1968*, pp. 38, 54. Eighty-nine percent of this total was allocated to the basic operation on the basis of data in Dietrich Wagener, "Development Trends in European Coke Plant Techniques," *Blast Furnace and Steel Plant*, vol. 56 (October 1968). The labor inputs for the subsidiary units discussed below are estimated independently and the total for the plant thus derived brackets the original assumed total, being slightly higher (0.44 man-hours per ton) or lower (0.39 man-hours per ton) depending on whether gas desulfurization and sulfur recovery are or are not operated.

Process costs. Since the model is designed to reflect an existing plant (save for treatment and certain by-product recovery options as discussed later), the only cost reflected in the vector objective function entries is equipment maintenance. This is based on a simple rule of thumb applied to capital costs: annual maintenance cost is assumed to be 4 percent of coke plant capital cost.

Hard data on coke oven and by-product plant capital costs are extremely difficult to obtain. The most recent published estimate of undiscounted coke plant investment costs discovered during this study is presented below, expressed in 1968 dollars per ton of coal input.[9]

	Range of Reported Construction Costs
New plant on greenfield site	
Coke plant exclusive of by-products	20.69–21.32
By-products plant	8.15– 8.78
Total for new plant	28.84–30.10
Rebuilding of existing battery	10.66–11.28

Industry sources have claimed that this published cost estimate is somewhat low for a coke plant of the capacity assumed in the model (0.7 million tons of coal annually). Accordingly, we take $43.00 per ton of coal as our estimate of the capital cost of our required coking installation, which includes coke oven, quench tower, ammonia absorber, and light oil recovery costs. Applying the maintenance cost rule of thumb to this figure yields a charge of $1.72 per ton of coal which is entered in the objective functions of the two essential coking activities.[10]

Process residuals. The residuals generated in the process block under consideration are contained either in escaped gases or captured liquor streams. The former, evolved from coke oven charging and pushing, are largely uncontrollable given the current technology. The latter are contained in the blowdown stream from the recirculating flushing liquor system from which they may be removed by by-product processing or

---

[9] Thomas M. Barnes, Albert O. Hoffman, and H. W. Lownie, Jr., *Evaluation of Process Alternatives to Improve Control of Air Pollution from Production of Coke,* PB 189 266 (Springfield, Va.: NTIS, January 1970), p. II-21. Their costs, expressed in 1969 dollars per ton of coke, were converted to 1968 dollars per ton of coal by application of the U.S. Department of Commerce Composite Construction Cost Index and an assumed ton of coke per ton of coal ratio of 0.70.

[10] Exclusive of utilities, our estimates yield a maintenance and labor cost of $3.53 per ton of coal for the entire coking operation if only the installed, required facilities are operated. If all facilities are operated, including the add-ons, the combined labor and maintenance costs amount to $3.98 per ton of coal. The total direct costs excluding the coal itself, but including labor, maintenance, utilities, and materials reported by Barnes, Hoffman, and Lownie in coke oven and by-product plant operations fall between $3.00 and $4.40 per ton of coal, close to our values when an allowance for utilities (electricity, steam, water, etc.) is made.

treatment prior to disposal in quenching or discharge to the watercourse. Per ton of coal, the uncontrolled escaping gases contain an assumed 2.10 pounds of particulates which settle locally, along with 0.032 pounds of sulfur compounds (hydrogen sulfide and thiophenes) from high sulfur coal blends or 0.016 pounds from low sulfur blends.[11]

Concentrations of residuals in the raw ammonia liquor (the flushing liquor blowdown stream) for high sulfur and low sulfur coke have been assumed after inspection of liquor analysis from a number of sources (see table 3.2).

The final cooler following the ammonia absorber is designed as a direct contact scrubber with a recirculating water system (figure 3.2). Here the coke oven gas is given its final cooling. Recirculated water is used in most final cooler applications, and we assume that a blowdown of 3.9 gallons per ton of coal must be discharged; this is 4 percent of the total recirculating volume. One thousand gallons of this blowdown are assumed to contain 1.82 pounds (218 ppm) of biochemical oxygen demand (BOD), 0.88 pounds (105 ppm) of phenol, and 1.67 pounds (200 ppm) of cyanides.[12]

Quenching

The incandescent coke, after being pushed from the coke ovens at a temperature of 1,800 to 2,000°F, is transported in rail cars to the quenching station where it is cooled to a temperature of 200 to 500°F by sprays of water to prevent it from simply burning up in the air. The sensible heat of the coke is sufficient to flash evaporate as much as half of the water applied to it. This water leaves the top of the quenching tower as an immense cloud of steam. The hot water that does not evaporate is drained and settled to remove coke fines before it is returned to the quenching tank for recirculation.[13]

---

[11] These emissions are difficult to quantify precisely. The particulate emission factor is reported by A. E. Vandegrift and L. J. Shannon, *Particulate Pollutant System Study*, vol. 3: *Handbook of Emission Properties*, report by Midwest Research Institute for U.S. Environmental Protection Agency, Air Pollution Control Office (Durham, N.C.: May 1, 1971), p. 120. The sulfur compounds lost are assumed to amount to 0.125 percent of the total sulfur output. In effect this means that less than 0.5 percent of the coke oven gas is lost, a conservative assumption based on conversations with Eugene Sheridan of the U.S. Department of the Interior, Bureau of Mines. For evidence of the wide variability in sulfur compound losses from coke ovens, see United Nations, Economic Commission for Europe, *Air Pollution by Coking Plants* (ST/ECE/Coal/26) (1968), pp. 25–30.

[12] BOD and phenol concentrations are derived from Nelson Nemerow, *Theories and Practices of Industrial Waste Treatment* (Reading, Mass.: Addison-Wesley, 1963), p. 399; cyanide concentration is from Fisher, "Coke and Gas," p. 227.

[13] We calculate the total heat removal requirement in quenching to be 1.01 million Btu per ton of coal. The removal of this heat is accomplished by the evapora-

In the basic production vectors described above, the requirements for evaporative and temperature change cooling of the coke are included separately. The evaporative component of quenching may be accomplished using river water alone or in combination with any of the untreated or treated process water streams (see figure 3.3). If the latter streams are employed for this purpose, atmospheric emissions of hydrogen sulfide, oil, phenols, and ammonia result that are directly equivalent to the amounts in the incoming stream or streams.[14] (As we shall see later, this tradeoff between water and air pollution is central in judging the impact of the 1972 Federal Water Pollution Control Act amendments on the industry and its surroundings.) The degree rise requirement is satisfied by water from the recirculating system which, we assume, loses 1 percent of its volume to evaporation and 4 percent to blowdown, requiring a makeup withdrawal of river water of 50 gallons per 10,000 recirculating gallons, or 12 gallons per ton of coal. This small blowdown is assumed to contain some BOD (240 ppm), oil (10 ppm), phenols (50 ppm), and suspended solids (100 ppm), but is not subjected to further treatment.

If process waste streams such as ammonia liquor are employed in quenching, the steel firm will incur extra costs regardless of the environmental implications of the resultant atmospheric discharges. This is because of the serious corrosion of exposed metals in the quenching area induced by chlorides and oxides of sulfur and nitrogen released during quenching, as well as the deposition on the coke of chlorides which attack the lining of the blast furnaces.[15]

Although steel mill personnel have admitted to the existence of this wholly private cost disincentive to quenching disposal of contaminated streams, only one estimate of the magnitude of this corrosion cost has been suggested, $0.143 per ton of coke.[16] On this slender thread we hang a base case charge of $3.33 per 1,000 gallons for the quenching alternative using high sulfur raw ammonia liquor, the most contaminated waste stream ($0.143 per ton of coke divided by 0.043×10^3 gallons of liquor

---

tion of some water and the heating of the unevaporated remainder. Roughly 100 gallons per ton of coal are reported to be evaporated. This translates into 0.94 million Btu removed by evaporation, leaving 0.07 million Btu per ton of coal to be carried off by the heated water. Assuming a 35° F rise in this water implies 240 gallons required per ton of coal. Therefore, the combined gross water requirement in quenching amounts to 340 gallons per ton of coal, of which 29 percent is evaporated.

[14] Some of these impurities may be absorbed by the coke, but they eventually end up as blast furnace gas washer water contaminants or atmospheric emissions from by-product blast furnace gas combustion.

[15] Ross Nebolsine, "Steel Plant Wastewater Treatment and Reuse," a paper presented at the annual meeting of the Association of Iron and Steel Engineers, New York, 1966 (Mimeographed), p. 9.

[16] Communicated in a letter to W. J. Vaughan from Henry C. Bramer, President, Datagraphics, Inc., Pittsburgh, Pa., August 3, 1973.

TABLE 3.2 *Residuals Concentrations in Various Liquor Effluents*

Residual	Raw ammonia liquor			Light oil decanter liquor			Combined ammonia still and dephenolizer liquor		
	ppm	lb./1,000 gal.[a]	lb./ton coal	ppm	lb./1,000 gal.[a]	lb./ton coal	ppm	lb./1,000 gal.[a]	lb./ton coal
Five-day BOD	10,000	83.40	2.50	635	5.30	0.060	4,036	33.66	1.32
Ammonia	6,900	57.50	1.72	10	0.08	0.001	100[b]	0.83[b]	0.03[b]
Phenol	2,960	24.69	0.74	100	0.83	0.009	157[c]	1.31[c]	0.05[c]
Oil	1,200	10.01	0.30	60	0.50	0.005	170[e]	1.42[e]	0.06[e]
Suspended solids	460	3.84	0.12	—[d]	—[d]	—[d]	350[e]	2.92[e]	0.11[e]
Sulfur									
High sulfur coal	2,020	17.68	0.53	—[d]	—[d]	—[d]	1,475[f]	12.30[f]	0.48[f]
Low sulfur coal	1,060	8.84	0.27	—[d]	—[d]	—[d]	737[f]	6.15[f]	0.24[f]
Cyanides	50	0.42	0.01	25	0.21	0.002	25	0.21	0.01

Sources: Ray O. Bowman, "Wilputte Centrifugal Extractor Phenol Plant," p. 234; Cousins and Mindler, "Tertiary Treatment of Weak Ammonia Liquor," p. 607; Elliot and Lafreniere, "Extraction of Phenolic Compounds," pp. 11–17; C. Fred Gurnham, ed., *Industrial Wastewater Control*, pp. 226–227; Fisher, Hepner, and Tallon, "Coke Plant Effluent Treatment," pp. 317–319; H. H. Lowry, ed., *Chemistry of Coal Utilization*, p. 1083; Nelson L. Nemerow, *Industrial Waste Treatment*, p. 399; Ohio River Valley Water Sanitation Commission, *Reducing Phenol Wastes*, p. 19; Patterson and Minear, *Wastewater Treatment Technology*, p. 196; and Wilson and Wells, table 23, p. 310.

[a] Pounds per 1,000 gallons is equal to parts per million (ppm) multiplied by 0.00834.

[b] Based on assumed ammonia still recovery efficiency of 98.5 percent.

[c] Based on a dephenolizer recovery efficiency of 95 percent for phenol and 86 percent for phenol-containing oil.

[d] Sulfur and suspended solids are entrained in the muck.

[e] No removal at the still or dephenolizer is assumed, so that the concentration in the influent is simply reduced by the ratio of incoming to outgoing liquor.

[f] Concentration in influent reduced by the ratio of incoming to outgoing liquor, with allowance for 0.05 pounds of sulfur in the high sulfur case and 0.025 pounds in the low sulfur case removed by sodium hydroxide. This calculation was performed on the basis of procedures outlined in Beychok, *Aqueous Wastes*, pp. 71–75.

per ton of coke). The other less-contaminated ammonia liquor streams are charged a fraction of this amount, depending upon their sulfur and ammonia contents relative to the base stream. Specifically, the estimated cost of corrosion associated with low sulfur raw ammonia liquor is $2.93 per thousand gallons; $0.57 for dephenolized high sulfur liquor; and only $0.30 for dephenolized low sulfur liquor. No charge is imposed upon any of the other process effluent streams or on ammonia liquor streams which have been treated biologically or by carbon adsorption, since they contain insignificant amounts of sulfur and ammonia.

Light Oil Recovery

Light oil contained in the gas leaving the final cooler can be recovered either from undesulfurized or desulfurized coke oven gas. The performance of the required light oil activities[17] in either case will be the same except for the fact that less insoluble muck will be formed in the latter instance because the hydrogen sulfide content of the desulfurized gases is lower. The most widely used method for recovery of light oil from coke oven gas is absorption in a higher boiling range oil called wash oil using countercurrent scrubbers. The enriched oil from the scrubbers is preheated and introduced into the top of a fractionating column in which the light oil is separated from the wash oil by direct steam distillation. The mixture of light oil and water vapor is then condensed, and the water is separated from the by-product light oil. The wash oil is cooled, and decanted to separate out any water it might contain before being regenerated and recirculated to the scrubbers for another round of absorption.

Since the wash oil absorbs dirt and contaminants such as hydrogen sulfide and tarry particles from the gas, as well as light oil itself, a precipitate that must be eliminated from the system forms in the decanters. This muck is boiled with steam to separate the good wash oil from the dirt and tarry matter, which become the final residual muck.

The products, utilities, and residuals associated with light oil recovery are shown in table 3.3. The waterborne residuals associated with this processing step are contained in the decanter effluents, the composition of which, along with the implied loads per ton of coal, are shown in table 3.2.

Raw light oil upgrading by acid treatment. The raw light oil can be sold as is, or it may be washed with sulfuric acid in order to remove sulfur-containing organic impurities which cannot be removed by fractional

---

[17] At steel plants which use coke oven gas as a fuel in their steel-making processes, light oil is generally recovered from the gas. See Wilson and Wells, *Coal, Coke, and Coal Chemicals*, p. 334.

TABLE 3.3 Products, Utilities, and Residuals Associated with Light Oil Recovery

(per ton of coal)

| Products, utilities, and residuals | Unit | Undesulfurized gas | | Desulfurized gas |
		High sulfur	Low sulfur	
Products[a]				
Light oil	lb.	18.1	18.0	18.1
Tar	lb.	0.16	0.16	0.16
Naphthalene	lb.	0.16	0.16	0.16
Forerunnings	lb.	0.45	0.42	0.45
Heavy solvents	lb.	0.58	0.58	0.58
Coke oven gas	lb.	338	334	331
Utilities				
Wash oil makeup[b]	lb.	0.60	0.38	0.16
Steam[c]	lb.	94.20	94.20	94.20
Heat removed from wash oil[d]	10⁶ Btu	0.10	0.10	0.10
Labor[e]	hr.	0.02	0.02	0.02
Residuals				
Muck	lb.	1.55	1.14	0.77
Decanter liquor blowdown[c]	gal.	11.3	11.3	11.3

[a] Our product yields are based on information in McGannon, The Making, Shaping and Treating of Steel, 8th ed., pp. 130, 131, and 137; and Wilson and Wells, Coal, Coke and Coal Chemicals, pp. 336 and 337. We have adjusted for the varying sulfur contents of the four entering gases.

[b] To replace wash oil lost in the muck.

[c] At the stripping still, 0.6 pounds of steam are required per gallon of recirculating wash oil. The blowdown volume is simply assumed to equal the condensate from this steam.

[d] Wilson and Wells, Coal, Coke and Coal Chemicals, p. 348.

[e] Wagener, "European Coke Plant Techniques."

distillation (table 3.4). In the model this process is assumed to be in place, but it need not be operated. After the light oil is washed with sulfuric acid, it is washed with water, neutralized with caustic soda, and then sold as is or fed to a series of continuous stills, where it is separated into benzene, toluene, and xylene (BTX) streams. Operation is optional for this process as well.

The resinous products of the reactions between the sulfuric acid and the organic compounds in the BTX form a sticky sludge (containing unused acid and entrained oil), which is separated from the BTX in an agitator. In the model this acid sludge can either be dumped in pits (assumed to be located some distance from the plant) or burned as an in-plant fuel.

Light oil fractionation. The final installed unit in the process flow sequence of figure 3.1 involves final fractionating columns which can be used to produce pure BTX from the acid-washed light oil, thereby yield-

TABLE 3.4 Treatment of Light Oil Extracted from the Four Coke Oven Gas Streams

(*per ton of coal*)

Products, utilities and residuals	Unit	High sulfur gas	Low sulfur gas
Acid washing			
Product			
Acid-washed light oil[a]	lb.	17.0	17.3
Utilities			
Sodium hydroxide[a]	lb.	0.30	0.15
Consumed sulfuric acid[a]	lb.	2.0	1.0
Steam[b]	lb.	0.10	0.10
Electricity[b]	kWh	0.006	0.006
Labor[b]	hr.	0.001	0.001
Maintenance[b]	$	0.001	0.001
Residual			
Acid sludge[a]	lb.	3.6	2.0
Final fractionization of acid-washed light oil			
Products			
Benzene	lb.	11.9	12.1
Toluene	lb.	3.6	3.6
Xylene	lb.	1.5	1.6
Utilities[c]			
Steam	lb.	3.2	3.3
Heat removed by cooling water	10^6 Btu	0.0022	0.0022
Electricity	kWh	0.005	0.005
Labor	hr.	0.002	0.002
Maintenance	$	0.0056	0.0057
Residuals			
Condensate[d]	gal.	0.39	0.40

[a] Based on data in Wilson and Wells, *Coal, Coke and Coal Chemicals*, pp. 358 and 360. We associate the high end of the reported use rates with high sulfur gas and the low end with low sulfur gas.

[b] W. L. Nelson, *Guide to Refinery Operating Costs*, pp. 113 and 120. Maintenance cost appears as an objective function entry in the model.

[c] Calculated assuming four fractionating towers with 120 barrels of daily capacity from information in W. L. Nelson, ibid., p. 45. Maintenance cost appears as an objective function entry in the model.

[d] The volumetric equivalent of the steam input. The BOD load per ton of coal is only about 0.002 lb. The phenol load is insignificant.

ing 0.70, 0.21, and 0.09 pounds, respectively, of the products per pound of input.[18] The only residual from this process is a fractionation condensate containing 5.3 pounds of BOD and 0.60 pounds of phenols per 1,000 gallons.[19] The products, utilities, and residuals associated with final fractionation are shown in table 3.4.

[18] Ibid., pp. 336 and 337.
[19] Nemerow, *Industrial Waste Treatment*, p. 399.

OPTIONAL BY-PRODUCT PRODUCTION ACTIVITIES

Our model contains several optional processes not always found at by-product coking installations. These processes may, however, prove to be profitable to install and operate from the firm's point of view under certain sets of relative prices, or, on the other hand, may be part of a least-cost adjustment to tightened residuals discharge restrictions. Specifically, we include removal of waste heat from indirect cooling water streams, recovery of ammonia and phenol from raw ammonia liquor, coke oven gas desulfurization, and recovery of sulfur from the hydrogen sulfide thus produced. Coke grinding is a minor process option which affects residuals discharges in an indirect way. (This produces additional coke fines for the sinter plant.)

Cooling Water and Waste Heat Removal

Waste heat requiring indirect cooling is generated in each process segment and is carried away by cooling water, which is allowed to rise 20° F in temperature in the coolers. This water is therefore capable of removing 20 Btu per pound, or 0.167 million Btu per 1,000 gallons. In the simplest case, when there is no pressure on the steel mill to reduce either its water withdrawals or its residual heat discharges, this cooling water is supplied on a once-through basis at an assumed cost of $0.015 per 1,000 gallons.[20] The heat picked up by the cooling water will be directly discharged to the watercourse in the unconstrained case.

If there is pressure to reduce either water withdrawals or waterborne heat discharge, the mill is permitted the option of installing cooling towers. The cooling system then becomes semiclosed with makeup withdrawals estimated to be 6.75 percent of gross cooling water flow. This makeup replaces water lost through evaporation (the method of cooling the circulating water) amounting to 2.0 percent of circulating water, windage (water not evaporated but blown out of the towers as mist) of 0.75 percent, and blowdown (necessary to control the concentration of solids in the circulating water) of 4.0 percent. The total cost of cooling tower use, net of makeup water cost but including operation, maintenance, and discounted capital costs is $0.025 per 1,000 gallons of circulating water.[21]

[20] This cost is low to reflect the fact that once-through cooling water may be of low quality and requires little or no pretreatment, even if it is withdrawn from polluted sources. Boiler-quality water does require preparation and is assumed to be ten times as expensive as a result.

[21] Information on the costs and operating characteristics of cooling towers was obtained from Paul Cootner and G. O. G. Löf, *Water Demand for Steam Electric Generation* (Baltimore: Johns Hopkins University Press for Resources for the Future, 1965), pp. 60–65; and Ian Wigham, "Designing Optimum Cooling Systems," *Chemical Engineering* (Aug. 9, 1971), pp. 95–102.

Product Transfer: Coke Crush and Grind

An insufficient supply of coke fines from coke screening might result if blast furnace activities using sinter burdens (the preparation of which requires coke breeze as well as ore fines and limestone) are lower in cost than blast furnace activities using direct ore charges. In order that the availability of sintering activities not be artificially limited by the supply of fine coke, we allow the plant to invest in coke-crushing machinery to grind coke into sinter plant fuel.

These activities operate on 2,000 pounds of either high or low sulfur coke, and produce 1,999 pounds of breeze, losing an assumed 1 pound of particulates in the process.[22] The pulverizing operation requires 0.005 man-hours and 14 kWh of electricity per ton of coke input.[23] A combined maintenance charge of $0.016 per ton and a capital charge of $0.040 per ton appear in the objective function.[24]

Coke Oven Gas Desulfurization and Sulfur Recovery

It is generally contended by industry people that, given the current and expected market price for sulfur, coke oven gas desulfurization and sulfur recovery are not profitable at the steel mill.[25] This has not always been so. In the early 1950s, for example, in a period of worldwide sulfur shortage, the Bethlehem Steel Company installed a desulfurizing–sulfur recovery unit at its Sparrows Point plant primarily to assure self-sufficiency in sulfuric acid and secondarily to upgrade coke oven gas so that it might be used at the open-hearth (OH) as a purchased fuel substitute. The process costs, if charged entirely to recovered sulfur, amounted to $77.40 per ton in the mid-1950s; this is obviously unrecoverable (if inflated to current prices) at the present low market price of sulfur.[26] In

[22] This was suggested by J. K. Delson, Electrical Engineering Department, Ben Gurion University of the Negev, Beer–Sheva, Israel.

[23] The man-hour requirement is assumed to be about 5 percent of the man-hour requirement at the sinter plant. The electricity requirement is taken from *Steam: Its Generation and Use* (New York: Babcock and Wilcox Company, 1963), p. 17–11.

[24] The maintenance charge is from ibid., p. 17–11. The discounted capital charge (10 percent interest rate and a ten-year life) for our small plant of 10 tons-per-hour capacity is based on information in Edward T. McNally, Robert C. Woodhead, and John L. Gamble, "Gauging the Costs in Coal-preparation Plant Selection," *Coal Age* (August 1966), pp. 78–82.

[25] This statement is based on an arbitrary assignment of all desulfurization costs to the recovered sulfur with no credit taken for the increased value of the desulfurized gas as a low sulfur, purchased fuel substitute at, for example, the OH and soaking pits. The situation may be contrasted with that existing in the petroleum refining industry where gas desulfurization appears to be profitable given the value of the petrochemical feedstocks thus produced. See C. S. Russell, *Residuals Management in Industry: A Case Study of Petroleum Refining* (Baltimore: Johns Hopkins University Press for Resources for the Future, 1973), pp. 103 and 114–120.

[26] J. K. Kurtz, "Recovery and Utilization of Sulfur from Coke Oven Gas," in Frederick S. Mallette, ed., *Problems and Control of Air Pollution* (New York: Reinhold Publishing Company, 1955), pp. 215–221.

fact, Bethlehem no longer operates this unit, according to the Maryland Environmental Service. The air pollution abatement benefits of the process were considered welcome but incidental at that time, probably because even undesulfurized coke oven gas has traditionally been regarded as a relatively clean fuel in comparison with other fuels available for industrial use. Current public concern with environmental quality has recently been reflected in the technical literature in the form of increased awareness of the environmental benefits resulting from the additional desulfurization cost.[27]

In the model, coke oven gas desulfurization is accomplished by a composite process which removes 96 percent of the hydrogen sulfide present. Steam is required and waste heat is generated in amounts depending on the sulfur content of the gas. Expressed per ton of coal input to the coke ovens, the gas from the high sulfur coal (about 2 percent sulfur) implies use of 1.19 pounds of steam and produces 0.05 million Btu of waste heat. The low sulfur coal produces a 1 percent sulfur gas, and desulfurization uses 0.92 pounds of steam, leaving 0.04 million Btu of residual heat. Capital and maintenance costs are estimated to be $0.178 for the high sulfur and $0.173 for the low sulfur gas stream.[28]

The hydrogen sulfide recovered in the first stage can either be flared to the atmosphere, producing sulfur dioxide emissions, or sent to a sulfur recovery plant, a process which is 90 percent efficient.[29] Thus, for every pound of sulfur entering the combined process, about 0.81 pounds can be recovered. The input requirements of the sulfur recovery activity are, per 100 pounds of hydrogen sulfide input,[30] 0.755 kWh of electricity, 24.5 gallons of water, 0.046 man-hours of labor, and $0.221 maintenance and discounted capital charge. Rejected heat amounts to 0.039 million Btu. About 6.01 pounds of salable sulfur can be recovered from the high sulfur gas per ton of coal, while half this amount is recoverable from the low sulfur gas.

Per ton of high sulfur coal, our calculated total cost of both desulfurization and sulfur recovery (including labor, capital, maintenance, and utility charges) amounts to about $0.41; or $0.58 per ton of coke. This

[27] J. B. Hyne, "Methods for Desulfurization of Industrial Gas Streams," *The Oil and Gas Journal* (August 28, 1972), pp. 64–70; and H. L. Richardson, "Control of Sulfur Emissions in an Integrated Steel Mill," *Iron and Steel Engineer* (July 1971), pp. 76–78.

[28] These costs and input requirements are based on W. L. Nelson, *Refinery Operating Costs* (Tulsa: Petroleum Publishing Company, 1970), pp. 103–104; W. L. Nelson, "Costimating No. 46: Cost of Plants for Recovery of Hydrogen Sulfide," *Oil and Gas Journal* (April 22, 1968), p. 199; W. L. Nelson, "What Does It Cost to Operate Gas Desulfurization Plants?" *Oil and Gas Journal* (August 5, 1968), p. 125.

[29] The inclusion of the flaring option appears redundant at first blush, but may conceivably be relevant because only low sulfur or desulfurized coke oven gas is allowed to be burned at the OH due to metallurgical considerations.

[30] Process utilities, residuals, cost, etc., are based on W. L. Nelson, "Cost of Sulfur Manufacture," *Oil and Gas Journal* (September 2, 1968), pp. 101–102.

translates into a cost of about $136.00 per short ton of recovered sulfur. Although it is not quite proper to assign the whole cost of recovery to the recovered sulfur product because of other linkages, the margin of five to one between the cost of recovery and the market price confirms the claim that sulfur recovery from coke oven gases is probably unprofitable if evaluated from a purely private point of view.[31]

The Recovery of Ammonia and Phenols from Ammonia Liquor

The liquid effluent from the so-called essential coking activities can, as previously mentioned, be discharged directly, used in quenching, stripped only of its contained ammonia, or processed to recover both its phenol and ammonia constituents, and then either discharged or used in quenching. The second alternative has already been covered, and the third, being a treatment activity rather than a by-product recovery activity, will be discussed in the section on optional waste treatment activities. Here, we describe the recovery of ammonia from the liquor in an ammonia still and the recovery of phenol in a dephenolizing unit. These two processes are treated as a single production process, producing the joint products ammonium sulfate and phenol in our model.

The ammonia still. The ammonia formed during coking exits in both the water and the gas that form part of the volatile products. We have patterned our activity for recovery on the semidirect process in which the ammonia is removed by distillation and alkali treatment and readded to the gas stream which, in turn, passes through an ammonia absorber containing dilute sulfuric acid for the extraction of ammonia.[32]

The activity requirements for this subprocess are identical for both the high and low sulfur liquor streams and are based on the following assumptions.

[31] As a check on our cost estimates based on Nelson's figures for petroleum refineries, consider the results given by R. W. Dunlap, W. L. Gorr, and M. J. Massey, "Desulfurization of Coke Oven Gas: Technology, Economics, and Regulatory Activity," in J. Szekely, ed., *The Steel Industry and the Environment* (New York: Marcel Dekker, Inc., 1973), pp. 70–72. They estimate that total costs for combined desulfurization–sulfur recovery, including capital and operating costs, fell between $0.36 and $0.54 per ton of coke in 1971 for processes operating on gas streams with hydrogen sulfide concentrations close to our high sulfur case. The authors apply a discount factor assuming a twenty-year life and an 8 percent discount rate to capital costs. Adjusting these costs to be compatible with our assumptions (ten-year life, 10 percent interest rate) reveals an adjusted range of $0.45 to $0.68 per ton of coke. Even without taking the additional step of deflating the 1971 Dunlap estimates to a 1968 base, we can reasonably conclude that our sulfur recovery costs are representative.

[32] In the model, the ammonia absorber must be operated to remove ammonia from the coke oven gas. Operation of the ammonia still, in conjunction with the dephenolizer, is optional and determines how much total ammonia is recovered.

1. The steam requirement is 2 pounds per gallon of entering liquor, or, given 30 gallons of liquor input per ton of coal, 60 pounds per ton of coal.[33]
2. Milk of lime is required and amounts to 11.4 gallons per ton of coal when the calcium hydroxide is in a typical concentration of 40,000 ppm. The calcium hydroxide component of the milk of lime amounts to 3.8 pounds per ton of coal.[34]
3. If the ammonia still is operated, 6.9 additional pounds of ammonium sulfate can be produced per ton of coal.
4. Total operating and fixed charges for the ammonia still and absorber in combination are assumed to be roughly 3.3 times the net sulfuric acid cost incurred at the absorber to recover 1 pound of ammonium sulfate, or $0.0248 per pound of sulfate, assuming a relatively low cost of $0.01 per pound for 100 percent pure sulfuric acid.[35] This total cost can be divided between acid ($0.0074), operating ($0.01), and fixed ($0.0074) charges. The operating and fixed costs calculated for the two units are allocated between them by their relative shares of sulfate production; so that the still alone, accounting for 34 percent of the sulfate, gets charged 34 percent of the combined total cost, giving it an operating cost of $0.0034 per pound of sulfate and a fixed charge of $0.0025 per pound. An assumed 60 percent of the operating cost is expressed as labor hours and the remainder as a maintenance charge.

Our calculations result in the ammonia recovery requirements per ton of coal in the combined vectors that are shown below.

Item	Unit	High and Low Sulfur Liquor
Product		
Ammonia recovered as sulfate	lb.	6.9
Utilities		
Sulfuric acid	lb.	6.9
Calcium hydroxide	lb.	3.8
Water	10³ gal.	0.011
Steam	lb.	60.0
Labor	hr.	0.003
Capital and maintenance	$	0.026
Residual		
Still waste	gal.	39.0

[33] Wilson and Wells, *Coal, Coke, and Coal Chemicals*, p. 312.
[34] McGannon, *The Making, Shaping and Treating of Steel*, 8th ed., p. 125.
[35] The only published source of costs available for this process is dated, and claims that the cost of sulfuric acid amounted to 42 percent of the total cost of

Dephenolizing unit. The raw ammonia liquor is processed for phenol recovery in a solvent extraction dephenolizer operating in conjunction with the ammonia still. The additional costs, which must be added to those already calculated for the still alone, involve a capital charge of $0.0474 per ton of coal and a maintenance charge of $0.0144.[36] Operating labor is assumed to be the same as the still requirement, that is, 0.003 man-hours per ton of coal.

These expenditures are rewarded by a yield of 0.93 pounds of marketable phenol and associated tar oils, the extraction of which requires 1.14 pounds of sodium hydroxide and adds 0.2 gallons of wastewater to the combined effluent stream.[37] The composition of this stream is shown in table 3.2.

OPTIONAL LIQUID WASTE TREATMENT ACTIVITIES

Where there are limits imposed on the steel mill's waterborne discharges, waste-water treatment activities may be required to supplant or supplement by-product recovery of ammonia and phenol. This certainly appears to be the case today, since separate recovery of ammonia from the liquor by means of the ammonia still has fallen into disuse because of poor markets for ammonium sulfate, and plant operators have sought other alternatives such as direct quenching with the liquor after ammonia removal, and biological and/or carbon treatment of the alternative streams followed by quenching or discharge. The model is set up to include all these alternatives (see figure 3.3).

The Ammonia Stripper

Instead of sending the flushing liquor blowdown to quenching, the ammonia still and dephenolizer, or the sewer, it can be prepared for bio-

---

production of ammonium sulfate in 1933, inclusive of operating (40 percent) and fixed charges (18 percent). We have adjusted these ratios on the assumption that the rate of increase in the cost of capital has exceeded the rate of increase in the price of sulfuric acid, so that total cost is redistributed between acid cost (30 percent), operating cost (40 percent), and capital cost (30 percent), assuming a net acid cost of $20 per ton. See, J. H. Black, "The Problem of Coke-oven Ammonia Recovery," in *AIME Blast Furnace, Coke Oven and Raw Materials Conference Proceedings,* vol. 18 (New York: AIME, 1960), p. 261.

[36] Calculated from information in A. C. Elliott and A. J. Lafreniere, "Solvent Extraction of Phenolic Compounds from Weak Ammonia Liquor," *Industrial Water and Wastes,* vol. 8 (September–October 1963), pp. 11–18.

[37] Figures are from calculations based upon the procedure outlined in Milton R. Beychok, *Aqueous Wastes from Petroleum and Petrochemical Plants* (New York: John Wiley and Sons, 1967), pp. 71–75.

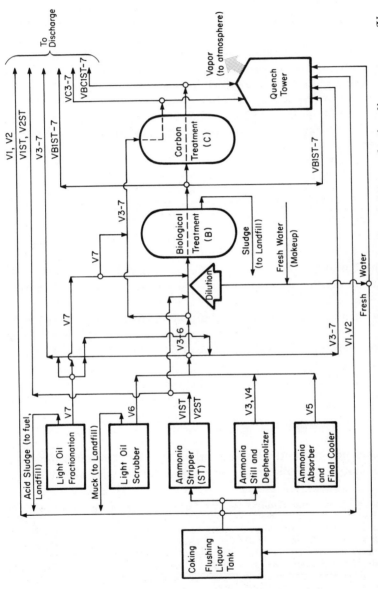

Figure 3.3. Alternative routings for contaminated coke and by-product production liquor streams (V; the numbers indicate sequence).

logical treatment by stripping it of its contained ammonia.[38] This ammonia is subsequently flared to the atmosphere instead of being converted to ammonium sulfate for sale. (This option is applied only to the liquor from the essential coking activities.) It costs an estimated $0.15 per thousand gallons of liquor, including capital, operating, and maintenance costs, to achieve 90 percent removal of ammonia in this fashion.[39] The effluent is assumed to have the same residuals concentration as the influent except for ammonia, which is now present in a concentration of 690 ppm.

Biological Treatment

Biochemical oxidation is an operation that converts water-soluble organic compounds into water-insoluble organic compounds. It is known that some bacteria will convert even phenols to harmless compounds if the toxic organics (phenols, cyanide) are not too highly concentrated in the liquor. If they are, the microorganisms are likely to be destroyed. To prevent this, dilution with fresh water is required, with the dilution requirement based upon a target cyanide concentration of 2 ppm.[40] This dilution rule also produces phenol concentrations within the range 50 to 500 ppm. This is usually considered suitable for biological processes.[41]

Our dilution rule implies the following additional water requirements per 1,000 gallons of entering liquor.[42]

[38] In the activated sludge process the ammonia content of the influent liquor must be below 1,200 ppm so as not to inhibit phenol removal. See, C. W. Fisher, R. D. Hepner, and G. R. Tallon, "Coke Plant Effluent Treatment Investigations," *Blast Furnace and Steel Plant*, vol. 58 (May 1970), p. 317; and Cousins and Mindler, "Tertiary Treatment," p. 608.

[39] This has been calculated on the basis of a flow rate of 60,000 gallons per day, a twenty-five year equipment life, and a 10 percent interest rate. See, Robert Smith and Walter F. McMichael, *Cost and Performance Estimates for Tertiary Wastewater Treating Processes*. Report for the U.S. Department of the Interior, FWPCA, Robert A. Taft Water Research Center (Cincinnati, O.: U.S. Department of the Interior, June 1969).

[40] This is a rule of thumb used to approximate the solution of a complicated problem, which is discussed at length in R. L. Cooper and J. R. Catchpole, "Biological Treatment of Phenolic Wastes," in *Management of Water in the Iron and Steel Industry* (London: British Iron and Steel Institute, 1970), pp. 97–100.

[41] J. W. Patterson and R. A. Minear, *Wastewater Treatment Technology* PB 204 521 (Springfield, Va.: NTIS), p. 203.

[42] Most of the dilution factors generated using our rule of thumb fall within the range reported in the literature for similar streams. For a low level of dilution of 3:1, see W. G. Cousins and A. B. Mindler, "Tertiary Treatment," p. 609. For a high level of dilution of 40:1, see Ohio River Valley Water Sanitation Commission, Steel Industry Action Committee, *Reducing Phenol Wastes from Coke Plants* (Cincinnati: Ohio River Valley Water Sanitation Commission, 1953), p. 27. A range of 20:1 to 40:1 is reported for waste ammonia liquors by Fisher, in "Coke and Gas," p. 230.

Influent Streams	Diluting Water (10^3 gallons)	Effluent Stream After Dilution (10^3 gallons)
Stripped ammonia liquor	24.0	25.0
Dephenolized ammonia liquor	11.5	12.5
Final cooler blowdown	99.0	100.0
Light oil decanter liquor	11.5	12.5
Light oil fractionation condensate	0.0	1.0

The assumed recovery efficiencies which apply to the residuals in the dilute streams are 80 percent for five-day BOD, 96 percent for phenols, 50 percent for cyanides, 30 percent for ammonia, 80 percent for suspended solids, 60 percent for oil, and 96 percent for sulfur occurring as hydrogen sulfide.[43] A sludge which must be landfilled is created by the process.[44]

Because of the dilution requirement, the capital and operating costs of the treatment plant must be calculated on the basis of a daily liquid input flow rate which is considerably larger than the undiluted flow. The plant is sized for cost-estimation purposes according to the maximum combined daily diluted liquor flow expected, given a daily coal input rate of about 2,000 tons. The operating, maintenance, and capital costs are evaluated on the basis of these respective throughputs, and the total cost per thousand gallons is allocated to each of the components of the composite stream.[45]

Carbon Treatment

Adsorption, usually on granulated carbon, often serves to remove trace concentrations of troublesome contaminants such as phenol from wastewaters. In our model, this process can be directly applied to undiluted waste liquid from the ammonia still, final cooler blowdown, light oil decanter liquor, and fractionation condensate without previous bio-

[43] Assumed after inspection of efficiencies reported in Cousins and Mindler, "Tertiary Treatment," p. 609; Fisher, Hepner, and Tallon, "Coke Plant Effluent," pp. 317–19; and George A. Sawyer, "Treatment and Recycle," *Chemical Engineering* (July 24, 1972), p. 121.

[44] The amount of sludge is assumed equal to 0.75 pounds of dry solids per pound of five-day BOD removed. See Beychok, *Aqueous Wastes*, pp. 267–268.

[45] Capital, operating, and maintenance costs were calculated from R. Smith, "Cost of Conventional and Advanced Treatment of Wastewater," *Journal of the Water Pollution Control Federation*, vol. 40 (September 1968), pp. 1546–1574. A capital recovery factor was applied to the total capital cost assuming a twenty-five-year life and a 10 percent interest rate. For example, the total capital, operating, and maintenance cost for the diluted combined stream containing ammonia still liquor and the other three streams amounts to $0.215 per 1,000 gallons. Since we must treat 12,500 gallons of dilute water per 1,000 gallons of incoming still liquor, the cost assigned per 1,000 incoming gallons of still waste is $12.5 \times \$0.215$, or $2.69.

logical treatment, although it is somewhat costlier than biological treatment of the same streams. In addition, all of the streams which have been biotreated and diluted can subsequently be carbon treated. Therefore, carbon treatment is either an alternative or adjunct to biological treatment in the model.

When carbon treatment is undertaken, the following removal efficiencies are assumed.[46]

Residual	*Previously Untreated Streams*	*Previously Biotreated Streams*
BOD	80	72
Phenols	90	81
Cyanides	90	81
Ammonia	0	0
Suspended solids	90	81
Sulfide	100	90
Oil	90	81

The secondary residuals from this treatment process are particulates and sulfur dioxide from carbon regeneration (that is, the reactivation of carbon by burning off the adsorbed residuals).

The carbon-adsorption facilities are costed on the basis of three separate flow rates: the rate expected if the contaminated streams are not previously biotreated (about 0.110 million gallons per day), and the rates expected if the contaminated streams have already been diluted and biotreated (about 2.05 and 2.56 million gallons per day). In the first case, the operating, maintenance, and capital cost amounts to $0.99 per 1,000 gallons of influent, and, in the other two, $0.25 to $0.22, respectively, because of the scale effect.[47]

In summary, then, we include both by-product recovery and treatment options as means of reducing the wasteload of ammonia and phenols (and other residuals) in the waste liquors. The effluents from any of the possible combinations of these methods can either be disposed of by quenching or direct discharge. The choice between by-product recovery

[46] See George J. Crits, "Economic Factors in Water Treatment," *Industrial Water Engineering* (October–November 1971), pp. 24 and 27; Sawyer, "Treatment and Recycle," p. 123; Smith and McMichael, *Cost and Performance*, pp. 22–27; and G. R. Van Stone, "Treatment of Coke Plant Waste Effluent," *Iron and Steel Engineer* (April 1972), pp. 63–66. Carbon treatment efficiencies for previously biotreated streams are assumed to be 90 percent of the efficiencies applying to previously untreated streams, since residuals removal becomes more difficult as contaminant concentration falls.

[47] Smith and McMichael, *Cost and Performance*, p. 26. The estimated total cost of installing and operating the smaller facility checks quite closely with that reported by Tom B. Henshaw, "Adsorption/Filtration Plant Cuts Phenols from Effluent," *Chemical Engineering* (May 31, 1971), pp. 47–49.

and treatment options in responding to a particular discharge standard will depend on the relative prices for the inputs and, especially, outputs of the recovery processes.

INPUT COSTS AND BY-PRODUCT PRICES

The set of prices assumed for the many purchased inputs and recovered by-products encountered in the coking unit was shown in table 3.1. The prices of the two metallurgical coal inputs deserve special attention.

In order to approximate the manner in which f.o.b. mine prices of coking coals vary with sulfur content, fixed carbon content, and ash content, a multivariate regression analysis was performed on a sample of forty-six bituminous coals from Pennsylvania, Kentucky, Indiana, Virginia, and West Virginia.[48] Ordinary least-squares procedures were employed to obtain estimates of the reduced-form coefficients for the predetermined variables (carbon, ash, and sulfur content) which explain coal price, the endogenous variable. No attempt was made to derive structural parameters for the coal demand or to supply equations, and therefore these prices should be viewed only as first approximations. The important matter of the sensitivity of the linear model to differential coal prices is explored in chapter 11.

As we shall discover in subsequent chapters, the coke plant is the key to most integrated steel mills' water pollution problems. The coking unit's problems arise in turn from the by-product oven technology, which stresses direct-contact cooling of the coke oven gas with water, and subsequent by-product recovery operations on both the gas and liquor streams. Furthermore, one of the vital characteristics of the coking process is the amount of sulfur introduced into the steel-making system by the metallurgical coal input. Appendix B provides detailed materials and sulfur balances for this process, including both coke and by-product production.

[48] A. C. Fieldner, W. E. Rice, and H. E. Moran, *Typical Analyses of Coals of the United States*, Bureau of Mines Bulletin No. 446; Bureau of Mines, *Minerals Yearbook*, vols. 1 and 2, *Metals, Minerals and Fuels*, pp. 338–344.

At least twenty-four of these coals are of metallurgical quality, according to information in Trozzo, "Technical Efficiency," appendix 1; and *Keystone Coal Buyers Manual* (New York: McGraw-Hill, 1963).

APPENDIX A

STEAM AND ELECTRIC POWER GENERATION

Many steel-making subprocesses require steam and electric power. Both of these inputs can be provided by using either internally produced or purchased fuels as an energy source. In the model, both steam and electric power are generally treated as if they were internally generated at the steel plant rather than purchased from an independent utility, in order to establish a common basis for comparing residuals discharges from the different mill types. (The effect of excluding the residuals associated with electricity production at the electric arc plant is discussed in chapter 9.) Because many of the internally produced fuels originate in the coking section of the plant, this is an appropriate place to discuss the production activities for steam and electricity.

Steam. Steam may be generated in boilers using either inplant by-product fuels such as acid sludge, forerunnings, tar, coke oven gas, and blast furnace gas, or purchased fuels such as residual fuel oil and natural gas. The heating values and residuals-generating properties of these fuels appear in table A.1.[1]

Our boiler vectors assume 80 percent boiler efficiency and require 1.61 million Btu of heat to produce 1,000 pounds of steam, the equivalent of 120 gallons of boiler-quality water.[2] An operating and maintenance cost,

---

[1] A crucial assumption here is that the capability for fuel substitution exists in the boiler plant. Although many boilers are capable of operating only with a single type of fuel, 23.5 percent of the electric power plants located in the Middle Atlantic region of the United States had a multiple-fuel boiler capability in 1969; therefore, our assumption is not wildly unreasonable. See "Clean Air Drive Creating Impossible Oil Supply Job," *Oil and Gas Journal* (Nov. 13, 1972), p. 95.

[2] The water required for steam production is assumed to cost $0.15 per 10,000 gallons, including the treatment required to reduce mineralization in order to protect the boiler tubes.

TABLE A.1   Boiler Plant Fuel Characteristics

Fuel	10^6 Btu/lb. fuel[a]	Lb. of fly ash/lb. fuel[b]	Lb. of SO_2 emitted/lb. fuel[b]	Fuel cost/ 10^6 Btu[c]
Internally produced				
Low sulfur acid sludge	0.007	0.001	0.350	n.a.
High sulfur acid sludge	0.007	0.001	0.396	n.a.
Low sulfur forerunnings	0.010	0.001	0.119	n.a.
High sulfur forerunnings	0.010	0.001	0.232	n.a.
Low sulfur tar	0.016	0.150	0.011	n.a.
High sulfur tar	0.016	0.150	0.022	n.a.
Desulfurized, low sulfur coke oven gas	0.016	...	0.002	n.a.
Desulfurized, high sulfur coke oven gas	0.016	...	0.003	n.a.
Low sulfur coke oven gas	0.016	...	0.020	n.a.
High sulfur coke oven gas	0.016	...	0.040	n.a.
Blast furnace gas	0.001	...	...	n.a.
Purchased				
Low sulfur (0.5%) fuel oil	0.019	0.001	0.01	0.57
Medium sulfur (1%) fuel oil	0.019	0.001	0.02	0.50
High sulfur (2%) fuel oil	0.019	0.001	0.04	0.39
Natural gas	0.019	0.0004	...	0.63

Abbreviations: n.a. indicates not applicable, ellipses (...) indicate too insignificant to record.

[a] These heating values have been chosen on the basis of data for comparable fuels given in W. L. Nelson, *Guide to Petroleum Refinery Operating Costs*, and Harold E. McGannon, ed., *The Making, Shaping and Treating of Steel*, 8th ed.

[b] Emission factors calculated from R. L. Duprey, *Compilation of Air Pollution Emission Factors;* and Ozolins and Smith, *A Rapid Survey Technique.*

[c] Residual fuel oil prices were obtained from Clifford S. Russell, *Residuals Management*, p. 83; and the *Journal of Commerce* (February 2, 1970). These prices were converted from dollars per barrel to dollars per million Btu by using factors reported in W. L. Nelson, *Guide to Petroleum Refinery Operating Costs*, p. 4. Our natural gas price is rather high in order to reflect the opportunity cost of natural gas in the absence of price regulation. See Leonard Waverman, "Remarks on a Continental Gas Model," pp. 410–412.

exclusive of capital charges, of $0.06 is associated with this output.[3] Parenthetically, it should be noted here that the OH itself is equipped with an installed waste heat boiler which can be operated to produce steam. In addition, the installation and operation of a waste heat boiler can be undertaken at the BOF. Operation of either of these activities will supplant part of the boiler operation in the utilities department proper. No such waste heat-utilization capability exists in electric arc operations.

Electricity. We assume that our thermal electricity generating plant operates with a gross thermal efficiency of 35.6 percent, so that 9,600 Btu of energy must be supplied by the fuel to produce a single kilowatt hour

[3] The cost is calculated from information from W. L. Nelson, *Guide to Petroleum Refinery Operating Costs* (Tulsa: Petroleum Publishing Company, 1970), pp. 23 and 25.

TABLE A.2   Energy Balance in Steam-Electric Power Plant

Plant characteristics	Unit	1 kWh net electrical output
Assumed overall efficiency	%	35.6
Assumed boiler efficiency	%	80.0
Assumed generator efficiency	%	97.5
Heat equivalent of 1 kWh	Btu	3,413
Fuel energy required	Btu	9,600
Heat losses from boiler furnace at 20% of fuel use	Btu	1,920
Energy in steam delivered to turbine (9,600 minus 1,920)	Btu	7,680
Energy required for generator equals energy output from turbine	Btu	3,500
Heat loss from electric generator, at 2.5% of generator input	Btu	87
Electric generator output	Btu	3,413
Energy remaining in steam leaving turbine, removed in condenser (7,680 minus 3,500)	Btu	4,180

Source: Adapted from Cootner and Löf, *Water Demand for Steam Electric Generation*, p. 13.

of electricity. Calculations based upon these assumptions appear in table A.2.

The link between steam generation and electricity production can be made using the information in table A.2. Specifically, the ratio of the heat equivalent of 1 kWh of generator output to the heat energy in the steam delivered to the turbine is 0.444. Therefore, 1,000 pounds of steam are capable of generating 167.3 kWh, or 598 pounds of steam are required per 100 kWh of electricity output. Producing this amount of electrical energy results in 0.418 million Btu of waste heat which must be removed by cooling water. An overall charge of $0.09 per 100 kWh, reflecting operating labor, supervision, and maintenance charges for a small power plant in the 20–39 megawatt capacity range, is entered in the objective function.[4]

[4] Leonard M. Olmstead, "16th Steam Generation Cost Survey," *Electrical World* 172 (Nov. 3, 1969), pp. 41–56.

APPENDIX B

SULFUR BALANCES IN COKE AND
COAL BY-PRODUCT PRODUCTION

The sulfur balances lying behind the activity vectors in the coking process are displayed in some detail in table B.1. Our product yields have been explained in the text. For verification of our calculated sulfur distribution, the reader is referred to the summary below which synthesizes the data from the table for the undesulfurized balances, and compares it to a typical sulfur balance reported in the literature. The two are in close agreement.

Percentage of sulfur in	Reported[a]	Calculated
Coke and breeze	50–65	63
Gas	25–30	29
Other	5–25	8

[a] Philip J. Wilson, Jr., and Joseph H. Wells, *Coal, Coke and Coal Chemicals*, p. 189.

TABLE B.1 Sulfur Balance in By-product Coking from High and Low Sulfur Blends

| | High sulfur coal blend | | | | Low sulfur coal blend | | | |
| | NGD | | WGD | | NGD | | WGD | |
Inputs and residuals	Sulfur (lb.)	Sulfur (%)	Sulfur (lb.)	Sulfur (%)	Sulfur (lb.)	Sulfur (%)	Sulfur (lb.)	Sulfur (%)
Input								
Coking coal	24.00	1.2	24.00	1.2	12.00	0.6	12.00	0.6
Products								
Coke and breeze[a]	15.20	1.0	15.20	1.0	7.60	0.5	7.6	0.5
Tar[b]	0.97	1.1	0.97	1.1	0.48	0.5	0.48	0.5
Light oil[c]	0.05	0.3	0.05	0.3	0.02	0.1	0.02	0.1
Forerunnings[c]	0.05	10.0	0.05	10.0	0.02	5.0	0.02	5.0
Gas[d]	6.90	2.0	0.56	0.2	3.45	1.0	0.28	0.1
Recovered sulfur	n.a.	n.a.	6.01	n.a.	n.a.	n.a.	3.00	n.a.
Residuals								
Particulates lost	0.03	1.4	0.03	1.4	0.02	1.0	0.02	1.0
Flared sulfur	n.a.	n.a.	0.67	n.a.	n.a.	n.a.	0.34	n.a.
Light oil lost in muck	0.34	21.2	0.02	5.0	0.17	14.2	..	..
Primary cooler condensate	0.53	0.9	0.53	0.9	0.26	0.4	0.26	0.4
Total products and residuals	24.07	n.a.	24.08	n.a.	12.02	n.a.	12.02	n.a.

Abbreviations: NGD, no gas desulfurization; WGD, gas desulfurization is practiced; n.a., not applicable; ellipses (...), too insignificant to record.

[a] On the basis of empirical work by P. H. Pinchbeck, E. W. Nixon, and C. Riley, "The Role of Sulfur in Carbonizing and Iron Making," in *Le Coke en Siderurgie* (Charleroi, Belgium: European Iron and Steel Community, September 1966), pp. 387–401, we assume that the sulfur content of the coke is 83.3 percent of that in the coal. This implies that about 63 percent of the sulfur in the coal ends up in the coke and breeze.

[b] We assume the sulfur content of the tar recovered from coking the high sulfur coal blend to be 1.08 percent. For the low sulfur coal blend, we assume 0.54 percent. This range spans the average observation, 0.8 percent, reported in H. H. Lowry, ed., *Chemistry of Coal Utilization*, Sup-

plementary vol. (New York: John Wiley and Sons for the National Academy of Sciences, 1963), p. 593.

[c] The amounts of sulfur in light oil and forerunnings are based on information in P. J. Wilson and J. H. Wells, *Coal, Coke and Coal Chemicals* (New York: McGraw-Hill, 1950), pp. 268, 334.

[d] The percentage sulfur in the coke oven gas prior to desulfurization is taken to be about 1.7 times the sulfur content of the coal blend being coked. This figure was derived from inspection of data given in Wilson and Wells, *Coal, Coke*, pp. 188–189; J. Varga, Jr. and H. W. Lownie, Jr., *A Systems Analysis Study of the Integrated Iron and Steel Industry*, PB 184 577 (Springfield, Va.: NTIS, May 15, 1969), p. V-51; and H. E. McGannon, ed., *The Making, Shaping and Treating of Steel*, 9th ed. (Pittsburgh: U.S. Steel Corporation, 1971), p. 89.

4

SINTER PRODUCTION

In the past, the preparation of iron ores for the blast furnace was limited to crushing and screening. The ore fines produced during the mining and preparation processes were either charged to the blast furnace with the lump ore or screened out and rejected as waste. As blast furnace height and wind rates increased, efficiency became impaired when a mixed burden of lump and fine ores was charged because of the low gas permeability of the burden and the appreciable loss of ore fines (containing iron and carbon) in the form of blast furnace dust. Efforts to circumvent these problems have led to the development of the iron ore upgrading technique which produces an iron ore agglomerate known as sinter.

The sintering process, developed between 1887 and 1906,[1] converts iron ore fines and recycled metallurgical dusts into an agglomerated product that is coarse enough for charging into the blast furnace. The iron-bearing materials are moistened and mixed with fine coke (breeze) and limestone (flux) and subjected to high heat under an ignition hood. After the coke in the top layer of the bed is ignited, combustion of the remainder of the carbon in the mix is supported by a forced draft of air from wind boxes along the sinter strand. If none of the strand length is used for cooling, the sintered product is discharged from the main grate when the burn-through point has been reached (that is, when the coke in the charge has been completely burned). The sinter product is then crushed, screened, and cooled, with fines under a specified minimum size being recharged as a process input. The flow chart presented in figure 4.1 outlines the main parts of the sintering process.

[1] United Nations, Economic Commission for Europe, *Economic Aspects of Iron Ore Preparation* (ST/ECE/STEEL/14, 1966), p. 28.

64

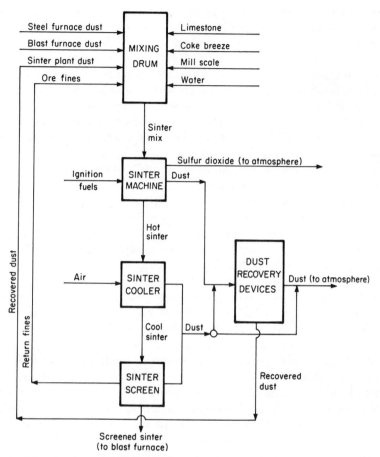

Figure 4.1.   A schematic diagram of sintering.

Significant quantities of dust are generated in both strand operations and materials handling, screening, and cooling. The dust can be either directly discharged to the atmosphere or partially collected (the captured dust is recycled as a process input), with the untrapped remainder being discharged to the atmosphere. Common practice is such that "control of sintering emissions is considered to be at a low level, especially in manufacture of fluxed sinters."[2]

The introduction of sintering as an intermediate link between the iron ore mine and the blast furnace made it possible to use ores containing high concentrations of impurities such as sulfur, which the

---

[2] J. Varga, Jr., and H. W. Lownie, Jr., *A Systems Analysis Study of the Integrated Iron and Steel Industry.* **PB** 184 577 (Springfield, Va.: NTIS, May 15, 1969), p. IV-6.

process drives off to the atmosphere.[3] The development of agglomeration also made it economically feasible to recycle various types of iron-bearing materials generated in steelmaking that were formerly regarded as wastes; especially flue dust recovered from blast furnace gas and mill scale recovered from rolling and finishing wastewaters. More recently, producers have included ground fluxes such as limestone and lime in the sinter mix, turning out self-fluxing sinters of almost any required composition.[4] This effectively means that the calcination of the limestone ($CaCO_3$ + heat $\rightarrow$ CaO + CO_2), which previously took place in the blast furnace using coke as a fuel, can be partially or wholly transferred to the sintering strand, where the fuel cost to achieve this reaction is much lower.

A related process is pelletizing, which has as a major purpose increasing the iron content of blast furnace charge material. Its major use is currently in the upgrading of low iron-content ores from the Upper Great Lakes. There are, however, other benefits which arise from the physical form of the pellets; that is, improved burden permeability, lower dust loss, and greater furnace productivity.

Pelletizing is of more recent origin than sintering and differs from it in that a damp, unbaked ore pellet or ball is formed before being hardened by heating in a furnace. During the heating process, magnetite is oxidized to ferric oxide, and sulfur is removed as sulfur dioxide. Customarily, pellets are prepared at plants located near the mine site, while sinter is made at the mill itself, principally because sinter suffers degradation in transit while pellets do not.[5] Our model maintains this locational distinction, permitting the purchase of pellets manufactured at the ore mine and the production of sinter at the steel plant. As a result of this convention, the residuals generated in pellet manufacture are not included in the model, while those evolved during sintering are. This is consistent with our interest in integrated iron and steel *plants,* as opposed to the overall industry from mine to consumer or scrap heap. On the other hand, this does introduce the possibility of misinterpretation of our results, since the use of pellets in the model will appear to be very much less pollution-intensive than the use of sinter. And it is—*at the steel plant*—but whether the actual decision

[3] As explained in chapter 5, the economics of the blast furnace are influenced to a great extent by the amount of sulfur contained in the inputs, which dictates in part the limestone and coke requirements per ton of iron product. A lessening of the amount of sulfur contained in the iron-bearing inputs prior to blast furnace charging will reduce these requirements, and hence reduce hot metal cost, *ceteris paribus*.

[4] A self-fluxing sinter is one which requires little or no additional flux in the blast furnace charge over and above that already contained in the agglomerate.

[5] Robert E. Power, "Economic Factors in the Site of Iron Ore Agglomerating Plants," *Skillings Mining Review*, vol. 4 (March 1961), p. 6.

between the two alternatives reflects the appropriate external costs will depend on whether the price of pellets (market or internal accounting) reflects residuals problems at the pelletizing plant. It is clear from the case of the notorious Reserve Mining plant that this has almost certainly not been so in the past.[6] Thousands of tons of tailings from the pelletizing process have been dumped each day into Lake Superior by this firm and, it is thought, have deposited large quantities of asbestos fibers in the lake and consequently in the water supplies of a number of communities.

The Sinter Burdening Problem

Our sintering and blast furnace activity vectors are designed to reflect the sorts of options outlined above. Specifically, we include possibilities for recirculation of recovered iron-bearing wastes and substitution of different grades of sinter for the different grades of ore which can be charged directly to the blast furnace.

Apart from pellets, three physically distinct ore types can be used as inputs in our model. The sinter plant operates exclusively on ores of fine particle size. The blast furnace operates on sinters made from these ore fines as well as on screened and unscreened ores.[7] Within any given physical category, we postulate four chemically distinct ore types, differentiated on the basis of iron and sulfur content. The high iron-, high sulfur-content ore contains 65 percent iron and 0.15 percent sulfur. The high iron-, low sulfur-content ore contains 65 percent iron and 0.015 percent sulfur. The low iron-, high sulfur-content ore contains 55 percent iron and 0.15 percent sulfur. The low iron-, low sulfur-content ore contains 55 percent iron and 0.015 percent sulfur.[8]

Ore fines in each of the four categories can be sintered with either high or low sulfur coke and the chemically homogeneous limestone input, which can be added to the sinter burden in either low, medium, or high proportions. Therefore, in sintering, the possible combinations of elements (in the absence of flue dust or mill scale additions) yield

[6] See, for example, Jane E. Brody, "Iron Ore Company vs. the Changing Times," *The New York Times* (Aug. 8, 1973), p. 58.

[7] Iron ore fines are obtained by screening natural ore and thus separating it into coarse and fine components.

[8] These are hypothetical ores and are intended to cover the range of available ore types with respect to iron and sulfur content either as mined or as blended, rather than to represent specific ores found in specific geographic locations. A more detailed statement regarding the chemical analyses of these ores and the sinters which can be produced from them appears in appendix C, but the brief description presented here is sufficient for an understanding of the model.

twenty-four distinct activities (eight low limestone, eight medium limestone and eight high limestone sinters) and can be displayed as:

$$
\begin{bmatrix} \text{High sulfur} \\ \text{coke} \\ \text{Low sulfur} \\ \text{coke} \end{bmatrix} \times \begin{bmatrix} \text{Low limestone} \\ \text{addition} \\ \text{Medium limestone} \\ \text{addition} \\ \text{High limestone} \\ \text{addition} \end{bmatrix} \times \begin{bmatrix} \text{High iron, high sulfur ore} \\ \text{High iron, low sulfur ore} \\ \text{Low iron, high sulfur ore} \\ \text{Low iron, low sulfur ore} \end{bmatrix} = 24
$$

When we consider the possibility of flue dust additions to the sinter burden, the total number of activities becomes forty-eight. And finally, when we include the possibility of mill scale additions to the sinter charge, the total number of activities becomes seventy-two (twenty-four low limestone, twenty-four medium limestone, and twenty-four high limestone sinters).

THE SINTER PLANT SUBMODEL

The vectors for sinter production have been developed by incorporating experimental and operating data on sintering within a system of materials balance equations based on the relationships between sintering inputs and product output and losses.[9] These equations account for the following losses which make the output of usable sinter product less than quantity of material inputs to the process: limestone calcination, ore ignition loss, coke-carbon oxidation, and dust loss. This approach allows us to calculate the yield and composition of sinters produced from a variety of input mixes. It may be distinguished from the burdening submodels used for the blast and steel furnaces, which solve for the inputs required to produce a desired chemically homogeneous output. Here, no a priori output-quality targets are specified; rather, we begin with different mixes of iron-bearing materials, limestone, and coke and accept whatever output qualities these imply.

A simple set of relationships, suggested by Doi and Kasai, which reflects these sources of weight loss, allows us to find the requisite quan-

---

[9] In the development of this model, we relied heavily on the work of Y. Doi and K. Kasai, "The Making of Self Fluxing Sinter and the Blast Furnace Practice with Its 100 Per Cent Sinter Burden," in *AIME Blast Furnace, Coke Oven and Raw Materials Conference Proceedings*, vol. 18 (New York: AIME, 1960). Our method is similar to that used by Trozzo except that the equations are not directly incorporated into our linear model. See Charles L. Trozzo, "The Technical Efficiency of the Location of Integrated Blast Furnace Capacity" (Ph.D. dissertation, Harvard University, 1966), p. 34.

tities of ore, coke, and limestone needed to produce 1 ton of sinter in the low, medium, and high limestone cases.[10] Specifically, the equations of the sintering submodel are:

(1) $$t \equiv m + c + r,$$

where (all expressed per ton of sinter output):

$t \equiv$ pounds of total input charge
$m \equiv$ pounds of raw mix [ore (b) plus limestone (a)], so that $m \equiv a + b$
$c \equiv$ pounds of coke
$r \equiv$ pounds of return fines.

We further require that:[11]

(2) $$m = 0.66t$$

(3) $$c = 0.04t$$

(4) $$r = 0.30t.$$

The key to the burden calculations is the amount of the gaseous loss (u) and this may be written as:

(5) $$u = c + 0.44a + 0.055b$$

so that we are essentially assuming that all the coke is burned and that about 5.5 percent of the ore is lost as gas (a phenomenon known as ignition loss in the technical literature). The 44 percent loss from the

---

[10] Doi and Kasai, "Self Fluxing Sinter," pp. 182–204. Since sintering involves continuous recirculation of some percentage of the original charge in the form of return fines, we approximate the steady-state conditions of the process by defining our sintering activity vectors net of return fines. We show the gross calculations in the text, however. That is, fines are shown as both input and output.

[11] In actual practice the coke requirement is a function of the nature of the ore charged, as well as a number of other variables, and can range from 3 to 8 percent of the total charge. However, the optimum carbon requirement generally appears to fall in the narrower range of 4 to 5 percent. See T. L. Myron, M. R. Faigen, and R. I. Franklin, "Fuels for Sintering," in *AIME Blast Furnace, Coke Oven and Raw Materials Conference Proceedings*, vol. 17 (New York: AIME, 1959), p. 287; Trozzo, "Technical Efficiency," p. 39; H. Rausch and H. Seidel, "Development Trends in the Agglomeration of Blast-Furnace Burdening Materials," *Neue Hütte*, vol. 11 (November 1966), pp. 647–657, trans. Henry Brutcher (Altadena, California: Henry Brutcher Technical Translations, no. 7540).

The percentage of return fines that are recirculated varies with the type of ore charged, but for simplicity the steady-state value is assumed to equal 30 percent of the total charge. See Doi and Kasai, "Self Fluxing Sinter," p. 190; Alan English, "Iron Ore Agglomeration—Sintering and Pelletizing," *Iron and Steel Engineer*, vol. 39 (March 1961) p. 14; and N. D. MacDonald, "The Effect of Screened Sinter on Furnace Productivity," in *AIME Blast Furnace, Coke Oven and Raw Materials Conference Proceedings*, vol. 20 (New York: AIME, 1962), p. 8.

limestone is simply the carbon dioxide lost in calcination.[12] Gross output from the process is then:

$$(6) \qquad G = 2000 + r + u.$$

But it must be true that $G = t$ so that we can write

$$(7) \qquad t = 2000 + 0.30t + u,$$

and our task is to express u in terms of t for different choices of limestone and ore proportions. Rather than carry out the algebra in the most general case, let us consider a medium limestone sinter, one which is made by including 10 percent limestone and 90 percent ore in the raw mix. Then, $a = 0.1\ m$ and $b = 0.9\ m$.

From equation 3 we know that $c = 0.04\ t$, and combining equation 2 with our equations for a and b, we obtain:

$$(8) \qquad u = 0.04t + 0.44(0.1)(0.66)t + 0.055(0.9)(0.66)t = 0.102t.$$

Then, from equations 7 and 8, we see that:

$$(9) \qquad 2000 = 0.598t \text{ or } t = 3344.$$

It follows that $m = 2207$, $c = 134$, $r = 1003$, $a = 221$, $b = 1986$, and $u = 341$. The results of similar calculations for low (5 percent) and high (15 percent) limestone additions, along with the medium limestone case, are shown in table 4.1.

A check on the reasonableness of our formulation can be obtained by comparing the yields implicit in table 4.1 with those reported by Doi and Kasai for similar cases. Yield, for this purpose, is defined as:

$$\frac{2000 + r}{m + r}$$

On this basis, our yields are 0.949 for low limestone, 0.936 for medium limestone, and 0.922 for high limestone. The comparable figures from Doi and Kasai are 0.943, 0.931, and 0.920, respectively.[13]

Adjustment of Baseline Vectors

The three baseline vectors calculated in the fashion outlined above and shown in table 4.1 must be modified to account for particulate and sulfur losses in order to obtain the final sintering activity coefficients. The adjustment procedure involves the calculation of a factor reflecting those losses that can be applied to the baseline vectors. First, the losses

[12] Calcination involves the following reaction: $CaCO_3 + \text{heat} \rightarrow CaO + CO_2$, which, by molecular weight ratios, implies a 44 percent loss as carbon dioxide.
[13] Doi and Kasai, "Self Fluxing Sinter," p. 190.

TABLE 4.1 Baseline Sintering Materials Balances for Three Limestone Addition Practices

(*pounds*)

Inputs and outputs	Low limestone (5%)	Medium limestone (10%)	High limestone (15%)
Inputs			
Ore	2,052	1,986	1,918
Limestone	108	221	338
Coke	131	134	137
[Returns][a]	[982]	[1,003]	[1,026]
Total net of returns	2,291	2,341	2,393
Outputs			
Sinter	2,000	2,000	2,000
[Returns][a]	[982]	[1,003]	[1,026]
Gaseous loss from:			
Coke	131	134	137
Other	160	207	256
Total net of returns	2,291	2,341	2,393

Note: For complete bibliographical information see the Table References at the end of the book.

[a] Sintering involves continuous recirculation of some percentage of the original charge in the form of return fines (bracketed above), which are netted out of the balances. See W. J. Vaughan, "A Residuals Management Model," pp. 127–128.

for a particular vector are subtracted from 2,000 to obtain net sinter. Each relevant input requirement in that burdening variant is then blown up by an adjustment factor, in order to obtain the adjusted input requirements. The factor is defined as:

$$\text{Adjustment factor}_i = \frac{2,000}{\text{net sinter}_i}$$

where $i = 1, \ldots, 24$.

A more specific discussion of the expansion of the three baseline vectors into the twenty-four net sinter vectors follows directly. After this discussion we will consider the possibility of flue dust or mill scale substitution for some of the ore input, giving us the full set of seventy-two vectors referred to above.

Particulate loss. The dust emissions in sintering are split into two categories, distinguished by location: sintering machine (strand) emissions, and tip-end (crushing and screening) emissions. Observations of the level of these emissions per ton of output show wide variations due to the influence of a number of variables such as burden quality (limestone practice, input size distribution, sinter bed permeability), wind volume per unit time, ratio of return fines, and type of sinter cooling.

Unfortunately, the relative impact of each of these factors cannot be sorted out, given the paucity of available information. In consequence, we have assumed that dust emission values of 30 pounds per ton sinter at the strand and 22 pounds per ton sinter at the discharge-handling point can be associated with 2,000 pounds of baseline sinter product in every limestone practice.[14]

Sulfur loss. The baseline sinter product must also be corrected for sulfur loss, since some sulfur in the inputs is driven off with the gases.[15] The range of opinion on the percentage of sulfur that is emitted this way (excluding sulfur generated from combustion of ignition hood fuels) is considerable. It does appear, however, that the desulfurization rate falls as the basicity of the sinter increases.[16] Accordingly, we assume that:

1. For low limestone sintering practices, 70 percent of the total sulfur entering the system in the coke, limestone, and ore is driven off with the stack gas as sulfur dioxide. The remaining 30 percent is allocated to the sintered product. Sulfur in the return fines input equals sulfur in the return fines output and drops out of the balance. For convenience all of the gaseous sulfur evolved is measured as sulfur dioxide.

2. In medium and high limestone additions, 50 percent of the sulfur in the inputs comes off in the gas, and 50 percent remains in the sintered product.[17] The other assumptions mentioned in item 1 still hold.

The following procedure was then used to obtain net sinter (and hence the adjustment factor): Gross sinter (2,000 pounds in baseline

14 A reported range of 5 to 100 pounds of dust generation per ton of sinter output for strand emissions and a value of 22 pounds for discharge, crushing, and screening emissions appear in R. L. Duprey, *Compilation of Air Pollution Emission Factors*, PB 190 245 (Springfield, Va.: NTIS, 1968), p. 27.

15 Implicit in the baseline calculations is the assumption that the coke, including whatever sulfur it contains, is completely burned. The ignition loss from ore has been assumed to reflect oxygen loss only.

16 One set of laboratory tests showed that the extent of sulfur removed in producing a sinter with a lime–silica ratio of 0.81 was 71 percent. However, when the lime–silica ratio was raised to 1.41 (relatively more lime added in the mix), the rate of desulfurization fell to 38 percent. [See B. Weilandt and F. Kruse, "Production of Lime-Containing Sinter and its Smelting with Special Reference to Sulfur Removal from Sinter and Pig Iron," *Stahl und Eisen*, vol. 81 (May 1961), pp. 295–302, trans. Henry Brutcher (Altadena, California: Henry Brutcher Technical Translations, No. 5110, p. 8.] Desulfurization data developed by Doi and Kasai also demonstrate this phenomenon. The desulfurization rate in cases where no limestone was combined with the ore was much higher (96.5 to 98.0 percent) than when limestone made up 15 percent of the ore–limestone mix (76.5 to 90.5 percent).

17 In fact, limestone addition is not a perfect proxy for sinter basicity, and our assumption results in some distortions. For example, our method treats all low limestone sinters as low-basicity sinters for desulfurization calculations. In fact, our low limestone sinter made from high iron-content ore has a basicity greater than 1, and probably should have a desulfurization rate lower than 0.70.

vectors) minus sulfur evolved from ore (in gas), sulfur evolved from limestone (in gas), and particulates evolved from ore (in gas)[18] plus sulfur from coke not contained in gas equals net sinter.[19]

The results of these calculations are small changes in the input and output values, along with residuals generation figures for particulates and sulfur dioxide as indicated. It is not necessary to display this enormous array of numbers since the baseline vectors will give the reader a sufficiently clear idea of what is going on.

Inclusion of Recovered Flue Dust and Mill Scale

Additional sintering vectors can now be constructed to include the option of recycling a number of potentially recoverable iron-bearing materials generated in iron and steelmaking.

Flue dust. Flue dust recovered from the sintering, blast furnace, and steel furnace operations can be recirculated to the sinter strand as a substitute for purchased ore fines. The method of introducing recovered flue dust into the final sintering vectors developed above is based upon the following simplifying assumptions.

1. Flue dusts from the sinter plant and dusts from blast furnace activities operating on 100 percent sinter burdens are associated with the four chemically different, fine ore inputs in the manner described in appendix C. Flue dusts from blast furnace activities operating upon 100 percent ore charges are assumed to be chemically equivalent to the respective blast furnace ores from which they originate. Flue dusts from steelmaking are associated with low iron-content, low sulfur-content ore fines. Therefore, a direct link is postulated between each flue dust generated at the sinter strand, blast furnace or steel furnace and one of the four alternative purchased virgin ore inputs. This means that the sulfur balance previously computed still holds.

2. The flue dust content allowed in the iron-bearing component of the sinter charge is 30 percent, and the carbon content of every flue dust is 10 percent.[20]

3. Each dust has the same iron content, net of carbon, as the ore that produced it, so that 1.11 pounds of flue dust substitute for 1 pound of associated ore.

[18] Assumed to be the sum of strand and discharge end particulates (52 pounds) net of 1.5 pounds of particulates from coke (5 percent of the 30 pounds of strand particulates), which have already been allowed for in the baseline weight balances.

[19] The initial assumption was that all coke disappeared in the form of carbon dioxide. Hence it is necessary to correct the vectors at this point for the sulfur not, in fact, driven off.

[20] This seems to be a reasonable upper limit based on information in the literature. See, for example, N. J. Cavaghan and F. B. Traice, "Utilization of In-Plant Fines," *Journal of the Iron and Steel Institute*, vol. 208 (June 1970), pp. 538–541.

On this basis, the correction required involves increasing total ore requirements by 3 percent; of the new total, 30 percent will be flue dust. The carbon content of the flue dust lowers the coke requirement in the charge.

Mill scale. Hot rolling of steel ingots produces on the product surface an iron oxide known as mill scale, which is objectionable if further processing such as drawing or cold rolling is required. After this scale is removed, it can either be disposed of or rerouted to the sinter strand. To reflect the latter alternative, we assume that:

1. The mill scale is all in the form of ferrous oxide so that it has an iron content of 70 percent. Its sulfur content is assumed to be zero.
2. Mill scale is allowed to substitute for 10 percent of the ore charge.[21]

Here the modification technique is as simple as that in the flue dust addition case.

1. Deduct 10 percent from the final ore charge requirement in the no-additions case.
2. Supply the compensating amount of mill scale which leaves the iron content of the sinter product unaltered. This is computed by dividing the predetermined iron content of the sinter output, less the iron content of the ore after a 10 percent deduction from the no-additions case, by the iron content of mill scale, 0.70.
3. All other entries (coke, limestone) remain unchanged from the no-additions case.

We have now determined the key raw materials requirements in the various sintering alternatives. Let us turn from product inputs to sinter plant utilities requirements and labor and operating expenses. The question of particulate recovery is treated in detail in chapter 8, and need not detain us here.

SINTER PLANT UTILITIES

The sinter strand requirements over and above raw materials are fuels for firing the charge, steam, electricity, and water.

Fuels for Hood Ignition

Heat is supplied in sintering by inclusion of a solid fuel, usually coke breeze, in the input charge. Ignition of this fuel in the burden

21 See Doi and Kasai, "Self Fluxing Sinter," p. 189.

can be accomplished in various ways. The general practice is to apply sufficient heat to the top of the bed to ignite the coke in the top layer, after which the airflow pulls the flame front down through the bed as it travels along the sintering grate. The initial heat is normally applied by torch burners directed onto the bed, or by passing the bed under a radiant furnace. In the model, fuel for ignition may be coke oven or blast furnace gas, or purchased residual oil or natural gas.

Although heat requirements necessarily depend upon many variables (type of ore charged, bed permeability, excess air conditions, and limestone practice), available sources fail to adequately explain the ignition heat requirement as a function of these variables. Hence, we assume the gross heat requirement to be 2 million Btu per ton of output for all practices.[22] To obtain the ignition heat requirement in Btus per ton of output, it is simply necessary to subtract from this figure the heat available from coke combustion. (We assume that this amounts to 12,600 Btu per pound of coke.)

The net ignition heat requirements of the seventy-two sintering activities computed according to the model span a range of 0.24 to 0.34 million Btus per ton of sinter output, which is compatible with reported requirements.[23] In the linear model, we allow a choice for the optimal combination of the fuels that can be burned to meet the requirement. The model reflects the sulfur dioxide emission attributable to these fuels on the basis of their respective sulfur contents, under the assumption that no matter whether oil, coke oven gas, natural gas, or blast furnace gas is utilized in sinter ignition, sulfur dioxide will be given off directly to the waste gas stack and will not alter the sulfur composition of the sinter.

Other Utilities

An electricity requirement of 20 kWh per ton of sinter output, unadjusted for relative burden weight, is assigned to all sinter vectors.[24] The steam requirement is 20 pounds per ton of sinter,[25] and in addi-

[22] Based on information in Harold E. McGannon, ed., *The Making, Shaping and Treating of Steel*, 8th ed. (Pittsburgh: U.S. Steel Corporation, 1964), p. 195.

[23] See R. W. Berry, "Trends in Energy Consumption," in British Iron and Steel Institute, Iron and Steel Engineers Group, *Energy Management in an Iron and Steelworks* (Margate, England: Eyre and Spottiswoode Ltd., 1968), pp. 32–33; Doi and Kasai, "Self Fluxing Sinter," p. 192; Yu A. Frolov, G. M. Maizel, D. P. Bubnov, V. P. Andreev, and Ya. L. Belotserkovskii, "Selection of Type of Fuel for Ignition and Combined Heating of Sintering Mixes," *Stahl und Eisen* (October 1970), p. 767.

[24] Calculated from Power, "Economic Factors," p. 8, assuming an electricity cost of $0.0075 per kWh. See also K. S. Kuka, "Planning the Electrical Power Supply for a Large, Integrated Steel Works," *Iron and Steel Engineer*, vol. 44 (February 1967), pp. 99–108.

[25] Calculated from Power, "Economic Factors," p. 8, assuming a steam cost of $0.50 per 1,000 pounds.

tion, 3 percent of the total charge weight must be added as water to improve sinter bed permeability in all activities.[26] All of this water is vaporized in sintering and thus represents an entirely consumptive use of water.

SINTER PLANT LABOR REQUIREMENTS
AND OBJECTIVE FUNCTION VALUES

The operating cost items in addition to raw materials and utilities inputs are explained below.

Labor

For moderate-size sinter plants having a capacity of about 2,200 tons per day, a 1961 labor cost of $0.65 per ton of sinter has been reported.[27] (It is reasonable to associate this size plant with a steel mill capable of producing about 1 million tons of steel per annum, which is the scale our model aims for.) The 1968 labor unit requirements for all vectors are taken to be the quotient of this 1961 cost divided by the 1968 wage rate of $5 per man-hour, or 0.13 man-hours per ton of sinter.[28]

Sinter Plant Maintenance Costs

This category, maintenance materials and supplies, is a component of sinter production cost which can be related to the plant capital cost, using a 4 percent rule of thumb. Since we obtained an estimate of $25 for undiscounted annual capital costs per ton of sinter in 1968 for a moderate-sized sinter plant, our maintenance cost is $1 per ton.[29]

Cost of Raw Materials Inputs Common to Sinter and
Blast Furnace Operations

Since limestone and iron ore inputs are charged to both the sinter strand and the blast furnace (to be discussed in chapter 5), this is

[26] E. W. Voice, S. H. Brooks, W. Davies, and B. L. Robertson, "Factors Controlling the Rate of Sinter Production," *Journal of the Iron and Steel Institute*, vol. 175 (October 1953), pp. 97–152, especially p. 99.

[27] Power, "Economic Factors," p. 8.

[28] This reflects our assumption that labor productivity in the industry has kept pace with rising wage rates. Thus fewer man-hours would be required in 1968, but the dollar cost would be the same per ton of sinter.

[29] Personal communication from Carlos Blanco, consulting engineer for Openchain Corp., Pittsburgh, Pennsylvania, January 11, 1972.

a convenient place to discuss the base case set of prices assigned to them.

Although a large component of the delivered price of limestone can be transportation cost, which obviously varies with quarry-to-mill distance, we are not particularly interested in changes in this cost. In consequence, we assume an invariant delivered limestone price of $4 per net ton in all model simulations.[30]

Iron ore production is controlled by a relatively small number of firms closely linked with the steel industry. Less than 10 percent of all iron ore consumed in the United States is traded on the spot market. Instead, most iron ore either comes from captive mines or is bought and sold under long-term contracts.[31] Unfortunately, the principal published price for domestic ores is the Lake Erie spot price, which refers to the Lower Lakes cost, insurance, and freight (c.i.f.) price of American and Canadian ores shipped down the Great Lakes from the Lake Superior region.[32] This price is based only upon the relative iron content and physical size of the ore; other quality indicators such as silica or sulfur content, although specified in individual sales, are not reflected in the Lake Erie price system.[33] Furthermore, although this system of base prices is widely quoted throughout the industry, there is considerable doubt whether it reflects any economically meaningful determination.

Despite its imperfections, the Lake Erie base system provides a useful bench mark for relative domestic ore prices and, in lieu of better information, we shall use it, recognizing that this raises the questions about quality differentials just discussed. The sensitivity of our model to different ore cost assumptions will be tested in chapter 11, however, by changing both the absolute and relative ore price levels.

[30] This is a reasonable cost for limestone consumed at east-coast blast furnaces. The cost of limestone has not varied much over time. See Battelle Memorial Institute, *Technical and Economic Analyses of the Impact of Recent Developments in Steelmaking Practices on the Supplying Industries* (Columbus: Battelle Memorial Institute, October 30, 1964), p. VIII–2.

[31] Gerald Manners, *The Changing World Market for Iron Ore 1950–1980: An Economic Geography* (Baltimore: Johns Hopkins University Press for Resources for the Future, 1971), p. 258.

[32] The spot price is discussed in L. Gregory Hines, "Price Determination in the Lake Erie Iron Ore Market," *American Economic Review*, vol. 41 (September 1951), pp. 650–661.

[33] Ibid., p. 654. Interestingly, Eastern European countries use statistical formulae for calculating the price of iron ores which are entirely determined on the demand side. The relative value of an iron ore is calculated by taking account of a number of ore chemical properties and assuming fixed prices for hot metal, coke and other inputs. These formulae are then used to decide to what extent it is economical to beneficiate each type of ore. Although this approach neglects the simultaneous nature of ore price determination, it is more exact in specification than the Lake Erie basis. See UN, ECE, *Iron Ore Preparation*, pp. 71–75.

TABLE 4.2   Ore Price Calculation

(*Constant Transport Cost: Lower Lake to Eastern Pennsylvania Mill*)

		Model inputs		
	Lake Erie base	Low iron-content ore	High iron-content ore	Pellets
Assumed iron content of ore (%)	51.50	55	65	66.19
Pounds of iron per 2,000 lb. ore	1,030	1,100	1,300	1,320
1968 Lake Erie price, 51.50 (%) iron natural standard Mesabi ore ($/gross ton)[a]				
Pellets	12.98	n.a.	n.a.	n.a.
Natural	10.55	n.a.	n.a.	n.a.
Coarse	11.35	n.a.	n.a.	n.a.
Fine	10.10	n.a.	n.a.	n.a.
Published Lake Erie price on contained iron basis (¢/lb. iron contained)[b]				
Pellets	1.12	n.a.	n.a.	n.a.
Natural	0.91	n.a.	n.a.	n.a.
Coarse	0.98	n.a.	n.a.	n.a.
Fine	0.88	n.a.	n.a.	n.a.
Calculated 1968 ore price: Lake Erie ports, actual basis ($/net ton)[c]				
Pellets	n.a.	n.a.	n.a.	14.85
Natural	n.a.	10.06	11.89	n.a.
Coarse	n.a.	10.82	12.79	n.a.
Fine	n.a.	9.63	11.38	n.a.
Freight charge: lower lake to Mill ($/net ton)[d]	n.a.	3.91	3.91	3.91
Delivered ore cost ($/net ton)				
Pellets	n.a.	n.a.	n.a.	18.76
Natural	n.a.	13.97	15.80	n.a.
Coarse	n.a.	14.73	16.70	n.a.
Fine	n.a.	13.54	15.29	n.a.

Note: n.a. indicates not applicable.

[a] Published prices are reported using standard of 51.50 percent iron content in terms of dollars per gross ton (2,240 lb.). A premium for coarse ore and a penalty for fines are also reported on the same basis. See *Steel*, vol. 163 (Dec. 30, 1968), p. 44.

[b] Dollars per gross ton divided by pounds of iron per gross ton, all times 100 (rounded).

[c] These values are the products of the assumed pounds of iron contained in the two ores times the respective prices per pound iron for fine, coarse, and natural sizes.

[d] From the *University of Minnesota Bulletin: Mining Directory Issue*, pp. 236–238.

The following method has been used to arrive at a baseline set of low and high iron-content ore prices.

1. All prices are computed using the Lake Erie method with the addition of a lower port-to-mill transport charge per short ton to arrive at the delivered price in the Philadelphia area, the region in which we locate our modeled mill.
2. No sulfur penalty is assessed in the base price set.[34] Table 4.2 shows how our hypothetical ore prices were computed as a function of iron content and size grade.

Now we have discussed the purchase and further processing of the key material inputs to the integrated steel mill: coal (coke) and ore (sinter). These first two substantive chapters have carried us up to the iron-making compartment of the mill, the blast furnace. The units we have discussed are, however, important in themselves, particularly when viewed from the perspective of residuals problems. We shall see in later chapters how strongly the mill operator's decisions about the use of coke and sinter influence the total daily residuals discharges from the mill complex. We now turn to a discussion of the blast furnace part of the model.

---

[34] In an interview with the authors, steel company personnel revealed no knowledge of such a price correction. (Interview with Messrs. K. Maxey, W. McShane, G. Dragonier, and A. Lame of the Wheeling–Pittsburgh Steel Corp., Pittsburgh, Pennsylvania, March 9, 1972.) It would be possible to employ the model to explore the steelmaker's willingness to pay for lower iron ore sulfur content, by using the method explained for coking coal in chapter 10. We have not followed up on this question.

APPENDIX C

CHEMICAL COMPOSITION OF IRON ORES AND THE SINTERS MADE FROM THEM

Idealized ore compositions, displayed in table C.1, have been chosen to reflect differences in ore sulfur and iron content. The remaining non-iron, non-sulfur compounds occurring in the ore are divided into acids (defined as alumina and silica), bases (defined as magnesium carbonate and limestone *gross*, magnesium oxide and lime *net*), and miscellaneous compounds. These decimal constituents, multiplied by the pounds of ore required in each blast furnace activity, are inputs into the blast furnace submodel explained in chapter 5. This set of hypothetical ores is intended to represent the greatest part of the spectrum of ore quality variations in the iron and sulfur content dimensions. These are not, however, extreme cases, since ores metallurgically inferior and superior to these are actually charged in the real world.

The composition of sinters derived from these ores and the materials balance assumptions explained in the text are displayed in table C.2, as is pellet composition derived from inspection of typical pellet analyses.[1] The calculations by which the assumptions are converted to the sinter compositions may be summarized as follows.

Let:

$f_{Si} \equiv$ decimal iron content of sinter i

$f_{Ri} \equiv$ decimal iron content of sinter i attributable to FeO in input mix

$f_{Oj} \equiv$ decimal iron content of ore j

$O_{ij} \equiv$ pounds of ore j used per ton of sinter output i

$D_F \equiv$ iron lost in flue dust.

[1] The hypothetical pellet composition was established from information in *Iron Ore 1969* (Cleveland, Ohio: American Iron Ore Association, 1969).

TABLE C.1 Composition of Iron Ores Charged Directly to Sinter Strand and Blast Furnace

	High iron high sulfur (65% Fe)	High iron low sulfur (65% Fe)	Low iron high sulfur (55% Fe)	Low iron low sulfur (55% Fe)
Fe_2O_3[a]	0.8579	0.8579	0.7832	0.7832
$Fe(OH)_3$[a]	0.0966	0.0966	0.0043	0.0043
Sulfur	0.0015	0.0002	0.0015	0.0002
Other[b]	0.0050	0.0050	0.0050	0.0050
Acids (gross)[c]	0.0260	0.0269	0.1373	0.1382
Bases (gross)[c]	0.0130	0.0134	0.0687	0.0691
Total	1.0000	1.0000	1.0000	1.0000

[a] Assumed on the basis of inspection of ore chemical analysis presented in Charles L. Trozzo, *The Location of Integrated Blast Furnace Capacity*, appendix II, pp. 444–446, subject to the requirement that total iron fraction be 0.65 for the high-iron ore and 0.55 for the low-iron ore.

[b] Especially phosphorus and manganese.

[c] The fraction of the ore accounted for by gross acids plus gross bases is computed as one minus the sum of the fractions for Fe_2O_3, $Fe(OH)_3$, sulfur and "other." Furthermore, from inspection of ore analyses in American Iron Ore Association, *Iron Ore*, 1969; Baldwin and Mathieson, "Fluxed Sinter," p. 220; and Trozzo, pp. 444–446, it has been assumed that: (1) gross acids equal two-thirds of the sum of gross acids and bases, (2) net bases (the input to the blast furnace submodel) are 52 percent of gross bases, or 48 percent of ore bases are lost to gas in blast furnace or sinter strand. This represents a 50–50 split between magnesium carbonate and calcium carbonate in gross bases. No loss of weight from acids is experienced.

Then, the following holds:

$$(1) \qquad f_{Si} = \frac{\Sigma f_{Oj} O_{ij} - D_F}{2000}$$

where only one of the four ores is used in making any given sinter. Furthermore, an indicator of sinter quality called the "oxidation ratio" can be used to split the iron contained in the sinter between iron contained as Fe_2O_3 and FeO. From Doi and Kasai, "Self Fluxing Sinter and the Blast Furnace Practice," p. 187; the ratio (R) can be defined as:

$$(2) \qquad R \equiv \frac{3f_{Si} - f_{Ri}}{3f_{Si}} = 1 - \frac{f_{Ri}}{3f_{Si}}.$$

We require that the oxidation ratio be 0.92 for all sinter practices. This allows us to solve for the ferrous oxide content of sinter as follows: Using (2) above we can write

$$(3) \qquad f_{Ri} = [3 - 3(0.92)]f_{Si} = 0.24 f_{Si}$$

TABLE C.2   Pellet and Sinter Characteristics and Composition

	Quality measures		Decimal constituents used in blast furnace model				
	Total Fe^b (f_{si})	Basic- ity^d	Fe$_2$O$_3$ (X)	FeO (Z)	Sulfur^b	Net bases^c	Gross acids^c
Low limestone sinter^a							
L1	0.667	1.39	0.724	0.206	0.001	0.037	0.027
L2	0.667	1.39	0.724	0.206	0.001	0.037	0.027
L3	0.666	1.36	0.724	0.206	0.000	0.037	0.028
L4	0.666	1.36	0.724	0.206	0.000	0.037	0.028
L5	0.564	0.47	0.612	0.174	0.001	0.067	0.141
L6	0.564	0.47	0.612	0.174	0.001	0.067	0.141
L7	0.564	0.47	0.612	0.174	0.000	0.067	0.142
L8	0.564	0.47	0.612	0.174	0.000	0.067	0.142
Medium limestone sinter^a							
M1	0.645	2.65	0.700	0.199	0.001	0.068	0.026
M2	0.645	2.67	0.700	0.199	0.001	0.068	0.026
M3	0.644	2.57	0.700	0.100	0.000	0.069	0.027
M4	0.644	2.57	0.700	0.199	0.000	0.069	0.027
M5	0.546	0.71	0.592	0.168	0.001	0.097	0.136
M6	0.546	0.71	0.592	0.168	0.001	0.097	0.136
M7	0.546	0.71	0.592	0.168	0.000	0.097	0.137
M8	0.546	0.71	0.592	0.168	0.000	0.097	0.137
High limestone sinter^a							
H1	0.622	4.06	0.675	0.192	0.001	0.101	0.025
H2	0.622	4.06	0.675	0.192	0.001	0.101	0.025
H3	0.621	4.06	0.675	0.192	0.000	0.101	0.026
H4	0.621	3.92	0.675	0.192	0.000	0.101	0.026
H5	0.526	0.98	0.572	0.162	0.001	0.129	0.132
H6	0.526	0.98	0.572	0.162	0.001	0.129	0.132
H7	0.526	0.97	0.572	0.162	0.000	0.129	0.132
H8	0.526	0.97	0.572	0.162	0.000	0.129	0.132
Pellets	0.662	0.61	0.633	0.281	0.000	0.030	0.050

^{a} Sinters 1–8 for each limestone practice are derived from input composition combinations as:

Sinter No.	Ore	Coke
1:	High iron, high sulfur	High sulfur
2:	High iron, high sulfur	Low sulfur
3:	High iron, low sulfur	High sulfur
4:	High iron, low sulfur	Low sulfur
5:	Low iron, high sulfur	High sulfur
6:	Low iron, high sulfur	Low sulfur
7:	Low iron, low sulfur	High sulfur
8:	Low iron, low sulfur	Low sulfur

^{b} Calculated from the sulfur balance assumptions explained in the text for sinters and taken from reported data for pellets.

^{c} For the sinter burden net bases originate from the ore and limestone, and gross acids originate from the ore. The acids and bases data for pellets were taken from reported analyses.

^{d} Basicity equals:

$$\frac{\text{Total net bases}}{\text{Total gross acids}} = \frac{\text{CaO} + \text{MgO}}{\text{SiO}_2 + \text{Al}_2\text{O}_3}.$$

TABLE C.3   Flue Dust and Iron Ore Substitution Linkages

	Sinter flue dust characteristics		Assumed ore equivalent of dust	
	% Fe	% S[a]	% Fe	% S
	Low limestone			
L1	67	0.007	65	0.150
L2	67	0.006	65	0.150
L3	67	0.003	65	0.015
L4	67	0.002	65	0.015
L5	56	0.007	55	0.150
L6	56	0.006	55	0.150
L7	56	0.003	55	0.015
L8	56	0.002	55	0.015
	Medium limestone			
M1	64	0.011	65	0.150
M2	64	0.009	65	0.150
M3	64	0.004	65	0.015
M4	64	0.003	65	0.015
M5	55	0.011	55	0.150
M6	55	0.009	55	0.150
M7	55	0.004	55	0.015
M8	55	0.003	55	0.015
	High limestone			
H1	62	0.012	65	0.150
H2	62	0.010	65	0.150
H3	62	0.005	65	0.015
H4	62	0.003	65	0.015
H5	53	0.012	55	0.150
H6	53	0.010	55	0.150
H7	53	0.005	55	0.015
H8	53	0.003	55	0.015

[a] Percent sulfur in sinter flue dust is equivalent to percent sulfur in sinter product.

But the ferrous oxide content of the ith sinter (Z_i) must be larger than the Fe content of the sinter attributable to the ferrous oxide. Since there is 0.778 pounds of iron in each pound of ferrous oxide, the decimal ferrous oxide content of the sinter is:

$$(4) \qquad Z_i = \frac{0.24 f_{si}}{0.778} = 0.308 f_{si}$$

The balance of the iron in the sinter is attributed to Fe_2O_3 and if we let the decimal Fe_2O_3 content of the ith sinter be denoted by X_i, we can solve for this from the relation:

$$(5) \qquad f_{si} = 0.70(X_i) + 0.778(Z_i) \text{ or}$$

$$X_i = \frac{f_{si} - 0.778(Z_i)}{0.70} = \frac{f_{si} - 0.778(0.308)f_{si}}{0.70} = 1.0863 f_{si}$$

A similar calculation has been made for pellets, where the assumed oxidation ratio is 0.89.[2]

Sintered flue dusts recovered directly from the sinter plant or recovered from the blast furnace activities using 100 percent sinter burdens are associated for substitution purposes with the four purchased fine ore inputs, as described in table C.3. Flue dusts from all steel furnace activities are associated with low iron, low sulfur ore fines for recycling purposes.[3]

[2] See, U.N. Economic Commission for Europe, *Iron Ore Preparation*, p. 75.

[3] Although OH and BOF steel-making dusts have variable iron contents, depending on furnace and practice, they can reasonably be linked to this ore, since the iron content of the dusts ranges from 55–60 percent. See P. G. Barnard, A. G. Starliper, M. W. Dressel, and M. M. Fine, Recycling of Steelmaking Dusts, USBM Technical Progress Report no. 52 (February 1972), p. 2. Electric arc dusts are not recirculated since no blast furnace–sinter strand is assumed for these plants.

5

IRON PRODUCTION: THE BLAST FURNACE

For decades the blast furnace was the symbol of industrial advance. Pictures of banks of these monsters in Pittsburgh or Gary were interpreted as evidence of the economic strength of the region and, indeed, the nation. In more recent times, developing countries have imported this symbolism, and several have stressed the creation of heavy industry based on iron and steel, often neglecting agriculture and the immediate needs of their populations. Meanwhile, in the developed world, the bloom has gone off this particular rose, and the blast furnace as often as not has come to symbolize dirty industry—the kind one does not want in one's own region, but is quite content to leave to Pittsburgh and Gary.

To some extent the symbolic freight carried by the blast furnace was and is excessive. True, the production of iron from iron ore has historically been a key step in the production of steel, but we suspect that in the past the blast furnace was singled out because it was large and because the boosters and picture takers were often confused about the distinction between iron and steel. A more accurate symbol would have been the Bessemer converter in which steel was made from iron, or the finishing mill in which the key products such as rails and sheet steel were produced from raw steel. Similarly today, the blast furnace answers for the sins of the integrated iron and steel mill even though it is a minor contributor to this pollution source. For example, the mill's water pollution problems stem largely from the coke ovens and finishing mills. Airborne residuals are dominated by the newer steel furnaces and the combustion of fossil fuels in the production of steam and electricity.[1]

[1] The roles of various parts of the mill as pollution sources will become clearer in chapters 9 and 10, in which several influences on millwide residuals loads are explored.

Nevertheless, there is still a sense in which the blast furnace signifies a vital choice open to the integrated producer, or more broadly, to the economy as a whole. This is the choice between emphasis on hot metal (iron) and on steel scrap in the production of new steel. This choice is central to the size of the integrated mill's residuals management problem. But the aggregate of these choices also determines the extent to which our current industrial throughput of steel products rests on further reduction of iron ore reserves as opposed to the recycling of obsolete steel scrap from buildings, bridges, rails, autos, and so on.[2] It is important then, to understand the blast furnace and to include a reasonable representation of its function in our model.

The operation of the blast furnace is semicontinuous. To begin a production round, the iron-bearing inputs (discussed in chapter 4 and in appendix C) are charged into the top of the blast furnace, along with coke and limestone. The proportions used depend on both physical requirements and economic considerations, and part of this chapter describes a submodel we used to reflect the former. The economic considerations, of course, emerge from the heart of the overall linear programming model. Heat is introduced at the bottom of the furnace in the form of blasts of superheated air. This heat ignites the coke and helps maintain generally high temperatures in the furnace. The incomplete combustion of the coke supplies the reducing agent, carbon monoxide, which separates the elemental iron from the ore. Molten iron collects in the bottom of the furnace. The limestone combines with impurities from the ore, forming a liquid slag which, being lighter than the metal, floats on top of it. As the slag builds up on the surface of the molten iron, it is periodically tapped off. Similarly, as a sufficient quantity of molten iron accumulates beneath the slag, it too is tapped off, ready for the steel furnaces. Meanwhile, the raw materials (sinter, pellets, ore, coke, and limestone) are periodically poured into the top of the furnace, and heated air is blasted into the bottom.

THE BURDENING PROBLEM

The determination of the proper quantities of ore, pellets, sinter, limestone, and coke which must be charged to produce the required amount of iron, given the variable chemical composition of the inputs and the desired composition of the homogeneous iron output, is called the blast furnace burdening problem. In our model, the aim is to ob-

[2] The future may belong to direct reduction (a process not included in the model) in which iron ore is transformed into "sponge iron" for charging to the steel furnace without the use of coke. These processes generally rely on another reducing gas, such as hydrogen. See H. E. McGannon, ed., *The Making, Shaping and Treating of Steel,* 9th ed. (Pittsburgh: U.S. Steel Corporation, 1971), ch. 14.

tain a molten iron 94.15 percent pure, known in the industry as hot metal. The inclusion of 0.10 percent alloy elements of chromium, copper, nickel, tin, and molybdenum brings the metallic content of the hot metal up to 94.25 percent. The balance of the hot metal is made up largely of materials assumed constant for our purposes and ignored in the burdening calculations. These materials are carbon (3.52 percent), manganese (1.00 percent), phosphorus (0.20 percent), and silicon (1.00 percent).[3] The sulfur content of the hot metal, on the other hand, is treated as a target in the burdening calculation, and is achieved by proper choice of charge material. We require that the sulfur content of the hot metal be 0.03 percent.[4]

In order to solve this first stage of the burdening problem, a variant of a model suggested by Tibor Fabian has been developed which permits the calculation of any number of technologically feasible blast furnace vectors.[5] Essentially this is a thermochemical submodel which solves simultaneously for the coke and limestone requirements per ton of hot metal once the ore requirement has been determined. The procedure involves restricting the sulfur and iron contents of the iron product and solving for the input quantities required to meet these restrictions. The major deficiency with the approach is that it does not reflect possibilities for the addition of other fuels, such as residual oil

[3] These specifications can be found in McGannon, *The Making, Shaping and Treating of Steel*, 8th ed., p. 431; and Battelle Memorial Institute, *Technical and Economic Analysis of the Impact of Recent Developments in Steelmaking Practices on the Supplying Industries* (Columbus: Battelle Memorial Institute, 1964), p. IV–13.
    Since we assume that 100 percent of the phosphorus and 50–70 percent of the manganese charged into the furnace exit in the hot metal, these specifications must be met by careful purchase and blending of ores.

[4] The upper limit on sulfur of 0.03 percent is a frequently mentioned value in the literature and can be found in McGannon, *The Making, Shaping and Treating of Steel*, 8th ed., p. 431. Sulfur concentrations above this limit would pose difficulties at later production stages because of the difficulty of achieving significant sulfur removal in the steel furnace, and the fact that sulfur in larger quantities increases the tendency of steel to tear and crack in rolling.

[5] Tibor Fabian, "A Linear Programming Model of Integrated Iron and Steel Production," *Management Science*, vol. IV, no. 4 (July 1958), pp. 439–448. This model represents a middle ground between very simple versions based on aggregate data (for example, J. P. Nelson, "An Interregional Recursive Programming Model of the U.S. Iron and Steel Industry" (Ph.D. dissertation, University of Wisconsin, 1970) and the sophisticated models which simultaneously account for most of the relevant thermochemical relationships and which can predict effects on the requisite charge of changes in blast temperature, ore moisture, etc. (for example, A. L. Hodge and F. R. Wyczalek, "A Mathematical Method for Analyzing and Predicting Changes in Blast Furnace Operation," *AIME Blast Furnace, Coke Oven and Raw Materials Conference Proceedings*, vol. 20 (New York: AIME, 1961), pp. 455–488; and T. E. Dancy, A. T. Sadler, and H. N. Lander, "Process Analysis of Blast Furnace Operation with Oxygen and Steam," *AIME Blast Furnace, Coke Oven and Raw Materials Conference Proceedings*, vol. 17 (New York: AIME, 1958), pp. 16–33. This Dancy–Sadler–Lander model is beautifully employed by C. L. Trozzo in "The Technical Efficiency of the Location of Integrated Blast Furnace Capacity" (Ph.D. dissertation, Harvard University, 1966).

or natural gas; or for the injection of steam or oxygen into the furnace. Thus, these productivity-enhancing alternatives are not available in our model.

The modified Fabian model, as described below, is applied in our model to sixty-six combinations of iron-bearing charge material and coke to produce sixty-six activities in the linear program, distinguished by sulfur, iron, and limestone content. These combinations are determined as follows:[6]

Coke Choice   *Iron-Bearing Input Choice*

$$\left.\begin{array}{c}\text{High sulfur coke}\\\text{Low sulfur coke}\end{array}\right\} \times \left\{\begin{array}{l}\text{Lump ores (4)}\\\text{Run-of-mine ores (4)}\\\text{Low limestone sinters (8)}\\\text{Medium limestone sinters (8)}\\\text{High limestone sinters (8)}\\\text{Pellets (1)}\end{array}\right\} = 66$$

Thus each of the two cokes may be combined with each of thirty-three iron-bearing materials. It is worth noting that this approach, in which a single iron-bearing charge material is used in each activity, is quite different from that adopted in steel furnace burdening (see chapter 6). Here we can meet the output quality requirements with a single input, and we depend on the linear model to show us if, in fact, the least-cost burden contains a combination of several iron-bearing inputs.

Iron-Bearing Input Requirements

The first step in our procedure is to determine the quantity of the iron-bearing input required per ton of hot metal based on the iron content of the input and flue dust losses from the furnace. In this connection we assume that no limestone is lost in the flue dust but that the composition of the dust from a particular burden is 90 percent iron-bearing material and 10 percent coke.[7] The quantity of dust generated is a function of the physical character of the metallic burden (that is, pellets, sinter, lump, or run-of-mine ore). We have three baseline flue dust estimates which can be associated with three of our metallic burden types.

1. There are 490 pounds of dust per ton of hot metal for a low iron content, run-of-mine ore charge.[8]

[6] The constituents of the ores, sinters, and pellets are discussed in chapter 4. Note that ore fines are not directly charged to the blast furnace.

[7] The limestone content of the dust may, in fact, be as high as 5 percent, according to J. Varga, Jr. and H. W. Lownie, Jr., *A Systems Analysis Study of the Integrated Iron and Steel Industry* (Columbus: Battelle Memorial Institute, May 1969), p. V–8.

[8] From H. M. Graff and S. C. Bouwer, "Economics of Raw Materials Preparation for the Blast Furnace," *Journal of Metals* (April 1965), p. 391.

2. There are 224 pounds of dust per ton of hot metal for a low iron content, lump ore charge.[9]

3. There are 40 pounds of dust per ton of hot metal for a low iron content, low limestone sinter.[10]

For high-iron-content lump, and run-of-mine ores and high-iron-content, low-limestone sinter we assume that dust generation is the same per ton of gross charge as for the corresponding low iron content burden. For medium and high limestone sinters we use the same dust generation factor as for low limestone sinter. Pellets are assumed to generate roughly half the amount of dust per ton of hot metal encountered in the high iron-content, low limestone sinter case.[11]

Given these assumptions about dust, and our requirement for the iron content of hot metal, the pounds of iron-bearing input required per ton of hot metal (b_h) are calculated as follows:

$$(1) \quad b_h = \frac{2000(0.9415)}{W_h} + 0.9D_h \text{ for } h = 1, \ldots, 11 = \frac{1883}{W_h} + 0.9D_h$$

where $W_h \equiv$ the iron content of the hth iron-bearing input, and $D_h \equiv$ the pounds of flue dust generated by the hth burden. These calculations produce the results shown in table 5.1.[12]

In this connection, the blast furnace has another link to other process units, for a large fraction of the flue dust generated in the furnace is assumed in our model to be recovered from the flue gas. The use of this recovered dust in sintering has already been discussed, and the dust recovery system that we assume to be in place is described in chapter 8. The quantity of the gas itself and its value as a fuel are dealt with later in this chapter.

Coke and Limestone Input Requirements

The amounts of coke and limestone required in an activity are interdependent and have to be determined simultaneously. An increase in the

[9] From D. C. Brown, "The What and Why of Future Blast Furnace Burdens," *Twenty-First Annual Mining Symposium Proceedings* (University of Minnesota, January 1960), p. E–2.

[10] The 40-pound figure is in the range reported by a number of observers, namely, Graff and Bouwer, "Economics of Raw Materials," p. 391; Varga and Lownie, *A Systems Analysis*, p. C–34; and Brown, ibid.

[11] Graff and Bouwer, "Economics of Raw Materials," p. 391.

[12] This relation neglects iron losses in the slag, a simplification which allows us to avoid the extremely complex matter of determining all of the elements of the burden simultaneously by ignoring the fact that slag quantity depends on the quantity of ore charged and on its sulfur content. This assumption was made by Hodge and Wyczalek in "A Mathematical Method," p. 458, a model which is considerably more complex than the one suggested here. In any event, the amount of ferrous oxides diverted to the slag is insignificant, amounting to 0.5 percent in commercial operations. See, Trozzo, "Technical Efficiency," p. 73.

TABLE 5.1   *Quantities of Iron-Bearing Inputs Required in the Blast Furnace Charge*

Type of iron-bearing input	Iron content of input (per lb. ore)	Pounds total flue dust[a]	Pounds iron-bearing input[a]	
			Lost as flue dust	Required
Ore				
Unscreened				
High iron	0.65	415.0	373.0	3273.0
Low iron	0.55	490.0	441.0	3868.0
Screened				
High iron	0.65	190.0	171.0	3071.0
Low iron	0.55	224.0	202.0	3629.0
Sinter				
Low limestone				
High iron	0.667	33.7	30.3	2856.4
Low iron	0.564	40.0	36.0	3378.0
Medium limestone				
High iron	0.645	34.9	31.4	2955.2
Low iron	0.546	41.2	37.1	3492.6
High limestone				
High iron	0.622	36.1	32.4	3063.0
Low iron	0.526	42.7	38.4	3622.2
Pellets	0.662	16.6	14.9	2862.7

[a] Figures expressed per ton of hot metal output.

limestone per unit of an activity will, for example, increase the coke requirement, because the calcination of the added stone and the increased slag quantity will require that additional heat be supplied. An increase in the limestone will also increase the volume of carbon dioxide, which implies a need for additional coke to reduce the carbon dioxide to carbon monoxide. The amount of stone in an activity is in turn dependent on the amount of coke, since the requirement for calcium oxide depends upon the quantities of acids, bases, and excess sulfur in the charge, and coke contains both acids (in the form of silicon dioxide) and sulfur.

Our approach to this part of the burdening problem is based, as we have indicated, on a modified version of the Fabian model. The essence of this method may be summarized as follows.[13]

1. Obtain one expression for the coke input required as a function of limestone input from the blast furnace *heat balance.*

2. Obtain a second such expression from definitions and empirical work concerning the *fate of sulfur* in the process.

[13] The derivation of the actual equations is described in considerable detail in W. J. Vaughan, "A Residuals Management Model of the Iron and Steel Industry: A Linear Programming Approach" (Ph.D. dissertation, Georgetown University, 1975).

3. Set these two expressions equal and solve the resulting nonlinear equation for the limestone requirement.[14]
4. Substitute into one of the earlier expressions to obtain the coke requirement and other quantities of interest.

The first expression for the coke requirement is obtained from the heat balance, where we have (ignoring minor heat sources and requirements) heat supplied in combustion of coke plus heat supplied in the blast air equals heat required in the reduction of the iron-bearing input to elemental iron[15] plus heat required in the calcination of the limestone charge plus heat required in the reduction of some carbon dioxide in the furnace to carbon monoxide.[16]

The derivation of the second expression for the coke requirement is more complicated since it depends on a mix of definitions and empirical results having to do with the chemistry of the blast furnace slag and the fate of the sulfur in the charge. The first definition is slag basicity, the ratio of the total weight of the acids in the coke, limestone, and iron-bearing material, to the weight of the bases in those inputs.[17] (*Acids* is a steel industry term for oxides such as alumina and silica. *Bases* refers particularly to calcium oxide, formed by calcination of the limestone, and magnesium oxide to the extent it is present.) Slag basicity is so called because nearly all these compounds are assumed to leave the furnace in the slag.

The next term we must define is much less exotic. The *partition ratio* is the ratio of the concentration of sulfur in the slag to the concentration of sulfur in the hot metal. The partition ratio and the slag basicity are related through the chemistry of the process, and empirical work has shown that the relation is approximately linear.[18] Writing the partition ratio as a linear function of slag basicity and making the necessary substi-

---

[14] We did not actually find a general solution to this equation. Rather we used a simple numerical technique to solve it for each specific burden type.

[15] This requirement varies with the specific iron compounds in the ore. Thus, for example, about 50 percent more heat per pound of iron is required to reduce ferric oxide, a common oxide in ore, than is required for ferrous oxide, the oxide found in mill scale used in some sinter.

[16] Fabian appears to have made two slips in his calculations at this point, or, at best, to have provided a misleading exposition of the steps which lead him to determination of this term. Fortunately, the errors tend to be mutually offsetting and the results in terms of coke rate obtained using this expression are reasonable. First, Fabian calculates the carbon dioxide equivalent of the total carbon input (some of which he claims must be reduced) incorrectly by using the wrong molecular weight for carbon dioxide (p. 443). This has the effect of lowering the coke requirement. Second, he ignores the heat available from oxidation of carbon monoxide (from coke carbon) to carbon dioxide. This has the opposite effect.

[17] In fact, outside industry definitions, there are no bases in the coke nor acids in the limestone.

[18] J. C. Agarwal and John F. Elliott, "High Sulfur Coke for Blast Furnace Use," Paper presented at the Iron-Making Conference, AIME, April 19, 1971, pp. 8, 13.

tutions so that everything is expressed in terms of the inputs of coke, limestone, and iron-bearing material, puts us in a position to solve for coke once again as a function of limestone. Setting the two expressions for coke equal, we can solve for limestone. Then the coke requirement is obtained by substitution back into the heat-balance coke expression.

The quantity of slag is determined from the calculated charge quantities of coke, limestone, and iron-bearing material, using information on the acids and bases contained in each of these inputs. As we have already noted, the slag is primarily composed of these acids and bases. The total weight of slag also includes, however, all the sulfur in the charge except that small amount leaving the furnace in the iron. (We assume that no sulfur leaves in the blast furnace gas.[19]) The slag is, of course, a solid residual, but it is also responsible for an addition to the mill's airborne residuals problem. When the sulfur-bearing slag is flushed from the furnace, some of the sulfur reacts with oxygen to form sulfur dioxide. In wet weather the sulfur in the slag may react with water to form hydrogen sulfide, which is released to the atmosphere. This reaction also occurs if the hot slag is granulated with water.[20]

It has been reported that about 15 percent of the sulfur in the slag oxidizes to produce sulfur dioxide fumes upon coming into contact with the atmosphere during the slag flush.[21] Assuming that the emission is by and large uncontrollable except by variation in charge inputs, and that it always occurs as sulfur dioxide, the weight of sulfur dioxide released from the slag per ton of hot metal amounts to 30 percent of the weight of sulfur in the slag.

Slag Disposal

It is debatable, according to the literature, whether the slag produced in the blast furnace is a net revenue-producing item or not.[22] This slag can be broken down into three categories: slag which is directly recycled within the mill as a substitute for lime and limestone, slag which is further processed to yield a metal-bearing slag that is recycled to the steel

---

[19] Varga and Lownie, *A Systems Analysis Study*, p. V–53.

[20] Ibid., p. V–54.

[21] This estimate is reported in Trozzo, "Technical Efficiency," p. 57. Although tenuous, this is the only numerical value for slag sulfur oxidation we found in the literature. For a more extensive discussion of this problem, see, R. S. Kaplan and G. W. P. Rengstorff, "Emission of Sulfurous Gases from Blast Furnace Slags," in Julian Szekely, ed., *The Steel Industry and the Environment* (New York: Marcel Dekker, 1973), pp. 199–224. This paper explains that the reaction between slag and water when the hot slag is quenched produces sulfur dioxide and hydrogen sulfide in quantities which, although small, can be detected by odor. Whether the hydrogen sulfide ultimately oxidizes to form sulfur dioxide appears debatable.

[22] The comments in this section apply generally to steel furnace slag as well, and we do not differentiate between the two in the model.

furnace as a substitute for no. 2 bundles, and a metal-free by-product slag which is either stockpiled or sold for railroad ballast, landfill, and road and highway base. It is difficult to make a quantitative judgment about the ratio of by-product slag sold to by-product slag stockpiled, but the existence of large slag stockpiles across the country indicates that there may be an excess supply of this material at current prices.

The model does not reflect the possibilities of substituting unprocessed slag for lime and metal-bearing slag for no. 2 bundles directly in our activity vectors. Instead, we handle the problem of slag disposal and recirculation as if these activities take place outside of the mill itself under the conservative assumptions that the mill pays an independent company a fee for trucking the slag to a process and disposal area and a rent for use of the area in order to process and stockpile the slag. The mill receives a credit for directly recycled slag and processed metal-bearing slag. Under these operating conditions the net cost of slag disposal is $0.33 per ton.[23]

Some Comments on Verification

The coke and limestone requirements resulting from the application of our blast furnace submodel defy precise verification, since it would be fortuitous indeed to discover published blast furnace performance tests based on the chemical and thermal characteristics which match our hypothetical furnace and its inputs. In addition, new developments in blast furnace operation, such as hotter blast temperatures, blast oxygen enrichment, and hydrocarbon injection, are not included in our model and thus make comparison of our results with recent coke and limestone requirements misleading.[24] It is, however, possible to compare our calculated coke requirements for different burdens to requirements reported in the literature during the 1950s and early 1960s, a period when recent

[23] This value is calculated from information presented in E. C. Baker, *Estimated Costs of Steel Slag Disposal*, U.S. Bureau of Mines Information Circular No. 8440 (June 1970). Baker's data, interpreted from our point of view, yield conclusions somewhat different from the authors'. Our procedure is as follows: (i) We assume the total processing cost, including transportation and stockpiling, is $2.00 per ton. This corresponds to Baker's present method. (ii) We assume the breakdown by end use is such that value of the processed slag is $1.67 per ton.

[24] Historically, the average U.S. coke rate was 1,700 pounds per ton in 1959, using an aggregate burden of 23 percent sinter; 1,540 pounds in 1960, using an aggregate burden of 53 percent sinter; and 1,456 pounds in 1961, using an aggregate burden of 55 percent sinter. The decline in the coke rate continued during the 1960s, falling to 1,020 pounds in the fourth quarter of 1967 for the top ten U.S. furnaces. See United Nations, Department of Economic and Social Affairs, *Proceedings of the United Nations Interregional Symposium on the Application of Modern Technical Practices in the Iron and Steel Industry to Developing Countries* (New York: United Nations, 1964), p. 47; and C. L. Kobrin, "Steel's Changing Uses of Energy," *Iron Age* (June 6, 1968), p. 146.

TABLE 5.2   A Comparison of Observed and Calculated Coke Requirements for Various Blast Furnace Burdens

(pounds per ton of hot metal)

Type of burden[a]	Observed requirements			Average calculated requirements[b]
	High extreme	Low extreme	Average	
Ore				
Low iron (100%)	3,000	1,340	1,944	1,819
High iron (100%)	n.a.	n.a.	n.a.	1,759
Mixed ore and sinter				
Ore (≥75%)	1,752	1,510	1,654	n.a.
Ore (25% to 75%)	1,826	1,218	1,530	n.a.
Ore (≤25%)	1,504	1,350	1,421	n.a.
Sinter				
Low iron/low basicity (100%)	n.a.	n.a.	n.a.	1,603
Unknown quality (100%)	1,969	1,230	1,455	n.a.
High iron/high basicity (100%)	n.a.	n.a.	n.a.	1,480
Pellets (>70%)	1,313	1,110	1,218	1,515

Notes: n.a., not available.
For complete bibliographical information, see the Table References at the back of the book.
Sources: Dancy, Sadler, and Lander, "Blast Furnace Operation with Oxygen and Steam," pp. 16–32; Graff and Bouwer, "Raw Materials Preparation for the Blast Furnace," p. 391; John Griffen, "High-Grade Iron Ores and Agglomerates," pp. 70–75; Hill and Epstein, "Pellet and Sinter Burdens," p. 80; Holowatty, Wilson, and Schwarz, "Evaluation of a Blast Furnace," pp. 317–343; Joyce, Dowhaniuk, and Marsden, "High Beneficiated Burdens," p. 63; Frank R. Kik, "Blast Furnace Sinter," pp. 100–105; E. Klein, "Sintering High Grade Hematite Ore," p. 372; C. M. Nitchie, "Improvements in Blast Furnace Operation," pp. 78–80; Stapleton, Lindbloom, and Regilin, "Ironmaking," pp. 304–318; J. H. Strassberger, "Experience at Weirton," p. 36; UN Economic Commission for Europe, *Iron Ore Preparation*, pp. 52, 58, 59, 63; Uys and Kirkpatrick, "Beneficiation of Raw Materials," p. 25; Varga and Lownie, *A Systems Analysis Study*, pp. C-31 to C-36; Richard J. Wilson, "Humidified Blast," p. 5.
[a] High iron burdens are taken to be those with an iron content greater than 60 percent. Mixed burdens are made up of sinter in combination with ore and/or pellets.
[b] Average calculated requirements obtained from the blast furnace submodel discussed in the text.

modifications in blast furnace technology were not widespread. Table 5.2 shows the results of this comparison, where we include average and extreme values for the literature data.

Table 5.2 is arranged roughly in order of decreasing coke rates from left to right. The situations assumed in our calculations are not, in most cases, matched by situations reflected in literature values, and this arrangement is designed to allow approximate interpolated comparisons. Thus, for example, we found no published data for high iron-content ore charges, but our calculated value lies in the range between low iron-content ore and mixed sinter–ore charge, a reasonable result. In general, it appears that our calculated coke requirements vary less between the low value for pellets and the high for low iron-content ore than do the observed coke requirements. Our value at the upper end (1,819 pounds per ton of hot metal) is about 6 percent lower than the average of the comparable values in the literature (1,944 pounds per ton of hot metal). At the other end of the scale, our calculated requirement for a pellet charge is almost 25 percent higher than the average reported value.[25] On the other hand, our calculated values, with the exception of the one for a pellet charge, fall within the reported ranges for the most nearly comparable charge type reported in the literature.

BLAST FURNACE PRODUCTIVITY AND THE PHYSICAL CAPACITY CONSTRAINT

Since a given blast furnace or set of furnaces has only so much total volume, and since producing a given quantity of hot iron from some particular charge (that is, of particular density, iron content, and permeability) requires a certain minimum amount of time, it is clear that there is an upper limit to iron production per day at an existing plant.[26] In order to include this constraint on the capacity of the existing plant in our model, we work with the inverse of hot metal production per hour. The structure of the constraint on daily capacity, for production of $X_1, \ldots, X_h$ tons per day of hot metal using practices 1 through h in a shop with two furnaces of given size is:

$$X_1 t_1 + X_2 t_2 +, \ldots, + X_{64} t_{64} \leq 2 \times 24$$

where the t_h is the hours required per ton of hot metal using practice h in the given-size furnace.

The data available for estimating the t_h are fragmentary and display considerable variability. We have, however, used data supplied by Trozzo and the UN to estimate hours-per-ton requirements by charge type for a furnace of 52,500 ft.³ working volume.[27] These estimates are summarized in table 5.3.

[25] Lower observed pellet coke rates reflect the benefits of a uniformly sized burden, which yields better contact between gases and solids in the furnace, superior heat transfer, better utilization of gases to remove oxygen from the ore, lower top gas carbon monoxide–carbon dioxide ratios, and lower top temperatures. (T. F. Olt, "Blast Furnace Performance Using Iron Ore Pellets," *Journal of the British Iron and Steel Institute*, vol. 200, pt. 2 (February 1962), pp. 88, 89, and 93.) These factors are not handled in our blast furnace submodel.

[26] As already noted, we are not including in our model some of the alternatives designed to expand hot metal capacity, such as natural gas injection. Hence our discussion here applies to a particular set of operating practices as well as to a given furnace volume and charge type.

[27] See Trozzo, "Technical Efficiency," pp. 615–636; United Nations Economic Commission for Europe, *Economic Aspects of Iron Ore Preparation*, ST/ECE/STEEL/24 (1968), p. 72; M. O. Holowatty, R. J. Wilson, and A. M. Schwarz, "Performance

TABLE 5.3   Blast Furnace Productivity and Labor Requirements

Practice[a]	Base[b] (t_h) (52,500 = ft.³ volume)	Corrected[b] (t_i) (21,000 = ft.³ volume)	Relative[c] produc- tivity (t_1/t_i)	Large-shop labor[d]	Small-shop labor[d]
Low iron ore	0.0150	0.03750	1.00	0.675	0.819
High iron ore	0.0135	0.03375	1.11	0.608	0.738
Low iron, low limestone sinter	0.0110	0.02750	1.36	0.493	0.598
High iron, low limestone sinter	0.0095	0.02375	1.58	0.425	0.516
Low iron, medium and high lime- stone sinter	0.0100	0.02500	1.50	0.452	0.549
High iron, medium and high lime- stone sinter and pellets	0.0085	0.02125	1.76	0.385	0.467

[a] All vectors involve 100 percent burden of the specific iron-bearing input.

[b] Quantities are expressed as furnace hours per ton of hot metal produced.

[c] The relative productivity values in column three (relative tons per hour) are expressed in relation to the least productive burden (low iron-content ore). These values are obtained by dividing the ton per hour value associated with each burden by the base ton per hour value, for example, t_1/t_h. A statistical estimation of the variation in blast furnace productivity with burden composition, based on company data, is presented in Myles Boylan, Jr., "The Economics of Change in the Scale of Production in the U.S. Iron and Steel Industry from 1900 to 1970," Eq. V-1, p. 209. This source became available to us only after our model was complete and most production runs had been made. It is, therefore, comforting to note that Boylan's equation (assuming a 21-ft. hearth diameter and no scrap in the burden) yields relative productivity values consistent with ours.

[d] Quantities are expressed as man-hours per ton of hot metal produced.

It is necessary, of course, to correct these figures for differences in volume between the furnaces we are interested in modeling which are 21,000 ft.³ and the baseline furnace of 52,500 ft.³ We perform this correction in the simplest possible way, by assuming that ratio of hours per ton in two furnaces is the inverse of the ratio of their volumes.

By-product Fuel, Heat Balance, and Utilities

In order to produce a reasonable model of the blast furnace, we must go beyond the considerations outlined so far to take account of the weight, volume, and heating value of the top gas generated in the smelting reaction as well as the waste heat which must be removed by blast

Evaluation of a Blast Furnace Burdened with Sized Ore, Sinter, and Pellets," in *AIME National Open Hearth Committee Proceedings*, vol. 22 (New York: AIME, 1963), p. 337.

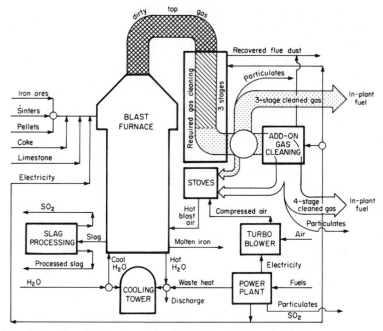

Figure 5.1. Simplified schematic of the blast furnace process.

furnace cooling water, and the heat input needed to heat the blast air. The overall system, including the furnace itself and the auxiliary equipment for dealing with the gas and slag, is shown schematically in figure 5.1.

Top Gas Generation

The total weight of the exit gas per ton of hot metal can be estimated as the sum of the nitrogen in the blast air, plus the carbon monoxide and carbon dioxide produced in the furnace. In fact, we assume that 10 percent of this is lost through leaks, so that only 90 percent is recovered for use as fuel. Since modern blast furnace practice generally yields a top gas with a heating value between 70 and 85 Btu per standard cubic foot (scf), we feel safe in assuming that our top gas has a value of 75 Btu per scf.[28]

Heat Balance

All the heat required at the stoves for heating the blast air to 1,000° F (estimated to be 1,152 net Btu per pound of carbon in the charge) is sup-

---

[28] See, C. L. Kobrin, "Steel's Changing Uses of Energy," p. 145; and Varga and Lownie, *A Systems Analysis Study*, p. C-41. We convert pounds to standard cubic feet (scf) using the factor 11.9 scf per pound based on the assumed gas composition.

plied by burning the top gas after it has been cleaned.[29] This leaves a quantity of gas, varying of course with the character of the charge, which is available for use elsewhere in the mill. It is this net gas availability which appears in each of the blast furnace vectors. In general, this amounts to 75–80 percent of the total quantity of gas generated.

The walls of the modern blast furnace are indirectly cooled by means of water passing through enclosed metal conduits known as cooling plates, which are laid in the brickwork of the furnace wall.[30] The predominant system in use today is of the once-through type, in which the heated water is discharged.[31] We incorporate this system in our base case, but allow the removal of heat from the cooling water by a cooling tower as an add-on option.

In order to estimate the quantity of heat which must be removed from the furnace wall per unit output, we treat the cooling requirement as a function of the heat carried in the hot blast. We use the rule of thumb derived from Bashforth that the ratio of the heat absorbed in the cooling water to the heat carried in the hot blast is 0.66.[32] This implies, for example, that 6,380 gallons of cooling water will be required per ton of hot metal when the coke rate is 1,400 pounds per ton of hot metal and the rise in water temperature is 20° F. When the coke rate is 1,700 pounds per ton, the cooling water requirement will be 7,750 gallons per ton. These coke rates span the range of our calculated rates (see table 5.2) and this range of cooling water usage falls well within the range reported in actual practice: 4,000 to 8,500 gallons per ton of hot metal.[33]

Utilities

Electricity and steam are the remaining utility entries required in the blast furnace portion of our activity matrix.

Electricity. The electricity coefficient per ton of hot metal in each of our sixty-six vectors is linked to the weight of burdens which must be hoisted and loaded into the furnace. A baseline value of 26 kWh per ton of hot metal is associated with the heaviest burden (low iron-content, unscreened ore and high sulfur coke).[34] The remaining sixty-five electricity

---

[29] The thermal efficiency of the stoves is assumed to be 85 percent.

[30] Hayse H. Black and Gerald N. McDermott, "Industrial Waste Guide–Blast Furnace Department of the Steel Industry," *Sewage and Industrial Wastes*, vol. 26, no. 8 (August 1954), p. 985.

[31] Frank A. Berczynski, "The Blast Furnace," *Blast Furnace and Steel Plant* (March 1971), p. 157.

[32] Calculated from George Reginald Bashforth, *The Manufacture of Iron and Steel*, vol. 1 (London: Chapman and Hall Ltd., 1948).

[33] Black and McDermott, "Industrial Waste Guide," p. 985. These figures actually reflect variation in the temperature rise allowed in the cooling water as well as the variation in furnace practice.

[34] *Watkins Cyclopedia of the Steel Industry*, 11th ed. (Pittsburgh: Steel Publications, Inc., 1967), p. 426.

entries are the product of this baseline electricity coefficient, multiplied by the ratio of the burden weight in each of these activities to the burden weight in the base activity.

Blast furnace wind compression: Turboblower steam requirement. Heated blast air blown into the bottom of the blast furnace must be compressed by blowing engines (steam turbine-driven compressors) to carry it through the stoves. We assume that the pounds of steam required for blast compression are directly associated with the blast air requirement per ton of hot metal (and thus indirectly with the coke requirement). According to data in a well-known industry publication, a reasonable figure to associate with our highest coke rate is 2,190 pounds of steam per ton of hot metal.[35] The quantities required in the other vectors are calculated on the basis of coke rate ratios.

LABOR REQUIREMENTS AND OBJECTIVE FUNCTION VALUES

The operating cost items not previously accounted for by the burdening and utilities estimation procedure, which are required to close out our discussion of the blast furnace, are explained below.

Labor

Past studies have taken different approaches to the determination of the labor hour requirement per ton of blast furnace hot metal. Some have used a constant coefficient for all blast furnace activities unadjusted for any difference in total burden weight or productivity.[36] Others have refined this procedure by adjusting a base coefficient by a burden iron-content ratio to obtain different labor requirements for different ore practices.[37] Although neither of these two methods is perfect, the second approach is a decided improvement over the first. Our procedure involves a refinement of this second approach, and is based upon two assumptions:

1. The labor coefficient is related to plant size, so that an adjustment should be made for economies in labor input as plant size increases.
2. The labor coefficient is a function of furnace productivity, which, we know from the previous discussion, is in turn a function of the type of burden.[38]

---

[35] This maximum requirement was calculated from McGannon, *The Making, Shaping, and Treating of Steel,* 8th ed., p. 387.

[36] Che S. Tsao, "Steel Production and Resource Allocation: An Empirical Study," *Applied Economics,* vol. 2, no. 3 (1970), pp. 203–223.

[37] See Nelson, "An Interregional Recursive Programming Model." For sinter burdens, the labor requirement is taken to be half that for domestic ore burdens—a rough attempt to reflect productivity differentials.

[38] Implicit here is the assumption that the absolute size of the labor crew at a

We associate a base requirement of 0.675 labor hours per ton of hot metal with the least-productive burden variant for large furnaces in a large shop (shop production ≥ 2.5 million tons of hot metal per year) and adjust this value by the appropriate productivity relatives (from pages 95–96) giving the set of large-shop labor coefficients found in table 5.3.[39]

Assuming economies of scale in labor, we estimate the requirement for smaller shops by correcting the large-shop value by the ratio of capital cost per ton of hot metal in the small shop to capital cost per ton of hot metal in the large shop, a value of 1.21.

Operating and Maintenance Costs

Treatment of blast furnace operating and maintenance costs in the iron-making literature generally involves considerable definitional and procedural confusion. Excluding utilities, there is some doubt concerning the appropriate accounting entries for blast furnace operating and maintenance costs. The most specific accounting breakdown available appears here, and gives figures for a hypothetical 1.2 million net ton per year blast furnace.[40]

Item	*1969 Cost/ton Hot Metal*
Labor	$0.50
Utilities	1.00
Refractories	0.15
Reline	0.60
Maintenance and repair	0.75
Supplies	0.78
General overhead	0.45
Total	$4.23

It would be difficult to use this estimate across the board for our activities for a number of reasons. First, no indication of the change of cost with change in furnace scale is given. Second, the labor estimate of 0.10 hours (based on a $5 per hour wage) is exceedingly low when compared to other sources, so that some labor must be buried in other categories.

---

shop of a given size is fixed, so that productivity increases due to changes in burdens are reflected in decreased labor requirements per unit output. This means that the annual wage bill at a given installation is assumed constant.

[39] The baseline value is taken from Nelson, "An Interregional Recursive Programming Model," p. 426.

[40] Thomas M. Barnes and H. W. Lownie, Jr., *A Cost Analysis of Air Pollution Controls in the Integrated Iron and Steel Industry* (Columbus: Battelle Memorial Institute, May 1969), p. III-16.

Third, it seems that gas cleaning, operating, and labor costs are included in the estimate.[41]

We approximate furnace maintenance costs, exclusive of the utilities previously discussed, and of gas cleaning and slag disposal costs, by applying the 4 percent rule of thumb. That is, the annual furnace maintenance charge is assumed to be 4 percent of furnace capital cost. To obtain these capital costs, we made use of several sources which indicated that the cost of a large blast furnace (28-ft. diameter; 50,000 ft.³ volume) was about $30 million in the mid-1960s.[42] Since our interest is in a smaller furnace (18-ft. diameter; 21,000 ft.³ volume), we are forced to make some assumption about the scaling factor in this cost function. We use 0.8 and, assuming that the smaller furnace (two of which are included in the model) produces about 300,000 tons of hot metal per year, this gives us a maintenance cost estimate of $1.68 per ton of hot metal.[43] The corresponding figure for the large furnace, producing about 800,000 tons of hot metal per year, is $1.38 per ton. No extra entries for refractory replacement or general overhead are added to this estimate, which already agrees with the cost range reported in the literature without them.

Before leaving the subject, we should note that by attaching this constant-dollar figure to every blast furnace vector, we are implicitly assuming that the annual total maintenance cost will vary directly with annual production. This is tantamount to assuming that each ton of production puts a constant strain on the facility which must be made good by maintenance. It is the opposite of the assumption made concerning labor costs.

We have now covered the iron production facilities of the typical integrated steel mill, and are in a position to consider the conversion of iron into steel and the shaping of the steel products which will finally be shipped from the mill. We shall find, however, as we go along that the several parts of the integrated plant are linked by more than the flow of hot iron and steel ingots. For example, by-product fuels from the coke ovens and blast furnaces may be used in subsequent sections, and certain

[41] Another approach is offered by H. M. Graff and S. C. Bouwer, "Economics of Raw Materials," p. 391, which is more reasonable than the above, but hardly as specific. The authors claim blast furnace processing costs, including labor, operation, and maintenance, can be estimated as $5,500 per day per furnace, plus $2.50 per ton of hot metal. A similar equation is employed by Trozzo, "Technical Efficiency," p. 473.

[42] From N. Bernstein, J. L. Reuss, and P. L. Woolf, "A Cost Comparison: Production and Smelting of Prereduced Sinter *vs.* Iron Ore Pellets," *Journal of Metals*, vol. 18 (May 1966), pp. 652–656; Graff and Bouwer, "Economics of Raw Materials," p. 393; and D. C. Brown, "The What and Why of Future Blast Furnace Burdens," p. E-2.

[43] In a total cost function of the form $C = \alpha(X)^B$, where X is some measure of size, B is often referred to as the scaling factor. $B < 1$ indicates the existence of economies of scale.

waste products, such as mill scale from the finishing section and dust from steel furnace flue gases, can be recycled to the production stream through the sintering process. Thus, the integrated mill forms a complex system and the resulting model will have many interesting options for adjusting to exogenous changes which are, at this stage, only implicit.

6

PRINCIPAL STEEL-MAKING PRACTICES

The three leading furnace types currently involved in steel production in the United States are the open hearth furnace (OH), the basic oxygen converter (BOF), and the electric arc furnace (EA). Over the past decade the OH has lost ground to the relatively newer BOF and EA furnace technologies in terms of actual annual production, as shown in figure 6.1.[1] The reasons for this shift in technologies and its timing have been the subject of extensive debate in both the economic and technical, steel industry literature. Most frequently, the principal question addressed has been whether the U.S. steel industry, especially the very large firms, was too slow in adopting the BOF technology.[2] The model being developed here can be used to address that question, and we have done so elsewhere,[3] but our purpose in this chapter is the narrower one of de-

[1] From J. Varga, Jr., and H. W. Lownie, Jr., *A Systems Analysis Study of the Integrated Iron and Steel Industry* PB 184 577 (Springfield: NTIS, May 15, 1969), p. IV-15.

[2] See, for example, W. Adams and J. B. Dirlam, "Big Steel, Invention and Innovation," *The Quarterly Journal of Economics,* vol. 80, no. 2 (May 1966), pp. 167–189, Peter T. Knight and G. S. Madalla, "International Diffusion of Technical Change—A Case Study of the Oxygen Steel Making Process," *The Economic Journal,* vol. 77, no. 9 (September 1967), pp. 531–558; Bela Gold, William S. Pierce, and Gerhard Rosegger, "Diffusion of Major Technological Innovations in U.S. Iron and Steel Manufacturing," *Journal of Industrial Economics,* vol. 18 (July 1970), pp. 218–241; David R. Dilley and David L. McBride, "Oxygen Steelmaking: Fact vs. Folklore," *Iron and Steel Engineer,* vol. 44 (October 1967), p. 135; Jon P. Nelson, "An Interregional Recursive Programming Model of the U.S. Iron and Steel Industry: 1947–1967" (Ph.D. dissertation, University of Wisconsin, 1970); William Reinfeld, "An Economic Analysis of Recent Technological Trends in the United States Steel Industry," (Ph.D. dissertation, Yale University, 1968); and Che S. Tsao and Richard H. Day, "A Process Analysis Model of the U.S. Steel Industry," *Management Science,* vol. 17, no. 10 (June 1971), pp. B588–B608.

[3] W. J. Vaughan and C. S. Russell, "Choice Among Technologies in the U.S. Steel Industry: Contributions from a Linear Programming Model," unpublished, Resources for the Future, Inc.

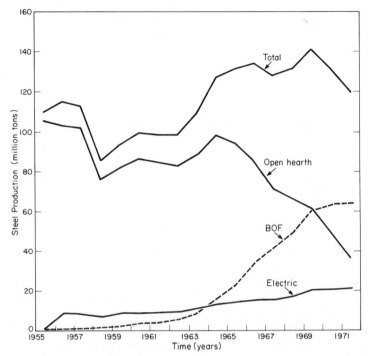

Figure 6.1. Steel production by various techniques. (Data from *1971 Yearbook*, American Iron and Steel Institute.)

scribing how we put together the steel furnace and related auxiliary vectors.

For each of the furnace types dealt with in our technical description, the relevant activities can be divided into:

1. Basic production vectors
2. Gas treatment vectors for particulate removal
3. Slag, recovered particulate, and gas disposal vectors
4. Purchase vectors for inputs specific to steelmaking

The rest of this chapter deals in sequence with the calculation of items 1 and 4 above. Parts of items 2 and 3 are covered in this chapter, and the remainder are discussed in chapter 8.

THE CHEMISTRY OF STEELMAKING

The chemical difference between iron and steel lies in the relative amounts of impurities in the two metals, the molten iron being saturated with carbon and containing undesirable amounts of silicon, manganese, phosphorus, and sulfur, which must be removed in the steel-making operation.[4] In the OH and BOF steel-making processes, an oxidizing atmosphere is employed to purify the metallic inputs of molten, blast furnace iron and steel scrap. In the EA furnace this atmosphere is used to purify the all-scrap charge. The oxidation of these impurities is followed by the solution of the oxides in the slag or their evolution as gases.[5] The required oxygen is introduced into the molten furnace charge from the furnace atmosphere, from iron ore additions, or from direct injection of pure oxygen, depending upon the furnace and practice.

There is, however, a new category of impurities of concern in steelmaking. These are the residual alloy elements or tramps; principally tin, copper, nickel, chromium, and molybdenum. These elements enter the steel cycle for three reasons: In controlled amounts and mixes they impart certain desirable properties to steel; or in the more common terminology, the additions are used to make different alloy steels. The most familiar of these is stainless in which high concentrations of the alloy elements produce resistance to rusting (oxidation of the iron). But there is an enormous range of steels differentiated by alloy contents and resulting physical properties. The second broad mechanism for the introduction of these metals is in the coating of steel, as in tin plating. And the third is the addition of parts containing the metals to consumer or producer products (as when copper-wound motors are added to cars and refrigerators). When the products are scrapped, the alloying elements may end up in the bundle.

In steel alloying, as in all our dealings with the world, we pay for what we get. In this case, when we add heavy doses of the alloy elements we obtain some undesirable properties along with the desirable ones. For example, high-alloy steels do not work as easily in the fabrication of sheet, strips, or tubes. In fact, it is difficult to produce thin sheets from high-alloy steels, because of brittleness. Thus, for applications where very high strength or great resistance to oxidation, for example, are of less importance than the ability to produce very thin cross sections, there will be strict upper limits on the allowable alloy content of the steel. In addition, copper and tin, particularly in combination with sulfur, tend to

[4] For a more extensive review of the physical chemistry of iron and steelmaking, see Harold E. McGannon, ed., *The Making, Shaping and Treating of Steel,* 9th ed. (Pittsburgh: U.S. Steel Corporation, 1971), ch. 13, pp. 281–402.

[5] Compared with the elimination of carbon, silicon, and phosphorus, the removal of sulfur from the metal is relatively inefficient at the OH, and only slightly better at the BOF, but no exact mechanism for sulfur removal at the steel-making furnaces has been established. See J. F. Elliott, "Application of Theoretical Principles to Desulfurization in Iron and Steel Making," in *AIME, Blast Furnace, Coke Oven and Raw Materials Conference Proceedings,* vol. 15 (New York: AIME, 1957), pp. 109–117.

produce surface defects in rolled products.[6] In these situations, the residual alloy elements become tramps.

If all steel were made by the purification of molten iron, alloy elements would be added to each batch (heat) in the amounts needed to produce the desired steel. In general, these elements do not enter the system in the ore, and thus there are only traces in the hot iron, these being introduced through the recycling of mill scale from the finishing mills via the sinter plant. But almost all steel production involves some use of steel scrap as an input along with molten iron, and with the scrap come the tramps. Of course, the scraps produced within the mill, principally in the course of finishing, are of known quality and could, in the extreme situation, simply be melted down in graded batches to produce additional steel of these grades. But the steel mill will also purchase steel scrap, and this makes the problem more complex for two reasons. First, there will be uncertainty about the actual quality of the purchased scrap until it has been melted, since there are only rough methods available for estimating the quality of cold scrap.[7] This is true even though scrap is graded by dealers and the definitions of the grades involve some restrictions on tramp content among other characteristics. (The specificity of these restrictions varies across the grades.) The second difficulty would exist even with perfect information about the tramp content of each shipment of purchased scrap, and it arises because even the highest-quality grades contain greater concentrations of tramps than are acceptable in the high-quality carbon steels—especially those used for auto body construction—which make up a large part of the output of the industry. (The exact percentage is impossible to obtain but it is probably in the neighborhood of 15–20 percent.)

Again, the explanation is somewhat complicated. Much of the highest-quality carbon steel (that is, steel with the lowest tramp content) goes into auto bodies, but once it is thus used it can be salvaged at the end of the auto's useful life as high-quality scrap only at great expense. The addition of generators, motors, and wires to the auto implies that if the

---

[6] Some authors have used copper content alone as a measure of scrap suitability and steel quality. An example of this approach can be found in R. A. Maggio, "A Simulation Model for Open Hearth Steelmaking" (Ph.D. dissertation, Ohio State University, 1966).

However, we follow the approach used by J. Silver, P. J. Koros, and L. R. Schoenberger in "The Effect of Use of Bundled Auto Scrap on Sheet Steel Quality," in Institute of Scrap Iron and Steel, Inc., *Facts*, 31 ed. (Washington, D.C.: ISIS 1970), pp. 71–83. The authors discovered that tin and sulfur, among the elements introduced by bundled scrap inputs, had the greatest effect on mechanical properties, while the influence of copper was found to be relatively slight and associated mainly with the effect of tin.

[7] One method depends on having available a person of extraordinary skill, since it involves holding randomly chosen pieces of the scrap against a grinding wheel and observing the colors and trajectories of the resulting sparks.

auto hulk is simply crushed into a bundle, the tramp content of that scrap will be very high. Extensive dismantling by hand or machine, burning, and shredding are all methods employed in dealing with auto hulks with the aim of producing higher-quality scrap.[8] But even after these assaults, the auto scrap contains a significantly higher concentration of tramps than what is allowed in the new steel for auto bodies (between 3.5 and 6 times higher, on the average; see table 6.1).

In fact, the highest-quality purchased scraps consist of steel pieces from fabricating operations and construction demolition. These steels at least do not present the problem of heavy admixtures of parts containing the alloying elements, but they are not generally the highest-quality carbon steels either. Finally, alloy elements are not removed in the steel furnace by the oxidizing reactions mentioned above.[9] The quantities present in the charge will be present in the steel. Thus, to cut short a long and complex story, the steel producer faces a dilution problem in making high-quality carbon steels from furnace burdens containing purchased steel scrap.[10] It is on this problem that we concentrate in the construction of our steel-making vectors. We deal with the thermal and chemical aspects of the problem in much rougher terms, on the basis of rules of thumb derived from the technical literature.[11]

Our model is constructed to be able to make three grades of steel, differentiated by carbon and, most significantly, by tramp alloy content.

Drawing quality (DQ) steel, a high-quality carbon steel with total tramp alloy concentration less than or equal to 0.13 percent
Commercial quality (CQ) steel, a medium-quality carbon steel with total tramp alloy concentration less than or equal to 0.21 percent
Alloy steel, a special steel with 1.75 percent total alloy content (pri-

[8] See James W. Sawyer, Jr., *Automotive Scrap Recycling: Processes, Prices, and Prospects* (Baltimore: Johns Hopkins University Press for Resources for the Future, 1974).

[9] The exception here is chromium, some of which does enter the slag.

[10] Clearly, the choice of burden—generally the choice between hot metal and purchased scrap—will depend on relative prices. This choice is made by the model, and we explore its implications in chapters 10 and 11. Here we concentrate on defining the technical possibilities.

[11] Full-scale steel furnace burdening models reflecting all these considerations apparently do exist but are treated as trade secrets by the companies that own them. See, for example, B. T. Bernacchi and E. F. Dudley, "Computerized Mathematical Analysis for Achieving Optimum Material Usage in Electric Steelmaking," *Journal of Metals,* vol. 18 (February 1966), pp. 205–209; Bernard Blum, John W. Schwartzenberg, and Frank C. Luxl, "Closed-Loop Computer Control of Basic Oxygen Steelmaking," *Iron and Steel Engineer,* vol. 44, no. 6 (June 1967), pp. 111–119; D. G. Boltz, "Charge Calculation—A Tool for BOF Process Control," *Iron and Steel Engineer,* vol. 44 (December 1967), pp. 117–124; and D. C. Hilty and T. F. Kaveney, "Economic Considerations of Various Charges for Stainless Steel Production," *Electric Furnace Conference Proceedings,* vol. 25 (New York: AIME, 1967), pp. 110–122.

TABLE 6.1 Assumed Characteristics of Metallic Inputs

(percent)

Item	Input and/or output							
	Molten iron or cold pig iron[a]	DQ steel/home scrap[b]	CQ steel/home scrap[b]	Alloy steel/home-purchase scrap[c]	Purchased no. 2 bundles[d]	Purchased shredded scrap[e]	Purchased no. 1 factory bundles[f]	Purchased no. 1 heavy melting[g]
Total residual alloy elements	0.100	0.130	0.210	≤1.75	0.770	0.462	0.175	0.230
Carbon	3.52–3.32	0.080	0.080	0.080	≤0.200	≤0.200	0.080	0.080
Silicon	1.00–1.20	≤0.030	≤0.030	0.130	0.200	0.200	≤0.200	≤0.200
Sulfur	0.03	0.017	0.017	0.017	0.080	0.035	0.025	0.035
Iron	94.150	99.440	99.300	97.910	85.000	97.000	99.000	97.000
Other[h]	1.20	≥0.330	≥0.360	≥0.113	≥13.650	≥2.110	≥0.52	≥2.455
Total	100	100	100	100	100	100	100	100

Note: For complete bibliographical information, see the Table References at the back of the book.

[a] All constituents from our blast furnace calculations. Cold pig assumed identical to molten iron.

[b] Tramp elements from Silver, Koros, and Schoenberger, "The Use of Bundled Auto Scrap," pp. 71–83; iron and silicon content from Battelle Memorial Institute, *Recent Developments in Steelmaking*, pp. IV-13, and 38.

[c] Composition synthesized from Harold McGannon, ed., *The Making, Shaping and Treating of Steel*, ch. 42; Gerhard Derge, ed., *Basic Open Hearth Steelmaking*, p. 378; and John Dearden, *Iron and Steel Today*, pp. 219–220.

[d] Tramp elements and iron content from Silver, Koros, and Schoenberger, p. 79. Silicon and carbon assumed approximately equal to shredded scrap analysis.

[e] Tramp elements from communication with Richard Burlingame of Luria Bros., Cleveland, Ohio, by analysis of 1971 ground product. Silicon, sulfur, and carbon content from Regan, James, and McLeer, *Increased Recycling of Ferrous Solid Waste*, p. 199.

[f] Iron content assumed close to DQ steel (from communication with James Fowler, Institute of Scrap Iron and Steel, Inc., 1972). Tramp elements and sulfur from C. C. Custer, "Cold Metal Practice *vs.* Hot Metal Practice"; carbon and silicon approximated from typical steel analysis reported in UN, Economic Commission for Europe, *Comparison of Steelmaking Processes*, pp. 31–42.

[g] Iron content from U.S. Department of Commerce, *Iron and Steel Scrap Consumption Problems*, p. 30. Tramp elements from Custer; carbon and silicon from UN, *Comparison of Steelmaking Processes*.

[h] Magnesium, phosphorus, dirt, etc.

marily nickel and chromium). (This is a low-alloy steel by industry standards.)

THE STEEL-MAKING FURNACES

All three furnace types treated here are capable of producing carbon and alloy steels of the same general grades,[12] albeit with differing technical and economic efficiencies. For example, until recently, EA furnaces were employed chiefly for the production of alloy steels, because of their ability to use high proportions (up to 100 percent) of alloy-containing scraps, thus reducing the requirement for virgin alloy additions. During the mid-1960s, however, over 60 percent of all EA furnace production was carbon steel. In our model, all furnaces are provided with burdens for each of the three steel types just described.

The Open Hearth Furnace

The OH is a rectangular furnace in which a long, shallow charge bath is heated by radiation from a flame generated from fuel nozzles built into the ends of the furnace. The fuel employed may be natural gas, coke oven gas, fuel oil, coal tar, or a combination of these, the choice of which will influence the sulfur dioxide generation per ton of steel. Oxygen may or may not be used for combustion air enrichment or decarbonization, giving two sets of practices, ore and oxygen, for all hot metal–scrap alternatives.

The OH is the most flexible furnace in its ability to handle different charge metallic proportions.[13] The basic open-hearth process can handle the full range of charges from 100 percent scrap down to no scrap at all.[14] Our model includes only a limited range of options, specifically 50–50 practice (50 percent hot metal–50 percent scrap) and high hot metal or 70–30 practice (70 percent hot metal–30 percent scrap).[15]

[12] Many excellent sources describing the production processes outlined here are available. Among the best are George Reginal Bashforth, *The Manufacture of Iron and Steel*, 4 vol. (2nd ed., London: Chapman and Hall Ltd., 1957); Gerhard Derge, ed., *Basic Open Hearth Steelmaking* (New York: AIME, 1964); McGannon, ed., *The Making, Shaping and Treating of Steel* (8th ed., Pittsburgh: U.S. Steel Corporation, 1964); *Watkins Cyclopedia of the Steel Industry* (12th ed., Pittsburgh: Steel Publications, Inc., 1969).

[13] See Derge, *Basic Open Hearth Steelmaking*, p. 263.

[14] "Basic" here refers to the use of nonacidic brickwork in the furnace lining.

[15] These are the two most common charge types according to McGannon, ed., *The Making, Shaping and Treating of Steel*, 9th ed., p. 520. Integrated mills seldom go below 35 percent hot metal in the charge, according to Derge, *Basic Open Hearth Steelmaking*, p. 264.

The Basic Oxygen Furnace

In the basic oxygen process, substantially pure oxygen is introduced above the surface of a bath of molten iron contained in a basic-lined cylindrical furnace. The process is characterized by: (1) use of oxygen as the sole refining agent; (2) a metallic charge composed largely ($\geqq 70$ percent) of blast furnace iron in a molten state; and (3) rapid chemical reactions giving rise to large quantities of gaseous red fume or dust. The only sources of heat are the sensible heat in the hot metal and the heat generated by exothermic reactions between the oxygen and the non-metals in the bath, especially carbon. Sulfur dioxide generation is negligible.

Basic oxygen steelmaking is relatively inflexible in its ability to use large proportions of cold pig iron or steel scrap in the charge due to the nature of its heat balance. The alternatives in our linear programming model are 70 percent hot metal–30 percent scrap, and 90 percent hot metal–10 percent high iron, low sulfur content iron ore.[16]

The Electric Arc Furnace

The direct arc furnace, the type most commonly in use today, is a squat cylinder set on end. The process itself consists of melting and refining a cold charge of pig iron and steel scrap. Graphite electrodes are the source of the energy required to melt the cold charge and to carry on the refining reactions.[17] Iron ore or oxygen lancing may be used to provide the oxygen. In this operation the selection of the proper scrap grade distribution for the charge is crucial, and depends mainly upon the steel grade to be produced, subject to charge density (volumetric furnace capacity) and productivity limitations.[18]

---

[16] Under certain hot metal–scrap relative price configurations, the BOF could conceivably charge more than 30 percent scrap (our assumption) by using injected fuel to preheat the scrap and alter the thermal constraint imposed by the furnace. (See Battelle Memorial Institute, *Technical and Economic Analysis of the Impact of Recent Developments in Steelmaking Practices on the Supplying Industries*, Columbus: Battelle Memorial Institute, October 30, 1964.) This alternative is not included in our model.

[17] Process variants in the industry include the addition of fuel burners to aid in scrap meltdown. This possibility is not reflected in our model.

[18] Interesting, although uncommon, charge variants include the case of molten blast furnace iron and direct-reduced materials (prereduced pellets). See McGannon, *The Making, Shaping*, 9th ed., p. 353. The EA shop could possibly charge molten metal or pellets in certain relative price situations. See E. L. Fogleman, D. O. Gloven, and H. B. Jensen, "Operational and Economic Aspects of Prereduced Iron Usage in Electric Arc Furnaces," *Blast Furnace and Steel Plant*, vol. 58, no. 10 (October 1970), pp. 733–743; and W. A. Hoff, "Use of Hot Metal in Electric Furnaces," in *Electric Furnace Conference Proceedings*, vol. 14 (New York: AIME, 1957), pp. 293–295.

RESIDUAL ALLOY ELEMENTS AND STEEL TYPE

As we have said, we concentrate on the problem of meeting residual alloy limits in our several steel types, using a number of different scraps. In the process we deal with the thermal and chemical aspects of the burdening question through rules of thumb, and we do not consider the difficulties raised by the differential densities of the several scraps and the restricted volumes of the assumed furnaces. Even so, the determination of alternative burdening possibilities across different furnace and steel types is not trivial, since we must simultaneously take account of the input of iron, the input of residual alloy elements, and the input of silicon. The silicon input, in turn, controls the production of slag and hence losses of iron to slag, and ultimately the output of iron (as steel).

The specific relations which we used to calculate the steel furnace burdens were (all are expressed per ton of steel ingot) : [19]

1. The iron balance:

    Iron input in molten iron, steel scrap, finishing additions (ferrochromium and ferromanganese) and iron ore equals iron output and losses in steel output, slag, and flue dust. [20]

2. The residual alloy element constraint:

    The input of alloy elements in molten iron and steel scrap must be less than, or equal to, the allowable alloy element concentration. [21]

3. The hot metal requirement:

    a. For the BOF, two practices were considered: 70 percent and 90 percent hot metal in the charge.

    b. For the OH, two practices were also considered: 50 percent and 70 percent hot metal in the charge.

    c. No hot metal is used in the EA. [22]

[19] One ton of steel ingot is equivalent to 2,060 pounds of molten steel, since we assume 60 pounds of steel are converted into scrap in pouring.

[20] Finishing additions are added at the final stages to the molten steel in order to bring silicon and manganese content up to specification, since the silicon in the charged material is largely removed in the slag. We assume these are constant, 14 pounds for given furnace and steel type, and are interested only in their iron contents. Silicon in the charge is the major influence on the quantity of slag produced in steelmaking, since sulfur is generally a very small part of the charge. We assume that slag quantity is directly proportional to silicon input and that iron lost is a constant fraction of slag weight.

[21] For alloy steel, the constraint has the opposite sense.

[22] In the electric arc, cold (pig) iron serves to provide the same dilution as does hot metal in the other two furnaces. Here, however, there is no thermal restriction to imply an upper or lower limit on the percentage of pig iron in the charge and the actual range in the vectors is from zero (alloy steel product) to 99 percent (DQ steel product with alloy scrap equal to 1 percent of charge).

The characteristics of the various possible iron-bearing charge constituents were summarized in table 6.1. Notice that the highest-quality purchased scrap (no. 1 factory bundles) has a tramp content 0.045 percentage points higher than the upper limit on DQ steel. This is simply numerical confirmation of the point made earlier about the importance of dilution in the steel cycle.

The rules of thumb used in combination with the tramp concentration data to calculate other elements of the steel furnace vectors may be summarized as follows.

1. Slag weight is taken to be 14.3 times the weight of silicon in the charge materials.[23]
2. Lime input (for BOF and EA) is 0.47 times the calculated slag weight from item 1.[24]
3. Limestone input (for OH) is 0.7 times the calculated slag weight from item 1.[25]
4. Fluorspar is added to make the slag workable (fluid). The quantity required depends on the weight of slag, but also on the furnace type and practice.[26]
5. Oxygen consumption at the BOF and the oxygen-lanced OH and EA furnaces per ton of ingot steel depends on furnace and practice (quantities per ingot ton).[27]
   a. OH 50 percent hot metal; oxygen use = 50 pounds
   b. OH 70 percent hot metal; oxygen use = 63 pounds
   c. BOF 70 percent hot metal; oxygen use = 138 pounds
   d. BOF 90 percent hot metal; oxygen use = 133 pounds
   e. EA oxygen use = 11 pounds
6. A small amount of low sulfur coke is consumed at the EA furnace: 6 pounds per ingot ton for all practices. Carbon electrodes are also consumed in this furnace: 10 pounds per ingot ton using ore practice and 9 pounds per ton using oxygen practice.[28]
7. Iron ore is added to all OH charges, to the EA when it is the sole source of oxygen, and to the BOF in 90 percent hot metal practice in making DQ steel. The amounts used are as follows:[29]
   a. OH, 50 percent hot metal, no oxygen, 100 pounds per ingot ton

---

[23] Suggested by Derge, *Basic Open Hearth Steelmaking*, p. 168.
[24] Based on information in ibid., p. 976; and S. L. Case, "Future of Desiliconized Pig Iron for the Electric Furnace," in *Electric Furnace Conference Proceedings*, vol. 14 (New York: AIME, 1957), p. 295.
[25] From Derge, *Basic Open Hearth Steelmaking*, p. 168.
[26] Calculated from Battelle, *Technical and Economic Analysis*, ch. IV.
[27] Taken directly from Battelle, *Technical and Economic Analysis*, ch. IV.
[28] Taken from ibid., ch. IV.
[29] Ibid.

TABLE 6.2   Steel Furnace Gas and Dust Generation Rates[a]

(pounds per ingot ton)

Furnace type	Ore practice	Oxygen practice
Open hearth		
50–50 practice		
Gas range	3,700–12,240	2,500–5,230
Dust range	12–40	22–46
70–30 practice		
Gas range	3,700–8,300	2,500–4,100
Dust range	12–27	22–36
Electric arc		
Gas range	25–287	22–272
Dust range	6–69	8–98
Basic oxygen		
Gas range	not	149–245
Dust range	applicable	40–66

[a] For every furnace and almost every practice, the low gas and dust generation rates are for DQ steelmaking, the high rates are for alloy steelmaking with burdens using purchased no. 2 bundles.

      b. OH, 50 percent hot metal, oxygen lance, 50 pounds per ingot ton

      c. OH, 70 percent hot metal, no oxygen, 387 pounds per ingot ton

      d. OH, 70 percent hot metal, oxygen lance, 122 pounds per ingot ton

      e. BOF, 90 percent hot metal, DQ steel product, 242 pounds per ingot ton

      f. EA, no oxygen, 40 pounds per ingot ton

  8. For the BOF and EA furnaces, the weight of gas and dust evolved is taken to be equal to the difference between the total weight of inputs and the sum of steel and slag output. Constant dust loadings were assumed as follows.[30]

      a. BOF, 70 percent hot metal, 0.27 pounds dust per pound of gas

      b. BOF, 90 percent hot metal, 0.22 pounds dust per pound of gas

      c. EA, ore practice, 0.24 pounds dust per pound of gas

      d. EA, oxygen lance, 0.36 pounds dust per pound of gas.

For the OH, we simply assumed dust generation rates and gas-to-dust

[30] Computed from ibid.; Varga and Lownie, *A Systems Analysis,* p. C-83; and A. E. Vandegrift and L. J. Shannon, *Particulate Pollutant System Study,* vol. 3, *Handbook of Emission Properties,* Report by Midwest Research Institute to U.S. Environmental Protection Agency (Durham, N.C.: May 1974).

ratios on the basis of literature values.[31] The results of all these calculations are summarized in table 6.2, where we show dust and gas generation per ingot ton at the furnace outlet.

Using the techniques and rules described above, we have constructed 145 steel furnace vectors broken down by furnace type, charge practice, and steel type as shown in table 6.3.[32] The rather strict thermal constraints on the BOF are reflected in the small number of alternative burdens available to it in the model; just as the flexibility of the OH shows up in the large number of burden choices available to it. As we shall see, the major effect of this difference lies in the ability of the furnace to react to changes in the relative prices of hot metal (iron) and scrap. To obtain flexibility similar to that displayed by the OH in this area, it is necessary to have available both an EA and a BOF furnace (referred to below as a duplex shop), where, of course, the actual degree of flexibility depends on the percentage of total output each furnace type can supply on its own.

Finally, by way of providing some evidence on the verification of our methods and assumptions, we have computed the average yield for each furnace and practice for the carbon steels.[33] These results are compared with yield values for carbon steels (generally no more closely defined than that in the quality dimension) in table 6.4.

In general, our vectors produce reasonable absolute-yield estimates, although our yields are somewhat higher than the corresponding yields reported by Battelle for open hearth operations. These yields will, of course, have an impact on the cost comparisons between furnace types mentioned in later chapters and will tend to make the OH look slightly better than it may actually be.

In terms of furnace yields relative to a base practice, 50–50 ore at the OH, the picture is cloudy. Our EA relatives seem much too low at first glance. However, omitting the drawing quality steel yield, because this steel type is probably not produced in great quantities at the arc, makes our arc–hearth yield relative (about 1.02) line up with the UN and Battelle relatives. Moving down to OH 70–30 ore practice, we find our relative falling in the lower end of the range of UN, Derge, and Battelle relatives. Our 70–30 hearth oxygen practice relative, although above

---

[31] The most important sources of this information were: Battelle Memorial Institute, *Technical and Economic Analysis*, ch. IV, pp. 17–18; and Derge, ed., *Basic Open Hearth Steelmaking*, pp. 23, 108, 845–848, and 875–877.

[32] In constructing the alloy steel vectors, one additional step is necessary; we must calculate the differences between the *desired* alloy contents and the contents implied by the burden. Any deficiencies must be made up by the addition of virgin alloy elements.

[33] Yield is defined by industry convention as the ratio of the weight of molten steel output to the total of the weight of scrap and hot iron, the weight of iron in any ore additions, and the *total* weight of the finishing additions.

TABLE 6.3   Breakdown of Steel Furnace Vectors

Furnace	Steel	Ore practice	Oxygen practice	Totals
Electric arc furnace				
	DQ	7	7	14
	CQ	13	13	26
	Al	7	7	14
Subtotals		27	27	54
Basic oxygen furnace 70–30 practice				
	DQ	n.a.	5	5
	CQ	n.a.	6	6
	Al	n.a.	7	7
90–10 practice				
	DQ	n.a.	1	1
	Al	n.a.	1	1
Subtotals		n.a.	20	20
Open hearth 50–50 practice				
	DQ	5	5	10
	CQ	6	6	12
	Al	7	7	14
70–30 practice				
	DQ	6	5	11
	CQ	5	5	10
	Al	7	7	14
Subtotals		36	35	71
Total				145

Abbreviation: n.a., not applicable.

both the Battelle and UN estimates, is sufficiently close to them for practical purposes.

A final heartening result, not displayed in any of the tables, is the percentage of no. 2 bundles which we calculate can be charged in BOF 70–30 practice without violating the DQ steel alloy element constraint. Our estimate is 2 percent of no. 2 bundles in the metallic charge, which checks with the same percentage reported in the literature for a BOF operation using a charge chemically similar to the one hypothesized in our calculations.[34]

DETERMINATION OF STEEL-MAKING CAPACITY CONSTRAINTS

Furnace productivity.   In order to compare furnace performance in particular areas of interest (for example, volume of residuals gener-

[34] Silver, Koros, and Schoenberger, "The Effect of Use," table IV, p. 80, Scrap Charge no. 1.

TABLE 6.4 *Comparison of Calculated and Reported Yields of Molten Carbon Steel*

(*in percentages*)

Alternative furnaces and practices	RFF[a]		United Nations[b]		Gerhard Derge[c]		Battelle Institute[d]	
	Unweighted average yield	Yield relative	Yield	Yield relative	Yield	Yield relative	Yield	Yield relative
Electric arc								
Ore practice	95.0	100.5	94.8	102.7	n.a.	n.a.	95.8	106.9
Oxygen practice	95.0	100.5	n.a.	n.a.	n.a.	n.a.	95.8	106.9
Open hearth								
50–50 ore	94.5	100.0	92.3	100.0	92.7	100.0	89.6	100.0
50–50 oxygen	94.4	99.8	n.a.	n.a.	n.a.	n.a.	89.6	100.0
70–30 ore	91.6	96.9	91.6	99.2	90.2	98.2	85.5	95.4
70–30 oxygen	91.6	96.9	89.0	96.4	n.a.	n.a.	85.7	95.6
Basic oxygen								
70–30	91.4	96.8	91.1	98.7	n.a.	n.a.	90.6	101.1
90–10	87.8	92.9	n.a.	n.a.	n.a.	n.a.	88.0	98.2

Abbreviation: n.a., not applicable.

[a] We use the simple average of our yields for DQ and CQ steels in computing the RFF yield relatives because the steels made in the other studies are carbon steels of undetermined tramp content.

[b] UN, Economic Commission for Europe, *Comparison of Steelmaking Processes*, p. 52.

[c] Gerhard Derge, ed., *Basic Open Hearth Steelmaking*, p. 226. Figures converted from ingot yield to molten yield.

[d] Battelle Memorial Institute, *Recent Developments in Steelmaking*, ch. IV. Figures converted from ingot yield to molten yield.

ated or discharged per ton steel, average and marginal cost per ton steel, and scrap use flexibility), hypothetical steel shops have been designed to produce approximately one million tons of molten steel per 350-day operating year. The resulting configurations (furnace number and dimension) yielding this annual output should not be construed as optimal, but instead as roughly representative.

Shop configuration. Assumed shop configurations are used to set the upper limit on furnace capacity, measured in tons of semifinished shapes per day, for the OH and EA. Each activity vector has a capacity use row entry expressed in hours per ingot ton. The right-hand side constraint of the appropriate capacity row is expressed as total daily furnace hours available (number of assumed furnaces multiplied by 24 hours per day). The values of these capacity use figures depend primarily upon the capacity of the refining vessel and the total time required to charge and refine one heat of steel (referred to as "heat time, tap to tap"). The potential (as opposed to nominal or rated) vessel capacity and the heat time in turn depend upon charge density, charge, chemical characteristics of the hot metal to scrap ratio, and furnace refining practice (ore or oxygen).[35]

The numbers arrived at are summarized in table 6.5. They are based on typical shop configurations and such data as were available in the literature on production rates and variations in productivity with charge composition.

FURNACE UTILITIES

The Open Hearth Furnace

The principal subcalculations required to fill out the rest of the OH operation involve the thermal balance and heat requirements of the process. The heat balances reported by Battelle are used for this purpose.[36]

Heat supplied by fuel combustion. The heat required for melting scrap and refining the charge at the OH is supplied by the combustion

---

[35] For the BOF we use the capacity and heat time assumptions only in the calculation of gas generation rates. Steel-making capacity is constrained indirectly by blast furnace capacity.

[36] Battelle, *Technical and Economic Analysis,* ch. 14.

TABLE 6.5 *Steel Shop Configurations and Production Rates*

Furnace type	No. of furnaces	Rated furnace capacity (tons/heat)[a]	Heat time (minutes)	Production rates		Productivity: furnace hours per ingot ton[c]
				tons per hr.	Appx. tons per yr.[b]	
Basic oxygen furnace[e]	2	140	45[d]	175	1.40×10^6	not used
Open hearth[f]	9	125	444	152	1.22×10^6	
70–30 oxygen						0.059
70–30 ore						0.074
50–50 oxygen						0.064
50–50 ore						0.080
Electric arc[g]	3	160				
Ore practice			240	120	0.96×10^6	0.025
Oxygen practice			226	128	1.02×10^6	0.024

[a] Steel-making terminology refers to a steel production cycle as a "heat."

[b] 8,000 hours operation per year assumed.

[c] Thus, daily ingot capacity at the electric arc is equal to
$$\frac{24 \text{ hours per day} \times \text{three furnaces}}{0.025 \text{ furnace hours per ton}} = 2,880 \text{ tons per day}.$$

[d] The BOFs operate only alternately; see Frank W. Dittman, "Oxygen Steelmaking Cost Comparison," pp. 372–379.

[e] Constraint on production in the model, based on blast furnace capacity, works out to about 1.12 million tons per year.

[f] Productivity differentials at OH shop are based on two assump-

tions: (1) change from 70 percent hot metal–30 percent scrap to 50–50 practice will decrease productivity (tons per hour) by 7 percent, and (2) ore practice is 20 percent less productive than oxygen practice, *ceteris paribus*. See Woods and Taylor, "A Statistical Method," pp. 847–901; Francis D. Nelson, "Utilizing Roof Lance Oxygen," pp. 142–152; Ralph A. Maggio, "A Simulation Model"; and Edgar B. Speer, "The Changing Open Hearth," pp. 71–79.

[g] Heat time differential is taken as a function of kWh required per ton of product. The ratio of electrical power input per ton of steel using oxygen practice to that for ore practice is about 0.94, according to the Battelle energy balances. This rule is suggested by McGannon, ed., *The Making, Shaping and Treating of Steel*, 9th ed., p. 572.

of one or another low sulfur fuel. This requirement varies with charge composition and source of oxygen, being 3.38 million Btu per ingot ton for 50–50 ore practice, 2.26 million for 50–50 oxygen practice, 3.28 million for 70–30 ore practice, and 2.05 million for 70–30 oxygen practice. The particular fuels we allow the model to choose among for this use are purchased natural gas or low sulfur (0.5 percent) residual fuel oil, by-product blast furnace gas, coke oven gas (undesulfurized low sulfur, and desulfurized high and low sulfur), and coal tar (high and low sulfur).

The fuels available are purposely limited to those with relatively low sulfur content in order to minimize the distortion caused by our simplifying assumption that all the sulfur in the fuel leaves the furnace in the stack gases as sulfur dioxide. In fact, sulfur in the combustion gases may be absorbed by the molten metal and slag; or sulfur from the bath may be picked up by the gases, depending on the sulfur contents of fuel, hot metal, and scrap, and on the type of scrap charged. The tendency to transfer sulfur from gases to slag increases with furnace temperature, the ratio of lime to silicate in the slag, and the slag iron oxide content. We are not prepared to deal with these factors. Our approach, however, has been suggested by others as a working approximation.[37]

The characteristics of the OH fuels are summarized in table 6.6.

Removal of rejected heat by cooling water and recovery of usable waste heat. To obtain sufficient flame temperature and economical fuel consumption, the air for OH fuel combustion must be preheated in a regenerative system of brick chambers called checkerwork. Waste gases from the furnace lose a large portion of their sensible heat to the checkers and this, in turn, is imparted to incoming combustion air in order to preheat it. A large part of the sensible heat remaining in the exit waste gases leaving the checkerwork can subsequently be recovered in the form of steam by use of a waste heat boiler located close to the stack.[38] At the same time, some heat must be removed from the furnace walls by cooling water, and further heat is lost directly to the atmosphere by radiation from the furnace and from the stack after the waste heat boiler. We are particularly interested in the first two heat quantities, and we estimate them using rules of thumb available in the literature,[39] along

[37] T. P. Colclough, "Sulfur in Iron and Steelmaking," in Frederick S. Mallette, ed., *Problems and Control of Air Pollution* (New York: Reinhold, 1955), pp. 209–210. Varga and Lownie in *A Systems Analysis*, pp. V54–V56, report that heavy scrap will pick up less sulfur than light scrap, *ceteris paribus*.

[38] McGannon, ed., *The Making, Shaping and Treating of Steel*, 9th ed., pp. 516 and 517.

[39] Derge, *Basic Open Hearth Steelmaking*, p. 869; and David H. Moore, "Cost Comparisons of the Open Hearth and Electric Furnace," *Iron and Steel Engineer*, vol. 31 (March 1954), p. 57.

TABLE 6.6 *Alternative Open-Hearth Furnace Fuels*

Fuel characteristics	Blast furnace gas	Natural gas	High sulfur tar	Low sulfur tar	Low sulfur coke oven gas (undesulfurized)	High sulfur coke oven gas (desulfurized)	Low sulfur coke oven gas (desulfurized)	Low sulfur residual fuel oil
Heat content[a]								
10^6 Btu per pound	0.0009	0.0192	0.0160	0.0160	0.0161	0.0161	0.0161	0.0194
10^6 Btu per scf	0.0001	0.0010	n.a.	n.a.	0.0005	0.0005	0.0005	n.a.
Sulfur content (%)	...	0.0004	1.08	0.54	0.99	0.16	0.08	0.50
Pounds of steam input per 10^6 Btu[b]	n.r.	n.r.	31.1	31.1	n.r.	n.r.	n.r.	25.8
Pounds of particulate emissions per 10^6 Btu[c]	...	0.018	0.94	0.94	...	...	...	0.053
Pounds of sulfur dioxide emissions per 10^6 Btu[d]	...	0.0004	1.36	0.68	1.23	0.20	0.10	0.55
Cost of purchased fuel ($ per 10^6 Btu)	n.a.	0.63	n.a.	n.a.	n.a.	n.a.	n.a.	0.57

Abbreviations: n.a., not applicable; ellipses (...), too insignificant to record; n.r., not required.

[a] Heat contents: *natural gas,* R. L. Duprey, *Air Pollutant Emission Factors,* W. L. Nelson, *Guide to Refinery Operating Costs,* p. 4; *coke oven gas,* see chapter 3; *low sulfur fuel oil,* 0.5 percent sulfur fuel oil has an average heating value of 6.43 million Btu per barrel, assuming 7.9 pounds per gallon (McGannon, ed., *The Making, Shaping and Treating of Steel,* p. 85); *blast furnace gas,* see chapter 5.

[b] According to Gerhard Derge, *Basic Open Hearth Steelmaking,* p. 86, 5 pounds of steam are required per gallon of tar combusted, and 3 pounds of steam are required per gallon of oil combusted.

[c] Blast furnace gas particulate emissions already accounted for elsewhere (see chapter 5). Oil and natural gas emission factors from Duprey, pp. 6 and 7. Tar factor from C. S. Russell, *Residuals Management,* table 14.

[d] Natural gas sulfur dioxide emission factor from Duprey, p. 6. Others calculated from known or assumed sulfur contents.

with the heat balances provided by Battelle.[40] The results of these calculations are summarized below.

	Practice (quantities per ingot ton)			
	50–50 Ore	50–50 Oxygen	70–30 Ore	70–30 Oxygen
Heat available for waste heat generation (10^6 Btu)	1.20	0.84	1.15	0.94
Waste heat lost to cooling water (10^6 Btu)	0.27	0.19	0.25	0.21

The heat available to the waste heat boiler (assumed to be in place) is converted to steam, and the surplus steam generated can be exported to the rest of the mill.[41] In the unlikely event that too much steam is available to the mill as a whole, the waste heat from the OH can be discharged up the stack. The heat removed in the cooling water is, in the base case, discharged to the aquatic environment, but if controls are instituted by some level of government, cooling towers may be installed.

Electricity. Electricity values are taken directly from Battelle,[42] and are equal to 14 kWh per 1.03 tons molten steel in all ore practices and 28 kWh in all oxygen practices.

The Basic Oxygen Furnace

The additional item of interest here involves the heat in the furnace exit gas after combustion, which can either be removed from the gas by cooling water or used for generating steam. Since the choices here in part depend upon the type of gas cleaning equipment being used to remove dust from the gas, a preliminary reference to the two alternative gas cleaning systems is necessary at this point. We have made a comparison of two gas cleaning systems: a wet system using a high-energy wet scrubber and a dry system using an electrostatic precipitator. The principal components of these two systems are set out in figure 6.2. This chapter deals with the component above the dotted partition line in figure 6.2 (the combustion hood, equipped either for cooling only, or for steam generation), since this component has a direct bearing upon cooling water requirements and steam generation possibilities. The portion below the line is discussed in chapter 8. The combustion hood captures the gas leaving the BOF vessel and in it the carbon monoxide in the gas

[40] Battelle, *Technical and Economic Analysis*, pp. IV-18 and IV-19.

[41] We assume an operating and maintenance cost of $0.03 per 1,000 pounds of steam produced in the waste heat boiler. The efficiency of this boiler is taken to be 80 percent.

[42] Battelle, *Technical and Economic Analysis*, p. XIII-13.

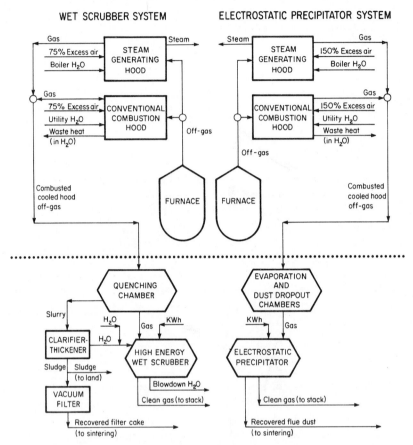

WET SCRUBBER SYSTEM   ELECTROSTATIC PRECIPITATOR SYSTEM

Figure 6.2.   Basic oxygen furnace gas treatment system alternatives.

is burned to carbon dioxide, while the temperature is lowered by about 1000° F.[43]

There are two distinctions important in the discussion of this part of the BOF gas-handling system.

1. *Wet versus dry subsequent collection system:* When the subsequent particulate collection system is to be based on wet scrubbers, combustion in the hood can be carried on with 75 percent excess air (75 percent more air than is strictly required in the reactions). On the other hand, to give a high degree of protection from explosion, when an electrostatic precipitator is to be used downstream, 150 percent excess air must be admitted to the hood. Thus there

---

[43] The gas at the furnace mouth is assumed to be 15 percent carbon monoxide.

TABLE 6.7   Wet and Dry Gas Treatment Systems with Alternative Hood Characteristics

Hood characteristics	Wet gas treatment system (quantities per ingot ton)	Dry gas treatment system (quantities per ingot ton)
All hoods		
Average furnace off gas (lb.)	168	168
Temperature (°F)	3,000	3,000
Gas leaving hood (lb.)	789	1,054
Temperature (°F)	2,000	2,000
Conventional hood only		
Btu removed in cooling water (10^6 Btu)	0.438	0.333
Cooling water required at 20°F (10^3 gal.)	2.62	1.99
Steam generation hood only		
Steam produced (10^3 lb.)	0.272	0.207
Boiler water required (10^3 gal.)	0.033	0.025
Cost[a]	$0.076	$0.052

Sources: Blaskowski and Sefick, "Economics of Gas Cooling and Gas Cleaning Systems with the BOF Process," p. 95; Brough and Voges, "Water Supply and Wastewater Disposal," p. A-26; Henschen, "Wet vs. Dry Cooling," p. 338; H. Hoff, "Treatment of Brown Fumes," pp. 562–566; Rowe, Jaworski and Bassett, "Waste Gas Cleaning Systems," p. 76.

Note: The quantities shown are for 70–30 practice, those for 90–10 practice are slightly different.

[a] The cost per 1,000 pounds of steam is $0.279 for the wet system and $0.251 for the dry.

will be a significant difference in the posthood gas volumes, depending on the type of collection equipment used.

2. *Capture versus discharge of waste heat:* Some of the sensible heat in the gases, which leave the BOF vessel at 3000° F (and leave the hood at 2000° F), and the heat of combustion of the carbon monoxide in that gas can either be discharged to the atmosphere or at least be partially utilized in the generation of steam. The hood in place in the base case is assumed to be of the cool-and-discharge type, so that the steam-generating hood is an investment decision in the model.

The cooling requirements for the hoods for both wet and dry systems, including the cooling water and steam generation options, are set out in table 6.7.

The reliability of these calculations can be subject to two indirect checks. First, the gallons of water required for hood cooling, assuming a 20° F rise, would amount to about 2,620 gallons per ingot ton in 70–30 practice, and Nebolsine reports that 2,730 gallons of water per ton steel are required in BOF practice for lance, hood, and miscellaneous gas cooling, which is close to our estimate.[44] Second, the quantity of steam produced in the model's steam-generating hoods is very close to the 280 to 400 pounds per ingot ton range found in the literature.[45]

The Electric Arc Furnace

When the EA furnace model is treated as a separate and distinct linear programming model, it is free from linkages to coke oven, sinter strand, and blast furnace requirements and involves very little complication. Any pig iron or coke which may be needed is assumed to be purchased in the market rather than manufactured at the mill. Amounts of inputs to the basic production vectors were estimated as above in the rules of thumb. The only other item of interest is the waste heat which must be removed from the furnace roof ring, the furnace doors, and the electrodes by cooling water. The amount of heat involved is taken to be 0.07 million Btu per ingot ton.[46]

FURNACE LABOR REQUIREMENTS AND OBJECTIVE FUNCTION VALUES

In deriving production labor input coefficients (man hours per ingot ton) for all steel production activities, we follow precedent and hypothesize that productivity increases within any given furnace type, attributable to charging and oxidation variants, are reflected in a diminished man-hour per unit output requirement, thus implicitly assuming that a furnace requires a fixed number of workers per unit time.

The principal source used for calculating the labor requirements was *Comparison of Steelmaking*.[47] For the OH production activities, a bench mark value of 0.50 labor man-hours per ingot ton is associated with 70–30 oxygen practice and is adjusted for previously explained productivity differentials between it and other OH processes. For all BOF activities, a value of 0.28 man-hours per ingot ton is required. For the EA furnace, a value of 0.40 man-hours per ingot ton is attached to ore practices and

---

[44] Ross Nebolsine, "Steel Plant Wastewater Treatment and Reuse," paper presented at the annual meeting of the Association of Iron and Steel Engineers, September 1966 (mimeographed), p. 11. Figures have been converted from gallons per minute to gallons per ton, assuming a 10-ton per minute production rate.

[45] H. J. Blaskowski and A. J. Sefick, "Economics of Gas Cooling and Gas Cleaning Systems Associated with the BOF Process," *Iron and Steel Engineer*, vol. 44 (May 1967), p. 95.

[46] David B. Moore, "Cost Comparisons of the Open Hearth Electric Furnace," p. 57.

[47] United Nations, Economic Commission for Europe, *Comparison of Steelmaking Processes*, p. 58 (ST/ECE/STEEL/4, 1962).

adjusted to 0.38 for oxygen practices by the assumed productivity differential explained in the preceding discussion.[48]

*Objective Function: Operating and Maintenance Costs Excluding
Capital Charges*

A general maintenance charge is taken as 5 percent of total capital
cost per ingot ton, expressed in 1968 dollars, for all furnaces at a typical
production level of one million annual ingot tons.[49] No correction for
productivity is included on the assumption that the total annual maintenance bill for more productive charging practices will be greater than
for less-productive charging practices, and therefore will be constant
per unit output for all vectors representing a given furnace's production
possibilities.

Jon Nelson's carefully calculated average investment costs for furnaces
of greater than one million tons annual capacity appear to give reasonable estimates of furnace capital costs in the United States.[50] Therefore,
after adjusting Nelson's costs to 1968 dollars and correcting for scale,
our maintenance costs are calculated directly as 5 percent of Nelson's
undiscounted average capital cost per ingot ton.

In addition to general maintenance, the objective function entries for
all furnaces include locomotive service, general overhead, and furnace
refractory replacement. Slag disposal cost does not appear here, but in a
separate slag disposal activity, as described in chapter 5. The replacement costs of ladle refractories and molds and stools, frequently reported
as a part of furnace-operating costs, are omitted because they are more
appropriately assigned to the rolling and finishing section of steel mill
operations. Table 6.8 shows the labor hours and direct operating cost
estimates based on our assumptions.

Cost of Inputs Specifically Required for Steelmaking

Finally, purchase activity vectors are provided for all of the requisite
steel-making raw material inputs not provided or called for elsewhere.[51]

[48] This procedure achieves percentage production labor requirement differentials
between furnace types correspondent with those reported by Madalla and Knight
in "International Diffusion of Technical Change," p. 538.

[49] A general plant maintenance rule of thumb of 5 percent of total capital cost
is used to reflect maintenance and repair costs for items other than the replacement of consumable materials (refractories, etc.), following the suggestion of Frank
W. Dittman in "Oxygen Steelmaking Cost Comparison: Kaldo *vs.* LD," *Journal of
Metals*, vol. 17 (April 1965), p. 376.

[50] Nelson, "An Interregional Recursive Programming Model," pp. 389–390.

[51] Electricity generation is required at the mill site and hence the cost of electricity is a function of the availability of recovered by-product fuels, purchased fuel
prices, and the level of environmental quality constraints.

TABLE 6.8   *Steel-making Labor Requirements and Operating Costs*

Process	Ore practice (per ingot ton)	Oxygen practice (per ingot ton)
Open hearth		
70–30 practice		
Labor hours[a]	0.625	0.500
Operating and maintenance cost[b]	$5.70	$5.59
50–50 practice		
Labor hours	0.672	0.538
Operating and maintenance cost[b]	$5.70	$5.59
Basic oxygen		
70–30 practice		
Labor hours[a]	n.a.	0.28
Operating and maintenance cost[b]	n.a.	$3.57
90–10 practice		
Labor hours[a]	n.a.	0.28
Operating and maintenance cost[b]	n.a.	$3.57
Electric arc		
Labor hours[a]	0.40	0.38
Operating and maintenance cost[b]	$4.09	$3.95

Abbreviations: n.a., not applicable.

[a] Based on UN, Economic Commission for Europe, *Comparison of Steelmaking Processes*, p. 58, with adjustment for productivity differentials except at BOF.

[b] Based on Battelle Memorial Institute, *Recent Developments in Steelmaking*, pp. A3–A8; Barnes and Lownie, *A Cost Analysis*, p. III-19; and Frank W. Dittman, "Oxygen Steelmaking Cost Comparison," p. 377.

Almost all these input prices can be assumed constant for all of our linear programming problems since wide variations in them are either infrequently observed in the market or are not particularly interesting from our point of view.

The price of purchased scrap is, however, very significant for the mill's operations and residuals load. In addition, wide swings in scrap prices are common—witness the quadrupling in the 1973–74 period. Nonetheless, it is necessary to choose some baseline price set, and our choice, consistent with the rest of the model, is the 1968 price. The base prices for all these inputs are shown in table 6.9.

This completes the description of the heart of the steel mill model, but we have by no means exhausted the significant sources of steel mill residuals, as we shall see in the next chapter, which develops our finishing section model. Thus far we have been moving over fairly well traveled ground—even though the most sophisticated maps (and, indeed, even some of the basic landmarks) are the secrets of the steel companies. From what is available publicly, it is reasonably straightforward to construct vectors for the several process units on a consistent basis. This situation changes as we move, in the next chapter, to consideration of the finishing section.

TABLE 6.9   *Prices for Steel Furnace Inputs*

Input	Furnace	Unit	Price ($)
Pig iron[a]	EA	ton	56.00
Coke	EA	ton	20.10
Carbon electrodes	EA	lb.	0.291
Finishing additions			
Ferrosilicon		lb.	0.101
Ferromanganese		lb.	0.101
Limestone	OH & EA	ton	4.00
Lime	BOF	ton	16.00
Fluorspar		ton	42.50
Alloying agents			
Ferrochromium		lb.	0.169
Nickel		lb.	1.03
Molybdenum trioxide		lb.	1.04
Oxygen		ton	12.00
Scraps (1968 prices)[b]			
No. 1 heavy melting		ton	25.97
No. 1 factory bundles		ton	29.49
Shredded		ton	25.97
No. 2 bundles		ton	19.87

Note: Effects of variation in scrap prices are explored in chapter 10.

Sources: Barnes, Hoffman, and Lownie, *Evaluation of Process Alternatives*, p. II-20; Barnes and Lownie, *A Cost Analysis of Air Pollution Controls*, p. III-19; Fogleman, Gloven, and Jensen, "Prereduced Iron Usage in EA Furnace," p. 733; James W. Sawyer, Jr., personal communication; Silver, Koros, and Schoenberger, "Use of Bundled Auto Scrap," pp. 52, 53–57, and 56; *Steel*, p. 45; U.S. Department of the Interior, *Minerals Yearbook*, 1968, pp. 516 and 772; for a complete discussion of sources with relation to figures quoted in this table, see W. J. Vaughan, "A Residuals Management Model," pp. 252–253.

[a] This checks with the marginal cost of hot metal calculated in supplementary model runs at relatively high-capacity blast furnace utilization.

[b] The scrap price in the table is the c.i.f. price plus a $2.50-per-ton unloading charge.

7

THE FINISHING SECTION

The *finishing section* is what we call the family of operations which take molten steel from the steel-making furnaces and produce the range of shapes and sizes the particular mill markets. In the awesome structure which is the modern integrated steel mill, this section is perhaps the most complicated part of all. It is also the section about which the least information is publicly available. The complexity arises because of the vast number of possible products, the array of process units used to produce any particular product, the different operating practices possible with each process unit, and the difficult relations between residuals generation and operating practice for each unit. In addition, of course, in designing and running an actual mill, it is necessary to solve difficult scheduling problems, since the primary input—molten steel—becomes available at discrete time intervals and since the product array must be produced using only a few very large process units, which must be adjusted to allow a shift from one product to another. We do not reflect these scheduling problems in the model, dealing instead with average daily production rates and assuming that the speed (including an allowance for roll adjustment) of the finishing mills is sufficient to keep up with the greatest possible daily production of steel at the furnaces.

The complexity of the finishing section and the lack of data forced us to make additional simplifications which will be made explicit in the more detailed description below, but for now we note the following guiding principles in choosing what to model.

1. We aimed to follow at least one important product type through from molten metal to finished condition in order to be able to show how the degree of finishing affects residuals generation.

2. We wanted to include the major finishing section residuals—as determined primarily from the amount of space devoted to them in the industry and government literature. These residuals are:

    a. The combustion residuals from the soaking pits or reheating furnaces in which ingots and semifinished shapes are brought to uniform temperature before hot rolling

    b. The water stream from the hot rolling mills containing heat, oil, and iron oxide scale

    c. The spent acid from the pickling bath in which the surface of hot-rolled sheet is cleaned before cold rolling.[1]

    d. The water stream from the cold-rolling mill with less scale but more oil than that from the hot mill (and no heat)

    e. The intermittent stream of oil–water emulsion blown down from the cold-rolling mill's cooling system.

3. We wished to show how the important and relatively new continuous casting option affects residuals generation.

As we have already noted, the literature concerning this section of the integrated mill is generally less useful than that for any other section. The articles and government reports tend to fall into either of two categories: (1) the detailed description of a particular hot or cold mill with data on motor and pump sizes, bearings, adjustment mechanism, etc., but nothing on actual operating results per ton of steel; or (2) the discussion of a particular residual (such as hot mill water or spent acid) and alternatives for its modification or recirculation based on some average quantity per minute, hour, or day, but with no data on quantities generated per ton of steel processed. This has made us heavily dependent on the few sources that do mention typical inputs, operating costs, residuals generation per ton of steel, and has also forced us to base some estimates on rather tenuous chains of assumptions. Nonetheless, we feel that this section of the model achieves our goals and provides a solid base from which future work can proceed.[2]

---

[1] Pickling is also used to prepare the surface of steel before galvanizing or other coating operations.

[2] The principal sources we relied on in constructing the finishing section of the model included: Thomas M. Barnes and H. W. Lownie, Jr., *A Cost Analysis of Air Pollution Controls in the Integrated Iron and Steel Industry*, PB 184 576 (Springfield, Va.: NTIS, May 1969); J. Varga, Jr. and H. W. Lownie, Jr., *A Systems Analysis of the Integrated Iron and Steel Industry*, PB 184 577 (Springfield, Va.: NTIS, May 1969). See especially pp. C-104 to C-119; Battelle Memorial Institute, *Technical and Economic Analysis of the Impact of Recent Developments in Steelmaking Practices on the Supplying Industries* (Columbus: October 30, 1964); K. S. Kuka, "Planning the Electrical Power Supply for a Large, Integrated Steel Works," *Iron and Steel Engineer*, vol. 44 (February 1967), pp. 99–108; U.S. Department of the Interior,

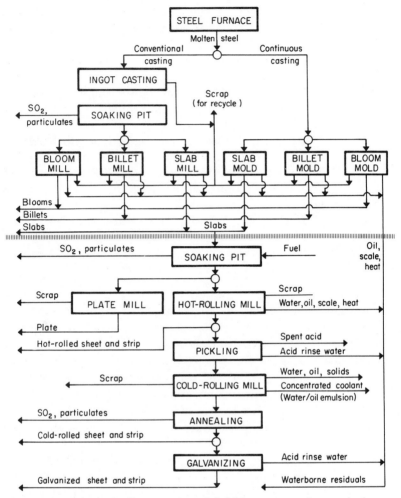

Figure 7.1. Schematic diagram of steel finishing: two casting methods.

FWPCA, "Industrial Waste Profile No. 1: Blast Furnaces and Steel Mills," *Cost of Clean Water, Vol. III* (September 1967); T. Joseph Ess, *The Hot Strip Mill: Generation II* (Pittsburgh: The Association of Iron and Steel Engineers, 1970); Harold E. McGannon, ed., *The Making, Shaping and Treating of Steel*, 9th ed. (Pittsburgh: U.S. Steel Corporation, 1971); D. R. Mathews et al., "Supplement on the Alan Wood Plant," in *Iron and Steel Engineer*, vol. 39 (March 1962), pp. AW-1 to AW-21. A more recent source which became available subsequent to the preparation of this manuscript is U.S. Environmental Protection Agency, Office of Water and Hazardous Materials, Efficient Guidelines Division, *Development Document for Effluent Limitations Guidelines and New Source Performance Standards for the Hot Forming and Cold Finishing Segment of the Iron and Steel Manufacturing Point Source Category*, EPA 440/1-75/048, August 1975.

The full-finishing section included in our model is shown schematically in figure 7.1. The truncated, surrogate finishing section described at the end of this chapter lies above the dotted line in figure 7.1. The basic features of the fuller version are easily summarized. First, we assume a particular product mix, specifying quantities of particular product sizes by steel type. This is described below. Second, we assume that the mill has in place the facilities, including pouring area, soaking pits, and rolling mills, for making semifinished shapes (blooms, billets, and slabs) via conventional casting and rolling of ingots.[3] The program may be altered to allow the choice of setting up a continuous casting process and bypassing the intermediate heating and rolling steps. Since this process is not assumed to exist at the mill, its capital cost is reflected in the objective function.

Some of the slabs produced by either of these methods are sold as is; the majority are subject to further rolling to produce plate or sheet. If they are to be rolled, the slabs must be reheated in another soaking pit, after which they are rolled into plate (0.25-inch thick) in the plate mill and into sheet (0.045-, 0.075-, or 0.1-inch thick) in the hot-rolling mill. The plate is sold, but some of the hot-rolled strip is cold rolled further to reduce its thickness and to improve surface finish. Cold-rolled strip is made in 0.05-, 0.15-, and 0.45-inch thicknesses. Before cold rolling, hot-rolled strip must be pickled to remove rust or scale and any oil left from the hot mill. After cold rolling, the strips are annealed to reduce the tensions created in the rolling process and improve workability. Finally, some cold-rolled sheet is galvanized (in our model this is done by the hot dip process) to give it corrosion resistance.

We assume that blooms and billets are sold as is and are not subject to further processing, though in a real integrated mill, blooms would be rolled into structural steel shapes, rails and the like, while billets would become wire rods. The processes by which these transformations are wrought would be similar to the ones we include explicitly here.

Now let us turn to a more detailed description of the activity vectors involved in the full finishing module.

MAKING SEMIFINISHED SHAPES: CONVENTIONAL CASTING

Conventional casting involves the pouring of ingots, their subsequent reheating in soaking pits, and then the rolling of semifinished shapes

---

[3] These shapes are distinguished roughly as follows: blooms are square in cross section and a typical size might be 8×8 inches; billets are also square in section, but much smaller, say 4×4 inches; slabs are rectangular in cross section and a typical size could be 6×60 inches.

from the ingots. In the course of all this handling, a considerable amount of the original melt of steel is lost from the direct process line in the form of scrap, scale, and dust. Scrap, which we assume is all made available for recycling in the steel furnaces, is produced in pouring, unmolding, rolling, trimming, and scarfing (surface preparation using torches). We have estimated on the basis of a number of conflicting sources that the overall losses to scrap from furnace to shape amount to 14.3 percent, of which about one fifth is pouring scrap and the rest produced in the subsequent stages. We do not differentiate between the various shapes in the estimate of scrap produced because we could find no single source giving consistently comparable yield figures for the three shapes, except for Battelle, which assumes the same yield.[4] Other losses of steel are 20 pounds of particulates from the process of pouring, from scarfing,[5] and from varying amounts of scale broken off by water sprays in the shaping mills.[6] (For alloy steel, we assume this scale loss is half that for carbon steel.) Overall, losses from furnace to shapes are about 16 percent, being slightly higher for slabs, and slightly lower for blooms and billets.

Labor, electricity, and heat inputs were estimated primarily on the basis of information in the Battelle study, although their figures were

[4] Our sources, and the yield they give the conventional process, from molten steel to shape are: Varga and Lownie, *A Systems Analysis* (79.5 percent); F. B. George et al., *The Effect of the Various Steelmaking Processes on the Energy Balances of Integrated Iron and Steel Works*, Special Report No. 71 (London: The Iron and Steel Institute, 1962), pp. 1–59 (82.5 percent); William Renfield, "An Economic Analysis of Recent Technological Trends in the U.S. Steel Industry," Ph.D. dissertation, Yale University, 1968, p. 120 (84.3 percent); Battelle Memorial Institute, *Technical and Economic Analysis*, p. VI-29 (83.4 percent to slabs, 77.6 percent to blooms and billets); and Kuka "Planning the Electric Power Supply," (91.7 percent) p. 100.

[5] The rolling of steel shapes involves only distortion of one shape into another. The surface of the original shape shows up in the surface of the new shape, so the surface of the shape is cleaned by torches before further rolling.

We assume that the particulates from scarfing are only a problem within the confines of the plant (local particulates) although if a machine is used and fans exhaust the work area, scarfing particulates will be emitted from a stack and may fall outside the plant boundaries. See A. C. Elliot and A. J. LaFreniere, "The Design and Operation of a Wet Electrostatic Precipitator to Control Billet Scarfing Emissions," presented at Air Pollution Control Association Meeting, Atlantic City, June 27–July 2, 1971.

[6] There is some question about how scale losses occur at this point, though there is no question that scale is formed in the process of soaking. (See E. A. Cook and K. E. Rasmussen, "Scale Free Heating of Slabs and Billets," *Iron and Steel Engineer*, March 1970, pp. 63–69.) The Battelle balances for the slab, billet, and bloom rolling processes show 10 pounds of mill scale lost, presumably to mill cooling water, but other sources indicate that scale removal is accomplished only by scarfing (Varga and Lownie, *A Systems Analysis Study*, p. C-107). Our numbers are based on information supplied by Henry C. Bramer in his technical review of the first version of the model, letter to Blair Bower, July 18, 1973.

also checked against other sources for consistency.[7] The electrical requirement for alloy steel is estimated to be 1.5 times that for producing the same shape in carbon steel.[8]

We have already mentioned the mill scale and particulate residuals generated in going from molten steel to semifinished shapes. The other major residuals involved are heat, oil, and the combustion residuals from the soaking pits.[9] Heat is introduced into the system in the hot ingots, the soaking-pit fuel combustion, and the electrical energy devoted to rolling. If one assumes that the shape produced ends up in a slab yard at ambient temperature, all this heat input must be given up to water or directly to the atmosphere. We have no data on the relative size of these two forms of loss, but various sources give us fragments of information which allow us to piece together some reasonable numbers. (A similar process is necessary in reconciling scale loss and cooling water use in the plate and hot-rolling mills.)

First, we know from Battelle that total water use is likely to be around 2,500 gallons per ton. Second, from information on the slab heating furnaces, it appears that about 25 percent of heat input to the soaking pits must be carried away by water circulating through and around the interior fittings used to hold and handle the ingots. This amounts to 0.25 million Btu for blooms and billets, and 0.28 million Btu for slabs, using Battelle's estimates of heat input requirements.[10] If we assume a 45° F temperature rise in the cooling water, this cooling duty implies water volumes of about 670 and 745 gallons per ton of product, respectively.

Third, the mill water, which comes in contact with the steel in the process of cooling and lubricating the rolling process, carries away scale, heat, and oil. The concentration of scale in this water is assumed to be 800 ppm or 6.67 pounds per 1,000 gallons.[11] Thus, using our estimates of scale loss, we require 1,500 gallons per ton of carbon steel

[7] Battelle Memorial Institute, *Technical and Economic Analysis*, p. VI-29. Additional information in Kuka, "Planning the Electric Power Supply," p. 105. Kuka's electrical power requirement is much smaller than that implied by Battelle's cost figures.

[8] Based on Ess, *The Hot Strip Mill*, figure 54.

[9] These last were discussed in chapter 2. We assume that coke oven gas, blast furnace gas, coal, coke breeze, or low sulfur residual fuel oil may be burned to provide the necessary heat.

[10] Based on Ess, *The Hot Strip Mill*, pp. 6–11. This source also suggests a 45° F rise in cooling water temperature.

[11] Based on R. Nebolsine, "Present Practice and New Concepts for Handling Effluents from Hot Rolling Mills," *Iron and Steel Engineer*, vol. 47 (August 1970), pp. 85–92. We assume that lower scale production but a greater heat load is associated with alloy steel. The mill water scale concentration is assumed to be 365 ppm with a 45° F temperature rise.

blooms, 1,200 gallons per ton of billets, and 3,000 gallons per ton of slabs. If this water is also heated through 45° F, on the average, it would carry away between 0.45 and 1.12 million Btu per ton, depending on the shape.[12] Total water use for carbon steel would then be 2,170 gallons per ton of blooms, 1,870 gallons per ton of billets, and 3,745 gallons per ton of slabs. The unweighted average of these figures is 2,600 gallons per ton, very close to the estimate we obtain directly from Battelle's cost figures.[13] If we again assume a basic similarity between the slabbing and hot-strip mills, we can use Nebolsine's estimate of 30 ppm (0.25 pounds per 1,000 gallons) oil concentration in the mill water effluent.[14] This amounts, then, to 0.375 pounds of oil per ton of carbon steel blooms; 0.30 pounds per ton of carbon steel billets, and 0.75 pounds per ton of slabs. The process vectors subsuming conventional ingot casting and subsequent milling of semifinished shapes are shown in table 7.1. In that table we also set out the vectors for continuous casting, discussed in the next subsection.

MAKING SEMIFINISHED SHAPES: CONTINUOUS CASTING

In continuous casting,[15] the molten metal is poured into a trough from which it flows into one or more water-cooled molds which force it directly into the cross section of the desired shape. The molds are so set up that the force of gravity acts to pull the hot metal through the mold, and the cooling taking place begins the solidification process. After exiting from the mold, the continuous piece of desired cross section is solid enough to be drawn on by rollers. Further cooling is achieved by direct water sprays, and finally pieces of the desired length are cut, either by hydraulic shears or torches. Thus, continuous casting short-circuits the chain of pouring, heating, and rolling implied by the

---

[12] Some of the water would, of course, boil away, but we have no basis for estimating how much cooling is accomplished in this way, since we have found no source which estimates consumptive use in rolling.

[13] Battelle Memorial Institute, *Technical and Economic Analysis*, p. VI-29.

[14] Our assumption of a single concentration of oil in all the wastewaters is made for simplicity in the full linear model. According to Bramer ("technical review"), the concentrations differ among shapes, being 10 ppm for blooms, 30 ppm for slabs, and 54 ppm for billets. Some small distortion of our residuals loads is thus introduced here because even though the unweighted average concentration is close to 30 ppm, slabs are, in fact, a relatively larger part of production at this stage.

[15] The descriptive material and specific estimates in this section are based primarily on two Battelle Memorial Institute reports which deal at some length with continuous casting (Varga and Lownie, *A Systems Analysis Study*, p. C-109 to C-112; and Battelle Memorial Institute, *Technical and Economic Analysis*, ch. VI).

conventional process. This means less scrap production and a smaller energy input (both fresh heat for soaking and electricity for rolling). The latter, of course, means less in the way of residuals from combustion and, indirectly, from electrical power generation.

We have assumed that the yield of the continuous casting process—reflecting metal losses from molten metal to shape—is 96.3 percent for all three shapes.[16] Of the loss, 60 pounds (or 2.9 percent) are scrap, produced mainly in pouring, but also in trimming to length; 12 pounds are local particulates also generated primarily in the pouring and cutting operations; and 8 pounds (for carbon steel, 4 pounds for alloy) are scale broken off and carried away by direct cooling water.[17]

Electricity, labor, and fresh heat inputs, capital and maintenance costs are based on Battelle.[18] For our mill, a size of about one million tons per year was assumed. Once again, the quantity of mill-water intake and the quantity discharged with a scale, oil, and heat load was determined from the scale estimate, using the same assumptions about concentration as discussed above. The cooling done by water circulating through the pouring molds we have assumed amounts to about 0.5 million Btu per ton of shapes.[19]

THE HOT-ROLLING MILLS: STRIP AND PLATE

Any mill which rolls hot steel to change its shape is a hot-rolling mill, but generally the term is taken to mean the hot-strip mill, where heated slabs are rolled out into thin steel strip, which is then either cut into lengths (sheet) or rolled onto cores (coil). The plate mill, in which hot slabs are rolled out into thicker plate (roughly over 0.25 inch in thickness), is clearly very similar in function to a strip mill, and we treat them similarly in setting up our process vectors.

The primary advantages of hot rolling are the high speeds and large thickness reductions per set of rolls achievable because of the plasticity of the hot steel. Hot rolling is limited, however, in the thickness to

[16] This figure represents a rough average of the yields given by Varga and Lownie, *A Systems Analysis Study*, p. C-111; Kuka, "Planning the Electric Power Supply" p. 100; and Renfield, "An Economic Analysis," p. 120.

[17] The estimate of 8 pounds is taken directly from Varga and Lownie, *A Systems Analysis Study*, p. C-111.

[18] Fresh heat is necessary to ensure that metal in the pouring trough remains molten.

[19] At a $45°$ F rise, this would require 1.33×10^3 gallons of water. Then, for carbon steel, total water use per ton of shapes is, for our process, about 2,500 gallons. This is somewhat lower than the 3,000 gallons implied by the cost figures in Battelle Memorial Institute, *A Technical and Economic Analysis*, p. VI-30.

TABLE 7.1 *Comparison of Conventional and Continuous Casting of Semifinished Shapes*

(*quantities per ton semifinished shape*)

Process vectors	Conventional casting			Continuous casting		
	Blooms	Billets	Slabs	Blooms	Billets	Slabs
Metal input						
Molten metal (tons)						
Carbon steel	1.184	1.184	1.190	1.040	1.040	1.040
Alloy steel	1.183	1.183	1.188	1.038	1.038	1.038
Scrap (tons)	0.169	0.169	0.170	0.03	0.03	0.03
Utilities and other inputs						
Electricity (kWh)						
Carbon steel	34.6	41.3	27.3			
Alloy steel	52.0	62.0	41.0	4.45	4.45	5.55
Water (1,000 gal.)						
Carbon steel	1.50	1.20	3.00	1.20	1.20	1.20
Alloy steel	1.64	1.31	3.28	1.32	1.32	1.32
Labor (hours)	0.584	0.714	0.444	0.140	0.116	0.052
Heat (10^6 Btu)	1.000	1.000	1.125	0.13	0.13	0.13

	20	20	20	12	12	12
Residuals						
Particulates (lb.)						
Mill water (10³ gal.)						
Carbon steel	1.50	1.20	3.00	1.20	1.20	1.20
Alloy steel	1.64	1.31	3.28	1.32	1.32	1.32
Scale (lb.)						
Carbon steel	10	8	20	8	8	8
Alloy steel	5	4	10	4	4	4
Oil (lb.)						
Carbon steel	0.375	0.300	0.750	0.30	0.30	0.30
Alloy steel	0.410	0.328	0.820	0.33	0.33	0.33
Heat (10⁶ Btu)						
Carbon steel	0.563	0.450	1.12	0.45	0.45	0.45
Alloy steel	0.615	0.491	1.23	0.495	0.495	0.495
Heat removed by indirect cooling (10⁶ Btu)	0.25	0.25	0.28	0.5	0.5	0.5
Costs						
Capital charges ($)	n.a.	n.a.	n.a.	1.33	1.43	1.94
Maintenance (plus molds) ($)	2.17	2.17	2.33	3.09[a]	1.64	1.94

Abbreviation: n.a., not applicable.

[a] According to Battelle, molds for blooms are much more expensive (per ton produced) than those for either slabs or billets.

which the steel can be rolled and in the quality of the surface produced. For very thin strip, or strip with a high quality finish, it is necessary to go on to cold rolling, which we discuss below.

We may think of the hot-rolling mill as consisting of:

1. slab-heating furnaces, which are similar to the soaking pits described above. Again, in the process of producing uniformly heated slabs, scale is formed.
2. the rolling mill itself, including:
   a. scale breakers which, through a combination of roll pressure and high pressure water jets, break up and remove surface scale before the size reductions begin.
   b. the rolling train, in which the required size reduction is achieved. Water is used as the coolant and lubricant during this process.
   c. the cooling area or run-out table in which the strip is cooled to a temperature suitable for handling and transfer.

Again we find that the major residuals problems involve fuel combustion and a water stream carrying scale, heat, and oil. (This last gets into the cooling water from leakage in the roll mechanism lubrication system.) There is, of course, some production of scrap in the process of side trimming and cutting to length.

Our activities for the hot rolling of plate and strip are summarized in table 7.2. Scrap production has been estimated on the basis of fragmentary data found in Fabian and adjusted in a rough way to reflect lower proportionate losses from rolling to thinner section (hence longer length).[20] Electrical power inputs are based on information in Kuka and Ess, and include an allowance for auxiliary machinery and a 50 percent greater requirement for alloy steel.[21] Labor hours have been related to electrical power requirements (for carbon steel) by the simple rule of thumb; labor hours = 0.0125 (kWh), based on the information provided by Battelle for the production of some finished shapes. The heat input to the slab furnaces is in the range quoted by

[20] Tibor Fabian, "A Linear Programming Model of Integrated Iron and Steel Production," *Management Science,* vol. 4, no. 4, July 1958. A second adjustment was made after the model was running to bring total scrap generation above 25 percent. (In fact, under the product mix described below, generation is 25.4 percent of molten metal poured, using conventional casting.) This is in line with Arsen Darnay and William E. Franklin, *Salvage Markets for Materials in Solid Wastes* (Kansas City, Mo.: Midwest Research Institute, 1972), pp. 58–59.

[21] Kuka, "Planning the Electrical Power Supply," p. 102; and Ess, *The Hot Strip Mill,* p. 54.

TABLE 7.2   Hot-rolling Mill Input and Residuals for Plate and Strip Production

(*quantities per ton product*)

Inputs and residuals	Unit	Plate	Strip 0.1 inch	0.075 inch	0.045 inch
Metal	tons				
Slab weight					
Carbon		1.156	1.149	1.139	1.129
Alloy		1.148	1.139	1.129	1.119
Scrap		0.14	0.13	0.12	0.11
Utilities and other inputs					
Electricity	kWh				
Carbon		90.5	76.5	85.5	104.0
Alloy		136.0	112.0	128.0	156.0
Mill water	10^3 gal.				
Carbon		4.80	5.64	5.70	5.85
Alloy		5.24	5.95	6.11	6.34
Labor	hours	1.13	0.955	1.07	1.30
Heat	10^6 Btu	2.0	2.5	2.5	2.5
Residuals					
Mill water	10^3 gal.				
Carbon		4.80	5.64	5.70	5.85
Alloy		5.24	5.95	6.11	6.34
Scale	lb.				
Carbon		32.0	37.6	38.0	39.0
Alloy		15.9	18.1	18.6	19.3
Oil	lb.				
Carbon		1.20	1.41	1.42	1.46
Alloy		1.31	1.49	1.52	1.58
Heat	10^6 Btu				
Carbon		1.81	2.11	2.14	2.19
Alloy		1.96	2.23	2.29	2.38
Heat removed by indirect cooling of slab furnace	10^6 Btu	0.5	0.65	0.65	0.65
Maintenance expenses	$	2.50	4.00	4.00	4.00

Ess.[22] Mill water intake to the processes is based on consideration of heat and scale residuals, as we discuss below. Maintenance expense comes from the *Cost of Clean Water* (table XVI), calculated as 4 percent of capital cost annually.

Process residuals and the volume of hot-mill wastewater have been estimated using a process similar to that described for the making of

[22] Ess, *The Hot Strip Mill*, pp. 6, 7. Heat inputs almost certainly vary with type of steel and rolling to be accomplished, but we have no information on the size of this variation. Battelle, *Technical and Economic Analysis*, p. VI-29.

shapes. First, roughly one quarter of the fresh heat added at the slab furnace is assumed to be removed by indirect cooling water within the furnace itself. Mill water volume and scale loss are estimated on the basis of two assumptions: first, that all the rest of the heat added to the process, including the heat equivalent of the electrical rolling power, is removed by mill water which is heated to 45° F and which comes in contact with the steel. Second, we assume that scale concentration in this water is 800 ppm for carbon steel (365 ppm for alloy).[23] The resulting figures check rather well with the sketchy information available on these problems.

1. Nebolsine (p. 85) gives a range of 3,000 to 10,000 gallons per ton for hot-mill water requirements.
2. Ess (p. 71) supplies a detailed breakdown of hot-mill water use, which implies a per ton use at peak production rate of 3,600–7,500 gallons per ton (exclusive of furnace cooling).
3. Nebolsine (p. 85) states that 1.5 to 4.0 percent of the slab is lost as scale in rolling. Ess (p. 71) suggests that 1.5 to 2.5 percent of steel is lost as scale. (It is safe to assume that this applies to carbon steel.)

Oil concentration in the hot mill wastewater is again assumed to be 30 ppm.[24]

ACID PICKLING OF HOT-ROLLED STEEL

Some steel products can be sold as is after hot rolling because the desired dimensions are attainable in the hot mill and because surface quality is not particularly important. For carbon steel sheet and strip, however, on which we concentrate in our model, somewhat more than half of the total production of the hot-rolling mill, on the average, is subject to further processing in the cold mill. As preparation for cold rolling, the surface of the strip is cleaned of scale formed in the hot mill and in storage. This cleaning is generally accomplished by passing the strip through baths of dilute hydrochloric or sulfuric acid, in which the scale dissolves.[25] The process is called pickling. For either

[23] The scale concentration is from Nebolsine, "Present Practice," p. 86.

[24] Bramer (technical review) has indicated that the volume of plate-mill wastewater ought to be about 13,000 gallons per ton, with about the same oil concentration and considerably lower solids load (20 pounds per ton). This change would have very little impact on residuals discharges and would require the inclusion of an entire new set of treatment and recirculation activities. (See below.)

[25] As we shall see, acid pickling produces some difficult residuals, and this reason, among others, has stimulated exploration of alternative cleaning methods. One such method involves blasting the strip with shot (roughly sand blasting). This method

acid, as the strip is pulled through the bath and the reaction proceeds, the acid is spent, and as the amount of free acid left falls toward zero, the effectiveness of the process decreases. To ensure effective descaling and maximum use of free acid, the process is generally set up as a countercurrent flow, with several connected tanks of increasingly spent acid, into the weakest of which the strip enters first. Spent acid from this tank is continuously drained off and fresh makeup acid is added at the last tank in the line.

The steel leaving the last bath is pulled through hard rubber rollers to remove acid being carried along on its surface, but some inevitably escapes. To remove these final traces of acid and thus prevent any loss of the steel itself, and to clean off vestiges of scale, the strip goes through a series of water rinse baths. These are also arranged countercurrently, with clean makeup water entering at the steel exit end, and water from the first bath being continuously drawn off to prevent excess acid buildup. Both the spent acid solution, containing free acid, a metal salt, and water, and the acid-contaminated rinse water are exotic residuals with which the steel producer has to deal. In a later section we shall discuss the difficulties he faces and some of the alternatives available to him.

The key numbers for the alternative pickling activities are shown in table 7.3. The amounts of spent acid and acid rinse water loss, and the constituents of these streams, are based on information supplied by Henry C. Bramer.[26] Since the alternatives do not show the same scale removal (36.9 pounds of iron using hydrochloric acid and only 12.8 pounds using sulfuric acid), it is difficult to make useful comparisons. It is, however, clear that the hydrochloric acid can be spent further, that is, used more completely, thus leaving less free acid to cause disposal problems. The electrical input comes from Kuka; labor hours are related to power consumption by our rule of thumb ($0.0125 \times$ kWh per ton for carbon steel) and costs are based on the information in the *Cost of Clean Water.*

COLD ROLLING OF STEEL STRIP

In cold rolling, because the steel is not heated to increase its plasticity, achieving the same proportional size reduction requires greater electrical energy input and requires a longer time per ton

---

is employed in shipyards to remove paint and rust from ship hulls and superstructures. For a discussion of its application in the steel mill, see K. Matheisus, "The Treatment of Water Wastes from Metal Pickling Plants," in *Reuse of Water in Industry* (London: Butterworths, 1963), pp. 143, 144.

[26] Letter to Blair T. Bower from Henry C. Bramer, August 3, 1973.

TABLE 7.3   *Pickling of Hot-rolled Carbon Steel Strip Prior to Cold Rolling*

Inputs and residuals	Unit	Hydrochloric acid	Sulfuric acid
Metal	tons		
Strip in (including scale)		1.0	1.0
Strip out		0.98	0.99
Utilities and other inputs			
Electricity	kWh	18.2	18.2
Mill water	10³ gal.	0.32	0.50
Makeup acid	lb.	n.a.	184
Sulfuric acid (25% solution)			
Hydrochloric acid (17% solution)		299	n.a.
Labor	hours	0.23	0.23
Residuals			
Spent acid	lb.	345	195
Iron	lb.	36.4	11.2
Free acidity[a]	lb.	2.8	20.3
Total acidity[a]	lb.	67.9	40.3
Sulfate	lb.	n.a.	38.7
Chloride	lb.	48.2	n.a.
Acid rinse water	10³ gal.	0.32	0.50
Iron	lb.	0.50	1.60
Free acidity[a]	lb.	0.96	2.89
Total acidity[a]	lb.	1.85	5.75
Sulfate	lb.	n.a.	5.52
Chloride	lb.	1.31	n.a.

Abbreviation: n.a., not applicable.

[a] Measured by limestone required for neutralization.

(rolling speeds are slower). The advantages of cold rolling are, as we have noted, that thinner strips may be attained in this way and that it produces a finer surface quality. (Cold rolling is generally used to attain strip thicknesses less than 0.05-inch.) As at the hot mill, the largest residuals problem is mill water contaminated with oil and solids. The relative quantities of these two entrained residuals are, however, different at the cold mill, reflecting the somewhat different function of the water here.

Instead of being used, as at the hot mill, primarily to remove surface scale and cool the steel after rolling, water is used here primarily as a lubricant and a rinse. In its role as a lubricant of the strip–roll interface, the water may be used alone, in combination with soluble oil, or as an oil–water emulsion. When used as a rinse, the water will tend to remove the oils and oil–water emulsions used at other rolling stands. Solids concentrations, on the other hand, tend to be low because scale has been removed in the pickling baths immediately preceding the cold mill.

For any real cold mill, the choice of oils; the arrangement of oil, oil–water, and water sprays over the mill stands; and the decision on quantities to be used per ton, will be based on the steel to be rolled, the reduction to be achieved, and most importantly, on the judgment of the mill supervisor. Needless to say, situations in which artistry or craftsmanship play such a large role are very difficult to model, and we have cut through the resulting thicket by assuming a roughly representative situation in which water is used both as a rinse and with soluble oils as a lubricant, while at one stand, a concentrated coolant–lubricant (an oil–water emulsion) is used. The quantities and concentrations involved are set out below.

We provide in the model for producing three thicknesses of cold-rolled strip in both carbon and alloy steels; starting from two thicknesses of hot-rolled strip, the input–output combinations in the model are:

Hot-rolled Strip	—to—	Cold-rolled Strip
0.1 inch		0.045 inch
0.1 inch		0.015 inch
0.075 inch		0.045 inch
0.075 inch		0.015 inch
0.075 inch		0.005 inch

Most of the items in the activity vectors shown in table 7.4 are taken from the same sources or are based on the same assumptions as for the hot mill. The only items on which special comments are in order are annealing heat, roll heat removed by indirect cooling, mill waste-water volume and its residuals load, and the emulsion blowdown.[27]

1. *Annealing* is a process of slow heating and cooling which removes stresses and makes the strip so treated less brittle. Since the process of cold rolling sets up considerable stress in the strip, we assume that all cold-rolled products are annealed, and the required heat input (0.93 million Btu per ton) is included directly in the cold-rolling vector.[28] In addition, each vector reflects 27 kWh per ton power consumption estimated necessary in annealing.

2. *Indirect cooling of rolls.* We assume that all power applied to the rolls is translated into heat and that this heat is carried away by water kept segregated and free of oil and solid contamination.

3. *Mill water volume and residuals load.* Here we first assume that total water use (including roll cooling), as once-through use, is proportional to electrical power applied. (Since heat load and,

[27] Scrap generation was discussed above in the section on the hot-rolling mill.
[28] See, for example, Miller and Rogers, *Manufacturing Policy* (Richard D. Irwin: Homewood, Ill., 1964), p. 584.

TABLE 7.4 Cold Rolling of Strip

(quantities per ton product)

Inputs and outputs	Unit	Thickness (inches)				
		0.1–0.045	0.1–0.015	0.075–0.045	0.075–0.015	0.075–0.005
Metal	tons					
Hot-rolled strip		1.115	1.110	1.115	1.110	1.105
Scrap out		0.115	0.110	0.115	0.110	0.105
Utilities and other inputs						
Electricity[a]	kWh					
Carbon steel		67.0	140	50.8	116	208
Alloy steel		87.0	196	62.6	160	298
Mill water	10^3 gal.					
Carbon steel		0.76	2.16	0.45	1.70	3.45
Alloy steel		1.14	3.21	0.68	2.55	5.55
Labor	hours	0.838	1.75	0.635	1.45	2.60
Heat (annealing)	10^6 Btu	0.93	0.93	0.93	0.93	0.93
Residuals						
Mill water	10^3 gal.					
Carbon steel		0.76	2.16	0.45	1.70	3.45
Alloy steel		1.14	3.21	0.68	2.55	5.55
Solids	lb.					
Carbon steel		0.47	1.32	0.28	1.04	2.12
Alloy steel		0.87	2.46	0.52	1.95	3.94
Oil	lb.					
Carbon steel		1.40	3.98	0.83	3.12	6.35
Alloy steel		2.82	7.90	1.67	6.28	12.70
Heat from indirect cooling of rolls	10^6 Btu	5.20	14.80	3.11	11.60	23.70
Emulsion	gallons					
Carbon steel		0.136	0.386	0.081	0.301	0.618
Alloy steel		0.204	0.576	0.121	0.455	0.925
Maintenance expense	$	3.60	3.60	3.60	3.60	3.60

[a] Power for rolling and annealing (27 kWh per ton).

hence, cooling water volume have already been assumed to be directly related to kilowatt hours applied, we are effectively adding the assumption that the needs of lubrication are also directly related to electrical power, hence, presumably to the difficulty of rolling.) For our base vector we pick carbon steel rolling from 0.075-inch to 0.015-inch, and for the base total volume we take 2,500 gallons per ton.[29] From the total water use figures thus implied for each vector, we subtract the quantity required, at 45° F rise, to carry away roll heat.

The residuals loads are based on the following assumptions.

a. *oil:* If all water were used once through and were allowed to become contaminated with oil, the concentrations would be

29 Based on *Cost of Clean Water*, p. 47, typical technology mill.

150 ppm for carbon steel rolling and 200 ppm for alloy steel rolling.[30]

    b. *solids:* Under these assumptions, solids would amount to 50 ppm for carbon steel and 62.5 ppm for alloy.[31]

    c. Blowing these concentrations up to reflect the segregation of the roll-cooling water gives us the following concentrations: for carbon steel, 220 ppm oil and 294 ppm solids; for alloy steel, 73.5 ppm oil and 92.0 ppm solids.

   4. *Emulsion coolant–lubricant.* In order to reflect the problems involved in using a coolant–lubricant based on an oil–water emulsion, we assume that at one of our rolling stands such a system is used and kept segregated from the systems of the other stands. The concentrated emulsion is recirculated and only occasionally blown down to maintain oil quality. Since our model will not handle intermittent blowdown, we average the quantity involved over the tons of steel produced from blowdown to blowdown. The average blowdown attached to the base vector is 11.6 gallons per ton,[32] and the volume varies with electrical power applied. The composition of this blowdown is assumed to be as follows:[33] total oil, 23,900 ppm; emulsified oil, 3,500 ppm; suspended solids, 1,000 ppm; BOD, 5,970 ppm.

BOD is here assumed to be 25 percent of total oil, and this, in turn, is based on a roughly estimated relation between the extent of emulsification and the BOD equivalent of rolling oil residuals.[34] The rule of thumb developed in this way is:

	Ratio of BOD Concentration to Total Oil Concentration
Hot mill waste water (30 ppm total oil)	2.0
Cold mill waste water (150 ppm total oil)	0.5
Cold mill concentrated coolant (24,000 ppm total oil)	0.25

[30] Ross Nebolsine, "The Treatment of Water-borne Wastes from Steel Plants," *Iron and Steel Engineer*, vol. 34 (December 1957), p. 137, estimates 100–200 ppm oil concentrations in cold mill water under these assumptions.

[31] Based on *Cost of Clean Water*, p. 47.

[32] Based on data in Armco Steel, "Treatment of Waste Water–Waste Oil Mixtures," Report to FWPCA, May 1970 (Water Pollution Control Research Series—12010 EZV 02/70), pp. 80, 81.

[33] Ibid., p. 59, except that total oil has been adjusted to make it consistent with oil recovery reported in this same source for a batch treatment process, pp. 63, 64.

[34] Based on data from Armco Steel, "Treatment of Waste Water–Waste Oil Mixtures," table XVIII.

GALVANIZING OF CARBON STEEL STRIP

In some uses, steel parts made from strip must be protected more or less permanently against corrosion, even though it would increase product cost by an unacceptable amount were a stainless alloy to be used. For these uses, carbon (or alloy) steels are normally coated with corrosion-resistant metals. Tin is the major such coating, but second only to tin is zinc, which is used to coat strip such diverse products as culvert pipe, roofing and siding, garbage pails, and auto rocker panels.[35]

Zinc coatings may be applied using either electrolytic solutions or baths of molten zinc. Our model concentrates on the latter, the so-called hot-dip process, because it is by far the most common, though not the most interesting from a residuals point of view.[36] In particular, while electroplating involves spent solutions and rinse waters in which are found dissolved metal ions and, frequently, cyanides, the hot-dip process itself produces essentially no liquid waste problems at all.[37] There are zinc fumes produced by the molten bath, but we ignore them here. We do assume that, before it is coated, the steel is subject to surface cleaning using acid pickling, and this, of course, produces spent acid and acid rinse blowdowns of (we assume) the same composition as those discussed above under pickling.[38] (The quantities involved are different since we assume that 19 pounds of ferrous oxide per ton are, on the average, to be removed by the pregalvanizing pickling step.)

In the model, all three cold-rolled strip gauges (0.045-, 0.015-, and 0.005-inch) in the commercial quality carbon steel may be galvanized. We assume that the zinc being applied to the 0.045- and 0.015-inch strip amounts to 1.5 ounces per square foot, roughly midway between culvert and roofing quality coatings.[39] For the thinnest gauge, 0.005-inch, we assume a 0.9 ounce per square foot coating, equivalent to roofing quality. These coatings translate into tons of zinc per ton of

[35] Zinc has two distinct advantages as a coating. First, it is cheap—compared, for example, to cadmium, a possible substitute. Second, its relation to iron in the electromotive series is anionic. That means that zinc will sacrifice itself by oxidizing while leaving adjacent iron in the elemental form. Thus, small breaks in the galvanized coating, as at sheared edges, are protected.

[36] The hot-dipping process was used to produce about 95 percent of total galvanized steel products in 1968. McGannon, *The Making, Shaping and Treating of Steel*, 9th ed., p. 1028.

[37] *Cost of Clean Water*, p. 47.

[38] Other pretreatment methods are also used, particularly caustic washing to remove oils, soaps, etc.

[39] McGannon, *The Making, Shaping and Treating of Steel*, 8th ed., p. 1031.

TABLE 7.5   *Galvanizing of Carbon Steel Strip (Including Acid Pickling)*

Inputs and outputs	Unit	Thickness (inches)		
		0.045	0.015	0.005
Metal	tons			
Strip in		1.0895	1.0795	1.0695
Zinc		0.05	0.15	0.31
Strip out		1.05	1.15	1.31
Scrap out		0.08	0.07	0.06
Utilities and other inputs[a]				
Electricity	kWh		45.3	
Acid	lb.			
Sulfuric (25%)			137	
Hydrochloric (15%)			130	
Labor	hours		0.57	
Mill water	10^3 gal.		0.182	
Residuals[a]				
Spent acid	lb.			
From sulfuric			153	
From hydrochloric			146	
Acid rinse water	10^3 gal.		0.182	
Maintenance expense[a]	$		3.60	

[a] Quantities of inputs and residuals are the same for all thicknesses.

steel as shown in table 7.5, where allowance is also made for the loss of scale and scrap losses.[40]

Inputs of electricity and labor have been estimated as for the other finishing vectors.[41] The scrap generation rate was adjusted in order to produce an overall rate above 25 percent of molten metal poured. It is, however, assumed that galvanized scrap cannot be recycled to the steel furnaces because of the harmful effects of the zinc.

Handling Major Residuals-Bearing Streams

In this section we describe the alternatives provided in the program for the major residuals-bearing streams identified with our simple finishing facilities. These streams are: hot-mill wastewater, cold-mill wastewater, cold-mill concentrated coolant, spent pickle liquor, and acid rinse water. For the mill wastewaters, the alternatives consist of: once-through use with simple settling to remove the largest scale par-

[40] Scrap based on balances given by Kuka "Planning the Electric Power Supply" p. 100, for cold rolling.
[41] Electricity from ibid., p. 104. Labor hours equal to $0.0125 \times$ kWh.

ticles, once-through use with settling plus coagulation and filtration to increase removal of both solids and oil, recirculation with simple settling (and cooling for the hot-mill water), and recirculation with settling, coagulation, and filtration (and cooling). For the concentrated coolant system blowdown, the alternatives are discharge or discharge after recovery of nearly all the emulsified oil at a quality level allowing burning. For the spent acid liquors, the set of alternatives is somewhat more complicated but basically the program may choose among uncontrolled neutralization, controlled neutralization with sludge dewatering, and some form of acid recovery.

Hot-mill Wastewater

The hot plate and strip mills produce very large quantities of wastewater heated, we assume, through 45° F and containing scale and oil. If no treatment of any kind were undertaken, enormous quantities of mill scale reusable as input to the sinter plant would be lost to the watercourse. For example, just in the rolling of 0.045-inch carbon steel strip from slabs, we have estimated the generation of 39 pounds of scale per ton. If 500 tons per day were rolled, the total scale loss would be nearly 10 tons, worth perhaps $10 to $20 per ton as an ore substitute in sintering, and imposing a very large suspended solids load on the watercourse.[42] For this reason, it has been standard practice in steel mills to provide an initial settling basin for this water, which allows the capture of the heavy scale particles (perhaps 90 percent of the total weight of scale). This same simple treatment process accomplishes some oil removal simply because some oil is trapped on the scale and settles out with it. This level of treatment is the minimum provided for in the model.

The other treatment and recirculation alternatives will be chosen only in response to charges or limits on discharges of solids, oil, or heat. The second level of treatment involves coagulation and sand filtration after settling. In addition, oil removal is greatly increased by the addition of skimming equipment.[43] For the recirculation alternatives, water which has been subject to either the first or second levels of treatment is cooled in forced draft towers and returned to the mill water system.

[42] Actually, since such a large fraction of this load would settle rapidly, the major effect would probably be to change drastically the bottom configuration in the neighborhood of the plant's outfall. Eventually some costs, in the form of dredging expenses or flooding losses, would probably be borne by the plant.

[43] Note that all oil recovered from hot and cold mill wastewaters is assumed fit only for sale as road oil. It contains too much scale and water to be burned in boilers, and open burning is assumed not to be an alternative.

In order to control the steady-state solids buildup, we assume that 10 percent of the gross use per ton must be blown down.[44]

In Table 7.6 we report the key information required for the vectors. The assumptions upon which we base these entries are summarized here.

	Removal Efficiencies[45] (in percentages)		
Alternative	Solids	Oil	Heat
Settling only	90	20	0
Settling + coagulation and filtration	95	80	0
Settling + recirculation (including cooling tower)	98.7	72	100
Settling + filtration + recirculation	99.4	98	100

Electrical power requirements were estimated on the basis of the following very rough rules of thumb: Plain settling requires 0.05 kWh per 1,000 gallons, filtration adds 0.1 kWh per 1,000 gallons, the cooling towers add[46] a further 0.67 kWh, and finally, recirculation requires 0.05 kWh per 1,000 gallons.

Costs, including only maintenance for the required minimum level and capital plus maintenance for the add-on alternatives, are based on data in the *Cost of Clean Water* (see especially pp. 92–94). The size assumed for costing is 20 million gallons per day.[47] Finally, the BOD equivalent of the oil is based on the rule given at the end of the section on the cold mill. Here the BOD concentration is assumed to be twice the oil concentration.

Cold-mill Wastewater

We provide the same set of treatment and recirculation alternatives for handling cold-mill wastewater as for the hot-mill water, despite its

[44] In addition, 5.8 percent of water is assumed lost through evaporation and windage at the cooling towers. Hence, makeup is 15.8 percent of gross use flow (measured after the tower).

[45] Based on *Cost of Clean Water*, pp. 72–75.

[46] Based on pumping and fan power requirements for a 50-ft. cooling tower with a relative rating factor of about 3. P. O. Cootner and G. O. G. Löf, *Water Demand for Steam Electric Generation* (Washington: Resources for the Future, 1965). The other rules are based on pumping heads of 10 ft. for settling, 20 ft. for filtration and 10 ft. for recirculation.

[47] This size is based on production of 2,860 tons per day (about a million tons per year) and an average of 7,000 gallons per ton gross mill water use per ton of poured steel. The *Cost of Clean Water* (p. 46) estimates 17.3 million gallons per day for the hot rolling sections of a million-ton-per-year mill.

TABLE 7.6   *Alternatives for Hot-mill Wastewater*

(all quantities per 1,000 gallons)

Process, inputs, and outputs	Unit	Carbon steel	Alloy steel
Settling + discharge			
Electricity	kWh	0.05	0.05
Scale recovered	lb.	6.00	2.74
Oil recovered (road quality)		0.05	0.05
Residuals discharged			
Suspended solids	lb.	0.67	0.30
Oil	lb.	0.20	0.20
BOD	lb.	0.40	0.40
Heat	10^6 Btu	0.375	0.375
Cost	$	0.017	0.017
Settling + filter + discharge			
Electricity	kWh	0.15	0.15
Scale recovered	lb.	6.34	2.89
Oil recovered	lb.	0.20	0.20
Residuals discharged			
Suspended solids	lb.	0.33	0.15
Oil	lb.	0.05	0.05
BOD	lb.	0.10	0.10
Heat	10^6 Btu	0.375	0.375
Cost	$	0.069	0.069
Settling + recirculation			
Electricity	kWh	0.77	0.77
Scale recovered	lb.	6.60	3.01
Oil recovered	lb.	0.18	0.18
Make up	10^3 gal.	0.158	0.158
Residuals discharged			
Suspended solids	lb.	0.069	0.032
Oil	lb.	0.068	0.068
BOD	lb.	0.137	0.137
Cost	$	0.09	0.09
Settling + filtration + recirculation			
Electricity	kWh	0.87	0.87
Scale recovered	lb.	6.64	3.02
Oil recovered	lb.	0.245	0.245
Makeup	10^3 gal.	0.158	0.158
Residuals discharged			
Suspended solids	lb.	0.033	0.015
Oil	lb.	0.006	0.006
BOD	lb.	0.012	0.012
Cost	$	0.12	0.12

different character, but we reflect this character in different assumptions about removal efficiencies at each stage.[48] In addition, since the

[48] The character of the solids is also different for the same reason. Instead of consisting almost entirely of scale, they will include some steel from the strip being worked, some steel worn from the rolls and some general dirt. For simplicity, we assume that the small quantity involved may be lumped in with scale from the hot mill for possible recycling to the sinter plant.

average daily flow is considerably smaller than for the hot mill, unit costs are higher.[49] (The size assumed for cost calculation here is 2.3 million gallons per day.[50])

In table 7.7 we present the activity vectors for these alternatives for carbon and alloy steel rolling. Below, we summarize the assumptions about removal efficiencies on which these vectors are based.

	Removal Efficiencies (in percentages)	
Alternative	Solids	Oil
Settling only	30	0
Settling + coagulation and filtration	50	50
Settling + recirculation	81.5	0
Settling + filtration + recirculation	91.6	91.1

These efficiencies are again based on information in *Cost of Clean Water,* and reflect the relatively small size (hence long settling time) of solids, and the assumption that the oil is emulsified or dissolved and hence nearly impossible to remove without the addition of heat, chemicals, or electrostatic forces. Electrical requirements are based on the same rules as for the hot-mill wastewater, though here, of course, no cooling towers are necessary since we have assumed that no significant heat load is picked up by the lubricating water.

Concentrated Coolant from the Cold Mill

The concentrated coolant which we assume is used at one stand of our cold-rolling mill is recirculated within its own closed system, and in the model we reflect only the blowdown necessary to control the buildup of solids in this system. This blowdown is, as we have noted, averaged over the tons of steel produced, while in a real mill the problem would be one of getting rid of a batch of coolant after some interval of use.

We provide two alternatives for this blowdown: discharge, and treatment to reclaim most of the oil. If the first alternative is chosen, the concentrations assumed in the cold-mill section may be used to estimate the quantities of residuals discharged per 100 gallons of coolant. These quantities are oil (total), 19.9 pounds; oil (emulsified), 2.9 pounds; solids, 0.8 pounds; BOD, 5.0 pounds. The reclamation process

---

[49] We assume that the two mill systems are kept separate because quality requirements, especially in terms of tolerance for solids, are stricter at the cold mill.

[50] Based on cold rolling about 40 percent of total steel produced (1,150 tons per day) and an average gross use of about 2,000 gallons per ton. *Cost of Clean Water,* (p. 47), estimates 1.37 million gallons per day.

TABLE 7.7   Alternatives for Treatment of Cold-mill Wastewater

(*quantities per 1,000 gallons*)

Processes, inputs, and outputs	Unit	Carbon steel	Alloy steel
Settling + discharge			
Scale recovered	lb.	0.184	0.230
Electricity	kWh	0.05	0.05
Residuals discharged			
Suspended solids	lb.	0.429	0.535
Oil	lb.	1.84	2.46
BOD	lb.	0.92	1.23
Cost	$	0.044	0.044
Sedimentation + coagulation and filtration			
Scale recovered	lb.	0.307	0.382
Electricity	kWh	0.15	0.15
Oil recovered	lb.	0.92	0.92
Residuals discharged			
Suspended solids	lb.	0.307	0.382
Oil	lb.	0.92	1.23
BOD	lb.	0.46	0.62
Cost	$	0.180	0.180
Plain sedimentation + recirculation			
Scale recovered	lb.	0.500	0.623
Electricity	kWh	0.10	0.10
Oil recovered	lb.	0	0
Residuals discharged			
Suspended solids	lb.	0.113	0.142
Oil	lb.	1.84	2.46
BOD	lb.	0.92	1.23
Cost	$	0.180	0.180
Sedimentation + coagulation, filtration and recirculation			
Scale recovered	lb.	0.562	0.701
Electricity	kWh	0.20	0.20
Oil recovered	lb.	1.68	2.24
Residuals discharged			
Suspended solids	lb.	0.051	0.064
Oil	lb.	0.16	0.22
BOD	lb.	0.08	0.11
Cost	$	0.204	0.204

removes 98.5 percent of the oil and 76 percent of the solids.[51] It produces a burnable oil product with about 14 percent water. When this oil is burned, we assume it produces 0.01 million Btu and 0.0025 pounds of particulates per pound. The cost of reclamation is estimated to be $0.71 per 100 gallons of blowdown for capital charge, chemicals,

[51] The reclamation process is based on one developed by Armco Steel and reported in *Treatment of Waste Water–Waste Oil Mixtures,* pp. 63, 64, 80–82.

and maintenance. Labor requirements are 0.048 hour, and electrical power requirements are 11.5 kWh per 100 gallons.[52]

After reclamation, discharge of the coolant implies the following quantities of residuals per 100 gallons: oil, 0.6 pounds; solids, 0.2 pounds; BOD, 0.15 pounds.

Spent Pickle Liquors and Acid Rinse Waters

One of the steel industry's most difficult residuals problems is that involving spent pickle liquors and acid-contaminated rinse waters. Both these liquid streams contain sufficient free acid to be dangerous, and their discharge untreated into the watercourse is, we assume, prohibited even in the absence of a comprehensive set of discharge regulations or ambient quality constraints.[53] But the obvious primary treatment step, simple neutralization with limestone, slaked lime, or other base, produces, not a relatively innocuous stream of neutral liquid, but a sludge which is nearly impossible to dewater.[54] We provide for this alternative and show as the secondary residual the cubic feet of sludge produced, since permanent storage lagoons seem currently to be the only way of dealing with the problem.

There is a considerable literature on alternatives to this simple, uncontrolled neutralization of pickling wastes, but it is a particularly difficult literature from which to extract the necessary information on costs, inputs, and efficiencies necessary to construct activity vectors. Our impression is that most of the literature amounts to promotion for new processes untested at large scale or in continuous operation. The costs, where provided at all, appear illustory and sometimes are not even internally consistent. We have attempted, nonetheless, to provide

---

[52] This power requirement is based on Armco's cost for "utilities" treated as though it were all for electricity.

[53] Such an assumption seems to reflect the actual pressures felt by the steel industry. One option we do not cover here is deep well injection. Except for certain limited areas, this seems to be potentially very dangerous and probably not a viable alternative over the longer run.

[54] See, for example, R. D. Wight, "Wastewater Treatment at an Integrated Steel Mill," *Journal of the Water Pollution Control Federation,* April 1972, pp. D–2, D–3. For the rinse waters, the quantities of acid and ferric chloride involved are small relative to the volume of water. We estimate the volume of sludge to be 1 percent of the volume of water. In other words we assume considerable dewatering is possible in the case of the rinse water simply because there is so little sludge formed. Bethlehem Steel has recently patented a new treatment process for handling heavily acid wastewater which cannot be discharged to surface or ground water because of environmental considerations. The Bethlehem process creates an especially dense sludge from metals precipitated from the wastewater: 15 to 50 percent solids instead of the normal 1 to 2 percent. This dense sludge is more easily handled than the sludge from the conventional disposal activities included in our model. See *Air and Water News,* vol. 7, no. 41 (October 1973), p. 7.

one alternative for spent sulfuric acid liquor and two for spent hydrochloric acid liquor. The sulfuric acid alternative is for recovery of free acid which can be recycled to the pickling baths.[55] For hydrochloric acid we had sufficient information to construct a two-stage set: first, the possibility of controlled neutralization plus filtration to recover ferrous oxide for recycling to the sinter plant and discharge of the remaining high solids water;[56] and second, the addition of a step to recover from this water fresh acid for recirculation to the pickling baths.[57]

For the acid rinse waters, we provide the alternatives of uncontrolled neutralization and controlled neutralization with iron oxide recovery. The very high dilution of these streams makes acid recovery extremely expensive, and we have ignored it. These alternatives are all presented in table 7.8.

PRODUCT MIX

The complexity of our product mix is limited by the alternatives available in the finishing section and, of course, by our use of three steel types to represent the large number of steels available from the industry. Within these limitations, we have attempted to provide a product mix that is consistent with publicly available data on aggregate U.S. production. Thus, our basic split between carbon and alloy steel is based on published AISI data for 1972. This is also true for the shape mix within carbon and alloy steels. Our assumption that drawing quality (DQ) steel is 25 percent of total carbon steel production has a weaker foundation.[58] The mix of DQ products and of strip thick-

[55] T. F. Barnhardt, "Evaluation of a Waste Pickle Liquor Treatment," in *Iron and Steel Engineer*, vol. 32 (December 1955), pp. 62–65.
Note that this recovery process is based on conversion of ferrous sulfate into sulfuric acid directly using concentrated hydrochloric acid. ($FeSO_4 + 2\,HCl \rightarrow FeCl_2 + H_2SO_4$). The hydrochloric acid is then recovered from the ferrous chloride. Some neutralization of free sulfuric and hydrochloric acid is necessary because none of the reactions go to 100 percent completion.

[56] Our process is a simplified version of the so-called Interlake process for controlled neutralization. In controlled neutralization the addition of the base is limited so that the iron salt (in this case $FeCl_2$) is converted only to an iron oxide rather than to $Fe(OH)_2$, the villain in the sludge problem. This process is mentioned in Daniel L. Brown, "Recovery of Acid from Spent Pickle Liquor," *Iron and Steel Engineer*, September 1970, pp. 68–73. Unfortunately, this article contains no cost information, and we have had to guess this important point.

[57] Ibid. The chemical processes involved in recovery are described very clearly, but as already noted, no costs are given.

[58] Aggregate data on this breakdown are not available. Our figure represents a rough average of information gained in several interviews with steel company personnel and a published product mix for a single Canadian plant, producing 38 percent of total carbon steel as DQ. L. Tellier, I. Mozer and S. F. Turcotte, "Direct Reduction in Steelmaking at Sidbec-Dosco," *Iron and Steel Engineer*, vol. 51 (December 1974), p. 37.

TABLE 7.8 *Alternatives for Handling Spent Acid and Acid Rinse Water from Pickling*

Process, inputs, and outputs	Unit	Sulfuric acid	Hydrochloric acid
Uncontrolled neutralization			
Spent acid	lb.	100	100
Electricity	kWh	0.0014	0.0014
Calcium carbonate	lb.	20.7	19.7
Residual sludge	ft.³	1.87	1.82
Cost	$	0.041	0.041
Acid rinse water	10³ gal.	1.0	1.0
Electricity	kWh	0.119	0.119
Calcium carbonate	lb.	11.5	5.8
Residual sludge	ft.³	1.3	1.3
Cost	$	0.37	0.37
Controlled neutralization[a]			
Spent acid	lb.	n.a.	100
Electricity	kWh	n.a.	0.015
Calcium carbonate	lb.	n.a.	0.8
Recovered scale		n.a.	13.6
Neutral liquor	lb.	n.a.	80.9
Residual high solids		n.a.	
wastewater	lb.	n.a.	6.3
Cost	$	n.a.	1.00
Acid rinse water	10³ gal.	1.0	1.0
Electricity	kWh	0.22	0.22
Calcium carbonate	lb.	5.8	3.0
Recovered scale	lb.	4.1	2.0
Residuals:			
Sludge	ft.³	0.14	0.14
High solids waste-			
water	10³ gal.	1.0	1.0
Cost	$	0.68	0.68
Acid recovery			
Spent acid	lb.	100	n.a.
Neutral liquor	lb.	n.a.	80.9
Recovered scale	lb.	7.38	n.a.
Steam	lb.	83.0	83.0
Electricity	kWh	0.015	n.a.
Concentrated acid input	lb.	1.3	15.4
		(HCl)	(H_2SO_4)
Recovered acid (dilute)	lb.	98.1	74.7
		(H_2SO_4)(25%)	(HCl)(15%)
Calcium carbonate	lb.	10.4	n.a.
High solids water	10³ gal.	0.001	n.a.
Gypsum	lb.	n.a.	30
Cost[b]	$	2.46	1.00

Abbreviation: n.a., not applicable.

[a] Controlled neutralization is not a separate option; it is included in the model as part of acid recovery.

[b] On the bases of subsequent calculations we have found that the capital and maintenance costs of acid recovery are probably overestimated.

TABLE 7.9   *Product Mix Assumptions*

Product mixes[a]	Proportions of mixes (percentages)
Split by steel type	
Carbon	91.5
Commercial quality (75.0%)	(68.6)
Drawing quality (25.0%)	(22.9)
Alloy	8.5
	100.0
Split by shape within steel type	
Commercial quality	
Hot-rolled strip	34.5
Cold-rolled strip	22.9
Galvanized strip (CQ only)	12.5
Plate	16.0
Total blooms, billets, and slabs[b]	14.1
	100.0
Drawing quality	
Cold-rolled strip	70.0
Blooms, billets, and slabs[b]	30.0
	100.0
Alloy	
Hot-rolled strip	7.1
Cold-rolled strip	1.4
Plate	27.0
Blooms, billets, and slabs[b]	64.5
	100.0

[a] Mill output is 2,340 tons of shape or 2,000 tons of product. For example, the model is required to produce as final output $(2,000 \times 0.915 \times 0.75 \times 0.345 \times 0.3)$ tons per day of CQ, 0.1 inch hot-rolled strip. Total production of this strip will be greater to the extent that the 0.1 inch size is used as input to the cold mill.

[b] Including those serving as proxies for wire rods, structural shapes, etc. Within this category, for each steel, blooms are assumed to be 45 percent, billets 45 percent, and slabs 10 percent.

nesses for each steel type is arbitrary; our only consideration was that the thinner gauges should predominate in DQ cold-rolled and CQ and alloy hot-rolled, while the reverse was assumed to be true for CQ and alloy cold-rolled. The complete set of product mix assumptions is set out in table 7.9.

THE TRUNCATED FINISHING SECTION

The full finishing section described in the preceding pages is rather unwieldy for the investigation of certain questions such as the effect on

TABLE 7.9 Continued

	Proportions of mixes (percentages)
Product mixes	
Split by thickness of strip	
Drawing quality	
Cold-rolled 0.045 inch	20.0
0.015 inch	40.0
0.005 inch	40.0
	100.0
Commercial quality	
Hot-rolled 0.10 inch	30.0
0.075 inch	35.0
0.045 inch	35.0
	100.0
Cold-rolled 0.045 inch	60.0
0.015 inch	35.0
0.005 inch	5.0
	100.0
Alloy	
Hot-rolled 0.10 inch	30.0
0.075 inch	35.0
0.045 inch	35.0
	100.0
Cold-rolled 0.045 inch	75.0
0.015 inch	25.0
	100.0

residuals generation of a change in steel type. Accordingly, we have constructed a truncated version of the finishing process which produces only semifinished shapes and which includes none of the residuals from the full finishing section. This simpler version does include average home scrap and mill scale generation factors as described below. It does not reflect the energy requirements (electricity and fuel for soaking) of the full section and consequently results in an altered energy balance for the plant as a whole. In particular, coke oven gas is available in surplus when the truncated finishing section is used.[59]

Relegating the final milling of semifinished shapes into finished shapes to the background is implicit in this procedure. Residuals generated in casting and final finishing which do not have backward links as input substitutes with prior steel-making processes are not included

[59] In order to distort later comparisons as little as possible, we include the sulfur dioxide residual from the combustion of the surplus gas as well as that from the combustion of the required portion when the truncated finishing module is substituted for full finishing.

in the metal transfer activities. In addition, these vectors obviously do not display an internal materials balance, because semifinished shapes are taken as a proxy for final output, while recoverable home scrap and mill scale are in fact generated in both the semifinished casting and rolling, and in final finishing steps.

We have estimated on the basis of a number of conflicting sources that the overall yield of semifinished shapes from molten metal in this process is about 0.84.[60] The yield in the pouring of ingots is known to be 0.971,[61] so the yield from ingots to semifinished shapes is roughly 0.868. The home scrap generation rate which can be expected when semifinished and finished shapes are fabricated is principally determined by final marketable product composition by shape but can be approximated as 0.27 tons recoverable home scrap per ton molten steel.[62] Therefore, ignoring incidental losses, the overall yield of finished shapes per ton molten steel is equal to 0.73, making the yield of finished shapes from semifinished shapes about 0.866.[63] Finally, we expect to find a maximum of 45 pounds of recoverable mill scale generated in primary and final finishing per ton of molten metal, 9.9 pounds of which come from the semifinishing stage.

[60] See footnote 4.

[61] Battelle Memorial Institute, *Technical and Economic Analysis,* ch. IV.

[62] This is an average of yield figures reported in U.S. Department of Commerce, BDSA, *Iron and Steel Scrap Consumption Problems,* p. 15; Battelle Memorial Institute, *Technical and Economic Analysis,* pp. VI-6, XIII-9; R. Tietig, Jr., and R. J. Kuhl, "Predicting Changes in Steelmaking Processes," p. 82; Darnay and Franklin, *Salvage Markets for Materials in Solid Wastes,* pp. 58–59.

[63] Since the yield of final shapes is 0.73 tons per ton of molten metal, and the yield of semifinished shapes is 0.843 tons per ton of molten metal, the yield of final shapes per ton of semifinished shapes is 0.73 divided by 0.843, or 0.866.

8

PARTICULATE EMISSION CONTROL

In the preceding chapters, the discussion of techniques available for removing residuals from liquid waste streams has been integrated directly into the process descriptions, while the discussion of removing particulates from the various off-gas streams has not. Instead, we have stopped our descriptions of these streams at the outlets of the major process units (for example, at the hood outlet from the BOF). Now, we will concentrate on the gas cleaning equipment assumed either installed or available for installation at the sinter machine, the blast furnace, and the several steel furnaces. We have postponed this discussion because of the substantial similarity of the problems encountered and calculations necessary across the several applications. We include only particulate removal options in the model, for although treatment processes are available to reduce the amount of sulfur dioxide in boiler stack gases, none seem to have been developed specifically for sulfur dioxide removal from steel mill process gases, apart from the coke oven gas desulfurization process discussed earlier. Furthermore, the performance of the power plant sulfur dioxide removal process has so far fallen short of expectations.

Even when we restrict ourselves to particulate removal from gas streams, a number of difficulties arise in ascertaining removal efficiency and cost of treatment equipment. The oft-repeated and frequently abused admonition "no typical practice, no typical shop" encountered in the technical steel-making literature can be applied without risk of exaggeration to the difficult problem of selecting the least-cost combination of gas cleaning equipment (cyclone, wet scrubber, electrostatic precipitator, fabric filter) from the many types which can be installed to remove a given percentage of particulates from a given process off-gas stream. The answer depends upon a maze of operating and performance variables, none of which can be assumed constant for all shops having similar process units. In our model, we have attempted to cut through this tangle, making reasonable assumptions along the way. However, the results should be interpreted with caution.

In constructing our model, we have established two sets of initial conditions or starting points, one being more stringent than the other. Specifically, in the base case we have assumed that for each process unit except the power plant some basic level of removal is accomplished, even in the absence of particulate emission charges or limits. The equipment employed to achieve this has been chosen from inspection of equipment cost comparisons by process application, surveys of installed equipment choices by furnace type, and reported equipment efficiencies.[1] In effect, the base case assumes either an equivalence between the economic level of particulate recovery and the actual level postulated, or the existence of regional environmental quality standards which require at least the postulated first-stage controls. The structure of the base gas cleaning case is displayed below.

Process Unit	Equipment Type	Efficiency (%)
Sinter plant wind box end	Dry cyclone	90
Blast furnace	Dry cyclone plus wet scrubber plus electrostatic precipitator	99
Open hearth furnace	Electrostatic precipitator	97
Basic oxygen furnace	Electrostatic precipitator[2]	94
Electric arc furnace	Fabric filter	97

We also have stipulated a case which assumes that no particulate emission control is required at any of the steel furnaces. We provide add-on options for each steel furnace type to allow the plant to react to the potential value of the recovered steel furnace dust as a purchased ore substitute or to exogenously imposed emission standards. The costs and input quantities for these devices are estimated using exactly the same techniques employed in the base case, except that capital cost becomes relevant for all the steel furnace options. The add-on options for both cases are shown in table 8.1.

[1] J. Varga, Jr., and W. H. Lownie, Jr., *A Systems Analysis Study of the Integrated Iron and Steel Industry*, PB 184 577 (Springfield, Va.: NTIS, May 15, 1969) Table VI-1, "Representative Emission Control Applications in the Integrated Iron and Steel Industry," p. VI-3, as well as appendix D, "Costs and Performance of Control Systems and Control Equipment," were used to infer the most popular equipment type in the base case for each furnace type. Actual efficiencies for these equipment types were derived from information in A. E. Vandegrift and L. J. Shannon, *Particulate Pollutant System Study*, vols. 1–3 (Durham, N.C.: Midwest Research Institute, May 1971); and Sabert Oglesby, Jr. et al., *A Manual of Electrostatic Precipitator Technology, Part II: Application Areas* (Birmingham: Southern Research Institute, August 25, 1970).

[2] Selected as superior to a high efficiency wet scrubber in trial runs not reported in this chapter.

TABLE 8.1 *Optional Gas Cleaning Equipment: Base Case and Steel Furnace Grass Roots Case*

Component	Equipment type	Base case	Grass roots case	Isolated removal efficiency (%)
Sinter plant				
Wind box end	Electrostatic precipitator or	O	O	90
	wet scrubber	O	O	92–95[a]
Discharge end	Fabric filter	O	O	90
Blast furnace	Electrostatic precipitator	O	O	90
Open hearth furnace	Stage I, electrostatic precipitator plus	R	O	97
	Stage II, electrostatic precipitator	O[b]	O	90
Basic oxygen furnace	Stage I, electrostatic precipitator plus	R	O	94
	Stage II, electrostatic precipitator or	O	O	82
	Stage I, wet scrubber plus	n.a.	O	94
	Stage II, wet scrubber	n.a.	O	82
Electric arc furnace	Stage I, fabric filter plus	R	O	97
	Stage II, fabric filter	O	O	90
Power plant	Cyclone 1 or	O	O	60
	Cyclone 2 or	O	O	75
	Cyclone 3	O	O	85

Abbreviations: O indicates that installation and operation are optional; R indicates that installation and operation are required; n.a. indicates not available.

[a] This efficiency is dependent upon the sulfur dioxide content of the wind box gas, i.e., the combination of charge materials chosen.

[b] We assume at the steel furnaces that additional equipment must be of the same type as preexisting equipment.

Our concentration on the steel furnaces in the grass roots case was dictated by the historical pattern of dust recovery and the lack of good cost estimates for equipment installable at the blast furnace itself. The development of the sintering process was originally spurred on by the realization that blast furnace dust had value as a recyclable material, and recovery of such dust has now become almost universal practice in the industry.[3] Another reason for cleaning blast furnace gas has been the desire to render it sufficiently clean for use in the mill as a by-product fuel. It seems pointless at this late date to explore the economic rationale for these long-standing decisions on the basis of the very rough cost estimates available for blast furnace gas cleaning equipment.

[3] Vandegrift and Shannon, *Particulate Pollutant System Study,* vol. 3, *Handbook of Emission Properties,* pp. 121 and 151.

GAS CLEANING VECTOR CONSTRUCTION

There are a number of reasons why the particulate removal cost estimation problem is complicated. Most of them revolve around the difficulties of calculating the actual volume of gas passing through the collector per unit time (or per unit production). Thus, the information we generally have concerning a process unit's gas and dust generation is the weight of the dust (and sometimes of the gas as well) and the temperature at the process unit exit. The first problem is to convert the gas weight (calculated or assumed) into volumetric terms. This depends on knowledge of the makeup of the gas. The actual cubic feet (acf) to be treated will then depend primarily on temperature unless there is a problem of large time variation in gas flow rates. At the BOF, for example, the peak gas flow rate may be four or more times greater than the average value for the steel-making cycle. These peak-to-average flow ratios are not easy to find in the literature, but clearly the equipment must be sized (hence the capital cost estimated for the grass roots case) on the basis of peak flows, even though other inputs, such as electricity, may be assumed to be related to average gas flows.

In this study, peak-to-average gas flow rate factors have been chosen which are consonant with those reported by Varga and Lownie, and other sources for shops of roughly the same steel output capacity.[4] Even though the appropriate peak flow rate may be known, the capital cost estimation problem remains, because there is an unfortunate disagreement in the literature regarding the functional forms and parameter values which relate installed capital costs to peak actual cubic feet per minute. Specifically, Battelle capital costs range from four to ten times higher than other available capital cost estimates for similar facilities.[5] Although the weight of authority seems to be against the independent estimates derived by Battelle from a small sample, inspection of

[4] Varga and Lownie, *A Systems Analysis Study,* appendix D.

[5] The following sources report similar gas treatment equipment capital cost estimating functions which generally yield costs lower than those reported by Varga and Lownie in *A Systems Analysis Study;* Vandegrift and Shannon, *Particulate Pollutant System Study,* vol. 3, appendix A, pp. 547–600; James E. Roberson and J. S. Henderson, "Planning for Air Pollution Control," *Plant Engineering,* vol. 41 (November 27, 1970); TRW Systems Group, *Air Quality Implementation Planning Program,* vol. 1: *Operator's Manual,* PB 198 299 (Springfield, Va.: NTIS, November 1970), ch. 5, pp. 35–42; Sabert Oglesby, Jr. and Grady B. Nichols, *A Manual of Electrostatic Precipitator Technology,* PB 196 381 (Springfield, Va.: NTIS, August 25, 1970); Norman Edminsten and Francis L. Bunyard, "A Systematic Procedure for Determining the Cost of Controlling Particulate Emissions from Industrial Sources," *Journal of the Air Pollution Control Association,* vol. 20 (July 1970) pp. 446–452; U.S. Department of Health, Education and Welfare, Public Health Service, NAPCA Publication No. AP-S1, *Control Techniques for Particulate Air Pollutants* (January 1969), pp. 155–182.

the alternative functions shows that they all originate in a single source published in 1969 by the National Air Pollution Control Administration (NAPCA), so in reality we are comparing only two conflicting sources, one which specifically refers to steel industry applications and one which does not. Therefore, in spite of the caveats expressed in the Battelle study, we have employed their gas cleaning equipment capital cost data whenever possible.

Electricity requirements for electrostatic precipitator fans and field, as well as wet scrubber, cyclone, and baghouse fans can all be estimated from the general electricity requirement equations and control device data presented in TRW, *Air Quality Implementation Planning Program* (p. 5–43 and table 7.5–2, p. 67). This publication also provides us with labor hours required per hour of operation of the various facilities over four gas flow rate ranges. Taking the midpoint of each range and plotting labor hours per hour of operation as a function of gas flow (in acfm) on a double log scale for the different equipment types gives us smooth relationships which can be used for each process unit gas flow.

GAS CLEANING AT SPECIFIC PROCESS UNITS

The calculations behind gas generation, flow rate, dust loading, equipment cost, and removal efficiency can now be examined in greater detail.

The Boiler Plant

The steam-generating boilers in the utilities component of the model are designed to burn a number of purchased and by-product fuels, all of which produce different particulate emissions per pound of steam output.[6] No treatment of these off gases is required either in our base or grass roots cases, because the recovered dusts have no value as a recyclable material.

We postulate an average (and peak) flow rate of 100,000 actual cubic feet per minute through all of these facilities. This rate is what would be expected from a plant capable of supplying between 400–600 megawatt hours of electricity daily, implying, for example, about 200 tons of coal consumed per day.[7]

---

[6] See appendix A.

[7] This estimate coincides with the flow rate reported by Varga and Lownie, in *A Systems Analysis Study*, appendix D, p. 53, for a power plant boiler of identical capacity. Since coal combustion, after allowing for excess air and temperature, evolves about 900,000 actual cubic feet of gas per ton, about 18 million actual cubic feet of dust-laden gas would be evolved per day. Dividing by 1,440 minutes of operation per day brings us close to our originally assumed flow rate.

Particulate loadings in the off gases from natural gas and coke oven gas combustion are insignificant, so no treatment is provided for them. Likewise, high efficiency (85 percent) particulate removal is necessary only for off gases from coal combustion, because these gases are very high in particulate concentrations compared to those evolved in the other fuel combustion activities. The equipment characteristics and costs associated with gas treatment in steam generation are set out in table 8.2.[8]

Sinter Plant Wind Box and Discharge Ends

At the sinter plant, separate control units are usually applied to the wind box and discharge-end gas streams.[9] Our model follows this pattern, and we assume that a dry cyclone with 90 percent removal efficiency is installed (and must be operated) on the wind box end, while assuming that no equipment is in place at the discharge end.

The sinter wind box gas emission is assumed to be 170,000 standard cubic feet of gas per ton of sinter produced in each sinter-producing activity. This gas generation rate is taken to be invariant across all activities because, as discussed in the text, productivity is assumed invariant and, in addition, combustion calculations based upon the gas evolved from the carbon and limestone in the assorted charges showed very little variation in gas generation between low, medium, and high limestone addition practices. Assuming a wind box off-gas temperature of $325°$ F, about 257,000 actual cubic feet of gas evolve per ton of sinter. At an average production rate of 1.7 tons of sinter per minute (a plant with a daily output of 2,450 tons of sinter), 437,000 actual cubic feet of gas flow through the collection device per minute.[10]

Two separate types of control devices can be installed to increase overall dust removal from wind box gases above 90 percent: an electrostatic

[8] All of the cost estimates, including electricity, labor, and capital, have been calculated from information presented in TRW Systems Group, *Air Quality Implementation Planning Program*, chapter 5, pp. 35–44 and chapter 7, p. 67. The capital cost estimate derived from the TRW estimating functions has been magnified by a factor of four. Doing so puts our boiler plant gas treatment equipment costs in the neighborhood of those reported by Varga and Lownie, *A Systems Analysis Study*, appendix D, p. 53, but differentiated by efficiency.

[9] Varga and Lownie, *A Systems Analysis Study*, appendix D, p. 17.

[10] Although reported estimates of the volume of wind box gas evolved per unit product and per unit time vary widely, figures roughly correspondent to those employed here can be calculated from information in S. H. Brooks and W. J. Calvert, "External Pollution from an Iron and Steelworks and Measures Towards its Reduction" in *Air and Water Pollution in the Iron and Steel Industry*, Special Report No. 61 (London: British Iron and Steel Institute, 1958), pp. 5–15; R. Jackson and R. A. Granville, "Measurement of Dust in Flue Gases," in *Air and Water Pollution*, pp. 119–128; Organization for Economic Cooperation and Development, *Air Pollution in the Iron and Steel Industry* (Paris: Organization for Economic Cooperation and Development, 1963), p. 52.

TABLE 8.2   *Boiler Plant Gas Treatment Characteristics: Add-on Dry Cyclones*

(equipment size averages 10^3 acfm)

Fuel burned	Efficiency (%)	Inlet dust loading (lb./ave. 10^3 acf)	Electricity requirement (kWh/ave. 10^3 acf)	Capital charge[a] (¢/ave. 10^3 acf)	Total cost[b] (¢/lb. removed)
Acid sludge and fore- runnings	60	0.002	0.007	0.028	63.3
	75	0.002	0.010	0.046	81.7
Tar	60	0.040	0.007	0.028	3.2
	75	0.040	0.010	0.046	4.1
Fuel oil	60	0.002	0.007	0.028	60.8
	75	0.002	0.010	0.046	78.7
Metallurgical coal	60	0.102	0.007	0.028	1.2
	75	0.102	0.010	0.046	1.6
	85	0.102	0.013	0.060	1.9

[a] Based on a capital recovery factor assuming a 10 percent interest rate and a 15-year equipment life.

[b] Electricity has been valued at $0.01 per kWh and labor at $5.00 per hour. The labor requirement is taken to be 0.083 hours per million actual cubic feet.

precipitator or a high energy wet scrubber. In power plant applications, precipitator removal efficiency appears to be adversely affected by low sulfur dioxide concentrations in the off gases.[11] In sintering applications, high lime content of sinter dust in the gas stream seems to have a similar effect on efficiency by increasing dust resistivity.[12] In our model we reflect only the first influence because of lack of good data on the second. We do so by assuming that the precipitator can remove 95 percent of the dust from gases having sulfur dioxide concentrations greater than 260 ppm, and only 92 percent from gases having lower concentrations.

The sulfur dioxide content of the wind box gases does not affect wet scrubber performance, and its efficiency is the same in all wind box gas applications. However, the wet scrubber does generate a liquid effluent containing sulfur compounds.

At the discharge end, 40,000 standard cubic feet of sulfur-free gas are assumed to be generated per ton of output. At a temperature of 135° F, this amounts to 46,000 actual cubic feet per ton, or 78,000 actual cubic feet per minute. A high efficiency fabric filter appears to be the least-cost method of dust removal in this application.[13]

[11] J. T. Reese and J. Greco, "Experience with Electrostatic Fly Ash Collection Equipment Serving Steam Electric Generating Plants," *Journal of the Air Pollution Control Association*, vol. 18 (August 1968), pp. 523–528.

[12] Oglesby and Nichols, *A Manual of Electrostatic Precipitator Technology: Part II*, p. 199.

[13] Varga and Lownie, *A Systems Analysis Study*, appendix D, pp. 21–23.

TABLE 8.3 Sinter Plant Gas Treatment Equipment Characteristics

Practice and equipment[a]	Efficiencies (%)	Inlet dust loading (lb./ave. 10³ acf)	Electricity requirement (kWh/ave. 10³ acf)	Labor requirement (hr./ave. 10⁶ acf)	Capital charge[b] (¢/ave. 10³ acf)	Total cost[c] (¢/lb. removed)
Wind box end						
Stage I using base cyclone						
All burdens	90	0.121	0.013	0.032	None	0.27
Stage II using add-on electrostatic precipitator						
Low sulfur burdens	92	0.012	0.007	0.104	0.068	11.2
High sulfur burdens	95	0.012	0.007	0.104	0.068	11.5
Stage II using add-on wet scrubber						
All burdens	95	0.012	0.065	0.073	0.078	15.7
Discharge end using add-on fabric filter						
All burdens	95	0.496	0.016	0.090	0.127	0.4

[a] Equipment size (average and peak 10³ acfm) is 437 at the wind box end and 78 at the discharge end.
[b] Based on a capital recovery factor assuming a 10 percent interest rate and a 15-year equipment life.
[c] Electricity has been valued at $0.01 per kWh and labor at $5.00 per hour.

These characteristics, along with the costs of treatment equipment in sinter plant applications, are displayed in table 8.3.[14]

The Blast Furnace

As already mentioned, the flue dust entrained in the blast furnace top gas is ordinarily subjected to a high degree of removal because this dust is valuable as an input to the sinter machines and because it is necessary to prevent the dust from entering the blast furnace stoves and the boilers elsewhere in the plant where the gas is used as a fuel. A survey of the literature revealed that established plants generally clean the gas in three stages: a preliminary cleaning stage employing dry cyclone collectors, a primary cleaning stage employing wet scrubbers, and a secondary cleaning stage employing electrostatic precipitators. The first two stages are used almost universally throughout the industry, and the third is common practice at a majority of furnaces.[15] In our model the dry dust catcher has an efficiency of 60 percent, the wet scrubber an efficiency of 80 percent, and the electrostatic precipitator an efficiency of 90 percent, giving an overall removal of 99.2 percent in the base case.[16]

In chapter 5 we identified sixty-six separate blast furnace activities which generate sixty-six different volumes of blast furnace gas. For simplicity in the model, equipment costs have been calculated for eight different sizes, each based on the average gas volume generated by a class of burdens based on iron content and sinter limestone content. Standard cubic feet of off gas have been converted to actual cubic feet on the basis of a gas temperature of 300° F.

[14] Labor and electricity requirements for all sinter plant gas cleaning equipment applications have been calculated from TRW Systems Group, *Air Quality Implementation Planning Program*. Capital cost has been obtained, where necessary, from a logarithmic plot of capital cost as a function of gas flow based on data in Varga and Lownie, *A Systems Analysis Study*, appendix D.

[15] Jean J. Schueneman et al. *Air Pollution Aspects of the Iron and Steel Industry*, U.S. Department of Health, Education and Welfare, Public Health Service publication No. 999-AP-1 (June 1963), p. 42.

[16] These typical stepwise removal efficiencies and the overall removal efficiency agree with those given by Hayse H. Black and Gerald N. McDermott, "Industrial Waste Guide—Blast Furnace Department of the Steel Industry," *Sewage and Industrial Wastes*, vol. 26 (August 1954), pp. 976–990; J. M. Uys and J. W. Kirkpatrick, "The Beneficiation of Raw Material in the Steel Industry and Its Effect upon Air Pollution Control," *Journal of the Air Pollution Control Association*, vol. 12, no. 1 (January 1963), p. 22; and Vandegrift and Shannon, *Particulate Pollutant Systems Study*, vol. 3, p. 120.

We assume that further dust removal from the gas above the base case level will be undertaken at the centralized blast furnace location rather than at the numerous points where the gas is burned. For simplicity, all particulates not removed from the blast furnace gas are treated as a point source emission from the blast furnace itself in the model, rather than as an emission from the combustion vectors employing the gas.

TABLE 8.4   *Blast Furnace Gas Treatment Equipment Characteristics*

Practice and equipment type	Equip-ment size (ave. and peak 10^3 acfm)	Inlet dust loading (lb./ave. 10^3 acf)	Labor re-quirement (hr./ave. 10^6 acf)	Capital[a] charge (¢/ave. 10^3 acf)	Total[b] cost (¢/lb. removed)
Stage I using base cyclone, wet scrub-ber, and electro-static precipitator					
Unscreened ore burdens	178	2.38	0.29	None	0.06
Screened ore burdens	178	1.09	0.29	None	0.14
Low limestone con-tent sinters	220	0.22	0.30	None	0.72
Medium limestone content sinters	234	0.23	0.29	None	0.64
High limestone content sinters	228	0.25	0.29	None	0.62
Pellets	254	0.10	0.27	None	1.41
Stage II using add-on electric precipitator					
Unscreened ore burdens	178	0.02	0.14	0.090	9.6
Screened ore burdens	178	0.01	0.14	0.090	21.1
Low limestone con-tent sinters	220	...	0.15	0.085	101.5
Medium limestone content sinters	234	...	0.14	0.084	94.6
High limestone content sinters	228	...	0.14	0.084	89.8
Pellets	254	...	0.13	0.082	13.6

Note: Ellipses (. . .) indicate less than 0.01 pounds per 1,000 acf.

[a] Based on a capital recovery factor assuming a 10 percent interest rate and a 15-year equipment life.

[b] Electricity has been valued at $0.01 per kWh and labor at $5.00 per hour. For all practices at both stages, the electricity requirement is taken to be 0.006 kWh/10^3 acf.

Gas flow rates can be obtained directly from the gas volumes per unit output by applying the inverse of the productivity coefficients (that is, tons of hot metal per hour) described in chapter 5. In table 8.4, the requirements of the facilities as well as the flow rates are displayed, after averaging over iron content for brevity of presentation.[17]

[17] All utility calculations have been performed using information in TRW Systems Group, *Air Quality Implementation Planning Program,* ch. 5, pp. 35–44; ch. 7, p. 67. Labor costs have been estimated on the basis of the total gas flow for both furnaces. That is, we assume one large gas cleaning installation for the multiple furnace shop rather than a separate set of devices for each furnace. In addition, because furnace top pressure is utilized to provide power for scrubbing, with a sufficient margin of pressure to distribute the gas through the rest of the system, no fan electricity requirement has been calculated for the cleaning equipment, so the electricity requirement applies to the electrostatic precipitator field only. See, Edward Basse, "Gases Cleaned by the Use of Scrubbers," *Blast Furnace and Steel Plant,* vol. 44, no. 11 (November 1956), pp. 1307–1312.

The add-on precipitator for each of the eight subsets of blast furnace gas is costed as a high efficiency piece of equipment requiring a high installation cost. Because Varga and Lownie provide no information on capital costs for such equipment in blast furnace applications, we have resorted to TRW capital cost estimating functions in this case. However, the result has been increased by a factor of two in order to make it consistent with the higher estimates reported by Varga and Lownie for other steel mill precipitator applications.

GAS TREATMENT AT THE STEEL FURNACES

The assumptions regarding gas generation, volume and weight increase, equipment type and efficiency for each steel furnace and practice are briefly explained in the following sections.

Open Hearth

Electrostatic precipitators have been the overwhelming choice for particulate control on open hearths.[18] Wet scrubbers are not economically attractive unless the shop either has no waste heat boilers or the existing boilers are unable to lower gas temperatures sufficiently to warrant precipitator installation. The corrosion problem attributable to sulfur dioxide and water in combination also militates against the use of wet scrubbers at the open hearth.[19] For these reasons no equipment type comparisons are included in the open hearth component of the model; an electrostatic precipitator is the only particulate control device provided for this application. Its assumed removal efficiency in the first stage is 97 percent.[20]

It is further assumed for simplicity that all ore practices (50–50, 70–30) have an identical dust loading which is lower than the dust loading for all oxygen practices (50–50; 70–30). In order to obtain a single dust loading across hot metal practices, the pounds of dust and gas obviously must move together in a compensating manner when one varies. Although this may not be exactly true in practice, it is true that the amount of excess air provided for fuel combustion makes up a large portion of

---

[18] Varga and Lownie, *A Systems Analysis Study*, ch. 6, p. 3. Of ninety-seven control applications cataloged by Varga and Lownie, ninety-three were of the precipitator type.

[19] Basse, "Use of Scrubbers," p. 1310.

[20] Vandegrift and Shannon, *Particulate Pollutant System Study*, vol. 3, p. 121.

the evolved open hearth gas, and would not have to vary greatly within any given practice in order for the above assumption to hold.[21]

As previously noted in chapter 6, our open hearth shop has nine furnaces, each having 125 tons per heat capacity. From the Battelle Institute balances, we know that approximately 3,700 pounds of gas are generated per ingot ton in ore practice, and 2,500 in oxygen practice.[22] Furthermore, the gas is calculated to have a volume of 16.4 standard cubic feet per pound (allowing for some steam augmentation). Its actual temperature is assumed to be 500° F, giving 30.3 actual cubic feet per pound. Allowing for air inleakage of 30 percent in the actual evolved gas volume,[23] the average volume of gas evolved per ingot ton amounts to 146,000 acf in ore practice and 99,000 acf in oxygen practice. The actual volume of gas flowing through the collector per minute is simply the actual cubic feet evolved per unit output multiplied by the productivity of each practice, expressed in tons per minute. This average flow rate has been converted to a peak shop flow rate for capital cost estimating by employing a factor of 1.33.[24] Utilities are related to average, not peak flow. The characteristics of the open hearth gas treatment system are set out in table 8.5.[25] All recovered dusts can either be disposed of as landfill or rerouted to the sinter plant as a substitute for low iron, low sulfur purchased ore fines.

[21] See the materials balances for open hearth operations in Battelle Memorial Institute, *Technical and Economic Analysis of the Impact of Recent Developments in Steelmaking Practices on the Supplying Industries* (Columbus: Battelle Memorial Institute, 1964), ch. IV.

[22] Battelle Memorial Institute, *Technical and Economics Analysis*, ch. IV, pp. 17–18.

[23] Gerhard Derge, ed., *Basic Open Hearth Steelmaking*, 3rd ed. (New York: American Institute of Mining, Metallurgical and Petroleum Engineers, 1964), pp. 23, 108, 845–848, 875–877.

[24] See, W. T. Purvance, "Atmospheric Pollution Control," *Chemical Engineering*, vol. 55, no. 7 (July 1959), p. 52 for a discussion of peaking and combined furnace gas collection in an open hearth shop. As a check on our peak values, see Thomas M. Barnes and H. W. Lownie, *A Cost Analysis of Air Pollution Controls in the Integrated Iron and Steel Industry*, PB 184 576 (Springfield, Va.: NTIS, May 1969), appendix C, p. 38.

[25] The articles upon which our remarks about open hearth gas cleaning are based include: David R. Anderson, "Air Quality Standards and their Application to Steelmaking Operations," *Iron and Steel Engineer*, vol. 46 (September 1969), pp. 76–85; C. A. Bishop et al. "Successful Cleaning of Open Hearth Exhaust Gas with a High Energy Venturi Scrubber," *Journal of the Air Pollution Control Association*, vol. 11 (February 1961), pp. 83–87; Carl U. Broman and Ronald R. Iseli, "The Control of Open Hearth Stack Emission with Venturi-type Scrubbers," *Iron and Steel Engineer*, vol. 45 (January 1968), pp. 128–133; W. A. Dickinson and J. L. Worth, "Open Hearth Waste-Gas Cleaning Systems," *Journal of Metals*, vol. 17 (March 1965), pp. 261–266; A. C. Elliott and A. J. Lafreniere, "Collection of Metallurgical Fumes from Oxygen Lanced Open Hearth Furnaces," *Journal of Metals*, vol. 18 (June 1966), pp. 743–747; and J. E. Johnson "Wet Washing of Open Hearth Gases," *Iron and Steel Engineer*, vol. 44 (February 1967), pp. 96–98.

TABLE 8.5   *Open Hearth Furnace Gas Treatment Equipment Characteristics*

Practice and gas treatment equipment type	Equipment size (ave. 10^3 acfm)	Equipment size (peak 10^3 acfm)	Inlet dust loading (lb./ave. 10^3 acf)	Labor requirement (hr./ave. 10^6 acf)	Capital charge[a] (¢/ave. 10^3 acf)	Total cost[b] (¢/lb. removed)
Stage I: Base [or grass roots] case, electrostatic precipitator[c]						
Ore practice	286	293	0.082	0.130	0.190	0.92 [3.34]
Oxygen practice	241	322	0.223	0.137	0.200	0.34 [1.27]
Stage II: Add-on electrostatic precipitator[c]						
Ore practice	286	293	0.002	0.130	0.190	[119.5]
Oxygen practice	241	322	0.007	0.137	0.200	[63.8]

Note: Total costs in brackets are for cases in which installation is optional.

[a] Based on a capital recovery factor assuming a 10 percent interest rate and a 15-year equipment life.

[b] Electricity has been valued at $0.01 per kWh and labor at $5.00 per hour.

[c] In all cases, electricity requirements measure 0.007 in kWh per average 10^3 acf.

Basic Oxygen

High energy wet scrubber and electrostatic precipitator gas treatment alternatives have both been programmed as options in our grass roots steel furnace model for BOF gas treatment because it appears from industry practice that at this furnace no single equipment type is clearly superior to the others.[26]

Two-step treatment is provided for by a first-level precipitator or wet scrubber designed to remove 94.4 percent of particulates generated (including some removal in ancillary chambers), and a second-level precipitator or wet scrubber designed to give an overall level of removal of 99 percent by removing 82 percent of the particulates not recovered in the first stage.[27] The first level becomes the base case situation after solution of the choice problem.

The electrostatic precipitator alternative. Reference to the simplified flow diagram of BOF gas treatment system alternatives (figure 6.2) shows hood effluent gases entering an evaporation chamber (or spark box) in

[26] Varga and Lownie, *A Systems Analysis Study,* ch. 5, p. 3, show in their tabulation of emission control applications that of thirty-eight BOF furnaces surveyed, fifteen had wet scrubbers while twenty-three had precipitators.

[27] No equipment cross combinations are allowed, such as a first-stage precipitator plus a second-stage wet scrubber or vice versa.

the electrostatic precipitator (ESP) system. The primary purpose here is to cool the hood gases with water sprays to about 500–600° F.[28] Pains are taken to evaporate all of the water sprayed, so that the only discharge is vapor-bearing gas at 500° F. A dust dropout chamber, in which the larger particles fall out of the gas stream, follows the evaporation chamber. This recovered dust is usually conveyed to storage and later recycled to the sinter plant. We also allow for landfill disposal for this dust.

The calculation of the quantity of water required to lower the gas temperature from 2,000° F to 500° F is straightforward and is based on the assumed specific heat of the gas (0.25 Btu per pound per degree Fahrenheit), the latent heat of evaporation of water, and the heat required for superheating steam from 212° F to 500° F. The result, 0.297 pounds of water (or 0.0356 gallons), is added per pound of incoming gas. The weight of exit gas is then 1.297 times the inlet weight.[29]

Because the dust-laden gas is transported through the type of hooding and ducting system assumed here, considerable agglomeration results before the dust enters the control device. We assume that 10 percent of the dust falls out in the dropout chamber.[30]

The gas enters the first-stage precipitator on leaving the evaporation chamber. Although reported design efficiencies for precipitators in this application range as high as 99 percent,[31] we employ here a first-stage precipitator with an efficiency of removal of 93.8 percent to produce direct comparability with the wet scrubber alternative discussed subsequently.

In precipitator applications, 1,370 pounds of gas enter the facility per ingot ton of molten metal in 70–30 practice, and 1,980 in 90–10 practice. One pound of the gas is equivalent to 13.1 scf and, at a temperature of 500° F, to 25.55 acf. Therefore, 35,000 acf per ingot ton enter the precipitator in 70–30 practice, and 51,000 in 90–10 practice. Given a rough production rate of 2.9 ingot tons per minute, we have 102,000 acf per minute entering in 70–30 practice, and 148,000 in 90–10 practice.[32] The

[28] H. C. Henshen, "Wet *vs.* Dry Gas Cleaning in the Steel Industry," *Journal of the Air Pollution Control Association,* vol. 18, no. 5 (May 1968), p. 339.

[29] As a check, see W. Muhlrad, "Removal of Dust from Basic Oxygen Furnace Brown Fumes by Means of Bag Filters," *Stahl und Eisen,* vol. 82 (December 1962), pp. 1579–1584, trans. Henry Brutcher (Altadena, California: Henry Brutcher Technical Translations, No. 5768), p. 17. Muhlrad reports that 26 gallons of water per ingot ton are consumed in spray cooling.

[30] Ibid., p. 16.

[31] Oglesby and Nichols, *A Manual of Electrostatic Precipitator Technology,* Part II, p. 559.

[32] The equipment is actually sized for peak flows which we assume are 3.9 times average flows. See, for example, Varga and Lownie, *A Systems Analysis,* appendix D, pp. 33–34. Capital costs are based on peak flow rates and are taken from the same source.

utility and capital requirements coming from these gas flow rates are displayed in table 8.6.[33]

The wet scrubber alternative. If the wet scrubbing alternative is to be used, after gas combustion (with 75 percent excess air) in the furnace hood, the hot dirty gases at 2,000° F enter a quenching chamber where they are cooled to about 175° F.[34] A considerable quantity of larger, heavier particles in the gas are removed at this stage. Lacking adequate data, we can only guess that the dropout percentage is about thirty percent. The quenching water containing this removed dust is then circulated to a thickener where a slurry is formed. The underflow slurry can then be filtered by a vacuum filter–air dryer system to form a recoverable filter cake (a substitute for purchased ore fines).

The total gross cooling water requirement is 6.80 pounds of water per pound of gas, and the gas is augmented by 0.29 pounds of water vapor per pound of gas entering the chamber. This gross water requirement would equal the net requirement if we had a once-through water system. However, in actual practice these systems employ recirculation of the water stream after some removal of solids in a clarifier–thickener, so that the steady-state fresh water requirement is considerably less than it would be in a once-through system. For the moment let us postpone consideration of the water problem and move on to the next stage of removal, the high energy wet scrubber.

In this unit, a high percentage of the remaining particles in the gas stream become entrained in water droplets after the two are brought rather violently together by the design of the scrubber. Much of the liquid is then removed from the gas in a separator where the droplets collect on surfaces and drain into a collection sump. At the wet scrubber itself, the gross water requirement is estimated to be 2.74 pounds of water per pound of entering gas for the first stage and 1.62 pounds of water per pound of entering gas for the second stage.[35]

Calculations similar to those explained in the preceding precipitator section have been made to estimate the actual average and peak volume of gas which passes through the device. For example, 1,016 pounds of gas enter the facility per ingot ton of output, which, at 12.7 scf per pound, is equivalent to 13,000 scf per ingot ton. At a temperature of 175° F, this

[33] Electricity and labor requirements have been calculated from the functions in TRW Systems Group, *Air Quality Implementation Planning Program,* ch. 5, pp. 35–44; ch. 7, p. 67.

[34] See Henschen, "Wet *vs.* Dry Gas Cleaning," p. 341.

[35] For the first stage, we use the high estimate from R. G. Winklepleck, "Conditioning and Wet Cleaning BOF Exhaust Gases," *Iron and Steel Engineer,* vol. 46 (September 1969), p. 89, who claims that 6–20 gallons are required per 1,000 acf of gas flow. We have converted to pounds of water per pound of gas, using a gas volume factor of 16.4 acf per pound. For the second stage, we assume the requirement to be 13.5 gallons per 1,000 acf.

TABLE 8.6 *Basic Oxygen Furnace Gas Treatment Equipment Characteristics*

Practice and gas treatment equipment type	Equipment size (ave. 10^3 acfm)	Equipment size (peak 10^3 acfm)	Inlet dust loading (lb./ave. 10^3 acf)	Electricity requirement (kWh/ave. 10^3 acf)	Labor requirement (hr./ave. 10^6 acf)	Water requirement[a] (gal./10^3 acf)	Capital charge[b] (¢/ave. 10^3 acf)	Total cost[c] (¢/lb. removed)
Stage I								
Base [or grass roots] electrostatic precipitator								
70% Hot metal practices	102	399	1.16	0.006	0.204	1.5	[0.66]	0.09 [0.63]
90% Hot metal practices	148	580	0.96	0.006	0.169	1.5	[0.60]	0.09 [0.68]
Base [or grass roots] wet scrubber								
70% Hot metal practices	49	191	1.88	0.130	0.232	68	[1.20]	0.10 [0.57]
90% Hot metal practices	71	277	1.56	0.130	0.193	68	[1.08]	0.10 [0.62]
Stage II								
Add-on electrostatic precipitator								
All practices	125	490	0.07	0.006	0.187	0	0.66	14.0
Add-on wet scrubber								
All practices	60	234	0.14	0.130	0.209	13.5	1.20	12.4

Note: Bracketed entries refer to costs assignable in the grass roots case.

[a] Includes water for gas cooling in the Stage I electrostatic precipitator system, and for both gas cooling and gas treatment in the Stage I wet scrubber system. Stage II includes gas treatment water requirements alone.

[b] Based on a capital recovery factor assuming a 10 percent interest rate and a 15-year life.

[c] Electricity has been valued at $0.01 per kWh and labor at $5.00 per hour.

amounts to 17,000 acf per ingot ton. Given the same production rate as before, we have 49,000 acf per minute entering the facility. The electricity, labor, and capital costs associated with the wet system flow rates are displayed in table 8.6, along with those for the precipitator system.[36]

Electric Arc

Fabric filters are by far the most widely used type of gas cleaning equipment in electric arc furnace applications.[37] We assume a first-stage fabric filter with a removal efficiency of 97 percent,[38] and allow an add-on second-stage installation to have a typical efficiency of 90 percent, yielding an overall combined efficiency of 99.7 percent. Recovered dusts are allowed to substitute for high iron, low sulfur content ore at the ratio of 2.17 to 1 in ore practices at the electric arc furnace. These dusts can also be sent to landfill at a cost of $2.00 per ton. Incidentally, it is hard to imagine why much dust at all would be recovered at electric arc furnaces located away from blast furnace shops, in the absence of environmental legislation. At these furnaces there would be a nearly complete lack of recycling alternatives, especially in the oxygen-lanced practices in which direct oxygen is substituted for ore.

The cost of particulate removal again depends on gas composition, temperature, and flow rate. Very little air is admitted to the electric arc furnace during meltdown, and during this time the furnace operates under an atmosphere which is predominantly carbon monoxide. After meltdown, if oxygen is lanced into the furnace, the atmosphere is also dominated by carbon monoxide, often as much as 80–85 percent.[39] However, gas composition varies with operating practice and period of the heat cycle. We assume that the average carbon monoxide content of the gas over the heat cycle is 30 percent.

The theoretical gas weight (and volume) calculated on the foregoing basis is still considerably less than the weight (and volume) which will pass through the dust collector because of provision of excess air in the combustion reaction as well as air inleakage to aid in cooling the gas to

[36] When the wet scrubber is used, the relevant constants employed in calculation of the dust loading at the scrubber inlet are: 6.05 pounds of gas per pound of original gas, 12.7 scf per pound of gas, 1.29 acf per standard cubic foot, and 30 percent dust removal in quenching.

[37] Varga and Lownie, in *A Systems Analysis Study*, ch. 6, p. 3, report twenty-nine fabric filters used for electric arc furnace gas cleaning out of a sample of thirty-nine installations.

[38] Vandegrift and Shannon *Particulate Pollutant System Study*, vol. 3, p. 164. The same authors report an application of control of 0.79 nationwide (p. 121).

[39] Oglesby and Nichols, *A Manual of Electrostatic Precipitator Technology*, Part II, p. 569; Varga and Lownie, *A Systems Analysis Study*, appendix C.

an acceptable temperature for cleaning. The actual amount of excess combustion air and air inleakage required depends on complex furnace hood design criteria which differ widely among shops. Most of the gas flow in electric arcs appears to be made up of atmospheric air drawn through the hood openings. This has been reported to range from five to ten times the original dirty gas volume for baghouse installations.[40] Although the authors neglect to inform us whether these factors should be applied to the actual or standard volume of gas either before or after combustion, we infer the volume of ambient air required by applying the high factor of 10 to the actual cubic feet of postcombustion gas, assuming that this factor accounts for both excess and cooling air. Taking the average furnace exit temperature of the combusted gas at 2,000° F,[41] and therefore the volume as 62 acf per pound, the actual cubic feet of gas entering the filter per ingot ton at 375° F can be obtained by multiplying the pounds of combusted gas per ingot ton by 620. From the steel furnace burdening submodel discussed in chapter 6, we find an average of 78 pounds of gas evolved in electric arc operations per ingot, after allowing for combustion of the carbon monoxide in the gas. Allowing for the increase in this volume due to the factors discussed above, roughly 50,000 acf of gas enter the precipitator per ingot ton of output. Adjusting for furnace productivity, this translates into an average shop flow of 99,000 acf per minute in ore practice and 106,000 in oxygen practice. The costs of the treatment system based on these flow rates appear in table 8.7.[42]

AUXILIARY EQUIPMENT REQUIRED BY WET CLEANING SYSTEMS

The water used to remove particulates from the gas stream entering a wet scrubber contains most of the particulates which otherwise would have exited to the atmosphere. Although this water could conceivably be directly discharged to the watercourse, thus resulting in the transference of an almost equivalent amount of solids discharge to a different receiving medium, recirculating systems involving solids removal and reuse of the water in the scrubber are more common.

[40] J. R. Brough and W. A. Carter, "Air Pollution Control of an Electric Furnace Steelmaking Shop," *Journal of the Air Pollution Control Association*, vol. 22, no. 3 (March 1972), p. 170.

[41] Oglesby and Nichols, *A Manual of Electrostatic Precipitator Technology*, Part II, p. 569.

[42] Electricity and labor requirements have been calculated from the TRW Systems Groups, *Air Quality Implementation Planning Program Functions*, ch. 5, pp. 35–44, ch. 7, p. 67. Capital costs as a function of shopwide flow have been estimated from data in Varga and Lownie, *A Systems Analysis Study*, appendix D, p. 43. We employed a peak-to-average flow factor of 1.7 to obtain reasonable peak flow rates.

TABLE 8.7 *Electric Arc Furnace Gas Treatment Equipment Characteristics*

Practice and gas treatment equipment type	Equipment size (ave. 10^3 acfm)	Equipment size (peak 10^3 acfm)	Inlet dust loading (lb./ave. 10^3 acf)	Labor requirement (hr./ave. 10^6 acf)	Capital[a] charge (¢/ave. 10^3 acf)	Total cost[b] (¢/lb. removed)
Stage I						
Base [or grass roots] fabric filter						
Ore practice	99	168	0.215	0.186	[0.195]	0.53 [15.09]
Oxygen practice	106	179	0.289	0.180	[0.193]	0.38 [11.66]
Stage II						
Add-on fabric filter						
Ore practice	99	168	0.006	0.186	[0.195]	[54.16]
Oxygen practice	106	179	0.009	0.180	[0.193]	[40.16]

Note: Brackets refer to cases where installation is optional.

[a] Based on a capital recovery factor assuming a 10 percent interest rate and a 15-year life.

[b] Electricity has been valued at $0.01 per kWh and labor at $5.00 per hour. For both stages and practices, the electricity requirement is taken to be 0.016 kWh per 1,000 acf.

We have assumed that wet particulate removal systems (gas washers or scrubbers as they are called) must be equipped with devices for recirculating the washer water. This assumption reflects two judgments.

1. Given the existence of a sinter machine at the plant, the costs of recirculation, with implied recovery of the captured flue dust, probably balance very closely with the value of the dust as an ore substitute. The information available to us on recirculation costs was too crude to permit us to make an accurate determination of whether or not recirculation was profitable.
2. In any case, public pressure, even in the absence of strict environmental quality laws and enforcement, would be great enough to prevent the dumping of once-through washer effluents into public watercourses.[43] The quantities involved are immense and would have severe impacts on stream quality. They might, in some situations, even result in destruction of shipping channels and thus necessitate dredging.[44]

In figure 8.1, we sketch the general form of all the wet-washer systems in the model. The actual determination of the numbers necessary in fitting such a system into the linear model can be quite complex if one begins from first principles and attempts to reproduce the few pieces of bench mark data available. We have adopted a much simpler approach. Starting from a few key assumptions about the specific system, we use the two relations which must hold in the steady state: (1) solids in equal solids out (per unit of time or of production) and (2) water in equals water out (per unit of time or of production), to determine all the quantities of importance.

The Blast Furnace System

This method may be illustrated by using the blast furnace gas washer system. Our initial assumptions here are based on information contained in a survey of blast furnace gas washer systems at a large number of integrated mills.[45] We may summarize these assumptions as follows.

---

[43] This assumption is clearly not universally valid. For example, the River Rouge in Detroit is said to run red or black depending on whether the steel furnace dust washer system water is being discharged.

[44] See "Blunders in Pollution Control: A Case Study," in *Air and Water News*, vol. 23 (August 1971), pp. 7, 8, for the history of a small foundry's problems with captured particulates.

[45] Ohio River Valley Water Sanitation Commission, Steel Industry Action Committee, *Dust Recovery Practice at Blast Furnaces* (Cincinnati: Ohio River Valley Water Sanitation Commission, 1958).

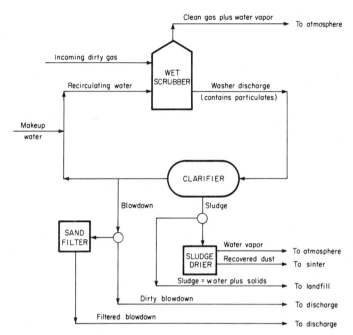

Figure 8.1.   The wet scrubber water system.

1. Of the solids removed from the gas, 95.5 percent are recovered in the clarifier sludge; 4.5 percent are blown down to keep the concentration of solids in the recirculation water at the desired level.
2. The concentration of solids in the blowdown is 200 ppm.
3. 4.2 percent of the water entering the scrubber is evaporated by the gas heat.
4. The concentration of solids in the water leaving the scrubber is 2,500 ppm.
5. The concentration of solids in clarifier sludge is 60 percent.[46]

Using these assumptions, then, and the water and solids balance requirements, it is straightforward work to obtain expressions for blowdown, evaporation, water lost in clarifier slurry, required water makeup, and the solids leaving the system via the several routes—all in terms of the original amount of particulates removed.

For the blast furnace recirculation system, we provide two other options. If the recovered dust is to be charged to sinter, its water content must be reduced. To accomplish this, we have provided vacuum filters which dewater the recovered sludge to form a filter cake whose moisture

[46] See Ross Nebolsine, "The Treatment of Water-Borne Wastes from Steel Plants," *Iron and Steel Engineer,* vol. 34 (December 1957), p. 131.

content is further reduced in an air dryer by evaporation. If the dust is not to be recovered, the sludge may be sent to landfill at a cost of $3.75 per wet ton.[47]

A second alternative of interest in the blast furnace system is the sand filter for removal of solids from the primary clarifier blowdown. This filter is optional and is assumed to remove 80 percent of the solids in the blowdown routed through it.[48] These solids are assumed not recoverable. The costs of the filter are based on the information on rolling mill filters in *Cost of Clean Water*.[49]

The recirculation system for the other wet scrubber applications was designed using a similar method, with specific numbers changed where necessary, of course, to reflect the different characteristics of the units. Because the wet system applied to the sinter strand wind box gases is a second stage unit, the concentration of solids in the gas washer water is relatively low because the dust loading in the inlet gas is low, so a once-through system is assumed in this case.

This completes our description of the model and our discussion of the techniques and calculations involved in its construction. In chapters 9–12, we move on to look at solutions under various combinations of exogenously given conditions, and we begin with the conditions which will form the basis for all later comparisons, the *bench mark* conditions.

[47] Calculated from information in "Emulsion Breaking Solves Oily Waste Disposal," *Oil and Gas Journal* (November 22, 1971), pp. 76–77. See also Philip A. Witt, Jr., "Disposal of Solid Wastes," *Chemical Engineering* (Oct. 4, 1971), pp. 62–78.

[48] The steel furnace and sinter applications do not have filters, but their clarifiers were assumed about 99 percent efficient, so the blowdown problem is small.

[49] See U.S. Department of the Interior, Federal Water Pollution Control Administration, *The Cost of Clean Water, vol. 3: Industrial Waste Profile, no. 1: Blast Furnaces and Steel Mills* (September 1967), pp. 86–87; and the description of rolling mill waste-water treatment in chapter 7.

Part II   ANALYTICAL APPLICATION OF THE MODEL

9

THE BENCH MARK CASE:
SOME RESULTS AND COMPARISONS

Now that the several major elements of an integrated iron- and steel-producing works have been explored and the relevant alternatives captured in the linear programming framework, we are nearly ready to ask the resulting model the sorts of questions raised in the introduction. There are, however, two important matters we must address before our explorations of the cost of residual discharge reduction and the impact of relative prices on residuals generation can be meaningful. First, we must find out what the bench mark situation looks like. That is, we want to know the costs of production, the pattern of input use, the residuals generation rates and other characteristics of the mill in the absence of assumptions other than those already outlined. Second, it is necessary to attempt some assessment of the realism of the model. Thus, although we have mentioned a number of checks on individual numbers used in the process and treatment vectors, we have no assurance that the whole model will produce anything but nonsense. Such assurance is clearly necessary, since there may be other numbers out of line or the basic structure may be flawed.

This chapter addresses these two concerns. First, we will pause to investigate the influence of furnace type and to set the stage for understanding the impact of the finishing section on the mill's residuals generation and its responses to various exogenous influences. Then we will present a set of bench mark solutions distinguished by furnace type and by how the mill deals with coke plant waste liquors. The final half of the chapter compares some of these solutions with actual steel mill data, particularly in the area of residuals discharge.

Before we begin, however, it is worth reviewing briefly the key assumptions of our model, all of which are covered in greater detail in the descriptive chapters:

- We assume 1968 price levels for ore, coal, scraps, and other inputs.
- Other costs, most importantly capital charges for optional equipment, are also given in 1968 dollars.
- We postulate the installed equipment configuration discussed in chapters 2 through 8, especially the required dust discharge control facilities summarized in chapter 8, p. 160.
- We require no other initial constraints on residuals discharge.

In this and the following chapters our discussion of residuals discharges and the various factors which influence them will be keyed to tables setting out data not only on residuals, but also on other aspects of each plant's operations. The residuals which we concentrate on are:[1]

1. Waterborne: five-day BOD, oil, phenols, cyanide, ammonia, suspended solids, sulfide, and rejected heat.
2. Airborne: sulfur dioxide, particulates, and, where applicable, phenols as a proxy for atmospheric discharges of volatilized residuals from quenching with coke plant liquors.
3. Solids: primarily stockpiled slag, but also collected boiler particulates, mucks, sludges, recovered furnace flue dusts not recycled to the sinter strand, and scrap from galvanized sheet.

The other aspects of plant operation on which we report include average steel cost per ton of semifinished shapes, marginal cost of iron production, percent of blast furnace capacity used, scrap use by type, coal and ore consumption, types and quantities of fuels purchased, and quantity of electricity required per ton of shapes. These data are intended to assist the reader in interpreting the residuals discharge results, but we emphasize that our choices represent only a sample of the information available from the solution printouts.

THE TRUNCATED CONVENTIONAL FINISHING VERSION

We are now prepared to pose a first, rather obvious, question: "Under the conditions assumed, can we expect a variation in residuals discharge among steel types and furnace types?" In table 9.1 we show the variation in residuals discharges attributable to steel and furnace type using the

---

[1] We ignore discharges of particulates where the conditions of discharge are such that the particulates can be assumed to fall out within the plant. These are assumed to be a housekeeping rather than an environmental problem.

truncated conventional finishing version of the model. Since the emissions reported in this table do not include the residuals from full finishing, the absolute levels of discharge are of minor interest, and are dominated on the water side by the residuals in the coke plant effluents. The highly contaminated raw ammonia liquor is discharged directly in these solutions, because the high corrosion cost penalty prevents it from being used in quenching, and the market value of ammonium sulfate and phenol does not warrant the erection of by-product recovery facilities.[2]

The differences among columns in table 9.1 suggest a number of observations which provide a useful introduction to the major features of the model and its responses. First, we notice that within a single furnace type the variation in residuals discharges due to a change in required steel type is very small. The only residual which varies noticeably with steel type is particulates, and this variation is assignable to changes in the quality of scrap charged, particularly the quantity of no. 2 bundles (auto scrap), which are high in nonmetal and hence in dust potential. The effect is most obvious at the electric arc, but also occurs at the open hearth.[3]

Furnace type, on the other hand, has a large effect on residuals generation, as one might expect. This influence arises from two causes: the characteristics of the furnaces themselves (especially the extent of particulate generation due to turbulence), and the extent to which the furnaces rely on molten iron rather than purchased scrap; hence the importance of the coke plant–sinter strand–blast furnace complex.[4] Direct evidence on this second feature shows up in the percentage utilization of blast furnace capacity, and in quantities of coal and ore purchased.

Because the BOF furnace is both particulate-intensive itself and uses a 70 percent molten iron charge, it enjoys, when the finishing section is truncated, the rather dubious distinction of being the largest discharger of particulates and every waterborne residual except heat. Compared to the open hearth shop, the basic oxygen plant discharges about 45 percent more of the relevant atmospheric, waterborne, and landfill residuals. This is partly the result of the fact that in 1968 scrap was cheap relative to molten iron (the price ratio having been 0.59), inducing the OH to

---

[2] Even if the ammonia still and dephenolizer are treated as installed equipment (their capital costs deleted from the objective function), they are not operated.

[3] The small change in particulates at the basic oxygen furnace between commercial quality carbon and alloy steel production is an artifact of our method of estimating particulate emissions for alloy production at that furnace.

[4] We have assumed the EA buys pig iron or a scrap of equivalent quality and have not reflected the residuals from the implied iron production in the electric arc plant model. To some extent this produces a misleading result whenever pig iron is used, since it leaves out of the account the residuals connected with pig iron production. For a similar problem, see the discussion concerning electricity generation.

TABLE 9.1 Mill Characteristics and Residuals Discharge Variation with Steel and Furnace Type (Using Truncated Finishing; Quenching with Raw Liquor Not Practiced)

Mill characteristics and residuals	Open hearth			Basic oxygen			Electric arc		
	DQ	CQ	AL	DQ	CQ	AL	DQ	CQ	AL
Average steel cost ($ per ton shape)	55	54	73	58	58	78	67	47	60
% Blast furnace capacity used	64	65	65	94	95	94	n.a.	n.a.	n.a.
Scrap purchased (tons per day)									
Pig	n.a.	n.a.	n.a.	n.a.	n.a.	n.a.	1440	0	0
No. 1 Factory	685	0	0	0	0	0	684	903	0
No. 1 Heavy melting	0	557	0	124	0	0	0	1160	0
Shredded	0	0	0	0	0	0	0	0	0
No. 2 Bundle	0	146	706	31	159	156	0	0	2340
Ore purchased (tons per day)[a]									
High iron content	1950	1960	1970	2770	2780	2750	n.a.	n.a.	n.a.
Low iron content	0	0	0	135	141	152	n.a.	n.a.	n.a.
Coking coal purchased (tons per day)									
1.2% Sulfur	88	89	88	128	129	128	0	0	0
0.6% Sulfur	1520	1540	1540	2230	2240	2230	11	11	11

Fuel purchased (10⁶ Btu per day)									
2.0% Sulfur fuel oil	0	0	0	0	0	0	13,000	12,400	12,500
Electricity produced (kWh per ton shape)	90	81	87	114	114	114	579	554	558
Residuals discharged									
Waterborne									
BOD-5 (lb. per ton shape)	1.73	1.75	1.75	2.54	2.55	2.54	0.01	0.01	0.01
Oil (lb. per ton shape)	0.21	0.21	0.21	0.30	0.30	0.30	...	...	...
Phenols (lb. per ton shape)	0.51	0.52	0.52	0.75	0.75	0.75	...	...	...
Cyanide (lb. per ton shape)	0.01	0.01	0.01	0.01	0.01	0.01	0.01	0.01	0.01
Ammonia (lb. per ton shape)	1.18	1.20	1.20	1.74	1.75	1.74	...	...	...
Suspended solids (lb. per ton shape)	0.40	0.40	0.40	0.58	0.59	0.58	...	...	...
Sulfide (lb. per ton shape)	0.19	0.19	0.19	0.28	0.28	0.28	...	...	...
Heat (10⁶ Btu per ton shape)	1.35	1.31	1.38	1.92	1.94	1.96	2.50	2.40	2.41
Airborne									
Sulfur dioxide (lb. per ton shape)	7.98	8.08	8.10	11.75	11.80	11.76	12.25	11.72	11.80
Particulates (lb. per ton shape)	6.56	6.89	7.37	11.69	11.94	12.27	0.58	0.72	2.82
Land									
Solids (ton per ton shape)	0.13	0.14	0.13	0.20	0.20	0.21	0.09	0.05	0.08

Abbreviations: n.a., not applicable; ellipses (...), too insignificant to record.

ᵃ Not differentiated by sulfur content or size.

opt for a high proportion of scrap in its charge by using 50–50 rather than 70–30 practice. The BOF, on the other hand, cannot capitalize on this relative price situation, because it does not have flexibility in the direction of greater scrap use and must charge at least 70 percent hot metal overall.[5] Hence the BOF needs to use roughly 45 percent more blast furnace capacity than the OH, implying a 45 percent higher consumption of coking coal and, consequently, an equivalently greater discharge of coke-related residuals.

This same argument helps to explain the position of the electric-arc plant in residuals generation relative to the open hearth and basic oxygen shops. The EA is able to use 100 percent scrap in its charge rather than 50 or 30 percent, and therefore requires only a nominal input of coke. However, the EA generates about as large a particulate load as the BOF, and produces more sulfur dioxide than either of the other furnaces. These very large emissions are caused by the required production of electricity at the in-plant generation station, for the electric arc plant requires the largest daily amount of electricity, and, to generate it, is forced to purchase residual fuel oil because by-product fuels such as coke oven gas are not available.[6] This last factor, combined with the thermal inefficiency of first producing electricity and then melting steel, makes the EA the leader in atmospheric emissions. This facet of the EA is almost never reflected in surveys of steel mill emissions, probably because a majority of electric arc plants purchase electricity from public utilities located away from the mill. However, we show the electrical generation as taking place at the electric arc shop itself for conceptual completeness. Ignoring the residuals from electrical generation makes the EA appear too clean from an environmental standpoint.[7]

If we did not have a more complete version of the finishing process, our discussion of the base case set of discharges would have to end here. Fortunately this is not the case, and the next section of this chapter will show the significant impact which the inclusion of a fuller finishing section has on discharges and operating costs.

---

[5] This stark contrast pictured in the model may not be so extreme in the real world, where certain techniques such as scrap premelting can increase the tolerable amount of scrap in the BOF charge.

[6] More accurately, they are available in the model in such miniscule quantities compared to the OH and BOF as to be unimportant.

[7] This is an important point. The internal electrical generation plant in the model is not subject to any required gas treatment for particulate removal, so the dust emissions from electricity generation represent the maximum possible from the fuel oils burned. However, application of control devices on oil-fired boilers appears to be limited, and in any event, the emission from an oil-fired unit without special collection equipment is comparable to that from a coal-fired unit subject to better than 99 percent collection efficiency, according to A. E. Vandegrift and L. J. Shannon, *Particulate Pollutant System Study, Vol. III: Handbook of Emission Properties*, Report by Midwest Research Institute to U.S. Environmental Protection Agency (Durham: May 1971), p. 72.

The introduction of a detailed representation of the processes which transform molten carbon and alloy steel into a wide assortment of semi-finished and finished products amends the results outlined in the preceding discussion. These impacts are not confined to residuals alone, but extend to many other aspects of mill operation such as operating costs and utilities requirements, which were given scant attention in the above discussion because the truncated finishing version of the model provides only incomplete information about them. In the context of a fuller model, these features are intrinsically interesting, and utilities requirements become particularly valuable as aids to an understanding of observed differences in residuals discharges over furnace types. Therefore, after setting out summaries of the model solutions with the full finishing section, we shall concentrate on the problems of heat sources and uses and the provision of electricity. A note on product cost–price comparisons will be included as further evidence bearing on the model's reliability.

Residuals

Attention can now be turned to the residuals discharge levels which will provide a foundation for subsequent analysis. Along with the usual mill characteristics, these discharges are displayed in table 9.2. In conjunction with table 9.1, table 9.2 shows us the impact of the inclusion of finishing, and in itself shows how discharges vary with furnace type for the complete model. Also included are additional columns for the open hearth and basic oxygen plants showing the impact of using raw ammonia liquor instead of purchased water for quenching the incandescent coke.

Abstracting from these two supplementary columns for the moment, we observe that the addition of the larger finishing section causes some modifications in discharges. Water-course discharges of BOD, oil, suspended solids, and heat all increase significantly. Phenol, ammonia, cyanide, and sulfide discharges associated exclusively with coking do not increase at all at the basic oxygen and electric arc plants, and increase insignificantly at the open hearth shop.

The large water-course discharge increases attributable to full finishing and its wider product mix are:

	Open Hearth	*Basic Oxygen*	*Electric Arc*
BOD (pounds per ton shape)	3.33	3.31	3.31
Oil (pounds per ton shape)	2.96	2.97	2.96
Suspended solids (pounds per ton shape)	5.83	4.58	4.58
Heat (10^6 Btu per ton shape)	3.89	3.52	3.89

Mill characteristics and residuals	Open hearth		Basic oxygen		Electric arc
	Fresh water quench-ing	Raw liquor quench-ing	Fresh water quench-ing	Raw liquor quench-ing	Fresh water quench-ing
Average steel cost ($ per ton shape)	70	70	73	73	68
Marginal iron cost ($ per ton hot metal)	41	41	42	42	n.a.
% Blast furnace capacity used	79	79	95	95	n.a.
Scrap purchases (tons per day)					
Pig	n.a.	n.a.	n.a.	n.a.	340
No. 1 Factory	150	150	0	0	799
No. 1 Heavy melting	436	436	35	35	821
Shredded	0	0	0	0	0
No. 2 Bundle	166	166	184	184	200
Ore purchased (tons per day)[a]					
High iron content	2,010	2,010	2,800	2,800	0
Low iron content	80	80	145	145	0
Coking coal purchased (tons per day)					
1.2% Sulfur	0	0	130	130	0
0.6% Sulfur	1,640	1,640	2,240	2,240	10
Fuel purchased (10^6 Btu per day)					
0.5% Sulfur fuel oil	451	451	0	0	7,290
2.0% Sulfur fuel oil	7,190	7,190	535	535	15,700
Electricity produced (kWh per ton shape)	215	215	254	254	700
Residuals discharged					
Waterborne					
Five-day BOD (lb. per ton shape)	5.08	3.32	5.86	3.33	3.32
Oil (lb. per ton shape)	3.17	2.96	3.27	2.96	2.96
Phenols (lb. per ton shape)	0.52	...	0.75	...	...[b]
Cyanide (lb. per ton shape)	0.01	0	0.01	0	...[b]
Ammonia (lb. per ton shape)	1.21	0	1.75	0	0.01
Suspended solids (lb. per ton shape)	6.23	6.15	5.17	5.05	4.58
Sulfide (lb. per ton shape)	0.19	0	0.28	0	...[b]
Heat (10^6 Btu per ton shape)	5.22	5.22	5.46	5.46	6.31
Airborne					
Sulfur dioxide (lb. per ton shape)	14.09	14.09	12.31	12.31	16.55
Particulates (lb. per ton shape)	5.91	5.91	12.06	12.06	1.11
Phenols (lb. per ton shape)	0.01	0.53	0.01	0.76	...[b]
Land					
Solids (ton per ton shape)	0.14	0.14	0.21	0.21	0.05

Abbreviations: n.a., not applicable; (...), too insignificant to record.
[a] Not differentiated by sulfur content or size.
[b] A very small amount of coking is done for the electric arc in this model. The amounts of residuals involved are correspondingly small and show up only in the third decimal place. Because of this, discharges when quenching is allowed are the same as when it is not.

BOD, suspended solids, and oil discharges increase mainly because of their presence in the rolling mill wastewaters, which were neglected in truncated finishing.[8] Heat discharge increases come from both the hot mill itself and from the increased level of electricity generation necessitated by the requirements of full finishing. However, the absolute increase in suspended solids is greater at the open hearth shop than it is at the other two mills, because the influence of finishing is felt both directly through an increase in solids exclusively associated with rolling mill wastewater, and indirectly through an alteration of activity use at the blast furnace where some run-of-mine ore displaces the sintered fines which were charged in the truncated version.[9] These ungraded ores have a blast furnace dust generation rate roughly ten times greater than sinter. Therefore, when they are charged, more dust is removed in the gas washer part of the blast furnace gas cleaning system, and hence a higher suspended solids load results from the gas washer water blowdown. This difference in load is great enough to offset the lower level of blast furnace use at the open hearth, compared with the BOF. (No change in blast furnace burdening takes place at the BOF plant.)

Regarding heat, the basic oxygen furnace feels both direct and indirect impacts from full finishing, while the OH and EA experience only the former. Heat discharges increase least at the BOF plant because of the new heat balance situation introduced by full finishing (discussed in greater detail below). It becomes profitable to recover waste heat from the BOF hood, a practice which was neither necessary nor profitable in the truncated case. No such changes take place at the OH, which must by assumption either recover waste heat or send it up the stack, or at the EA, which has no recovery capability.

Atmospheric discharges do not follow the same pattern as water-course discharges; particulates emitted by the open hearth shop actually drop when full finishing is introduced. However, sulfur dioxide discharges increase across the board at all plants, albeit most dramatically at the OH and EA. Counterintuitively, after all interactions are accounted for, the BOF is no longer a larger discharger of sulfur dioxide than the OH at the reigning fuel oil price set. This phenomenon can only be understood by

---

[8] We require that all hot- and cold-rolling mill waters be passed through primary settling facilities at a minimum. These are assumed to remove 90 percent of suspended solids and 20 percent of oil from the hot mill water and 30 percent of solids but no oil from the cold mill water. In these base solutions the model does not choose to go beyond these minimum levels because recovered scale is not valuable enough as a sintering input to offset the additional costs of further treatment.

[9] A sign of this change is given by the increase in blast furnace capacity utilization at the open hearth shop between tables 9.1 and 9.2 indicating the choice of less technically efficient blast furnace activities in the full finishing case. (Less efficient here means fewer tons of iron per hour for fixed physical capacity.) The trivial increases in phenol, ammonia, cyanide, and sulfide are caused by the slightly higher coke rate involved.

TABLE 9.3   Steel Mill Heat Sources and Requirements Net of Blast Furnace Thermochemistry (full finishing; bench mark solutions)

(quantities for 10^6 Btu/day)

	Open hearth (50–50)	Basic oxygen (70–30)	Electric arc[b] (100–0)
Sources of available heat[a]			
Intramill			
High sulfur acid sludge	0	. . .	0
Low sulfur acid sludge	. . .	. . .	. . .
High sulfur forerunnings	0	. . .	0
Low sulfur forerunnings	. . .	. . .	. . .
High sulfur coke oven gas	0	700	0
Low sulfur coke oven gas	8,800	12,100	100
Blast furnace gas	8,000	11,000	0
Recovered steel furnace heat	2,300	700	0
Subtotal	19,100	24,500	100
Percentage of available heat	(71.6)	(97.9)	(0.3)
External[c]			
Purchased 0.5% sulfur fuel oil	500	0	7,300
Purchased 2.0% sulfur fuel oil	7,200	500	15,700
Subtotal	7,700	500	23,000
Percentage of available heat	(28.4)	(2.1)	(99.7)
Total available heat	26,800	25,000	23,100
Heat requirements[a]			
Underfiring	3,300	4,700	. . .
Power plant boilers	7,200	11,300	15,700
Waste heat boilers	2,300	700	0
Sinter ignition hood	400	1,000	0
Steel furnace (direct)	6,300	0	0
Soaking pits	7,300	7,300	7,300
Sludge dryer	. . .	. . .	0
Total heat required	26,800	25,000	23,000

Note: Total available and required heat may not agree because of rounding.

[a] Heat sources exclude heat available in coking coal and in blast furnace gas used to heat air injected into the blast furnace. Heat requirements exclude heat required for calcination of limestone and reduction of ferrous inputs in the blast furnace. The tar produced in coking is sold in the bench mark solution.

[b] The small amount of coking done to provide coke for the electric arc furnace produces some intramill by-product heat sources and requires an underfiring heat input.

[c] 1.0 percent sulfur fuel oil may also be purchased, but is not in the bench mark solutions.

reference to the altered heat balance situation introduced by full finishing.

The Heat Balances

In truncated finishing, both the open hearth and basic oxygen furnace plants generate more by-product fuel than is needed to meet overall heat requirements. These surpluses, indicated by the absence of fuel oil purchases in table 9.1, must be disposed of by flaring because the model includes no provision for by-product fuel sale or storage. The sulfur dioxide discharges associated with truncated finishing consequently reflect the sulfur dioxide generated when these zero-opportunity-cost gases are burned. Naturally the basic oxygen plant is a larger sulfur dioxide discharger than the OH in this case because its higher coke requirement leaves it with a larger fuel surplus.

The increased heat requirement introduced by the soaking pits and the additional electricity needed in full finishing work together to eliminate the OH and BOF fuel surpluses, and force the purchase of outside fuel to a differing degree at each of the three shops. The magnitude of the change in sulfur dioxide discharges taking place between the truncated and full finishing solutions is directly related to the quality and amount of additional fuel which must be purchased by each mill to fill the gap created between the heat available from its by-product fuels and its total requirement. The electric arc shop, which had no surplus in truncated finishing, meets the whole of this additional requirement through the purchase of more fuel oil, and sulfur dioxide discharges per unit output increase in proportion to these purchases. Because the BOF has the largest surplus of blast furnace and low sulfur coke oven gas (zero and 1.23 pounds of sulfur dioxide emitted per million Btu respectively), when an equal amount of additional heat must be supplied because of finishing, it must obviously rely least on purchased high sulfur fuel oil, which emits 2.20 pounds of sulfur dioxide per million Btu. Hence the BOF shop enjoys the lowest proportional increase in sulfur dioxide emissions of the three plants when full finishing supplants truncated finishing.

A closer look at how in-plant and external heat sources balance with full finishing requirements is provided in table 9.3. Although these heat balances do not canvass all sources and requirements—omitting those directly related to the metallurgy of the blast furnace—they do demonstrate the essence of the argument.[10]

[10] Because these balances neglect the blast furnace metallurgical requirements, they make the three paths to finished steel appear roughly equal in energy intensity. In fact, of course, it is considerably more energy-intensive to start with iron

Particulate discharges generally increase because of the increased use of fuel oil at either the power plant or the soaking pits. The open hearth plant is the exception, and this can be traced to the partial shift away from sinter production in favor of the use of run-of-mine ore in the blast furnace. Because of our assumptions that a very high level of particulate control is required at the blast furnace and that control at the sinter discharge end is optional, this shift results in a net decrease in particulate emissions. Thus, even though sinter charges emit only 10 to 20 percent of the dust that run-of-mine ore charges do at the blast furnace itself, when the discharges from the sinter plant are also accounted for, sinter charges yield a higher dust generation rate per ton of iron produced than do run-of-mine ore charges.

In sum, then, the consequences of introducing the full finishing section are strongly felt in several residuals categories. However, it is only in its effect on the plant's heat balances that full finishing actually changes furnace discharge rankings. This happens for sulfur dioxide emissions; the basic oxygen plant no longer ranks just below the EA in this category, but instead becomes the lowest bench mark case discharger of this gas.

A Comment on Quenching

When we look at the two supplementary columns of table 9.2., which display the consequences of removing the corrosion cost charge attached to activities which quench with contaminated coke plant liquor streams, we observe that water-course discharges of the residuals generated solely in the coke plant, such as phenols and ammonia, fall by 100 percent. Other water-course discharges which fall are BOD (33 percent reduction at the OH, 43 percent reduction at the BOF), oil (respective 7 and 9 percent decreases), and suspended solids (respective 1 and 2 percent decreases). Discharges of various noxious gases to the atmosphere of course increase. As a proxy for this, we indicate the weight of phenols vaporized in quenching and show it as phenol gas discharge. In fact, of course, some of the cyanide, phenols, sulfide, and ammonia would be oxidized and we would have discharges of sulfur dioxide, NO_x, carbon dioxide, water vapor, and other compounds.

This table points out a very important tradeoff available to the steel industry—the exchange of waterborne for atmospheric residuals—though the extent to which quenching with contaminated liquors is currently practiced in the industry is an open question. Some authoritative

---

ore than with steel scrap, and measuring total energy use shows us how much more. The BOF process overall requires 2.7 times as much energy per ton of product as does the electric arc process (with nearly 100 percent scrap charge). For the open hearth plant, the corresponding ratio is 2.2. None of these numbers reflect mining or transportation energy requirements.

sources claim that the practice is widespread: "Most modern plants, of necessity, quench with contaminated water as there seems to be no other practical method of disposal of these wastes."[11]

If we read between the lines, we see the implication that steelmakers believe there is no less expensive method of disposing of these wastes, and feel themselves under no compulsion to discover one in the absence of strict constraints on their atmospheric discharges. However, another source[12] reports that this situation is rapidly changing as coke plant managers recognize the ultimate futility of exchanging contaminated water for contaminated air. According to Battelle, over the past few years many plants have actually disconnected the lines that formerly carried contaminated liquors to quenching. In the chapters to come, we will see that a prohibition of quenching with contaminated liquors will have a significant effect on costs (both marginal and total) implied by various levels of discharge limitations on coke plant residuals.

COMPARISON OF ESTIMATED AND OBSERVED RESIDUALS DISCHARGES

Without further confirmation, our impressive array of bench mark discharge data would remain unconvincing since, after all, a mathematical model merely performs according to a stated criterion on the basis of the information at its disposal. Although verification of our solutions is difficult, several reassuring sets of comparisons can be made. We first compare our model's bench mark discharges with discharge generation coefficients which others have estimated from inventory data on actual emissions at operating mills.

Table 9.4 compares the bench mark discharges from our three different mills both when coke plant liquors are discharged directly and when they are evaporated in quenching. Placed alongside these discharges are actual discharges calculated from information contained in alternative sources and designated as *CEP (Council on Economic Priorities) subsample, Delaware Region Mill, and Cost of Clean Water (CCW)*. The CEP subsample estimates have been calculated from information in

---

[11] Harold E. McGannon, ed., *The Making, Shaping and Treating of Steel,* 9th ed. (Pittsburgh: U.S. Steel Corporation, 1971), p. 131. The United States Department of the Interior's Federal Water Pollution Control Administration agreed with this observation. In their report *The Cost of Clean Water, Vol. III, Industrial Waste Profile No. 1: Blast Furnaces and Steel Mills* (September 1967), p. 76, they estimated that 90 percent of integrated mills would follow this practice by 1972. This judgment may be biased by the report's nearsighted concentration on water pollution alone.

[12] Thomas M. Barnes et al., *Evaluation of Process Alternatives to Improve Control of Air Pollution from Production of Coke,* PB 189 266 (Springfield, Va.: NTIS, January 31, 1970), p. III-60.

TABLE 9.4 *Comparison of the Full Finishing Bench Mark Solutions with Other Data*

(quantities per ton semifinished shape)

Furnace and source	Water[a] (10³ gal.)	Waterborne residuals						Heat (10⁶ Btu)	Airborne residuals	
		BOD (lb.)	Oil (lb.)	Phenols (lb.)	Cyanide (lb.)	Ammonia (lb.)	Suspended solids (lb.)		SO₂ (lb.)	Particulates (lb.)
Open hearth										
Bench mark solution										
No quench	32.5	5.08	3.17	0.52	0.01	1.21	6.23	5.22	14.1	5.9
Quench	32.4	3.32	2.96	...	0	0	6.15			
CEP subsample										
Mean	37.0	1.11	0.84	0.01	0.03	0.91	4.93	4.05	10.7	14.4
−1 S.D.	5.3	0	0	0	0	0	0	0.84	2.2	2.8
+1 S.D.	68.7	2.29	1.84	0.03	0.08	2.98	10.85	7.26	19.3	26.0
Delaware Region Mill (U.S. Steel Fairless)	34.6	2.30[b]	0.51	0.01	...	0.06	0.85	3.75	1.6 to 3.7[c]	5.1[d]
CCW										
Typical	11.5	n.r.	3.13	0.07	0.03	0.09	144.00[e]	n.r.	n.r.	n.r.
Basic oxygen										
Bench mark solution										
No quench	33.3	5.86	3.27	0.75	0.01	1.75	5.17	5.46	12.3	12.1
Quench	33.3	3.33	2.96	...	0	0	5.05			

CEP subsample									
Mean	33.3	0.50	1.22	0.01	0.05	0.52	4.54	2.91	11.2	17.0
−1 S.D.	14.3	0	0	0	0	0	1.06	1.46	0	0
+1 S.D.	52.3	1.14	3.55	0.03	0.13	1.14	8.02	4.36	22.6	35.4

Delaware Region Mill (Alan Wood)

	n.r.	n.r.	n.r.	n.r.	n.r.	n.r.	n.r.	n.r.	6.3[c]	5.4[f]

Electric arc

Bench mark solution

Internal (kWh)	38.1	3.32	2.96	...	...	0.01	4.58	6.31	16.6	1.1
External (kWh)	20.1	3.32	2.96	...	...	0.01	4.58	3.39	1.8	0.8

CEP subsample

Mean	8.3	0.22	0.07	0.01	0.01	0.11	2.32	1.04	1.0	3.7
−1 S.D.	0	0	0	0	0	0	0	0	0	1.5
+1 S.D.	17.5	0.53	0.18	0.02	0.04	0.37	7.59	2.25	2.6	6.0

Note: Ellipses (...) indicate too insignificant to record. n.r. indicates "not reported."

a Bench mark data refer to total water withdrawals. CEP data refer to total water discharges. The CCW definition of wastewater is on a gross basis, and appears to exclude water discharged from indirect cooling.

b CEP data indicate that Fairless water discharges have a lower BOD concentration (4.3 ppm) than withdrawals (5.0 ppm), implying a negative BOD discharge. The withdrawal concentration used by CEP appears high, according to average Delaware River BOD concentrations reported near the mill's intake. Unpublished data collected by the Delaware River Basin Commission (DRBC) available from EPA's "STORET" data bank indicate that the appropriate concentration is 2.9 ppm, not 5.0. Using this figure yields a 1968 discharge of 0.40 lb. of BOD per ton of shapes.

c Neglects sulfur dioxide emissions from slag and from steel furnace fuels (where applicable).

d Based on 99 percent particulate removal from open hearth gases.

e Based on the unrealistic assumption of once-through use for all water streams, including blast furnace gaswasher water.

f Based on 99.75 percent particulate removal from BOF gases.

James S. Cannon's *Environmental Steel*, and include only those discharges from particular plants in the CEP document which produce steel in a single type of furnace.[13] The CCW estimates come from the U.S. Department of the Interior's *Cost of Clean Water*,[14] and represent discharges from a typical technology mill characterized by a coke plant quenching with contaminated liquor, a sinter plant equipped with wet gas cleaning equipment, an OH furnace similarly equipped, a conventional rolling and finishing facility, and once-through water use.[15] The Delaware Mill entries are included supplementally because these two mills are similar in equipment design and operation to the modeled mills.

The most striking feature of the table is the high degree of within- and between-source variation in discharges it reveals. The extent to which coke plant liquors are used in quenching is obviously one of the causes of this variation. We can infer from the low discharge coefficients in the observed discharge cases that disposal of these liquors by evaporation at the quenching station (perhaps in conjunction with some treatment) is

---

[13] James S. Cannon, ed., *Environmental Steel* (N.Y.: Council on Economic Priorities, 1973). This careful study of the environmental impact of the steel industry was conducted under the auspices of the nonprofit Council on Economic Priorities during 1972. The CEP group optimistically sent questionnaires to seven major steel companies requesting information about the extent of their pollution control programs, but none responded. This universal reticence forced CEP to rely primarily on air emission data compiled by state and local pollution control agencies in accordance with the 1970 Clean Air Act and water emission data available from Refuse Act permit applications filed with the Army Corps of Engineers and EPA. CEP's tenacity was rewarded by what appears to be the most complete collection of discharge information publicly available at this time for the seven major producers who jointly accounted for 68 percent of production in 1971.

The CEP daily discharges were converted into discharges per unit shapes using plant raw steel production capacities reported by the NUS Corporation, Cyrus William Rice Division, in *Development Document for Effluent Limitations Guidelines and New Source Performance Standards: Iron and Steel Industry*, a draft report prepared for U.S. Environmental Protection Agency under contract No. 68-01-1507 (June 1973), and a factor of 0.77 reflecting ingot to semifinished steel yield and plant utilization. The twelve basic oxygen plants in the subsample account for 65 percent of the production from all BOF furnaces in the full CEP sample, and 57 percent of the total 1971 U.S. production from all BOF furnaces. The eight open hearth plants in the subsample account for 87 percent of the production from all OH furnaces in the CEP sample, and 68 percent of total 1971 U.S. production from all OH furnaces. The eight electric arc plants in the subsample account for 36 percent of the production from all EA furnaces in the CEP sample, and 23 percent of total 1971 U.S. production from all EA furnaces.

[14] In FWPCA, *The Cost of Clean Water*, discharges per ingot ton steel were converted to pounds per ton semifinished shape using our yield factor of 0.868.

[15] A careful reading of the literature suggests that many of these characteristics are hardly typical, especially wet scrubber use at the hearth and the absence of water recirculation. Therefore, these estimates, based primarily on secondary sources and tenuous assumptions, should be given less weight than the CEP estimates.

widespread.[16] Therefore, the appropriate comparison is between the observed discharges and the bench mark solution discharges when quenching is allowed.

For each residual, two statistics have been calculated from the CEP subsample—the mean and standard deviation. To establish a basis for evaluating our bench mark estimates, the table presents a range of one standard deviation on either side of the CEP mean discharges.[17] (If the parent population distribution of discharges were normal, this range would include about 68 percent of the distribution.) When quenching with coke plant liquors is allowed in the model, we find that eight of our ten estimates at the OH and BOF, and seven of our ten estimates for the EA (purchasing its electricity from an outside supplier) are within the ± 1 S.D. range. The open hearth plant estimates for BOD and oil fall outside the upper limit, the latter barely exceeding a more liberal ± 2 S.D. limit. The basic oxygen shop estimates for heat and BOD are also high, the latter exceeding a ± 2 S.D. limit. The electric arc estimates for water, BOD, oil, and heat fall above their respective ± 1 S.D. upper limits. Of these, BOD and oil exceed a ± 2 S.D. limit. Particulate discharges are on the low side.

One possible explanation for the model's apparent overstatement of a few of the waterborne discharges lies in the extent of finishing actually undertaken at the observed plants, as well as the actual level of BOD and oil removal from finishing wastewaters. It is impossible to tell from the CEP data whether a majority of the surveyed plants actually carry the finishing process as far as the model does. If a few large mills cut finishing short at the ingot or semifinished shape stages, measure discharges might fall short of estimated discharges, as we know from the truncated–full finishing comparisons. Comparing the CEP range with truncated discharges (if quenching with contaminated liquor is allowed) would bring all of the open hearth discharges in line. So doing would also improve the electric arc discharge comparison for everything except heat and particulates, although heat would not remain very far above the target. The same comparison, if made for the BOF, would bring the heat discharge within the acceptable limits. However,

[16] FWPCA, in *The Cost of Clean Water* (p. 75) claims quenching removes 92.7 percent of coke plant chemicals from coke plant wastewaters. Taking about 7 percent of either the open hearth or basic oxygen discharges of phenols and ammonia, in the absence of quenching, gives discharges of the same order of magnitude as *The Cost of Clean Water* discharges.

[17] Conceivably, watercourse discharges could be negative when the quantities of the several residuals in the intake water are taken into account. In our judgment this is an unlikely possibility (see note *b* in table 9.4). Accordingly, the lower limit of the range has been assumed to be zero in cases where subtraction of the standard deviation from the mean yields a negative number.

the BOD discharge would remain high and the suspended solids discharge would be pushed below the tolerable lower limit.

Therefore, the extent of finishing can be at best a partial explanation. However, observed discharge levels could also be influenced by the extent of by-product recovery and waste-water treatment actually undertaken, especially the degree to which hot- and cold-mill wastewaters are subjected to sedimentation, coagulation, and filtration at the observed plants. The model chooses only to undertake the settling step in the bench mark solutions, but it is likely that between 15 and 25 percent of the observed mills took further treatment steps, which would have a greater effect on the remaining oil than on suspended solids, making our estimated discharges of oil and BOD appear somewhat high.[18] Furthermore, there is no assurance that over the reporting period all relevant external influences and relative prices were exactly the same as those assumed in the model. Any divergence could well cause a different set of optimal treatment and by-product recovery activities and a different set of water-course discharges. On balance, the model estimates on the water side are not distressingly inaccurate, especially in view of the CCW oil discharge estimate of table 9.4.[19]

For airborne emissions, our sulfur dioxide estimates are quite good, especially when a correction for external electricity purchase at the EA is made. Again, relative purchased and by-product fuel prices have a large bearing on sulfur dioxide discharges, explaining the wide range observed. For example, plants having favorable access to natural gas at a cost lower than our high opportunity cost would emit less sulfur dioxide than the model predicts.

For particulates, much of the observed between- and within-source discharge variation can be explained by the level of particulate control applied. That is, although the observed removal efficiency of control equipment installed at open hearth, basic oxygen, and electric arc furnaces in the United States ranges between 97 and 99 percent, application of this equipment is universal only at the BOF.[20] Only 41 percent of all open hearth shops are controlled, and 79 percent of EAs.[21] If we were to blow up the model's particulate discharges for these shop types to account for this extent of application, we would

18 See FWPCA, *The Cost of Clean Water*, vol. III, p. 76.

19 The Cyrus William Rice Division of NUS Corp., in *Industry Profile Study on Blast Furnace and Basic Steel Products*, Draft, Report for U.S. Environmental Protection Agency under contract No. 68-01-0006, Washington, D.C., June 1971 reported, based on observation of a number of mills, a standard raw waste load (prior to any treatment) of over 3.2 lb. of BOD per ton of shapes, *exclusive* of the finishing load.

20 The large deviation around the mean in the CEP basic oxygen particulates discharge cannot be due to this reason, but must involve blast furnace charge characteristics instead.

21 Vandegrift and Shannon, *Particulate Pollutant System Study*, vol. III, p. 121.

raise the model's estimate of particulate discharges from the electric-arc shop into the acceptable range, and bring the open hearth estimate even closer to the observed mean.

Keeping in mind the possible discrepancies between actual and assumed operating practice which serve partially to explain discrepancies between observed and estimated discharges, a broader gauge comparison between the CEP discharges and our own can be made. The complete CEP sample discharge averages and standard deviations provide an estimate of the average discharges emanating from all mills.[22] Comparing these statistics to our estimated discharges weighted by furnace-type shares in total output demonstrates how well the model would predict discharges for the industry as a whole, assuming that each plant must produce the typical full finishing product mix.[23]

Referring to table 9.5, we find that for airborne discharges, our estimates compare well with the CEP statistics, since sulfur dioxide is quite close to the sample average and particulates are at least well within ±1 S.D. of it.

On the water side, our bench mark estimates are close to the sample average for water withdrawals and suspended solids discharges. Our heat discharge, although high, is within 2 S.D. above the sample mean. The fact that the model does not require removal of heat from most indirect cooling water in cooling towers explains this divergence, since some existing mills operate them. The discrepancies in the other waterborne discharges are generally large, and some likely explanations have been discussed. However, they do not tell the full story, which is even more complicated.

First, relative input price constellations vary in space as well as in time. Mills located in some regions of the country find that, given the relative prices confronting them, their optimal choice of operations differs substantially from the best practice elsewhere. Many vertically integrated mills may have favored access to certain key inputs at costs which are at variance with published prices, and hence may choose to

[22] The CEP average discharges per ton of output are weighted by plant production. We calculated the standard deviation.

[23] The bench mark discharges have been weighted by the share of output by furnace type implicit in the CEP sample to arrive at bench mark industry aggregate discharges. The output of plants covered in the CEP sample has been estimated from information in the NUS Corporation's *Development Document,* after application of the usual conversion factors. As a result, on the water side open hearth plants in the CEP sample account for 28.5 percent of total sample production, basic oxygen plants 57.4 percent, and electric arc plants 14.1 percent. On the air side, open hearth plants account for 33.1 percent, basic oxygen plants 52.8 percent, and electric arc plants 14.1. This distinction between air and water output shares is necessitated by the lack of synchronization in air and water discharge information, because some plants effected a changeover in furnace type between air and water discharge measurement periods.

TABLE 9.5   *Aggregated Steel Industry Bench Mark Discharges Compared with CEP Sample Data*

(per ton semifinished shape)

Residual	Unit	CEP sample low (−1 S.D.)[a]	Bench mark weighted average[b] (quench-ing)	CEP sample average	Bench mark weighted average[b] (no quench-ing)	CEP sample high (+1 S.D.)[a]
Waterborne						
Water[c]	10^6 gal.	23.5	31.2	36.6	31.2	49.8
Five-day BOD	lb.	0.20	0.33	1.20	5.28	2.20
Oil	lb.	0.60	2.96	1.00	3.20	1.40
Phenols	lb.	0	...	0.04	0.58	0.08
Cyanide	lb.	0.03	0	0.08	0.01	0.13
Ammonia	lb.	0.30	0	0.60	1.24	0.90
Suspended solids	lb.	3.90	5.30	5.90	5.39	7.90
Heat	10^6 Btu	2.00	5.10	3.40	5.10	4.80
Airborne						
Sulfur dioxide	lb.	5.7	11.4	10.2	11.4	14.7
Particulates	lb.	6.8	8.4	14.6	8.4	21.4

Abbreviation: Ellipses (...), too insignificant to record.
Sources: CEP sample statistics calculated from information in James S. Cannon, *Environmental Steel.*
[a] Figures show ± S.D.
[b] These represent production-weighted full finishing bench mark discharges. Open hearth and basic oxygen plants produce electricity internally. Electric arc plants purchase electricity.
[c] CEP sample data represent discharges. Bench mark data represent withdrawals.

burden their blast furnaces differently than the model, which contains published input prices. Furthermore, the output capacity of some company-owned iron ore and coal mines may be limited, and mill operators do not look on the supply curves for their inputs as perfectly elastic, though we have done so in our simplifying assumption for the model.

To show heuristically the potential influence of these factors on the potential range of residuals discharge, the linear programming model can be forced to choose a subset of the potential inputs by setting zero upper limits on the availability of all but one possible ore and coal. Table 9.6 shows the consequences of some of the more extreme pair-wise possibilities. As expected, the atmospheric discharges of sulfur dioxide and particulates are affected most dramatically, but some variation in water-course discharges is also evident as a direct result of the different blast furnace coke rates required by the charges.

TABLE 9.6 *The Influence of Limited Ore and Coke Input Availability on Basic Oxygen Furnace Steel Mill Characteristics and Residuals Discharge (using full finishing; quenching with raw liquor not practiced)*

Mill characteristics and residuals	Charge type[a]					
	1	2	3	4	5	6
Average steel cost ($ per ton shape)	77	81	75	73	78	75
Marginal iron cost ($ per ton metal)	46	53	46	42	49	46
Percentage blast furnace capacity required[b]	110	164	94	94	149	94
Ore purchased (tons per day)	3570	4070	3030	2960	3470	3030
Coking coal purchased (tons)	2510	2800	2320	2370	2650	2270
Fuel purchased (10^6 Btu per day) 2.0% sulfur	119	0	0	525	0	0
Electricity produced (kWh per ton shape)	267	237	222	253	230	221
Residuals discharged (per ton shape)						
Waterborne						
BOD-5 (lb. per ton shape)	6.01	6.33	5.81	5.87	6.16	5.76
Oil (lb. per ton shape)	3.28	3.32	3.26	3.27	3.30	3.25
Phenols (lb. per ton shape)	0.80	0.89	0.74	0.76	0.84	0.72
Cyanide (lb. per ton shape)	0.01	0.02	0.01	0.01	0.01	0.01
Ammonia (lb. per ton shape)	1.85	2.07	1.71	1.75	1.95	1.67
Suspended solids (lb. per ton shape)	5.27	11.09	4.92	5.16	10.15	4.92
Sulfide (lb. per ton shape)	0.57	0.64	0.53	0.27	0.30	0.26
Heat (10^6 Btu per ton shape)	5.55	5.99	5.74	5.46	5.92	5.71
Airborne						
Sulfur dioxide (lb. per ton shape)	28.2	23.7	18.5	11.4	10.6	9.0
Particulates (lb. per ton shape)	12.0	6.2	3.0	10.2	5.9	3.0
Land						
Solids (ton per ton shape)	0.42	0.67	0.29	0.22	0.43	0.27

[a] Charge types numbered 1–6 above are defined as follows:

	1	2	3	4	5	6
Ore size:	Fine	Run of Mine	Pellets	Fine	Run of Mine	Pellets
Iron content:	Low	Low	High	High	High	High
Sulfur content:	High	High	Low	Low	Low	Low
Coke sulfur content:	High	High	High	Low	Low	Low

[b] Because of the technical inefficiency of some of the charges, more than 48 hours of blast furnace capacity are required to produce the targeted output of steel. Therefore, in order to assure 100 percent burdening for all ore–coke pairs, the constraint on blast furnace capacity has been relaxed. Required capacity is expressed as the ratio of hours needed by each charge to bench mark hours available, 48.

What of inputs excluded from consideration in the model but available in the real world? In most cases our exclusions do not create serious problems in residuals discharge estimation. Our ore and coal input combinations seem varied enough to adequately represent the intermediate and extreme portions of the actual range. However, one exclusion which is potentially important is that of nonmetallurgical coal as a source of fuel.[24]

A second possible source of variation in discharges is to be found in the seasonal shifts in demand for finished steel products, which cause fluctuations in the overall level of mill operations, the nature of these operations, and the consequent discharge of residuals. When blast furnace and steel furnace capacities are severely pressed because of the need to produce a higher output level, the discharges per unit output change, though for most residuals the change is slight. For example, when the open hearth shop is forced to operate at a physical maximum daily output level of 3,555 tons of semifinished shapes, discharges of suspended solids decrease by 1.24 pounds per ton of shapes while the other waterborne residual loads change by less than 0.1 pounds per ton. Airborne particulates increase by 0.13 pounds and sulfur dioxide increases by 1.15 pounds. Small changes in the opposite direction are experienced at the basic oxygen plant; discharges fall when a maximum daily output level of 2,518 tons of shapes is reached.[25]

OTHER OBSERVATIONS AND COMPARISONS

For residuals discharges, the groundwork of the bench mark solutions has been laid. The other aspects of mill operation which have a bearing on these discharge levels may now be discussed.

Utilities

In the bench mark version of the model, electric power requirements must be provided internally; no purchase of externally generated electricity is permitted. The marginal cost of providing this power is 5.5 mills per kilowatt hour (kWh) at each plant. This marginal cost repre-

---

[24] We do not allow for the burning of nonmetallurgical coal in the power plant because our data indicated such a small price differential (per million Btu) between coal and fuel oil that the cost of particulate reduction was nearly zero over a very wide range. This, to judge from the actions of electric utilities prior to the 1973–74 crisis, was indeed the way the world looked. It did not add anything to our presentation, though in today's situation coal is probably an important alternative.

[25] The lower maximum output level at the BOF is due to its required 70 percent hot metal in the furnace charge instead of the open hearth's 50.

sents the cost of producing electrical energy by combustion of purchased 2 percent sulfur fuel oil after all internal sources of by-product fuel have been exhausted. Interestingly enough, even if all electricity had to be purchased from a utility at a cost of 9 mills per kWh instead of internally generated, none of the plants would alter their daily electricity consumption one whit. This suggests that the steel mill's demand for electricity is price inelastic over the range of 5.5 to 9.0 mills. In fact, the estimated arc elasticity of demand for electricity by the basic oxygen shop over the wider range of 5.5 to 20.5 mills per kWh is only 0.054.

Naturally the quantity of internally produced electricity required by the open hearth, basic oxygen, and electric arc steel mills has an impact on the quantity of fresh heat required daily, as well as on the amount of water withdrawn and steam generated. Concentrating on the latter two categories of utilities for the moment, we observe the following total daily requirements for all purposes.

	Open Hearth	*Basic Oxygen*	*Electric Arc*
Electricity (10^6 kWh)	0.504	0.594	1.634
Steam (10^6 pounds)	5.921	7.570	9.780
Water withdrawals (10^6 gallons)	75.991	78.084	89.154

These figures reveal the striking fact that in order to produce the same amount of steel, the electric arc shop requires about three times the amount of electricity needed at the OH and BOF. However, steam and water requirements at the EA are not commensurately greater because of the high steam and water requirements at the coke oven–blast furnace departments of the two hot metal shops. For example, the basic oxygen plant requires only 47 percent of its total steam generation specifically for electricity production; the remaining 53 percent is used elsewhere in the mill for other purposes. Similarly, the open hearth shop utilizes 51 percent of its total steam generation for power production.[26] In contrast, the electric arc shop uses nearly all of its steam for generating electricity. Other requirements are minuscule because purchased scrap rather than internally produced hot metal is charged into the steel-making furnace.

The open hearth mill also benefits from a greater waste heat capturing capacity than the other two shops. It is able to produce 24 percent

[26] The fact that the open hearth shop employs a lower percentage of its steam for other purposes than does the basic oxygen shop is due to the familiar influence of low scrap prices. Although requiring a daily output of electricity almost equal to the basic oxygen shop, the open hearth shop operating on 50–50 practice requires a lower utilization of coke oven–blast furnace capacity, and hence less steam input for nonelectrical purposes.

of its total daily steam requirement from its waste heat boilers, whereas the waste heat boilers on the BOF can only produce 7 percent of total requirements in this manner. The EA has no waste heat recovery capability at all.

In a like manner, water withdrawals, although not widely variant between shops, are strongly influenced by electricity requirements at the electric arc plant, and by other process and cooling considerations at the open hearth and basic oxygen mills. In the absence of heat discharge constraints, none of the shops elect to erect cooling towers. Therefore, merely because of electricity generation, the electric arc shop discharges 6,841 million Btu of waste heat in 41 million gallons of cooling water daily; this volume amounts to 46 percent of total withdrawals for all purposes at the mill. Contrast this to open hearth and basic oxygen shop withdrawals undertaken to provide heat rejection for steam and electricity production, which respectively amount to only 17 and 19 percent of total withdrawals.[27]

It is also quite clear that the question of whether or not electricity production ought to be internal to the model is more than academic if our interest is in a comparative analysis of residuals discharge by furnace type. Failing to internalize this generation understates the discharges of heat, sulfur dioxide, and particulates[28] from all the furnaces, but does so in an uneven manner, understating most severely the emissions from the electricity-intensive EA. The figures below illustrate the magnitude of such understatement, and are expressed in terms of the percentage decrease in emissions from each furnace's bench mark level when the discharge of residuals from electricity production is not accounted for.[29]

	Open Hearth	Basic Oxygen	Electric Arc
	(percentage decreases)		
Water withdrawals	17.1	12.8	47.3
Heat discharge	9.9	12.5	46.3
Sulfur dioxide discharge	32.3	4.1	89.4
Particulates discharge	1.9	0.1	32.2

In the following chapters we shall assume that all electricity generation is internal unless stated otherwise.

Turning now to fresh heat requirements, another set of comparisons can be drawn. Table 9.7 displays the model's estimates of by-product

[27] Adding boiler water withdrawals to cooling water withdrawals associated with electricity production raises these ratios one percentage point for all shops.

[28] Similarly affected would be NO_x, hydrocarbon, and other combustion residuals not considered in our model.

[29] All other discharges are unaffected by this change.

TABLE 9.7 *Comparison of Aggregate U.S. Energy Consumption at Steel Plants in 1968 and 1968 Production Weighted Model Estimates*

(*quantities in million Btu per ton ingot steel*)

	Model open hearth	Model basic oxygen	Model electric arc	Model weighted average	1968 actual
Fuels					
Noncoking coal	n.a.	n.a.	n.a.	n.a.	1.4
Coke	11.3	16.3	0.1	11.7	11.1
Fuel oil	2.8	0.2	8.6	2.6	1.4
Tar and pitch	Sold	Sold	Sold	Sold	0.3
Liquefied petroleum gases	n.a.	n.a.	n.a.	n.a.	...
Natural gas	0	0	0	0	4.4
Coke oven gas	3.3	4.8	...	3.4	3.3
Other (sludge and forerunnings)	...	...	...	...	n.a.
Nonfuels					
Purchased electricity	n.a.	n.a.	n.a.	n.a.	2.4[a]
Total	17.4	21.3	8.7	17.7[b]	24.3

Abbreviations: n.a., not applicable; ellipses (...), too insignificant to record.

Sources: Model estimates calculated from results obtained in the bench mark case using full finishing. U.S. aggregate estimates calculated from data in American Iron and Steel Institute, *Annual Statistical Report, 1971.*

[a] Converted at the rate of 9,600 Btu per kWh, which implies 36 percent efficiency. All electricity in the model is internally produced.

[b] Obtained by weighting fuel consumption by furnace type by each furnace's share of production in 1968 (i.e., 50.1 percent open hearth; 37.1 percent basic oxygen; 12.8 percent electric arc).

and purchased fuel energy consumption by furnace type, along with a weighted average estimate of what the model would predict such consumption to be for the industry as a whole, given the 1968 furnace distribution. Alongside this estimate appears the actual consumption of energy at steel mills observed in 1968.[30]

Of the separate model estimates, it can be said that the electric arc plant requires less heat input than either the OH or BOF, given the extent to which we have traced the steel-production cycle. The comparison of our weighted average estimate of consumption by fuel type to the observed 1968 total is also revealing. Our estimates of coke and coke oven gas consumption, which are in close concert with actual consumption, provide some additional confirmation of the model's reasonableness. Furthermore, the actual heating value of the noncoking coal

[30] The method employed in determining the total heat equivalent of the physical quantities of fuel consumed, reported by the American Iron and Steel Institute is detailed in J. Varga, Jr. and H. W. Lownie, Jr., *A Systems Analysis Study of the Integrated Iron and Steel Industry*, PB 184 577 (Springfield, Va.: NTIS, May 15, 1969), chapter V, pp. 21–27.

plus fuel oil of 2.827 million Btu is approximately the same as our estimate for fuel oil alone of 2.592 million Btu, and we do not include the possibility of coal combustion for steam and power production. Overall, the model reproduces 73 percent of the energy consumption per unit output observed in 1968. Several considerations help to account for the difference: the most important of these, we suspect, is that we do not reflect as much annealing in the finishing area as is carried on in the real mill. This category makes up a large part of the 1968 AISI totals. Space-heating requirements are not included in our model either. Other minor distortions may be attributable to the 100 percent utilization of available waste heat recovery equipment at both hot metal shops, which reduces the overall heat required from purchased or by-product fuels.

Costs

Another interesting type of information available from the linear programming model concerns the marginal cost of the steel produced. Because the model is driven by the minimum production constraints described in chapter 7, it is possible to calculate the increase in cost (the increase in the objective function value) implied by a unit (ton) increase in any of the final products, and this information is routinely reported by the solution package we used. Each bench mark solution yields over thirty such final product marginal cost estimates. Published market prices, on the other hand, are available only for broad product categories. We therefore computed composite marginal costs as the ton weighted averages over all three furnace types, for six product categories chosen to match those reported in *Steel* magazine. The observed 1968 prices and our calculated costs are compared in table 9.8.

It should be noted that our cost estimates reflect the cost of hot metal, scrap, processing costs, and revenues from the sale of by-products, but do not include any allowance for sales and administrative overhead costs or long-run profits. Essentially they are short-run marginal costs. Because of these omissions (and because of the oligopolistic structure of the industry), one would expect the marginal costs in the model to lie below the ex-mill prices quoted by the industry. The data shown in table 9.8 conform to this pattern and show that our production costs amount to roughly 67 percent of the observed market prices.[31] A general rule of thumb used to transform steel pro-

31 The galvanized sheet and strip shadow price–market price ratio appears aberrant, indicating that we may have overestimated the cost of galvanizing. For alloy steels an opposite pattern appears. At the molten and semifinished stages, the alloy steel shadow–market ratio is in line with carbon shadow–market ratios. However, as one moves through the finishing steps, the ratio of the alloy shadow price to the

TABLE 9.8   *Carbon Steel Product Price Comparison*

(prices in 1968 $ per ton)

Product	Weighted bench mark shadow prices[a]	Actual 1968 mill base prices[b]	Ratio of shadow price to mill base price[c]
Ingots	47.84	83.00	0.58
Blooms, billets, and slabs	57.90	89.00–108.50	0.53–0.65
Plates	71.35	120.00	0.58
Hot-rolled sheet and strip	73.31	88.50–113.50	0.65–0.83
Cold-rolled sheet and strip	95.52	144.0–169.50	0.56–0.66
Galvanized sheet and strip	140.70	159.50–169.50	0.83–0.88

ᵃ These three-furnace composite shadow prices were derived by applying weights based on the typical product mix discussed in chapter 8 and the 1968 share of carbon steel production by furnace type reported in the American Iron and Steel Institute, *Annual Statistical Report*, 1971, to the appropriate shadow prices.

ᵇ Mill base prices from *Steel*, pp. 41–42.

ᶜ The ratio of the variable cost of a steel ingot to its market price was calculated to be between 0.53 and 0.66 by Thomas Hall, and this ratio was confirmed to be representative in a letter to Professor Hall by an Armco Steel Corporation executive. See "Production and Investment in the European Steel Industry" (Ph.D. dissertation, University of Missouri, 1971).

duction costs into selling prices states that distribution and selling costs, taxes, and a margin for profits together add 30 percent to production costs or that the average production cost is 75 percent of market price.[32]

In sum, then, the main contribution of this chapter has been first to establish our base level of discharges, and then to investigate how well or poorly they match observed discharges and to attempt to explain the differences. We believe that the model does rather well at mimicking the world when allowance is made for our assumptions. The estimated and observed atmospheric discharges match well for all furnaces. Our water-course discharge estimates on balance appear high relative to observed discharges. This is primarily attributable to the tremendous range of operating, by-product recovery, and treatment possibilities available on the water side since the choice among these is very sensitive to assumptions about base cost and price conditions and base operating equipment. The next chapter will show what happens when some of these assumptions are altered.

carbon shadow price, although always greater than one, falls, as does the alloy shadow–market ratio. This indicates that we have been unable to fully capture the cost of transforming alloy steel into finished shapes, since the only difference in finishing the two steel types in our model involves electricity required and home scrap produced.

[32] See United Nations Industrial Development Organization, *UNIDO Monographs on Industrial Development*, No. 5, *Iron and Steel Industry* (New York, UN, 1969, ID/40/5/1969), pp. 17–18.

10

INDIRECT INFLUENCES ON RESIDUALS GENERATION AND DISCHARGE

Associated with given production technology, mill configuration, input price set, product demand levels, and set of public policies on environmental quality, is a least-cost vector of residuals discharges from the mill.[1] Our bench mark discharges, for the several steel furnace types, are such vectors, corresponding to a single chosen constellation of exogenous forces. If these forces were stable our job would be nearly done, and the coefficients displayed in the last chapter (pounds of BOD per ton of shapes, million Btu's of waste heat per ton of shapes, etc.) might be used with confidence in projections of economic activity and its environmental implications. In fact, one might question the necessity of creating an elaborate and expensive linear programming model to produce a few numbers which could presumably have been calculated from historical data, were those data to be made available. (There would, of course, remain the matter of developing cost functions for discharge reductions, but even here it could be argued that concentration on treatment options would allow a much-truncated model, without severely distorting the results.)

But of course the world is not static, and demands, prices, technology, and public policies impinging on all these factors are constantly changing. In a fundamental sense that is why an activity model of iron and steel production may be useful, for it provides us with predictions of how a firm will respond to hypothesized changes. As we shall see

[1] For purposes of this discussion, public attitudes, which may or may not be reflected in legislation, may be taken as part of the set of exogenous forces. Changes in attitudes are, of course, difficult to reflect in the model—they must be translated into specific prohibitions.

in this chapter and the next, the predicted reactions often involve highly complicated relationships among the mill components—relationships which very quickly carry us beyond the capacity of unaided reasoning.

One lesson of the investigation we are about to undertake will be that changes in certain exogenous influences can have dramatic effects on a steel mill's residuals discharges, even when these influences superficially appear to be unrelated to residuals. This strong evidence casts doubt on the constant-coefficient approach to either environmental quality forecasting or management, though it may be nearly impossible in a given application to reflect the range of potential variation in an industry's discharges. We shall also find areas, however, in which a mill's response to very large changes in some underlying condition is so small as to be negligible. Another way of using the model, then, is to separate the sheep from the goats—to identify the market forces or policy areas which really cannot be ignored in assessing future prospects, while allowing us to set other forces aside.

The method followed in the next two chapters may be seen as an exercise in comparative statics, using the bench mark solutions of the preceding chapter as a reference point. In turn we shall show what happens to mill characteristics and discharges when a new technology (continuous casting) is introduced, what happens when some finishing water treatment equipment costs are decreased, what happens when the composition and level of the final output are altered and when the relative prices of some vital inputs change, and finally, what occurs when some important by-product prices are varied. Of course, not all these events are equiprobable,[2] nor need they occur singly. By attacking several possibilities, however, we hope to come through with a clearer understanding of the potential magnitude of the changes in discharge levels and the reasons for these changes, which are attributable to some of the major indirect influences. The reaction of the various plant types to altered public tolerance of their discharges, expressed either through effluent charges or discharge standards, will be left to chapter 11.

For taxonomic convenience in what follows, we shall label as direct all influences reflecting actions undertaken by public institutions explicitly to alter the residuals discharges of the plant itself. All other influences, arising from whatever source, will be designated as indirect. This is not

[2] For example, published ore prices demonstrate a remarkable stability over time, changing infrequently, while scrap prices appear to fluctuate violently. Hence, it seems that changes in the price ratio between scrap and molten iron are more likely to originate on the scrap side, which is a segment of the steel supply system not subject to backward integration.

to imply that indirect influences are not related to public policies.[3] For example, the same authority which is responsible for effluent standards could also undertake actions aimed at changing the characteristics of the plant's inputs or outputs for environmental reasons not immediately related to discharge levels, and a policy of this sort might ultimately have unforeseen and perhaps unintended repercussions on the preexisting levels of discharge.[4]

CHANGING TECHNOLOGY: CONTINUOUS CASTING

One of the most important technological improvements currently being adopted in the steel industry is continuous casting. By transforming molten steel directly into semifinished shapes, this process by-passes the traditional ingot-forming stage and with it, the necessity for ingot reheating and shape milling. We expect that the adoption of continuous casting would result, at a minimum, in the reduction of combustion residuals associated with reheating and of waterborne milling residuals (BOD, oil, and suspended solids).

Although one investigator has made the assertion that the continuous casting process unhappily "increases the volume of pollutants produced by steel mills,"[5] table 10.1 presents some contrary evidence from the model, contrasting the conventional and continuous casting situations for all three plant types.[6] From the table we observe that the impact of continuous casting is not confined to the finishing section and the residuals generated there, but is felt throughout the mill. At all three plants continuous casting establishes new relationships within each set of principal subprocesses, especially at the steel furnace, where new activities replace bench mark activities or where the bench mark activities are no longer operated in the same proportions as previously.

[3] Furthermore, indirect influences need not be entirely exogenous either to firm or industry. That is, product-improving or cost-reducing innovations are consciously undertaken after extensive research and development inside the industry, but nonetheless are classified as indirect in our scheme.

[4] As an extreme example, if automobile junkyards were prohibited, it is likely that the scrap market would be flooded with automobile hulks, and, *ceteris paribus*, the prices of shredded and no. 2 bundle scrap would plummet. In the short run, the change in the price ratio of scrap to molten iron induced by this policy would bring about a change in the optimal steel furnace burden and ultimately affect the quantity of residuals discharged per unit of steel produced. Conversely, a policy of setting aside public lands as automobile scrap storage centers, although improbable, would affect relative prices, burdens, and discharges in an opposite direction.

[5] Sheldon Novick, "Steel: The Obsolete Giant," *Environment*, vol. 15, no. 9 (November 1973), p. 8.

[6] This comparison should not be interpreted as implying that the process is equally suitable for installation at all three plant types; other outside considerations may render it infeasible at some, especially if molten steel is not available in the appropriate time pattern over the production period.

Without going into excessive detail about these changes, however, some general observations can be made which distill the essence of the comparison. At the open hearth and basic oxygen plants the generation of the waterborne phenol, ammonia, and sulfide residuals, which do not emanate from finishing itself, falls by about 12 percent from the conventional casting case. These decreases arise from a diminution in the relative importance of molten iron, and hence of coking, when the continuous casting alternative is introduced.[7] This change is betrayed by the fact that scrap purchases increase while blast furnace capacity utilization and ore purchases decline after the switchover in casting technology is made.

A very simple example will serve to demonstrate why these changes occur, especially why the coke rate falls. Consider a hypothetical steel plant required to produce T tons per day of finished steel. Assume that in the conventional casting route, home scrap generation in finishing is 20 percent of molten steel output, while in continuous casting it is only 10 percent. Further, assume that steel furnace charge practice is always 30 percent scrap, and neglect all furnace losses, flue dust recovery, or mill scale recirculation. Then we have the following two simplified situations.

(a) Conventional Casting:

total steel to be poured	$= T/0.8 = 1.25\ T$
hot iron required	$= 0.7\ (T/0.8) = 0.875\ T$
total scrap required	$= 0.3\ (T/0.8) = 0.375\ T$
home scrap available	$= T/0.8 - T = 0.25\ T$
purchased scrap	$= 0.375\ T = 0.25\ T = 0.125\ T$

(b) Continuous Casting:

total steel to be poured	$= T/0.9 = 1.111\ T$
hot iron required	$= 0.7\ (T/0.9) = 0.778\ T$
total scrap required	$= 0.3\ (T/0.9) = 0.333\ T$
home scrap available	$= T/0.9 - T = 0.111\ T$
purchased scrap	$= 0.333\ T - 0.111\ T = 0.222\ T$

---

[7] An interesting check is available here on our cost assumptions. The superior yield in continuous casting implies that the costs of steel production are lower after its introduction than in the bench mark situation, even though capital charges are included in the former and not the latter casting activities. D. J. Blickwede estimates that continuous casting enjoys a $5 per ton operating cost advantage over the conventional route. He claims that this advantage is effectively cancelled by very high capital costs, but using Battelle's capital cost estimates (about $2.00 per ton discounted at 10 percent over a conservative 10-year life), his operating cost figures imply a difference in total costs of about $3 per ton. In the model, average production costs fall by $3.50 to $4.00 per ton using continuous casting. Battelle Memorial Institute, *Technical and Economic Analysis of the Impact of Recent Developments in Steelmaking Practices on the Supplying Industries* (Columbus, Ohio: October 1964), ch. 6.

TABLE 10.1 *Mill Characteristics and Residuals Discharge Variation with the Substitution of Continuous for Conventional Casting*[a]
(quantities based on output of 2,340 tons per day semifinished shape)

Mill characteristics and residuals discharge	Open hearth			Basic oxygen			Electric arc		
	Con-tinuous casting	% Change from bench mark	Absolute change from bench mark	Con-tinuous casting	% Change from bench mark	Absolute change from bench mark	Con-tinuous casting	% Change from bench mark	Absolute change from bench mark
Average steel cost ($ per ton shape)	66	−5.8	−4	68	−6.0	−4	64	−5.1	−3
Percentage blast furnace capacity used	58	−26	−21	83	−18.2	−12	n.a.	n.a.	n.a.
Daily iron production (daily tons)	1300	−10.3	−150	1860	−12.2	−260	n.a.	n.a.	n.a.
Scrap purchases (daily tons)									
Pig	n.a.	n.a.	n.a.	n.a.	n.a.	n.a.	336	−1	−3
No. 1 Factory	83	−44.8	−67	46	n.a.	46	790	−1	−8
No. 1 Heavy melting	647	48.3	211	206	495	171	812	−1	−9
No. 2 Bundle	123	−25.8	−48	182	−1	−2	199	−1	−2
Ore purchased (daily tons)									
High iron content	1830	−8.7	−174.6	2860	−12.1	−338.6	0	0	0
Low iron content	67.0	−16.7	−13.4	129.9	−10.4	−15.0	0	0	0

Coking coal purchased (daily tons)									
1.2% Sulfur	80	n.a.	80	113.0	−12.3	−16	0	0	0
0.6% Sulfur	1380	−16.0	−262	1970	−12.2	−274	9	0	−1
Fuel purchased (10⁶ daily Btu)									
0.5% Sulfur fuel oil	0	−100.0	−451	0	0	0	5030	−31.1	−2270
2.0% Sulfur fuel oil	5060	−29.5	−2120	0	−100.0	−535	1360	−13.5	−2130
Electricity produced (kWh per ton shape)	181	−15.8	−34	215	−15	−39	605	−13.6	−95
Residuals discharged									
Waterborne									
Five-day BOD (lb. per ton shape)	4.27	−15.9	−0.81	4.94	−15.7	−0.92	2.71	−18.4	−0.61
Oil (lb. per ton shape)	2.84	−10.4	−0.33	2.92	−10.7	−0.35	2.65	−10.5	−0.31
Phenols (lb. per ton shape)	0.46	−11.5	−0.06	0.66	−12.0	−0.09	...	...	...
Cyanide (lb. per ton shape)	0.01	...	...	0.01	...	...	...	...	...
Ammonia (lb. per ton shape)	1.07	−11.6	−0.14	1.53	−12.6	−0.22	...	...	...
Suspended solids (lb. per ton shape)	3.96	−36.4	−2.27	4.11	−20.5	−1.06	3.59	−21.8	−0.99
Sulfide (lb. per ton shape)	0.17	−10.5	−0.02	0.24	−14.3	−0.04	...	...	...
Heat (10⁶ Btu per ton shape)	4.59	−12.1	−0.63	5.16	−5.5	−0.30	5.56	−11.9	−0.75
Airborne									
Sulfur dioxide (lb. per ton shape)	12.5	−11.1	−1.57	10.4	−15.8	−1.9	14.0	−15.3	−2.5
Particulates (lb. per ton shape)	6.17	4.4	0.26	10.7	−11.6	−1.4	1.0	−13.5	−0.1
Land									
Solids (ton per ton shape)	0.12	−14.3	−0.02	0.18	−14.3	−0.03	0.04	−20.0	−0.01

Note: n.a. indicates not applicable; ellipses (...) indicate too insignificant to record.   [a] Raw ammonia liquor not used for coke quenching.

This example reveals that, *ceteris paribus,* purchased scrap, as a fraction of required output T goes up, while molten iron, also as a fraction of T, declines when continuous casting supplants conventional. Less molten iron of course means less coke, and therefore the residuals associated exclusively with coking fall by the same percentage as the requisite fall in the coke rate. This happens to be about 12 percent for the open hearth and basic oxygen plants represented in table 10.1. For the electric arc plant, changes in these residuals are negligible simply because coking requirements are minor with either casting variant.

BOD and oil are generated in both the coking and finishing processes at the two hot metal shops and only in finishing at the cold melt electric arc shop. Therefore the 16 percent decrease in BOD and the 10 percent decrease in oil discharge at the former two plants (OH, BOF) represent weighted average decreases from the original bench mark quantities, whereas the respective 18 and 10 percent decreases in these residuals at the electric arc plant are unequivocally attributable to continuous casting.[8]

The percentage changes in suspended solids, SO_2, and particulates involve a more complex response pattern. If continuous casting's introduction caused no significant changes in the sinter strand–blast furnace–steel furnace activity set which was optimal in the bench mark case, combustion residuals ought to fall merely because of the smaller amount of electricity and direct heat the process requires. The suspended solids load should fall because the elimination of the conventional milling steps produces less scale. This is precisely what happens at the basic oxygen and electric arc plants, where the percentage decreases in suspended solids, sulfur dioxide, and particulates are almost alike. The open hearth plant, however, responds in a more extreme degree to the innovation by switching away from direct run-of-mine ore blast furnace burdens to sinter burdens. Higher sinter production yields a net increase in particulates because of a greater loss of dust at the partially controlled sinter strand. This is accompanied by a very large (36 percent) decrease in suspended solids, because of a reduction

[8] That is, if continuous casting itself causes a fall of 18 percent in the BOD discharged in the casting subprocess, and the 12 percent fall in the coke rate causes a 12 percent fall in coking-associated BOD, we can multiply these factors by the amounts of the residual emanating from these two subprocesses in the bench mark case to get the overall percentage decrease. Specifically from the truncated–full finishing BOF comparison, we infer that of the total 5.86 pounds of BOD, 2.54 are from coking, and 3.32 are from finishing. Therefore the total percentage decrease equals roughly

$$100 \left[\frac{(0.12 \times 2.54) + (0.18 \times 3.32)}{5.86} \right] = 15.4$$

which, with allowance for rounding error, is the percentage decrease found in table 10.1.

in the amount of dust captured in the blast furnace gaswasher water; it is a pattern quite unlike that demonstrated by the other shops.

In conclusion, our results show that continuous casting is economically superior to conventional casting over a reasonable range of relative input prices, even for installation at an existing mill. Not only does the process permit the same final output to be produced at a lower total cost when residuals discharges are unconstrained, but it also involves the generation of smaller quantities of these residuals. If the mill is charged for residuals discharged to the environment, then continuous casting will have an even bigger cost advantage over conventional casting. We will return briefly to this point in chapter 11.

CHANGING WATER TREATMENT EQUIPMENT COSTS: HOT ROLLING

So far, we have shown that an entirely new process can have a significant impact on mill-wide residuals discharges when it replaces an established technology. We can also expect that the model will be sensitive to the equipment structure assumed in the base case, as well as the capital and operating expenses charged to optional equipment that can be introduced to alter this structure, even though such equipment is not necessarily innovative.

Let us, for example, assume that our base-case cost estimates for the combined operating, maintenance, and capital costs of the alternatives which recirculate treated hot mill wastewaters rather than discharge them directly are too high. Table 10.2 shows what happens to overall basic oxygen plant discharges if the costs of these two recirculation alternatives are in fact lower than their base levels by different amounts, assuming that the costs of the direct discharge alternatives are correct at the base levels of $0.017 per 1,000 gallons for settling and $0.069 per 1,000 gallons for settling plus filtration.

A 7.4 percent reduction in the cost of the alternatives encourages the recirculation of settled wastewater generated in hot rolling of carbon steel in place of settling plus discharge, while an 11.4 percent reduction additionally encourages recirculation of settled wastewater from hot rolling of alloy steel. From table 10.2 we see that after this latter change, the residuals directly connected with the hot mill wastewater (BOD, heat, oil, and suspended solids) fall by large but varying amounts, compared to the bench mark case. Because the recirculation system involves a more complex circuit than the direct discharge system, it has a higher pumping, and hence electricity requirement. Thus, a secondary repercussion of hot mill wastewater recirculation is a larger sulfur dioxide discharge, because more fuel must be burned at

TABLE 10.2   *Discharge Variations at the Basic Oxygen Plant with Reduction of Hot Mill Waste water Recirculation Costs*

(based on 11.4% cost reduction)

BOF conditions	Hot mill water recirculated	Absolute change from bench mark[a]	Percentage change from bench mark
Ore purchased (tons per day)			
High iron content	2,790	−7	−0.2
Low iron content	145	0	0
Fuel purchased (10^6 Btu per day)			
2.0% Sulfur fuel oil	644	108	20.2
Electricity produced (kWh per ton shape)	259	5.0	1.9
Residuals discharged			
Waterborne			
Five-day BOD (lb. per ton shape)	4.10	−1.76	−30.0
Oil (lb. per ton shape)	2.39	−0.88	−26.9
Suspended solids (lb. per ton shape)	1.29	−3.88	−75.0
Heat (10^6 Btu per ton shape)	2.98	−2.48	−45.4
Airborne			
Sulfur dioxide (lb. per ton shape)	12.4	0.10	0.8
Particulates (lb. per ton shape)	12.1	0	0
Land			
Solids (ton per ton shape)	0.21	0	0

[a] The quantities of scrap and coal purchased daily remain unchanged.

the inplant power station. Notice, in this connection, that the purchase of 2.0 percent sulfur fuel oil goes up by 20 percent, while sulfur dioxide discharges increase by only 0.8 percent, and electricity production by only 1.9 percent. The reason for these wildly different numbers is, of course, that the fuel oil is the marginal heat source. The plant very nearly has an internal heat balance without any outside fuel purchases in the bench mark case, with total heat inputs on the order of 60 billion Btu per day. The extra heat requirements for the recirculation system must be met with additional fuel oil purchases, but the resulting change in sulfur dioxide discharges is tiny. Although this also means a larger heat discharge from power generation, the decrease in heat discharge due to cooling and recirculating the hot mill water is more than offsetting, leaving a net decrease in waterborne heat discharge as the final result.[9]

9 Some informed readers may feel that table 10.2 provides a better representation of the base steel mill discharge situation than table 10.1 if they feel it is more realistic to assume the operation of finishing water recirculation equipment. Because of the sensitivity of the model to a rather small change in hot mill wastewater recirculation costs, when BOD, oil, and suspended solids discharges are either constrained below their bench mark levels or penalized with an effluent charge, the same large absolute (and percentage) reductions will initially be achievable at

CHANGING RELATIVE INPUT PRICES:
WITHIN-GROUP PRICE VARIATION

Each broad input category such as ore, coal, and fuel is composed of a number of alternative inputs which serve the same general purpose. The quality variations in the inputs falling in any one of these general categories imply that some perform the same function better than others, and if nothing else were different, their market prices would also differ. In this section we will show the effects of varying the price of a single input while keeping the prices of other inputs in its category, as well as all other prices, constant at their 1968 bench mark levels. Because this procedure implies that the price of the relevant input changes in relation to inputs in its own group as well as in relation to all other inputs, we call it "within-group" price variation.

Specifically, there are two important inputs whose base price levels seem to exclude them from the optimal solutions in most cases: pellets and high sulfur coal.[10] Our aim here is to find the prices which would induce the model to substitute these specific inputs respectively for the other preferred ores and for low sulfur coal. We will then be able to discover whether the resulting discharge levels are much different from the bench mark case discharges. The exercise will also yield the relationship between the quantity of the specific input demanded and its price; this is our qualified version of the elasticity of derived demand.

Pellet Price Variation

As it stands, the base price of pellets is too high to warrant their selection as part of the optimal blast furnace burden because sinters can be produced which provide a lower cost molten iron. However, steel industry spokesmen appear to be confident that pellets will dominate blast furnace burdens in the future.[11]

---

relatively low shadow prices (or effluent charges) by taking advantage of the hot mill water recirculation alternative. This fact should be borne in mind by those who favor table 10.2; their interest should focus on the shape of the cost of reduction curves beyond their initial region.

[10] We will look at within-group scrap price variation in chapter 12.

[11] The importance of pellets was stressed in a technical review of this study submitted to Resources for the Future on July 18, 1973, by Henry C. Bramer, president of Datagraphics, Inc., Pittsburgh, Pennsylvania. Confirming this opinion is the estimate of Varga and Lownie, *A Systems Analysis Study*, PB 184 577 (Springfield, Va.: May 15, 1969), chap. IV, p. 7, that by 1980 almost 54 percent of all the ore consumed in the United States will be in pellet form, a projected increase of 21 percentage points over the 1967 figure. Our coke rate for a pellet burden at the blast furnace may be too high, and this may explain why pellets are not used in the bench mark case.

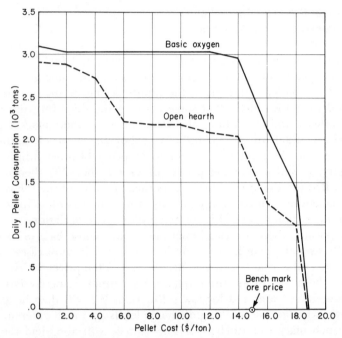

Figure 10.1. Response of the open hearth and basic oxygen steel plants to changes in the cost of pellets. Weighted average price of ores used in basic solution: OH, $15.48; BOF, $15.21.

From figure 10.1 we observe that in order for pellets to displace other ores completely at the basic oxygen plant, their price would have to fall below $14.00 per ton.[12] Some pellets would enter the burden sooner, actually comprising almost 50 percent of all ore inputs at a price of $18.41 per ton, only $0.34 below the bench mark pellet price level. The elasticity of the basic oxygen shop's demand for pellets is understandably high between $18.41 and $14.00 per ton (amounting to 7.35 over this range) because pellets are such a close substitute for the other iron-bearing inputs.[13] Thereafter, of course, there are no more opportunities for ore displacement, so the demand for pellets is almost completely inelastic.

---

[12] In this and other graphical presentations, and dependent variable, quantity, is represented on the y axis, and the independent variable, price, on the x axis.

[13] Pellet production costs, including mining, processing and transportation charges, were estimated to vary from $12.30 to $16.20 per ton in the U.S. Lake Superior District, and from $12.95 to $18.75 in Ontario and Labrador in 1972. See Jack Robert Miller, "The Inevitable Magnitudes of Metallurgical Iron Ore," paper prepared for the 1972 Annual Convention of the Association of Iron and Steel Engineers, Pittsburgh, September 1972 (mimeographed), Table 7.

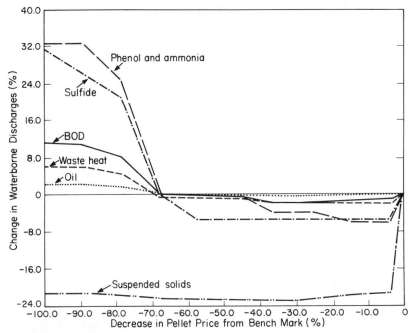

Figure 10.2. The influence of the pellet price level on open hearth water-borne discharges.

The open hearth plant's derived demand curve for pellets lies inside that of the basic oxygen plant, because the low absolute 1968 scrap price level induces it to opt for 50 percent hot metal in its steel furnace burden rather than 70, thus requiring less of all ore inputs. If absolute scrap prices were higher, the two curves would be nearly identical. The open hearth curve also exhibits two distinct elasticities, 7.45 between the price range of \$18.41 to \$14.00 per ton, and 0.18 thereafter.[14]

Does the displacement of other ores by pellets cause any significant changes in residuals discharge? The answer is equivocal. Reference to figure 10.2 shows that for waterborne discharges, nothing exceptional happens at the OH over the elastic range of the demand curve except for the sharp fall in suspended solids discharges resulting from the almost immediate displacement of run-of-mine ores by pellets as the price of pellets falls. Discharges change by even less at the basic oxygen

[14] The slightly greater slope of the open hearth curve over the inelastic region is due to its ability to move away from 50–50 practice toward 70–30 at the steel furnace at pellet prices below \$6.00 per ton, whereas the basic oxygen plant is technologically constrained to use at least 70 percent hot metal whatever the pellet price.

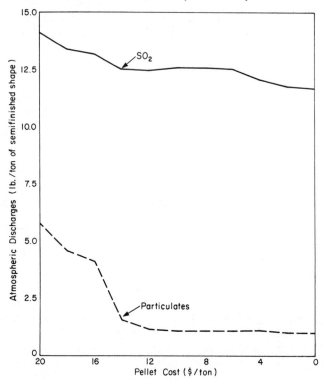

Figure 10.3 The influence of the pellet price level on open hearth atmospheric discharges.

plant. Therefore, we conclude that even though pellet burdens do not appear in the bench mark solutions because of their high relative price, waterborne discharges are about the same as they would be under any price for pellets, given our coke rates.

The situation for air is quite different, as can be seen in figure 10.3. At the open hearth facility, a decrease in the pellet price from $18.75 to $12.00 (36 percent) stimulates a 12 percent decrease in sulfur dioxide emissions (14.09 to 12.09 pounds per ton shape) and an 82 percent decrease in particulate emissions (5.91 to 1.09 pounds per ton shape). At the basic oxygen plant the same percentage decrease in the pellet price causes respective 26 and 75 percent decreases in discharges of these two residuals. Since the pellet price could reasonably be anywhere between $12.00 and $18.75 per ton, the possible range of atmospheric discharges is extremely wide for any steel mill, even if it has installed flue dust removal equipment. (This point was already mentioned in chapter 9, in connection with the comparison of our bench mark results with data from samples of real mills.)

This wide discharge variation in atmospheric residuals refers only to the steel mill itself. In a broader view, because pellet processing usually takes place at the mine while sinter processing takes place at the mill, when pellets have a cost advantage over sinter the real impact may not be a net decrease in atmospheric discharges from the steel supply system, but rather a shift from mill to mine in the location of the discharges. This point must be borne in mind whenever pellets replace other ore burdens in response to effluent charges or discharge constraints.

Coal Price Variation

The overwhelming preference for low sulfur coal at both the open hearth and basic oxygen plants in the bench mark case is a product of the base coal price set determined from the multiple regression analysis referred to in chapter 3. This exercise gave us nothing more than a starting point from which we can now expand our understanding of the role sulfur content plays in the steel manufacturer's demand function for metallurgical quality coal.[15] For simplicity, we shall confine this investigation to the basic oxygen plant.

If there were only two production activities using coal (one using high and one low sulfur coal), a "coal sulfur penalty" could be defined as the absolute difference in price (expressed per percent sulfur) between two coals of differing sulfur contents, but otherwise similar in all relevant respects, which leaves the steel producer indifferent between the two inputs. Our iron and steel production model is, of course, quite complex. In fact, we have sixty-six alternative blast furnace activities. Many of these are linked to sintering, which has its own sulfur removal characteristics, and all of them face a common capacity constraint. Both of these aspects of iron production influence the mill's evaluation of the internal cost of introducing sulfur into the smelting system. Therefore, we cannot expect to find a unique coal price differential (given the absolute price of one coal) which delineates the crossover from exclusive low sulfur coal use to exclusive high sulfur

[15] Because of data inadequacies, our coal price estimating equation had to be structured in such a way that supply considerations were not included. For this reason alone, the regression estimate of the price differential between high sulfur and low sulfur coal cannot be equated to the demand side price premium on coal sulfur content.

Apart from this problem, the regression estimate may be distorted simply because of the inclusion of nonmetallurgical coal prices and characteristics in the sample. This means that the regression coefficient for coal sulfur may reflect the additional boiler corrosion cost incurred by utilities from combustion of higher sulfur coals, not the additional metallurgical costs of including them in the blast furnace burden.

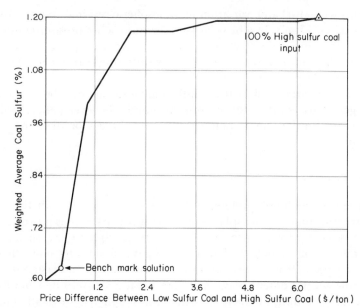

Figure 10.4.   Coal sulfur penalty in basic oxygen steelmaking. (Pure metallurgical basis. No environmental constraints on sulfur dioxide discharges; price of high sulfur coal at $10.25/ton.)

coal use. Instead, as the relative price of the two coals is varied, we discover a number of places where marginal substitution of one coal type for the other occurs.

Figure 10.4 demonstrates the response of the model to different relative prices of the two coals created by varying the low sulfur coal price above the high sulfur coal price of $10.25 per ton. This figure substantiates our reasoning that on the demand side there exists a range of so-called coal price penalties corresponding to the range of process alternatives, the penalty at any point being defined by the marginal process entering the basis of the linear programming solution in response to the price change. There is no unambiguous or unique penalty. The first substitution away from low sulfur coal is made when the low sulfur coal price is only $0.073 per ton above the high sulfur price, implying a marginal penalty of $0.12 per ton per percent sulfur.[16] At this point the majority of the coal consumed is still low sulfur. Finally, when the price differential becomes $6.56 per ton, the last substitution is made. Here, high sulfur coal completely replaces low sulfur coal, and the implied penalty is $10.90 per ton per percent sulfur. The best that can be said of the regression estimated penalty is that it falls within these limits.

[16] Simply the difference in the two coal prices divided by the difference in sulfur content between coals, 0.6.

Table 10.3 displays the discharges associated with seven different low sulfur–high sulfur coal price differentials created by raising the low sulfur coal price while holding the high sulfur coal price constant at $10.25 per ton. A differential of about $1.00 instead of $0.37 per ton (the bench mark level) encourages a large change in high sulfur coal use, and produces significant changes in the obvious residuals categories: sulfide and sulfur dioxide, along with very small changes in several other discharges. The bench mark coal price set decreases the latitude of response available to a mill faced with sulfur dioxide and sulfide constraints; the first stages of removal will be more costly per pound removed under the bench mark conditions than they would be at a higher relative price although the latter stages will be coincident.[17]

As might be expected, the two coals are very close substitutes, and the elasticity of demand for one of them is very high, given a constant price for the other. The derived price elasticity of demand for low sulfur coal corresponding to table 10.3 is 4.13. This estimate refers to a given base, so that when a new absolute price is chosen as the base, the elasticity changes. In fact, there is a demand surface for the two coals, and a two-dimensional demand curve for any one of them really represents a slice out of this surface. Figure 10.5 illustrates a set of piecewise linear slices out of such a surface; each slice begins from a different absolute low sulfur coal price level. This surface demonstrates that the familiar law of demand holds; since, given a particular low sulfur coal price, as the price of high sulfur coal increases, the quantity of high sulfur coal demanded falls. Concurrently with the decrease in high sulfur coal consumption, there occurs a nearly equivalent increase in low sulfur coal consumption.

CHANGING RELATIVE INPUT PRICES: BETWEEN-GROUP PRICE VARIATION

Variations in relative prices between broadly defined input categories are oftentimes at least as interesting as variations in the relative prices of specific inputs within a category. In this section we create a number of situations in which the relative price of one entire group of inputs varies while the price relatives of the specific inputs within that group remain constant.[18] Derived demand curves for all the principal inputs are a product of this exercise; and a major theme of this section

---

[17] This statement does not mean that the cost of meeting a sulfur dioxide emission standard set below the bench mark level of discharge is higher than it would be if high sulfur coal were relatively cheaper.

[18] In the real world there is no reason to expect that price changes will exclusively be either intragroup or intergroup in nature; mixed changes undoubtedly occur. Since there are an infinite number of possibilities of the mixed variety, for systematic purposes we have confined our investigation to the two extremes.

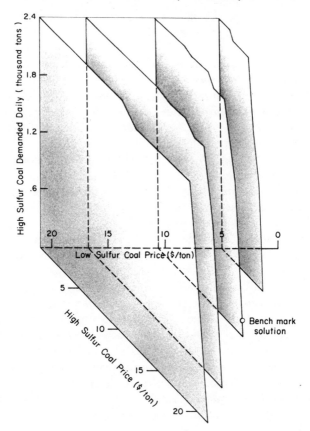

Figure 10.5.   The basic oxygen plant's demand surface for high sulfur coal.

will be to show that the elasticity of many of these curves depends on the underlying plant situation assumed, and the absolute price level of other cooperant inputs.

Ore and Scrap Price Variation

The effects of ore and scrap price variation can be explored in two distinctly different situations. The first centers on the effect of different absolute ore price levels on each plant type (OH, BOF) viewed in isolation.[19] The second, which attempts to replicate the future economy-wide plant situation, involves a composite electric arc–basic oxygen shop.

The open hearth plant.   Let us begin with the OH plant having the base level of steel furnace gas treatment equipment. Because ore

[19] The electric arc plant is very insensitive to the ore price. Both the basic oxygen and electric arc shops viewed separately are insensitive to the scrap price.

TABLE 10.3 *Residuals Discharge Variation at the Basic Oxygen Plant with Variation in the Price of High Sulfur Coal Relative to Low Sulfur Coal*

Inputs and residuals	Difference between low- and high-sulfur coal price[a]						
	0[b]	$0.37[c]	$1.00	$2.00	$3.00	$4.00 to 6.47	$6.56[d]
Coal purchased (tons per day)							
1.2% Sulfur	0	129	1610	2290	2300	2400	2420
0.6% Sulfur	2370	2240	792	124.0	124.0	22	0
Residuals discharged							
Waterborne (per ton shape)							
Five-day BOD (lb.)	5.86	5.86	5.90	5.91	5.91	5.92	5.91
Phenols (lb.)	0.75	0.75	0.77	0.77	0.77	0.77	0.77
Ammonia (lb.)	1.75	1.75	1.77	1.78	1.78	1.78	1.78
Suspended solids (lb.)	5.17	5.17	5.54	5.28	5.28	5.64	5.25
Sulfide (lb.)	0.27	0.28	0.46	0.53	0.53	0.55	0.55
Heat (10^6 Btu)	5.46	5.46	5.49	5.49	5.49	5.59	5.49
Airborne							
Sulfur dioxide (lb.)	11.4	12.3	17.8	20.8	20.8	21.4	21.7
Particulates (lb.)	12.1	12.1	11.8	12.1	12.1	11.8	12.1

a Absolute high sulfur coal price held constant at $10.25 per ton.
b No high sulfur coal consumed.
c Bench mark solution.
d No low sulfur coal consumed.

TABLE 10.4   *Mill Characteristics and Residuals Discharge Variation at the Open Hearth Plant with Variation in the Ore Price Level*

Mill characteristics and residuals	Percent increase in ore prices above bench mark level			
	0[a]	10	20	≥36
Average steel cost ($ per ton shape)	70	72	73	76
Marginal iron cost ($ per ton hot metal)	41	43	45	49
% Blast furnace capacity used	79	78	65	64
Scrap purchased (tons per day)				
No. 1 factory	150	150	150	164
No. 1 heavy melting	436	436	436	426
Shredded	0	70	70	70
No. 2 bundle	166	92	92	94
Ore purchased (tons per day)				
High iron content	2010	2000	1990	1980
Low iron content	80	78	78	79
Residuals discharged (per ton shape)				
Waterborne				
Five-day BOD (lb.)	5.08	5.07	5.06	5.05
Oil (lb.)	3.17	3.17	3.17	3.17
Phenols (lb.)	0.52	0.52	0.52	0.51
Ammonia (lb.)	1.21	1.21	1.20	1.19
Suspended solids (lb.)	6.23	6.23	4.98	4.98
Heat (10^6 Btu)	5.22	5.22	5.21	5.21
Airborne				
Sulfur dioxide (lb.)	14.1	14.1	15.0	15.0
Particulates (lb.)[b]	5.91	5.83	6.94	5.99

[a] Bench mark solution.
[b] Base gas treatment.

prices are already high enough to make 50–50 practice more attractive in general than 70–30,[20] we would not expect much response to any ore price increases above the bench mark level. What we might expect, however, is less particulate discharge at higher ore prices due to the increased value of internally recovered flue dust. Strangely, this does not happen consistently because of other compensating changes. Table 10.4 shows the response pattern, which has significant implications, principally for airborne discharges.

As ore and pellet prices are raised 10 percent above their base levels, the only major change occurs at the steel furnace itself. Here, alloy steel which was formerly produced using no. 2 bundle scrap in an ore practice activity is now made in an oxygen practice activity using shredded scrap, so particulate discharges fall. The cleaner shredded

[20] The only exception is that 5 percent of the drawing quality steel output is produced by a 70–30 ore practice.

scrap is a more attractive source of iron units than no. 2 bundles at higher ore prices because molten iron becomes an increasingly expensive alloy dilutant in carbon steel production.

At the next step (a 20 percent increase in ore and pellet prices), however, particulates discharges rise as run-of-mine ore is replaced by sinter at the blast furnace.[21] This change brings with it an increase in sulfur dioxide emissions and a decrease in suspended solids. At or above a 36 percent increase in ore prices a final response occurs;[22] the small amount of drawing quality steel which was produced in a 70–30 ore practice is now produced in a 50–50 ore practice because the increased cost of hot metal has finally rendered all 70–30 activities inferior. Less hot metal production causes sulfur dioxide and particulate discharges to fall below their previous peak.

Over this entire range, second-stage gas treatment equipment installation is unprofitable at the steel furnace. In fact, the only response in terms of treatment equipment involves the erection of a fabric filter at the discharge end of the sinter plant to capture a small amount (1.12 tons per day) of low iron-content flue dust when ore prices are more than 23 percent above the base level.

Three other features of this particular solution stand out. First, while ore prices rise nearly 40 percent, total costs increase only 8 percent, yielding a cost response ratio of 0.22.[23] This ratio is low because ore is not originally as great a factor in total cost as it would be if 70–30 practice were the bench mark burden. A 100 percent increase in the prices yields a ratio of 0.26, larger because the mill is locked into using the same quantity of ore at all prices above 40 percent of the bench mark level.

The price elasticity of demand for iron ore is very low (0.05) when ore prices rise above the base.[24] This is because the open hearth shop has a limited number of avenues of escape from ore use. All it can do

[21] The evidence of this switch in table 10.4 is the fall in the percentage of blast furnace capacity utilized.

[22] All solutions out to a 100 percent increase are identical (except for daily costs).

[23] The ratio of the percentage change in costs to the percentage change in input price (using high iron content fines to define the price change) is not associated with a single cost curve, since each input price change redefines (shifts) the plant's total cost curve. The response ratio is defined over the chosen range by the formula:

$$\frac{C_1 - C_0}{P_1 - P_0} \cdot \frac{P_1 + P_0}{C_1 + C_0}$$

Obviously this is not strictly equivalent to the ratio of the increase in costs from the base to the increase in prices

$$\frac{C_1 - C_0}{C_0} \cdot \frac{P_1 - P_0}{P_0},$$

although it yields nearly the same result.

[24] Of course, the elasticity will be higher for ore price changes below the base due to the shop's ability to move toward 70–30 practice.

as ore prices rise is switch away from ore practice to oxygen practice at the steel furnace, reshuffle its scrap mix in order to extract more iron units, and recover some sinter strand dust. For these reasons the cross price elasticity of demand for scrap is less than 0.01. Given the inflexibility of response alternatives in this situation, the two iron-bearing inputs are not very close substitutes.[25]

The basic oxygen plant. The basic oxygen shop is even less responsive than the OH plant to increased ore prices, and no tabular or graphic presentation of the response pattern is warranted. Ore prices increase 23 percent before anything happens at all, and this response is again the installation of dust recovery equipment at the sinter strand. Because this solution does not alter the blast furnace burdening situation very much, its only impact is to lower particulate discharges per ton shape 1.77 pounds from the bench mark case. Beyond this point, the only change that occurs involves a substitution away from no. 2 bundles toward shredded scrap, this time at an ore price level roughly 62 percent above the base. Although water-course discharges fall slightly from their bench mark levels, the major result is a reduction in particulate discharges to 10.0 pounds from 12.3 pounds per ton of shapes.

At the basic oxygen plant, the ratios of the percentage increase in costs to 40 and 100 percent increases in ore prices are 0.30 and 0.36, respectively. The effect of ore prices on total daily costs is larger than it was in the isolated open hearth case after all burdening options have been exhausted, simply because of the basic oxygen furnace's greater technical dependence on molten iron, and hence ore, because it must always use at least a 70 percent iron charge. The price elasticity of demand for ore is consequently very low (0.02) and the cross elasticity of demand between scrap purchased and ore prices is actually negative, for the reason mentioned below.

Plants without installed steel furnace dust recovery equipment. In chapter 8 we constructed two gas cleaning cases for each mill, a base case and a grass roots case. The former represents our version of the status quo at tightly controlled mills. The latter exists so that we might discover under what circumstances this status quo would actually be desired for motives of purely private profit. That is, at what ore price level would it pay steel producers to erect steel furnace gas treatment equipment in the absence of any public pressure?

---

[25] Because of the iron content differences between the scraps, higher ore prices in some circumstances might even lead to a decrease in the total quantity of scrap demanded, as high iron content scrap is substituted for low iron content scrap, making ore and iron appear to be complementary inputs. In these circumstances a more appropriate measure would be the percentage change in scrap iron units consumed induced by a percentage change in the price of ore iron units.

Survey data reveal that only about 40 percent of open hearth furnaces are equipped with particulate emission control equipment, whereas 99 percent of basic oxygen furnaces are so controlled.[26] Part of this disparity may be explained by the desire to be prepared in advance for expected tight environmental standards on the part of steel companies engaged in existing-shop modernization and new plant construction during the late 1950s and early 1960s, since generally gas treatment equipment is more expensive when it is added to an existing shop than when it is built as part of a grass roots plant.[27] This problem may have been severe at many older open hearth mills, explaining why a majority of them remain uncontrolled. As stated by a Bethlehem Steel Corporation executive, "The age, space requirements and nature of operation of the conventional open hearth furnace are such as to make it impracticable in most instances to apply well designed and effective air pollution control equipment."[28]

The model can be employed to show that in many instances the installation of dust control equipment at an existing BOF is a paying proposition, while under the same circumstances it is not at the OH. It is our aim here to delineate the situations in which dust recovery and recycling are profitable, and therefore to introduce some economic content into statements like the following, made by a Japanese steel expert at the Fifth Annual Conference of the International Iron and Steel Institute: "In terms of costs, we consider such waste [recovered iron-bearing flue dust] almost priceless, or in other words, cost free."[29]

We should first note that the capital cost information used in this study refers to the minimum cost of gas treatment equipment at a completely new facility. Since the decision to allow for such equipment in the design of a basic oxygen furnace has generally been made concurrently with the decision to build the furnace (whether or not the equipment was actually installed at the same time as the furnace itself), our implicit assumption that the furnace is in place without treatment equipment probably involves no distortion in treatment

[26] Vandegrift and Shannon, *Particulate Pollutant System Study,* vol. III, p. 121.

[27] Thomas M. Barnes and H. W. Lownie, Jr., *A Cost Analysis of Air-Pollution Controls in the Integrated Iron and Steel Industry,* PB 184 576 (Springfield, Va.: NTIS, May 15, 1969), appendix C, pp. 11–13.

[28] Allen D. Brandt, "Current Status and Future Prospects—Steel Industry Air Pollution Control," a paper presented at the National Conference on Air Pollution sponsored by the U.S. Department of Health, Education and Welfare, Public Health Service, Division of Air Pollution, Washington, D.C., December 1966 (mimeographed), p. 5.

[29] International Iron and Steel Institute, *Fifth Annual Conference Proceedings,* Toronto, 1971, p. 99.

equipment capital costs.[30] However, our capital costs probably under-
state the real cost of tacking on a gas treatment system to an existing
OH because we make no special allowance for the added installation
cost caused by the space problem referred to above. As we shall see,
however, at the OH the installation of control equipment is virtually
never a profitable move from a private point of view *even* given our
sanguine capital cost estimates. Thus it is not hard to understand why
only 40 percent of these facilities are controlled.

For the moment, let us focus on the steel furnace gas treatment operating decision. Assume that, for whatever reason, the equipment is in
place. Under our bench mark conditions this equipment must be operated, but there is no reason to believe that this would always be the
case; it may pay to leave the equipment idle.

If the furnaces are allowed to bypass their dust treatment equipment, under the bench mark conditions the OH would actually do so,
and the BOF would not. Operating labor requirements, which depend
on average gas flow rates, are too high at the open hearth shop to make
operation of steel furnace flue dust recovery equipment a viable alternative. As a result, the open hearth shop's particulate discharges sky-
rocket, from a bench mark value of 14.09 pounds per ton of semifinished shapes to 31.96 pounds.[31] At the basic oxygen shop there is no
payoff in leaving the steel furnace dust collectors idle, so the bench
mark solution remains unaltered.

This simple experiment reveals an important lesson for environmental policy makers. That is, government subsidizing of pollution
control equipment capital costs offers no guarantee that the devices
will be operated once they are installed. If the subsidy route is chosen
to attain a desired level of environmental quality, in some instances
equipment operating costs might also have to be covered by public
revenues in order to ensure the maintenance of that quality level. For
example, in order to achieve a daily decrease of 60,960 pounds of particulate emissions by the installation and operation of a steel furnace
electrostatic precipitator at a medium-sized open hearth plant, the
public must be willing to spend about $51.00 per day over and above
the capital cost of the equipment.

On the other hand, equipment capital cost subsidies may work in
certain other situations. That is, although it may not be profitable to
privately install control equipment, if the installation cost is borne by
the public instead of the producer, he may find it profitable to operate
the installed equipment even if he assumes the operating cost burden

---

[30] Design of the furnace's gas hooding and ducting system is an integral part of
the basic oxygen shop design problem, since the off gas must always be combusted
and cooled even if it is not subject to dust removal.

[31] The value is high because the model for the most part prefers to employ
oxygen lancing, which generates more dust than ore practice.

himself. This is the case at the basic oxygen plant. Given the bench mark conditions (especially ore prices and capital costs), the producer would not willingly install steel furnace dust recovery equipment. In this situation his total daily cost would be $170,300 and his plant would discharge 137,600 pounds of dust daily. If, however, the public were to bear the capital cost burden of the control equipment, the producer's costs would be reduced by about $200 per day, while the public would enjoy a 109,400-pound reduction in dust discharges. The daily equivalent of the electrostatic precipitator capital cost subsidy—that is, the daily cost borne by the public at large—would be $660. The net daily cost of the reduction is then about $460, or about 4 mills per pound of dust removed. Contrast this to the open hearth net daily operating and capital costs which the public must bear: $820, or more than $0.01 per pound removed.[32]

Although the basic oxygen plant would not erect gas cleaning equipment given the bench mark conditions, it is not true that it would never do so. For example, if ore prices were to increase by 83 percent above their bench mark levels, the producer would install a first stage electrostatic precipitator at the BOF. In contrast, it would require a 211 percent increase in ore prices to induce the OH operator to do the same thing. Viewed from a different angle, precipitator capital costs would have to be 60 percent lower than the bench mark estimate (given the operating costs) to make the equipment's installation profitable at the BOF.[33] At the OH, of course, capital costs could be reduced by 100 percent and the operation would still not be undertaken, since, as we have seen, the internal value of the recovered dust is insufficient to offset operating costs.

Even though these ore price increases or capital cost decreases seem substantial, they may give an exaggerated impression of the unprofitability of BOF flue dust recovery equipment since the comparisons assume that the recovered dust contains an average 55 percent iron. If, on the other hand, the dust really contained an additional 10 percent iron, it would pay the mill to erect a first stage precipitator immedi-

---

[32] Remember, however, that the postremoval discharge levels at the two plants are not the same, because of their different generation characteristics. Costs to achieve a given daily discharge will be discussed in chapter 11.

[33] The percentage decrease in precipitator capital costs required to make recovery attractive is not a mirror image of the percentage increase in ore prices needed to achieve the same result because of the complementary nature of low iron content purchased ore fines and low iron content recovered flue dust. That is, every sinter burden can contain no more than 30 percent flue dust because of desired physical sinter characteristics such as permeability and strength (see ch. 4, p. 73). Thus, as the price of ore rises two things happen. First, potentially recoverable flue dust becomes a more attractive substitute for purchased ore. At the same time, in order to use the dust to make a quality sinter, it must be combined in fixed proportions with purchased ore fines, whose price is rising along with the price of all the other ores.

ately and to recycle the dust to the sinter strand.[34] Total daily costs (now including a discounted capital cost for treatment equipment) would be $89 higher than in the bench mark case. In exchange, sulfur dioxide discharges per ton shape would fall to 12.20 pounds, and particulate discharges to 10.19 pounds, respectively 0.11 and 1.87 pounds per unit output below the bench mark.[35] (Water-course discharge would be the same as in the bench mark case.) It would take a 25 percent increase in precipitator capital costs to make equipment installation unprofitable if the dust in the furnace off gas contained 65 percent iron.

The fact that dust recovery from BOF off gas is, at least potentially, more likely to be privately undertaken than recovery from OH gases is demonstrated in the model by the absence of investment in such equipment at the latter furnace even when dust is defined as containing 65 percent iron. Even given our probably understated OH treatment equipment installation costs, ore prices would have to increase by at least 72.6 percent above their bench mark level to make erection of open hearth precipitators profitable.

Plants in combination. The basic oxygen and electric arc plants (at least as we have modeled them) lack sufficient flexibility to allow significant response to changes in the relative price of ore and scrap. In order to further explore the impact of such changes on residuals discharge, we have created a composite plant, containing both basic oxygen and electric arc capacity, which can fruitfully be compared to the open hearth plant. The composite plant's response can either be interpreted narrowly as pertaining to a single shop or, more broadly, as the expected response for the industry as a whole some time in the future when OH capacity has been completely replaced.[36]

First, to delineate the limits of residuals discharge variation, let us create an admittedly unrealistic situation by assuming that each steel furnace type in the composite plant has gas cleaning equipment and can independently produce the required 2,340 tons of semifinished shapes per day. Given the bench mark conditions for all else but ore prices, we observe from table 10.5 that ore prices must rise considerably

[34] To the extent that contaminants in the dust (such as zinc) make it difficult to recycle, this conclusion does not hold.

[35] A higher iron content in the recycled dust implies different sinter and blast furnace activities than the bench mark, and hence less sulfur dioxide and particulates.

[36] At the micro level, when more than one furnace type is installed at the same location, the shop can be labeled a duplex plant, although this term customarily has been more narrowly defined to mean only a combination of the acid Bessemer converter and the basic open hearth processes. In the present day, the BOF–electric arc combination is much more common than the Bessemer–open hearth combination. See Harold E. McGannon, ed., *The Making, Shaping and Treating of Steel*, 9th ed. (Pittsburgh: United States Steel Corp., 1971), pp. 544–547.

TABLE 10.5 *Mill Characteristics and Residuals Discharge Variation at a 100 Percent Excess Capacity Basic Oxygen–Electric Arc Plant with Variation in the Ore Price Level*

Mill characteristics and inputs and residuals	Percent increase in ore prices above bench mark level			
	0[a]	20 to 100	120	140
Average steel cost ($ per ton shape)	64	65 to 68	68	68
Marginal iron cost ($ per ton hot metal)	39	43 to 59	59	59
% Blast furnace capacity used	18	17	...	...
% Steel produced by electric arc	82	82	100	100
Price ratio: No. 1 heavy melting scrap to Iron	0.67	0.61 to 0.44	0.44	0.44
Price ratio: No. 1 heavy melting scrap to high iron content ore fines	1.70	1.42 to 0.85	0.77	0.71
Scrap purchased (daily tons)				
Pig	0	0	339	339
No. 1 factory	770	770	799	799
No. 1 heavy melting	821	821	821	821
Shredded	0	0	0	0
No. 2 bundle	200	200	200	200
Ore purchased (daily tons)				
High iron content	473	473	...	0.3
Low iron content	24	24	...	0
Residuals discharged (per ton shape)				
Waterborne				
Five-day BOD (lb.)	3.79	3.79	3.32	3.32
Oil (lb.)	3.02	3.02	2.96	2.96
Phenols (lb.)	0.14	0.14	...	...
Ammonia (lb.)	0.33	0.33	0.01	0.01
Suspended solids (lb.)	4.70	4.70	4.58	4.58
Sulfide (lb.)	0.05	0.05	...	...
Heat (10^6 Btu)	6.13	6.13	6.31	6.31
Airborne				
Sulfur dioxide (lb.)	16.4	16.4	16.5	16.5
Particulates (lb.)[b]	3.09	3.07	1.11	1.11
Land				
Solids (tons)	0.06	0.06	0.05	0.05

Note: Ellipses (. . .) indicate too insignificant to record.
[a] Bench mark solution.
[b] Base gas treatment.

(103 percent) before any significant changes in discharges occur. Even before that point, the low price of scrap relative to ore causes most (81.5 percent) of the steel output to be produced in the EA, since the BOF has economic superiority only in the drawing quality carbon steel line. Once the shadow price of molten iron exceeds the (constant) price of purchased pig iron, the BOF surrenders its superiority even in this product category, and coke plant-related discharges fall accordingly.[37]

In contrast with the OH solution represented in table 10.4, the ratio of the combined shop's change in daily costs to a 100 percent increase in ore prices is now only 0.07, because the combined shop is less dependent on ore as a factor of production. The price elasticity of demand for ore is considerably higher: 2.43 over the full price range shown in table 10.5. The cross elasticity of demand between the quantity of scrap consumed (including iron purchased) and ore prices is 0.22, indicating that the two iron sources are better substitutes at the combined shop under these circumstances than they would be in the isolated shop cases.

Neither the open hearth shop viewed in isolation nor the composite shop as seen above show any strong reactions to increased ore prices. Scrap prices already are so low in the bench mark situation that most of the potentially ore-intensive activities (which generally are residuals-intensive as well) are already suboptimal, and hence never appear in the solutions. Therefore, to bring some of the hot metal intensive activities into focus, let us double the bench mark scrap price level and again sequentially increase ore prices above the 1968 base at the combined shop.[38]

Table 10.6 depicts the principal features of the combined shop's response in this new situation. Now the band of response to ore prices is much broader, because the new starting point when scrap prices are doubled involves more basic oxygen-produced steel, and thus higher

---

[37] Watercourse discharges are not altered if the combined shop is allowed to operate without steel furnace dust control equipment. Furthermore, ore price rises are felt so strongly in the relative competitive positions of the two furnaces that it does not pay to erect the equipment even at prices 200 percent above the base level because recycling alternatives (sinter strand–blast furnace–basic oxygen furnace) are phased out due to the inferiority of molten iron vis-à-vis purchased scrap.

[38] Although a doubling of scrap prices in constant 1968 dollars may appear extreme, this situation is fairly representative of what has happened between 1968 and 1974. Namely, the increase in scrap prices has far outstripped the price increases observable in other major input categories over this period. For example, the ratio of the quoted no. 1 heavy melting scrap price to the quoted pig iron price (calculable from prices in *American Metal Market*) was roughly 0.46 in 1968, and 1.18 in February of 1974. Hence a preliminary indication of what has happened to a particular mill type's discharges between 1968 and 1974 as a result of relative price change can be obtained by comparing the benchmark solutions to the doubled scrap price solutions.

coke oven and blast furnace use and residuals discharge. Now, for example, a 120 percent increase in ore prices induces a 43 percent decrease in BOD discharge, while formerly (table 10.5) the same ore price increase led to only a 12 percent reduction in BOD. This is a direct result of the greater fall in blast furnace use dictated by the ore price increase, given the higher level of absolute scrap prices. The same reasoning holds true for airborne discharges. Sulfur dioxide discharges escalate more rapidly with the ore price increase at a doubled scrap price level than they did at the bench mark scrap price level, because a given percentage increase in ore prices induces more electric arc steel production at the expense of basic oxygen steel production than formerly, and hence implies more electricity production and purchased fuel combustion. This also means that the absolute and percentage fall in particulates over the same ore price span is greater than it was in table 10.5, since the electric arc segment of the plant generates fewer particulates, even before dust removal, than the displaced basic oxygen component.

Also noteworthy is the fact that when a given scrap–ore price ratio is generated from different sets of absolute scrap and ore prices, there is no assurance that discharges and mill characteristics will be similar. For example, when scrap prices are at the bench mark levels and ore prices are 1.5 times scrap prices, the electric arc share of output is about 82 percent and hence the residuals discharges associated with this point are quite different from those associated with the same relative prices, but a scrap price twice the bench mark level. What this means, of course, is that we must be quite clear about what other factors are or are not held constant when discussing changes in discharges with respect to changes in a single relative price.

In any particular region, or even in the economy as a whole, we would not often expect to find the 100 percent excess capacity situation represented by the above version of the combined basic oxygen–electric arc shop. *A priori* we might think that the swings in residuals discharges represented in tables 10.5 and 10.6 delineate the limits of the potential range, for it could be reasoned that the limits of this band will be narrowed insofar as capacity by furnace type is circumscribed, and no furnace is able to meet the whole of the production requirement by itself. This line of reasoning might be expected to apply in the aggregate as well as to a single plant if the economy is operating near full capacity.

To show that this argument, however intuitively appealing, is not correct for every residual, let us make the duplex shop more realistic by altering the furnace capacity constraints in the model in such a way that the electric arc component of the duplex shop can produce no more than 34 percent of the requisite steel output, while the basic

TABLE 10.6 *Mill Characteristics and Residuals Discharge Variation at a 100 Percent Excess Capacity Basic Oxygen–Electric Arc Plant with Variation in the Ore Price Level (Scrap Prices Double the 1968 Base)*

Mill characteristics and residuals	Percent increases in ore prices above bench mark level						
	0[a]	20	40	60	80	100	≥120
Average steel cost ($ per ton shape)	75	78	82	85	87	87	88
Marginal iron cost ($ per ton hot metal)	42	47	51	55	56	59	61
% Blast furnace capacity used	95	89	85	79	24	22	1
% Steel produced by electric arc	1	8	11	17	74	77	100
Price ratio: No. 1 heavy melting scrap to iron	1.23	1.12	1.02	0.94	0.93	0.88	0.85
Price ratio: No. 1 heavy melting scrap to high iron content ore fines	3.40	2.83	2.43	2.12	1.89	1.70	1.54
Scrap purchased (daily tons)							
Pig	0	0	0	0	280	291	743
No. 1 factory	0	0	0	0	0	0	0
No. 1 heavy melting	0	0	35	180	1200	1240	1250
Shredded	0	0	0	0	0	0	0
No. 2 bundle	206	358	414	388	208	200	200

Ore purchased (daily tons)							
High iron content	2810	2620	2490	2310	659	600	4
Low iron content	146	133	137	127	35	31	1
Residuals discharged (per ton shape)							
Waterborne							
Five-day BOD (lb.)	5.87	5.70	5.60	5.44	3.97	3.91	3.33
Oil (lb.)	3.27	3.25	3.23	3.22	3.04	3.03	2.96
Phenols (lb.)	0.76	0.71	0.68	0.63	0.20	0.18	0.01
Cyanide (lb.)	0.01	0.01	0.01	0.01	...	...	...
Ammonia (lb.)	1.75	1.64	1.57	1.46	0.45	0.41	0.02
Suspended solids (lb.)	5.17	5.13	5.11	5.08	4.75	4.73	4.60
Sulfide (lb.)	0.28	0.27	0.25	0.24	0.07	0.07	...
Heat (10^6 Btu)	5.50	5.55	5.56	5.61	6.08	6.09	6.28
Airborne							
Sulfur dioxide (lb.)	12.5	13.1	13.3	13.9	16.4	16.4	16.4
Particulates (lb.)[b]	12.1	11.5	9.5	8.9	3.9	3.7	1.2
Land							
Solids (ton)	0.21	0.19	0.19	0.17	0.07	0.07	0.06

Note: Ellipses (...) indicate too insignificant to record.
[a] Not equivalent to bench mark solution due to doubled scrap price level.
[b] Base gas treatment.

oxygen component can produce no more than 84 percent.[39] The capacity-constrained version of the composite shop represents in a rough way the kind of aggregate capacity situation likely to exist in the industry in the near future.[40] Table 10.7 shows us what to expect under these conditions, when scrap prices are set at twice their 1968 levels.

The above argument breaks down at ore prices higher than twice their base values, simply because furnace switching is not the only way the model can react to an indirect influence. There are finishing treatment alternatives common to the output of both furnace types which will sometimes be used to increase the amount of mill scale recovered when the increased ore price makes the scale a valuable ore substitute. As a result, suspended solids discharges actually fall farther in the constrained than in the unconstrained capacity case. In fact, as soon as ore prices increase by 101 percent of their base levels,[41] the hot mill wastewater which was formerly settled and discharged is settled and recirculated. This investment results in substantial decreases in BOD, oil, suspended solids, and heat discharges, as is evident in column 3 of table 10.7.

In summary, then, in terms of the absolute and percentage decreases in most water-course discharges associated with ore price increases, the constrained capacity duplex shop is not much different from the outmoded OH shop (given the same background conditions and either scrap price level). The reactions on the atmospheric side are not as consistent. Increased ore prices mean increased sulfur dioxide discharges at the duplex plant, and the opposite at the open hearth. The results further show that, given the base price set, it is difficult to say that the open hearth technology, if subject to steel furnace dust control, offers a much worse picture of aggregate discharges than the similarly controlled basic oxygen–electric arc technology. However, in terms of private daily costs, it is definitely inferior.

The influence of a doubled scrap price level (given bench mark ore prices) on plant residuals discharges is implicit here and does not merit extensive discussion. Appearing on page 242 is a summary of the estimates of the price elasticity of derived demand for scrap and the price

[39] Operating to satisfy the daily output requirement hence implies an 85 percent utilization of aggregate productive capacity, i.e., $100/(34 + 84)$.

[40] J. Varga, Jr. and H. W. Lownie in *A Systems Analysis Study*, p. IV-2, predict that by 1980, the OH will provide only 20 percent of raw steel production. Of the remaining 80 percent, 31 will be produced by the EA and 69 percent by the BOF.

[41] This change occurs slightly above a 100 percent increase in ore prices. Its results hold up to and beyond an ore price increase of 200 percent, which is the point at which the full solution is reported.

TABLE 10.7 *Mill Characteristics and Residuals Discharge Variation at a Constrained Capacity Basic Oxygen–Electric Arc Plant with Variation in the Ore Price Level*

(*twice base 1968 scrap prices*)

Mill characteristics and residuals	Percent increase in ore prices above bench mark level		
	0	100	200
Average steel cost ($ per ton shape)	75	90	102
Marginal iron cost ($ per ton hot metal)	55	64	86
% Blast furnace capacity used[a]	100	78	78
% Steel produced by electric arc[b]	16	34	34
% Steel produced by basic oxygen	84	66	66
Price ratio: No. 1 heavy melting scrap:			
(1) iron	0.95	0.81	0.61
(2) high iron content ore fines	3.40	1.70	1.13
Scrap purchased (daily tons)			
Pig	0	84	84
No. 1 factory	0	0	0
No. 1 heavy melting	155	484	484
Shredded	0	0	0
No. 2 bundle	393	334	334
Ore purchased (daily tons)			
High iron content	2340	1810	1810
Low iron content	124	100	100
Residuals discharged (per ton shape)			
Waterborne			
BOD-5 (lb.)	5.47	5.00	3.33
Oil (lb.)	3.22	3.16	2.33
Phenols (lb.)	0.64	0.50	0.50
Cyanide (lb.)	0.01	0.01	0.01
Ammonia (lb.)	1.48	1.16	1.16
Suspended solids (lb.)	5.08	4.98	1.18
Sulfide (lb.)	0.24	0.19	0.19
Heat (10^6 Btu)	5.60	5.75	3.38
Airborne			
SO_2 (lb.)	13.8	15.5	15.6
Particulates (lb.)	10.6	7.3	7.3
Land			
Solids (ton)	0.18	0.14	0.14

[a] A total of 38.4 hours of blast furnace capacity are available.
[b] A total of 21.6 hours of electric arc furnace capacity are available.

cross elasticity of demand for ore calculated from the solutions discussed above and from some supplementary solutions.[42]

[42] Scrap price changes are represented by using the change in the price of no. 1 heavy melting in the elasticity calculation. All elasticities are for a doubling of scrap prices given the base ore price level. All plants have installed steel furnace gas treatment equipment which must be operated.

Plant Type	Price Elasticity of Demand for Scrap	Cross Price Elasticity of Demand for Ore
Isolated open hearth	2.68	0.52
Isolated basic oxygen	0.24	0.03
Isolated electric arc	0.33	n.a.
100% excess capacity duplex	2.41	2.14
Constrained capacity duplex	0.71	0.39

Purchased Heat Price Variation

In this era of rising energy prices, the popular and scientific press have both demonstrated a renewed interest in the energy intensity of transport modes and industrial processes. In the steel industry each of the typical plant types has its own fuel balance situation, and in two of them the demand for purchased fuel is nearly zero elastic.[43]

The basic oxygen plant can meet the bulk of its fuel needs from by-product fuels captured during coking and smelting, and consequently is almost entirely independent of the purchased fuel market. In contrast, the electric arc shop produces no by-product fuel, so it is almost entirely dependent on purchased heat (or its electricity equivalent). However, because none of the modeled electric arc activities differ radically in their electricity intensity, the EA has almost no leeway in this regard, whatever the cost of fuel or electricity.

Let us concentrate then on the reaction of the open hearth shop to higher fuel oil and natural gas prices, holding the metallurgical coal price constant at the base level.[44] The data in figure 10.6 indicate that the elasticity of demand for purchased fuels is rather low, in fact being 0.31 over the price range represented. However, in the range above the bench mark level, which is of more interest, the elasticity of demand is higher but still inelastic: 0.61. As fuel prices ascend beyond the bench mark level, the decrease in purchased heat consumption is obtained by the withdrawal of by-product tar from the market in order to burn it internally, as well as by reordering of blast furnace activities toward those which generate more blast furnace gas. Very little of the decrease is, in fact, achieved by lowered electricity production. Furthermore, total fresh heat requirements are nearly constant, as the figure indicates.

Again we find a familiar pattern in the discharge of residuals as the change in the price of external fuels induces run-of-mine ore blast furnace activities (which cause the generation of a large quantity of blast

[43] New technological variants not represented in the model may not exhibit this characteristic.

[44] Fuel price changes are represented in the elasticity calculations by using the change in the price of 2 percent sulfur fuel oil.

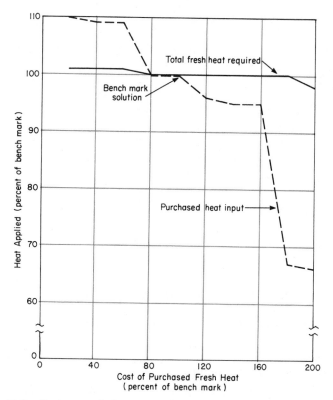

Figure 10.6. Response of the open hearth plant to changes in the cost of purchased heat.

furnace gas) to displace some sinter burdens (which generate less gas). Associated with fuel prices 60 percent below the bench mark level is a suspended solids discharge of 4.98 pounds per ton of shapes produced, a 1.25 pound decrease from the bench mark. Other water-course discharges are nearly the same as they were in the base solution. Sulfur dioxide and particulate discharges increase respectively by 0.95 and 1.16 pounds per unit output due to the increased importance of sintering at lower fuel prices.

For prices above the bench mark set, water-course discharges remain basically unaltered. On the air side, the combustion of tar which was formerly sold causes a decrease in sulfur dioxide discharges since it replaces 2 percent sulfur fuel oil as the price of the latter rises. At the same time, however, we observe a shift toward predominantly high sulfur coal use. Because the recovered gas from this coal has a higher sulfur content (as well as a higher Btu content) than low sulfur coke oven gas, the increase in sulfur dioxide emissions from this source is sufficient to more than wash out the decrease involved in the afore-mentioned substitution of tar for 2 percent sulfur fuel oil. Hence, at fuel prices 80 percent above the base, sulfur dioxide emissions are 2.09 pounds greater per unit output. That is, an 80 percent increase in fuel prices in-duces a 15 percent increase in OH sulfur dioxide emissions. It also causes a 16 percent increase in particulate discharges. In conclusion, then, we can say that any set of fuel prices close to the bench mark set (±40 per-cent) is unlikely to significantly affect open hearth discharges. Fuel price changes in either direction exceeding this amount will cause increased sulfur dioxide and particulate discharges.

Water Price Variation

Even though in industry the problem of waterborne residuals dis-charges is probably far more significant than that of the volume of water required by the manufacturer, there nonetheless exists a long tradition of interest in water use.[45] But the concept of requirements implied in many of these studies generally abstracts from price considerations. That is, the studies implicitly or explicitly assume completely inelastic water demand functions, although there is some evidence that even household demand for water in some use categories is far from zero elastic.[46] We can show that the same holds true for steel plants.

Recall that at the steel plant water is withdrawn for three different purposes: cooling, steam production, and processing. The model deter-mines separately the quantities of untreated and treated water with-drawn. Base water costs differ among uses to reflect the amount of treat-ment required:[47]

Untreated water	$0.015 per 10^3 gallons
Boiler water	0.150 per 10^3 gallons
Hot rolling mill makeup water	0.060 per 10^3 gallons
Cold rolling mill makeup water	0.075 per 10^3 gallons

Now imagine a situation where water treatment costs remain constant (intake water has not declined in quality) but the cost of raw water rises,

[45] Faulkner B. Walling and Louis E. Otts, Jr., *Water Requirements of the Iron and Steel Industry* (U.S. Geological Survey Water Supply Paper 1330-H) 1967.

[46] For a summary of many statistical estimates of the price and income elastici-ties of demand for water by use category available in the literature, see C. S. Rus-sell, "Restraining Demand," in B. M. Funnell and R. D. Hey, eds., *The Management of Water Resources in England and Wales* (Westmead, England: D. C. Heath, Ltd., 1974), pp. 67–98.

[47] If a cooling tower is erected, the objective function entry in this activity re-flects the cost of treating the recirculated water, which may be as high as $0.04 per thousand gallons. If cooling water is not recirculated, it is assumed to cost the same as untreated process water.

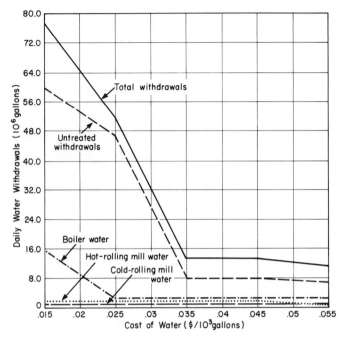

Figure 10.7. Basic oxygen shop response to changes in water cost.

due, perhaps, to a new water withdrawal charge imposed by a river management authority on all riparian abstractors. Then, how high will this constant charge have to rise to induce a significant reduction in total steel mill water withdrawals? Figure 10.7 shows that a charge of about $0.02 per 1,000 gallons over and above the base untreated water cost will induce an 83 percent reduction at the basic oxygen shop. Both the OH shop and the EA shop (purchasing its electricity from a public utility) respond in the same way. For an electric arc shop generating its own electricity, a $0.02 levy will induce an 81 percent reduction in withdrawals. Obviously, given the absence of required recirculation in the bench mark case at all three plants, considerable latitude exists for water withdrawal reduction by engaging in more recirculation as the surcharge on withdrawals escalates.

The average price elasticity of demand for water at the basic oxygen shop between the 0 and $0.04 per 1,000 gallon surcharges is in fact 1.31.[48] Demand is completely inelastic thereafter. For a privately borne cost of $1,080 per day ($0.46 per ton of semifinished shapes) a 67 million gallon

[48] Water price changes are represented by using the change in the price of untreated water in the elasticity calculation.

per day reduction in basic oxygen shop water withdrawals can be achieved, and this cost will completely exhaust all possibilities for further reduction.

The impact of increased water withdrawal costs on the basic oxygen shop's discharges is set out in table 10.8. The first major process changes take place at a surcharge of $0.006 per 1,000 gallons, and involve the recirculation rather than direct discharge of hot mill wastewater. Consequently, in the second column of the table we observe decreases in the BOD, oil, suspended solids, and heat discharges. Sulfur dioxide discharges increase because more electricity must be produced to run the pumps in the new recirculating system.[49]

The next major change involves the erection of a cooling tower to recirculate the cooling water from all other parts of the mill. Its impact is revealed in column three. Finally, at a charge of $0.034 per 1,000 gallons, the cold mill wastewaters which were formerly discharged are recirculated, and the result of this appears in column four. Note that the only discharge categories enjoying major reductions are BOD, oil, suspended solids, and heat.

CHANGING BY-PRODUCT PRICES: PHENOL AND AMMONIUM SULFATE RECOVERY

The coke plant of an integrated steel mill produces a number of liquid and gaseous waste streams containing chemicals which, under certain recovery cost and market price conditions, will be converted into salable by-products instead of being discharged. However, under the bench mark conditions, phenol and ammonia in the ammonia liquor are not recovered. In this section we will explore the by-product market prices which would induce their recovery.

Given the bench mark market prices for phenol and ammonia, ammonia liquor disposal is a headache for the plant managers who cannot dump the untreated liquor into an adjacent watercourse. The trend of rising sulfuric acid costs, coupled with falling ammonium sulfate prices since 1958, has made ammonia recovery increasingly unprofitable. This situation has caused many plants to discontinue crude ammonia liquor distillation entirely in favor of quenching station disposal, exacerbating the coke plant's air pollution problem.[50] The bench mark solution of the model reflects this worst of all possible worlds by reporting the quan-

---

[49] The quantity of boiler quality water withdrawn rises very slightly with the general price increase because additional electricity must be provided to run the recirculating system.

[50] H. A. Grosick, "Ammonia Disposal—Coke Plants," *Blast Furnace and Steel Plant*, vol. 59 (April 1971), pp. 217–222.

TABLE 10.8   Response of the Basic Oxygen Plant to a Surcharge on Water Withdrawals

Inputs and residuals	Surcharge per 10^3 gallons			
	$0[a]	$0.01	$0.02	≥$0.04
Average steel cost ($ per ton shape)	73	73	73	73
Water cost ($ per 10^3 gallons):				
Untreated	0.015	0.025	0.035	0.055
Boiler	0.150	0.160	0.170	0.190
Hot mill	0.060	0.070	0.080	0.100
Cold mill	0.075	0.085	0.095	0.115
Water withdrawals (daily 10^3 gallons)				
Untreated	59,900	47,000	8,100	7,100
Boiler	900	900	900	900
Hot mill	15,600	2,500	2,500	2,500
Cold mill	1,700	1,700	1,700	700
Total	78,100	52,100	13,200	11,200
Electricity produced (kWh per ton shape)	254	259	259	259
Residuals discharged (per ton shape)				
Waterborne				
Five-day BOD (lb.)	5.86	4.11	4.11	4.11
Oil (lb.)	3.27	2.39	2.39	2.39
Phenols (lb.)	0.75	0.75	0.75	0.75
Cyanide (lb.)	0.01	0.01	0.01	0.01
Ammonia (lb.)	1.75	1.75	1.75	1.75
Suspended solids (lb.)	5.17	1.28	1.28	1.12
Sulfide (lb.)	0.28	0.28	0.28	0.28
Heat (10^6 Btu)	5.46	2.98	0	0
Airborne				
Sulfur dioxide (lb.)	12.3	12.4	12.4	12.4
Particulates (lb.)	12.1	12.1	12.1	12.1
Land				
Solids (tons)	0.21	0.21	0.21	0.21

[a] Bench mark solution.

tities of potentially recoverable ammonia and phenol as water-course discharges, since the quenching corrosion penalty prevents the vaporization of these chemicals.[51]

Figure 10.8 shows two price sets for the joint phenol and ammonium sulfate by-products: one would induce the operation of an installed ammonia still–dephenolizer, and another would encourage its installation and operation. It is obvious from this figure that as long as some method of free liquor disposal is available, phenol and ammonium sulfate would not even be partially recovered at a mill where the recovery equipment

[51] Often the direct water-course disposal option for ammonia liquors may be blocked by explicit or implicit discharge standards. We will discuss the impact of prohibiting both direct discharge and use in quenching in the next chapter.

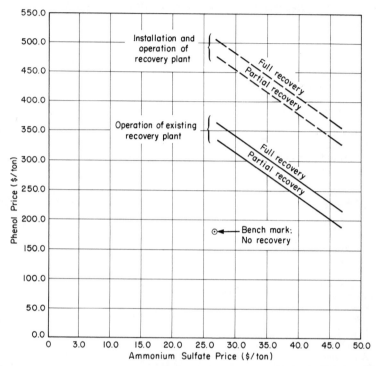

Figure 10.8. Price combinations of phenol and ammonium sulfate which render recovery profitable at the basic oxygen plant. Corrosion cost penalties are associated with the use of the ammonia liquor at the quench station. Solid lines indicate operating and maintenance costs, dotted lines, capital, operating, and maintenance costs.

is in place unless: (1) the ammonium sulfate price were to rise about 78 percent above the base level (given the 1968 phenol price), (2) the phenol price were to rise 88 percent of its base level (given the 1968 ammonium sulfate price), (3) some weighted average of the two price increases reported above occurred, or (4) recovery equipment operating and maintenance costs were considerably reduced, given the base prices.[52]

Table 10.9 shows the discharges associated with zero, partial, and full by-product recovery. Partial recovery results in significant decreases in waterborne residuals discharges: 19.3 percent for BOD, 7.3 percent for oil, 88.0 percent for phenols, and 92.6 percent for ammonia. The final

---

[52] Since a mix of high and low sulfur coal appears in the optimal basic oxygen plant solution, two separate ammonia liquor streams must be processed or disposed of. There are two steps in the choice of recovery because the sulfur concentrations in the liquors imply that the low sulfur stream requires slightly less sodium hydroxide input at the dephenolizer than the high sulfur stream.

TABLE 10.9   Residuals Discharge Variation at the Basic Oxygen Plant with Various Levels of Ammonia and Phenol By-product Production (Quenching Penalized)

(quantities per ton shape)

By-products and residuals	Level of phenol and ammonia recovery		
	Zero[a]	Partial	Full
Phenol sold (lb.)[a]	0	0.89	0.94
Ammonium sulfate sold (lb.)	13.3[b]	19.9	20.3
Residuals discharged			
Waterborne			
Five-day BOD (lb.)	5.86	4.73	4.67
Oil (lb.)	3.27	3.03	3.02
Phenols (lb.)	0.75	0.09	0.06
Cyanide (lb.)	0.01	0.01	0.01
Ammonia (lb.)	1.75	0.13	0.03
Suspended solids (lb.)	5.17	5.17	5.17
Sulfide (lb.)	0.28	0.26	0.26
Heat (10^6 Btu)	5.46	5.47	5.47
Airborne			
Sulfur dioxide (lb.)	12.3	12.5	12.5
Particulates (lb.)	12.1	12.1	12.1
Land			
Solids (ton)	0.21	0.21	0.21

[a] Bench mark solution.
[b] Recovered from gas in the ammonia absorber. Includes no ammonium sulfate recovered in the ammonia still.

step increases these percentages to 20.3, 7.6, 94.7, and 98.3 percent, respectively. Notice that heat and sulfur dioxide discharges increase slightly because of the additional electricity and steam required to run the recovery unit.

RECOVERED SULFUR PRICES AND SULFUR DIOXIDE EFFLUENT CHARGES

Although it seems unlikely that sulfur prices will rise much in the future because of the millions of tons added to domestic supplies through recovery dictated by environmental regulation, let us see how far the price of elemental sulfur would have to rise to encourage its recovery at a basic oxygen steel plant.[53]

In view of our prior discussion of the costs of installing and operating coke oven gas desulfurizing equipment, it is not surprising to find that the price of sulfur would have to increase very far indeed above the base

[53] "Should the U.S. Slam the Door on Sulfur Imports?" *Chemical Week*, April 12, 1972, pp. 11–12.

TABLE 10.10 Mill Characteristics and Residuals Discharge When Sulfur Recovery is Induced at the Basic Oxygen Plant by Increases in the Price of Sulfur

Sulfur price ($ per long ton)[a]

Mill characteristics and residuals	No recovery	Partial recovery				Full recovery	
	20[b]	200 (190)	260 (249)	280 (277)	300 (287)	320 (309)	340 (335)
Change in total daily resource cost from base ($)[c]	0	60	130	740	780	1110	1440
% Blast furnace capacity used	95	95	95	100	100	100	100
Sulfur sold (daily long tons)	0	0.35	0.67	3.04	3.20	4.34	5.40
Coal purchased (daily tons)							
1.2% Sulfur	130	130	250	1,130	1,190	1,620	1,620
0.6% Sulfur	2,240	2,240	2,120	1,260	1,200	790	790
Residuals discharged per ton shape							
Waterborne							
Five-day BOD (lb.)	5.86	5.86	5.87	5.89	5.89	5.90	5.90
Oil (lb.)	3.27	3.27	3.27	3.27	3.27	3.27	3.27
Phenols (lb.)	0.75	0.75	0.76	0.76	0.76	0.77	0.77
Cyanide (lb.)	0.01	0.01	0.01	0.01	0.01	0.01	0.01
Ammonia (lb.)	1.75	1.75	1.75	1.77	1.77	1.77	1.77
Suspended solids (lb.)	5.17	5.17	5.17	5.64	5.64	5.64	5.64
Sulfide (lb.)	0.28	0.28	0.30	0.40	0.41	0.46	0.46
Heat (10^6 Btu)	5.46	5.47	5.47	5.51	5.51	5.52	5.54
Airborne							
SO_2 (lb.)	12.3	11.8	11.7	11.0	11.0	10.7	9.0
Particulates (lb.)	12.1	12.1	12.1	11.7	11.7	11.7	11.7
Land							
Solids (ton)	0.21	0.21	0.21	0.21	0.21	0.21	0.21

[a] Plant cost information is associated with the first price listed, while prices in parentheses are the values associated with major process changes. Hence recovery actually begins when sulfur can be sold for $190 and is complete when sulfur can be sold for $335. Average out-of-pocket cost of steel production is about $73 per ton for all sulfur prices.

[b] Bench mark solution.

[c] Assuming the increase in the sulfur price is achieved via a subsidy over and above the market price ($20), the resource cost is equal to the total daily objective function value reported in the optimal solution adjusted by addition of the total daily subsidy paid to the producer (i.e., tons of sulfur sold daily multiplied by the subsidy per ton).

of $20 per long ton before a steel producer would, of his own accord, install and operate gas desulfurization equipment. Table 10.10 shows the response of the basic oxygen plant. The results shown in the table reveal two significant conclusions. First, we cannot expect that steel mills having coke ovens will build gas desulfurization equipment in the future without direct public policy encouragement in the form of effluent charges, discharge standards, or sulfur price subsidies. Gas desulfurization is just too expensive over a reasonable sulfur price range to induce privately motivated recovery. Second, even in the unlikely event that sulfur prices were to soar 1,600 percent above their 1968 constant dollar base, the effect on plant discharges would not be entirely welcome. The desulfurization of all of the coke oven gas produced at the coke plant is accompanied by the replacement of low sulfur coal with high sulfur coal in order to obtain the maximum amount of potentially recoverable sulfur from the coke oven gas. Unfortunately, the 27 percent decrease in atmospheric sulfur dioxide emissions resulting from a $315 increase in the price of sulfur over the base involves as well a 64 percent increase in water-course sulfide discharges, and minor increases (less than 3 percent) in all other water-course discharges.

Perhaps an effluent charge on sulfur dioxide emissions could be a more certain and efficacious means of reducing steel plant discharges. Since a tax of 5–7.5 cents per pound of sulfur dioxide emitted has actually been proposed by government spokesmen,[54] let us explore this possibility. Table 10.11 shows the basic oxygen plant's discharges and characteristics associated with four different sulfur dioxide emission charge levels, given the 1968 price of recovered sulfur.

Here, a $0.05 tax per pound of sulfur dioxide discharged causes the substitution of some run-of-mine ore blast furnace charges for some sinter burdens in order to capture some sulfur in the blast furnace slag rather than allowing it to be discharged to the atmosphere at the sinter strand. It yields a 15 percent reduction in sulfur dioxide emission. A charge of $0.10 causes some sulfur recovery as well as the substitution of 1 percent sulfur fuel oil for 2 percent sulfur fuel oil at the power plant, in order to reduce sulfur dioxide discharge by 60 percent. A charge of $0.15 involves a move further away from sinter by the introduction of pellets, as well as the use of some natural gas at the sinter hood. It gives us a 68 percent reduction in sulfur dioxide discharges, which is maintained for any charge between $0.15 and $0.50 per pound of sulfur dioxide discharged.

Comparing tables 10.11 and 10.10, we can see that an effluent charge is a better way of achieving a given sulfur dioxide discharge reduction

[54] Nicholas P. Chopey, "Taking Coal's Sulfur Out," *Chemical Engineering*, July 24, 1972, pp. 86–88.

TABLE 10.11   Mill Characteristics and Residuals Discharge When Sulfur Recovery is Induced at the Basic Oxygen Plant by a Sulfur Dioxide Effluent Charge

Mill characteristics and residuals	SO$_2$ effluent charge ($ per pound)			
	0[a]	0.05	0.10	0.15
Change in total daily resource cost				
from base ($)	0	50	1,150	1,440
Average steel cost ($ per ton shape)	73	73	74	74
% Blast furnace capacity used	95	100	100	100
Sulfur sold (daily long tons)	0	0	3.20	3.09
Coal purchased (daily tons)				
1.2% Sulfur	130	0	0	0
0.6% Sulfur	2,240	2,380	2,380	2,290
Residuals discharged (per ton shape)				
Waterborne				
Five-day BOD (lb.)	5.86	5.87	5.87	5.78
Oil (lb.)	3.27	3.27	3.27	3.26
Phenols (lb.)	0.75	0.76	0.76	0.73
Cyanide (lb.)	0.01	0.01	0.01	0.01
Ammonia (lb.)	1.75	1.75	1.75	1.69
Suspended solids (lb.)	5.17	5.64	5.64	5.55
Sulfides (lb.)	0.28	0.27	0.27	0.26
Heat (10^6 Btu)	5.46	5.47	5.51	5.46
Airborne				
Sulfur dioxide (lb.)	12.3	10.4	4.9	4.0
Particulates (lb.)	12.1	11.6	11.6	9.40
Land				
Solids (ton)	0.21	0.21	0.21	0.22

[a] Bench mark solution.
[b] The total daily resource cost is equal to the total daily out-of-pocket cost (i.e., the reported objective function value) less the total daily effluent tax (i.e., pounds of sulfur dioxide discharged times the charge per pound).

than a subsidy on the price received for recovered sulfur. For approximately the same increase in the total daily resource cost, the former procedure yields a 68 percent decrease in sulfur dioxide emissions while the latter gives us only a 27 percent reduction. Furthermore, the subsidy would worsen the discharge picture for all the other residuals, whereas a $0.15 charge on sulfur dioxide would improve the situation for all residuals except suspended solids.

This short example of the basic oxygen shop's response to an effluent charge on its sulfur dioxide emissions is a prelude to chapter 11, the principal concern of which will be the cost of residuals discharge reduction undertaken in response to direct public management intervention. What we have learned in this chapter will be helpful in understanding the context of the next. That is, before one can speak of managing the level of residuals discharge in an industry, it is helpful to know something about the way discharges vary in response to economic influences outside the purview of the managing authority. A process analysis model which is capable of characterizing the discharge situation for a number of different plant types within a broad industry category under a variety of conditions is a particularly helpful device in this regard for a number of reasons.

Preparation of the activity matrix demands that data be collected in an informed and structured manner in order to describe the production processes available within an industry. Therefore, the economist is forced to come to grips with the engineering attributes of the technical production function. The insight gained during this descriptive stage becomes an invaluable aid in understanding the rationale behind observed responses when the model is used as an analytical tool for predicting the consequences of changes in underlying circumstances (new technologies, different relative prices).[55]

Furthermore, a process analysis model like the one developed here is capable of answering questions not directly related to residuals reduction but likely to be important in the future. Specifically, estimates of the responsiveness of plant types to the costs of inputs such as iron-bearing ore and scraps, coal, purchased fuels, and water can be obtained through price parameterization.

Finally, the model can be used to demonstrate the fact that the cost of reduction to a given residuals discharge level is a function not only of treatment equipment costs, but also of underlying background conditions (technology variants, input prices, and by-product prices) as well.

[55] The estimation of production functions with residuals by regression analysis rather than linear programming suffers three shortcomings in this respect. First, adequate data connecting technology, costs, output and residuals discharge are difficult to obtain. Second, *a priori* mis-specification of the functional form of the equations because of ignorance will introduce bias into the results. Finally, the learning process is cut short to the extent that although we may be able to estimate the likely effect of an influence, we may remain uncertain about the chain of causality. For a discussion of the methodological differences between the estimation of cost functions using statistical and process analysis methods, see James M. Griffin, "The Process Analysis Alternative to Statistical Cost Functions: An Application to Petroleum Refining," *American Economic Review*, vol. 62 (March 1972), pp. 46–56.

11

DIRECT INFLUENCES ON RESIDUALS GENERATION AND DISCHARGE

Given an assumed set of background conditions, the linear model has provided us with a calculated set of bench mark discharges for each plant. Further, the sensitivity of these discharges to altered background conditions has been explored. Now, as the second half of our inquiry, we will discuss selectively the cost implications of and operating responses to discharge constraints on steel mill residuals which are set below the bench mark levels. Further, we will show that exogenous (indirect) influences can have a significant impact on the costs of residuals discharge reduction, given a publicly desired level of discharge which must be attained; and, conversely, that a given effluent charge will produce different levels of discharge when the underlying conditions are different.

In this connection, it is worth noting that though we concentrate in the early sections of the chapter on presenting the marginal and average cost curves implied by the imposition of various discharge constraints, we do not wish to be interpreted as holding a brief for this policy instrument. Indeed, the points we make in the last section of the chapter cast some doubt on the efficacy of both charges and standards in a nonstatic world. In using the standards for our exposition, we are merely making use of the model in a particularly convenient way; we are also able to use effluent charges explicitly, but in doing so we create an additional calculation for ourselves in finding increases in total resource costs (counting effluent charge payments as transfers). We may also take advantage of the rough symmetry between charges and standards in the linear model in interpreting our results.[1] We emphasize, however, that

[1] There is no strict effluent charge–shadow price equivalence in a linear model because of discontinuities at the points of process changeover. The general sym-

the familiar ground of the quarrel between proponents of charges and standards is not within the scope of this study.[2]

There are, of course, many methods which an industrial plant can employ to reduce its waste discharges in the face of public policies. The quantity of wastes discharged per unit time can be reduced by changes which decrease residuals generation, such as input mix alterations, changes in production processes, and output mix alterations.[3] Further, materials recovery, by-product production, and waste treatment methods can reduce waste discharges after generation. Often, more than one of these reactions can occur simultaneously. If, for example, a restriction on sulfur dioxide discharges causes a particular steel mill to reduce its use of the sintering strand, both a process change and an input mix change will occur as pellets supplant sinter in the blast furnace burden (the amount of dust recovered may be affected as well). In fact, the distinction between process change and subsequent residuals modification is not always clear-cut in practice. As noted by Kneese and Bower: "Materials recovery, for example, is in a sense a change in production process because it involves a change in the mix of raw product inputs; process change may be necessary before inplant water recirculation is possible; and product output changes may require some changes in production processes."[4]

Therefore, in order to avoid confusion about the kind of abatement response that occurs in the model, it is perhaps best to categorize the alternatives selected as "treatment" and "nontreatment" without making the finer distinctions discussed above.

In displaying the results of our experiments, we shall concentrate on graphs of cost response, reserving for the text a discussion of some of the operating changes that lie behind the cost figures. We shall generally show both marginal and average cost curves related to discharges of the

---

metry between constraints and objective function changes is discussed by C. S. Russell in *Residuals Management in Industry: A Case Study of Petroleum Refining* (Baltimore: Johns Hopkins University Press for Resources for the Future, 1973), pp. 133–136.

[2] Effluent charges and standards are compared in Allen V. Kneese and Blair T. Bower, *Managing Water Quality: Economics, Technology, Institutions* (Baltimore: Johns Hopkins University Press for Resources for the Future, 1968), pp. 131–142. For a rigorous theoretical discussion of the merits of the two instruments in the face of imperfect information, see Karl Göran Mäler, "Effluent Charges *vs.* Effluent Standards," in J. Rothenberg and Ian G. Heggie, eds., *The Management of Water Quality and the Environment* (London: MacMillan, 1974), pp. 189–212. A case against the practicability of effluent charges in real world situations is made by Susan Rose-Ackerman in "Effluent Charges: A Critique," *The Canadian Journal of Economics*, vol. 6 (November 1973), pp. 512–528.

[3] The cost-minimizing structure of our linear model does not enable us to cover this last response, since the output mix must be chosen as an initial condition.

[4] Allen V. Kneese and Blair T. Bower, *Managing Water Quality*, pp. 41–42.

residual in question, but sometimes, where it appears more interesting, we shall use some transformation of discharges, such as quantity of discharge reduction (from the base case) or percentage reduction.[5]

The Cost of Waterborne Residuals Discharge Reduction

In this section we will investigate the marginal costs implied by satisfying discharge requirements which are progressively further below the bench mark for a number of waterborne residuals considered separately. In each case the discharge of the other waterborne and atmospheric residuals from the plant will not be constrained.[6] Since a significant proportion of all waterborne residuals generation is accounted for in either the coke plant or the finishing section, it will, as we shall see, be sufficient to confine ourselves to a single steel furnace type. We choose the basic oxygen plant because it is quantitatively most important in the national picture and because, with our assumed price set, it uses the most hot metal, and thus has the most severe water-course discharge problem. When we look at particulate emissions to the atmosphere, we must deal separately with each plant type, because in this area steel furnace characteristics become important in determining the set of responses open to the plant. The cost-of-reduction schedules resulting from this exercise are simplified in the sense that they assume no variation in background conditions. Later we show that altered background conditions may or may not significantly alter the location and shape of the marginal cost-of-reduction curves.

Biological Oxygen Demand

In figures 11.1 and 11.2, we show the marginal removal costs per pound of residual and the implied increase in average costs per unit output[7] for limits on BOD discharges below the bench mark levels reported in

[5] These curves can either be drawn precisely as step functions or approximated piecewise line segments drawn through several sets of steps. In order to do the former, we would have to know the exact points at which basis changes (and hence changes in marginal removal costs) occurred. However, we have kept the size of the discharge decrement rather large and the number of steps in the decrement process small in order to reduce computer expense. This means that a number of intermediate marginal cost changes often occur within a given step, complicating the process of constructing the price step functions. The more such changes within a step, however, the better the linear approximation.

[6] Multiple constraints simultaneously imposed on the discharge of many residuals are discussed in chapter 12.

[7] The added costs of meeting discharge constraints include a capital charge for the equipment that must be constructed. The base level of costs is calculated for an existing plant and does not include capital costs. Further, it should be noted

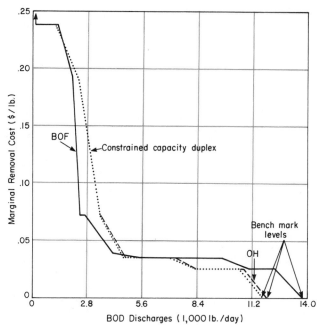

Figure 11.1. BOD Discharges and related marginal removal costs for three plant types.

chapter 9; all other conditions remain as in the bench mark solutions, including the imposition of a quenching penalty. We do this for three mill types—BOF, OH, and duplex (BOF plus EA)—in order to illustrate the basis for our decision to rely on a single kind of mill in much of the rest of the section.

We can see from the figures that the locations and shapes of the three curves are very similar. This is, of course, because the initial loads and the routes taken to achieve BOD discharge reductions at the three plants are very similar. (So nothing significant is lost by concentrating on the BOF.) This BOD reduction sequence involves both treatment and nontreatment adjustments in plant operating practice. Thus, for a marginal removal cost of $0.025 per pound, discharges can be reduced

---

that each distinct marginal removal cost implies a set of optimal activities which are unique to the associated constraint. If we view the constraint parameterization process as an analogue for the two-stage standard implementation procedure outlined in the Federal Water Pollution Control Act, we must realize that the model is not able to look ahead and anticipate what should be done to satisfy a later constraint. Hence we often observe the erection of physically distinct equipment at each distinct constraint level. The model has no way of knowing that previously satisfactory equipment would have to be torn down and replaced with more sophisticated designs: each solution represents a snapshot of static optimality.

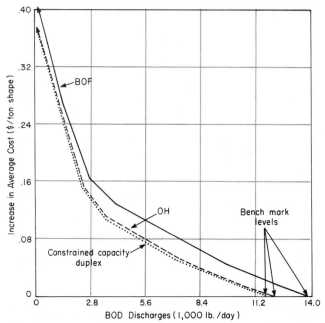

Figure 11.2.   Cost of BOD discharge reduction for three plant types.

roughly 30 percent by the settling and recirculation of hot-mill waste-waters in the finishing section, where the bench mark practice had been once-through use preceded by a settling step. This result is not surprising given the small cost difference between the once-through and recirculation alternatives discussed in chapter 10. Further substantial reductions (up to almost 70 percent) are available at a marginal cost of $0.035 per pound removed, and come about by supplementing the recirculation of finishing water with quenching station disposal of low sulfur, raw ammonia liquor.[8] The quenching option is attractive here because our estimated corrosion cost penalty is low compared to the relative costs of coke plant liquor treatment and by-product recovery.

To move above 70 percent removal, sedimentation, coagulation, filtration, and recirculation of hot- and cold-mill wastewaters become necessary, along with reclamation of oil from the blowdown of the concentrated cold-mill coolant. Even though these processes involve marginal

---

[8] This marginal removal cost is the quotient of the $2.93 corrosion cost penalty per 1,000 gallons of low sulfur liquor divided by the 83.41 pounds of BOD contained per 1,000 gallons, so that discharge reductions for all other residuals in the stream are essentially free.

removal costs between 7 and 24 cents per pound, their introduction allows the plants to achieve better than 99 percent removal at an increase of less than 0.5 percent in daily cost (figure 11.2).

All these processes cause other waterborne residuals discharges to decline along with BOD—especially oil, phenols, ammonia, and suspended solids. It may bother the economist to see the entire costs of various treatment and nontreatment alternatives assigned in this chapter to the single residual being constrained when, in fact, other residuals loads are being reduced simultaneously by the nature of the processes involved. In the model the costs of these processes are expressed per unit of the carrying stream (for example, raw ammonia liquor) and if, in the context of a regional management problem, effluent charges were assigned to several residuals, decisions about removal levels would reflect the concentrations of those residuals in each of the streams, and the model would take into account the possibilities for joint discharge reduction. In the context of this chapter, it is only necessary to caution the reader that the individual cost curves are not additive.

Oil

The daily oil discharge can be reduced more than 70 percent by adjustments made exclusively in the finishing section of the mill, since this is the source of most of the mill's oily waste. The abatement pattern is, however, quite different from the one observed for BOD. Specifically, a discharge reduction of 26 percent is achieved for a marginal cost of $0.042 per pound of oil by replacing the settling and direct discharge of cold-mill wastewater by the more complicated sedimentation, coagulation, filtration, and recirculation system. The first steps in BOD reduction were made, in contrast, by changes in hot-mill wastewater treatment. Moreover, oil discharge reductions between 30 and 70 percent are made possible by supplementing the treatment process mentioned above with the reclamation of oil from the cold mill's concentrated coolant and the settling and recirculation of hot mill wastewater. The quenching alternative is chosen for oil removal only after large reductions have first been accomplished in finishing, because the low oil loading in the raw ammonia liquor means that the corrosion cost penalty, when allocated wholly to the oil removed, is relatively high ($0.29 per pound removed) compared to the marginal removal costs in finishing waste-water treatment. For large percentage reductions (those in excess of 90 percent), the marginal removal cost is rather high (nearly $0.50 lb). On the other hand, oil discharge reduction is about as expensive, on an *average* cost basis, as BOD reduction, for a similar percentage discharge reduction.

This is hardly surprising, since the same changes, albeit in different orders of appearance, are involved in both cases.

Phenols

Because quenching is only penalized, not prohibited, in the bench mark situation phenols can be vaporized by quenching station disposal of low sulfur, raw ammonia liquor; final cooler blowdown; light oil decanter effluent; and light oil fractionation condensate. The marginal removal cost is $0.118 per pound for low sulfur, raw ammonia liquor.[9] This cost holds up to 96 percent reduction level (about 110 pounds discharged daily) and is the quotient of the $2.93 quenching penalty per thousand gallons divided by 24.7 pounds of phenol contained per thousand gallons of low sulfur, raw ammonia liquor. The model can achieve 99.5 percent removal of phenols by routing the high sulfur, raw ammonia liquor stream to the quenching station as well. The marginal removal cost in this upper removal range is $0.134 per pound of phenol, and is calculable in the same manner as the $0.118 marginal cost. Overall, 99.5 percent removal can be achieved for an increase in average steel cost of only $0.09 per ton of shape; or about an 0.1 percent increase in daily cost, which is very much cheaper than the highest attainable reductions for BOD and oil.

It is interesting to note that the method of phenol removal undertaken depends on whether or not we assume the plant has an ammonia still–dephenolizer unit installed. The quenching route is chosen under the bench mark conditions because the combined operating and capital costs of the dephenolizer are greater, per pound of phenol removed, than the quenching penalty. However, when these capital costs are deleted from the objective function, as if the by-product plant were installed already, the net operating costs fall below the quenching penalty. For a marginal removal cost of $0.107 per pound, phenol discharges to the watercourse can be reduced from 1,770 pounds per day to 220 pounds (an 87.6 percent reduction) by by-product recovery from the low sulfur, raw ammonia liquor, and therefore, by-product recovery would be practiced in preference to quenching. Extraction of phenol and ammonia from the high sulfur liquor implies a marginal removal cost of $0.126 per pound, and lowers the discharge level to about 140 pounds daily (a 92 percent reduction). Beyond this point, because by-product recovery possibilities are exhausted, discharges are reduced further by the familiar quench-

---

[9] The other streams, of course, have different shadow prices associated with their evaporation, because they have different phenols concentrations. They are, however, so tiny by comparison with low sulfur, raw ammonia liquor that no violence is done by ignoring them in figure 11.5.

ing option, now using the liquid effluent from the by-product recovery equipment rather than the raw liquor. Doing so allows the mill to achieve better than 98 percent removal at a marginal removal cost of $0.218 per pound.

Two key points emerge from the two sets of solutions. First, whether or not we assume that the by-product recovery equipment is installed at the plant, we observe the extremely discontinuous marginal removal cost curves. The practical importance of schedules having this shape is that they make effluent charges a much less efficient policy instrument than discharge standards. Let us suppose it has been determined that marginal damages from phenol disposal equal marginal removal costs at the 60 percent ($0.118 per pound) reduction level. Now, given a plant without a dephenolizer, if the effluent charge is less than $0.118, no reduction will be achieved; if it is equal to $0.118, the firm will be indifferent between zero and 92 percent reduction (or anything in between), and if it is greater than $0.118, too much reduction, in terms of economic efficiency, will be undertaken. Only a discharge standard set at the 60 percent removal level (710 pounds allowed) will ensure the economically efficient solution.[10] Hence we see that the superiority of charges over standards in real world situations is an empirical question, whose answer is dependent, at least in part, on how well the firm's cost-of-reduction curves approach the continuous versions employed most often in the theoretical literature.

The second observation which the results on phenol discharge limitation allow us to make is that even though the marginal removal cost schedules for a particular residual may be quite similar in shape and location whether or not a plant has by-product recovery equipment in place, the impact of a given discharge standard or effluent charge on the emissions of residuals other than the one of immediate concern can sometimes be severely affected by the configuration of the plant. Specifically, when we assume that the dephenolizer-still is not installed, atmospheric discharges of phenolic and other vapors increase as a direct result of the use of the quenching station to eliminate water-course phenol emission, while this is not the case when we assume that the equipment is already in place.

On the other hand, quenching with raw liquor reduces cyanide discharge to the watercourse by over 80 percent, and sulfide discharges are also lower, but by only 35 percent. By-product recovery has much smaller effects on the residuals other than phenols and ammonia. For example,

[10] See Robert F. Byrne and Michael H. Spiro, "On Taxation as a Pollution Control Policy," *Swedish Journal of Economics*, vol. 75, 1973; and C. S. Russell and W. J. Vaughan, "On Taxation as a Pollution Control Policy: A Comment" *Swedish Journal of Economics*, vol. 77, no. 2 (June 1975) for a discussion of the limitations of effluent charges as a least-cost method of reaching a specified level of ambient quality.

cyanide discharges go down by only 30 percent, and sulfide by only about 8 percent. The BOD reduction is just half of that observed in the quenching case. In either case, however, the increase above the bench mark in average cost per ton of semifinished shape is only $0.07. These features of the two routes are shown in table 11.1, for a required phenol discharge reduction of 80 percent. Clearly, this kind of tradeoff contrast implies that a regulatory authority would have to impose multiple constraints (or charges) on water-course and atmospheric emissions or, in the extreme, prohibit quenching entirely.

Ammonia

Since ammonia disposal and by-product recovery are so closely linked with phenol disposal and by-product recovery, we might anticipate the same reactions just discussed for phenols. However, neither the quenching nor by-product recovery alternatives are superior to the ammonia stripping treatment option if ammonia is considered separately. In fact, it is cheaper to build an ammonia stripper (which recovers no salable ammonia product) than it would be either to build a new dephenolizer-still or to utilize an existing one in order to reduce ammonia discharges up to 90 percent. The marginal removal cost over this range is $0.014 per pound of ammonia, and the mill can arrive at the 90 percent ammonia reduction level (408.9 pounds discharged per day) for an increase in average shape cost of only $0.022—0.03 percent above the bench mark cost.

To do better than 90 percent removal, the plant replaces (not merely supplements) the stripper by quenching station liquor disposal. This is an example of the static nature of the model. That is, for any standard set once and for all up to 90 percent removal, the stripper would be built. If the standard were set beyond that point, the stripper would not be built, and quenching would be chosen instead. Another important implication here is that no other waterborne residuals are removed when the constraint is at or below the 90 percent removal level, while, when it is above that level, they are.

Suspended Solids

Although suspended solids originate at a number of places in the mill such as the coke plant, the blast furnace, and the finishing stands, once again the least expensive place to begin discharge reduction is the hot mill. As figure 11.3 shows, the discharge level can be reduced by more than 8,466 pounds (70 percent) at a marginal removal cost of $0.011 per pound. This is accomplished simply by introducing a settling and recir-

TABLE 11.1 Comparison of Residuals Discharge Vectors at the BOF: 80 Percent Phenol Removal; Quenching versus By-product Recovery

(quantities per ton shape[a])

Residuals	Quenching with raw liquor: no recovery equipment installed	No quenching with raw liquor, by-product recovery equipment installed
Residuals discharge		
Waterborne		
Five-day BOD		
lb. per ton shape	3.83	4.83
% change from bench mark	−34.8	−17.7
Oil		
lb. per ton shape	3.02	3.05
% change from bench mark	−7.5	−6.6
Phenols		
lb. per ton shape	0.15	0.15
% change from bench mark	−80.0	−80.0
Cyanide		
lb. per ton shape	...	0.01
% change from bench mark	−80.6	−30.1
Ammonia		
lb. per ton shape	0.34	0.27
% change from bench mark	−80.4	−84.8
Suspended solids		
lb. per ton shape	5.04	5.17
% change from bench mark	−1.8	0
Sulfide		
lb. per ton shape	0.07	0.26
% change from bench mark	−76.3	−7.5
Heat		
10^6 Btu per ton shape	5.46	5.47
% change from bench mark	0	...
Airborne		
Sulfur dioxide		
lb. per ton shape	12.31	12.51
% change from bench mark	0	1.6
Particulates		
lb. per ton shape	12.06	12.07
% change from bench mark	0	...
Vaporized phenols[b]		
lb. per ton shape	0.62	0.01
% change from bench mark	4570	0

Note: Ellipses (...) indicate too insignificant to record.

[a] The average cost per ton is $72.78.

[b] When quenching is practiced, vaporized cyanide, sulfur, and ammonia compounds also appear.

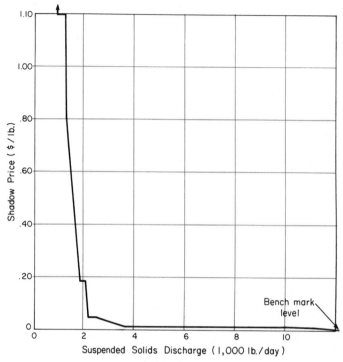

Figure 11.3.   Suspended solids discharges and related shadow prices (BOF).

culation system for hot-mill wastewater. After the 70 percent removal level is reached, the other principal means of further reducing discharges are, in turn, the erection of a sand filter for removal of solids from the blowdown originating in the blast furnace's recirculating gas-washer water system; the introduction of quenching with coke plant ammonia liquors; the sedimentation, coagulation, filtration, and recirculation of hot- and cold-mill wastewaters; and the treatment of concentrated coolant from the cold-rolling mill. But marginal cost increases very rapidly as discharge reductions greater than 70 percent are required. Indeed, the curve is nearly vertical for reductions below about 2,000 pounds per day (representing about 85 percent removal).

For suspended solids, as for the other waterborne residuals, reaching quite high removal levels does not involve large average steel cost increases. This is shown in figure 11.4. We see that a 92 percent reduction, for example, entails an average cost increase of $0.34 per ton of semi-finished shapes, only 0.5 percent above the bench mark cost. (The maximum possible suspended solids discharge reduction level in the model is, however, 94.3 percent, and this involves a large increase in costs, to 4.4

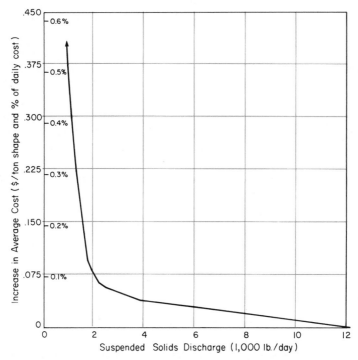

Figure 11.4.   Cost of suspended solids discharge reduction (BOF).

percent above the base.) The average cost curve is thus much more nearly L-shaped than was the corresponding curve for BOD.

Waste Heat

Reduction of waste heat discharge to the local watercourse involves the straightforward application of cooling towers and the consequent in-plant recirculation of water. As a first step, these heat discharges can be lowered 45.4 percent below the base level of 12,800 million Btu per day by the construction of facilities, including cooling towers, which allow for the recirculation of hot-mill wastewater. (The waste heat is, of course, still discharged; the cooling towers simply change the immediate accepting medium to the atmosphere.) The marginal cost of removal over this span (0 to 45.4 percent reduction) amounts to $0.018 per million Btu. As a consequence, daily water withdrawals fall from 78 million gallons to 55 million gallons. Due to the increase in the amount of mill scale recovered from the finishing water and used in sintering, daily ore purchases decrease by 6 tons between the bench mark and the 45 percent removal level. This is an example of how a combined materials-recovery–waste-treatment process designed to reduce waste discharges after generation can affect the input mix of iron-bearing materials consumed.

Discharges of other waterborne residuals such as BOD, oil, and suspended solids fall as the heat discharge is reduced, since the recirculation of hot-mill wastewater involves the joint removal of these residuals. At the same time, the increase in the in-plant generation of electricity required to run the recirculating system forces sulfur dioxide discharges to rise 0.8 percent above the base.

In order to move to complete waste heat removal, cooling towers must be added which remove heat from the indirect cooling water needed at other locations within the plant, especially at the blast and steel furnaces. The marginal removal cost for levels above 45 percent is $0.066 per million Btu, and is constant up to 100 percent removal since we have assumed no difference in cooling tower costs in these several applications. In this connection, it is interesting to note that 100 percent reduction of waterborne waste heat discharge involves an increase of $0.24 above the average shape cost in the base case, which represents a mere 0.3 percent increase in total daily (and average) cost at the given output level.

The Cost of Acid-Neutralization Sludge Reduction

On the solid waste side of the model, there is little flexibility for reduction in discharged quantities except where the sludge resulting from uncontrolled neutralization of spent pickling acid and acid rinse water is concerned. In the base case, the basic oxygen plant must provide storage space for 4,370 cubic feet of this substance daily. As we shall discover, it is an expensive proposition to significantly decrease this volume.

To understand the process changes which occur as the discharge constraint on pickling sludge is tightened, we should first note that all of the pickling in the base case is done with sulfuric acid; the hydrochloric acid pickling option is inferior. As figure 11.5 shows, to reach a 10 percent reduction in the volume of sludge discharged, a marginal removal cost of $0.172 per cubic foot is incurred. The treatment process change associated with this marginal cost involves the replacement of the (required) uncontrolled neutralization of acid rinse water with (optional) controlled neutralization.

A 20 percent discharge reduction (874 ft.^{3} decrease in sludge discharge) may be implemented for a marginal cost of $0.387 per cubic foot by the replacement of some sulfuric acid pickling with hydrochloric acid pickling at the galvanizing line, and the simultaneous controlled neutralization of spent hydrochloric acid and acid rinse water. This is

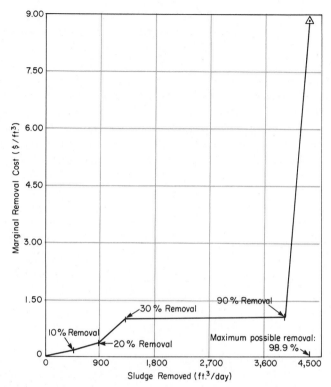

Figure 11.5. Acid-neutralization sludge discharge reduction and related marginal costs (BOF).

another good example of the potential linkage between treatment and production process change in the face of required discharge reductions.

To decrease discharges by 30 percent, the aforementioned activity changes are supplemented by the partial recovery of free sulfuric acid for recycling to the main pickling baths, which continue to use it in preference to hydrochloric acid. The marginal removal cost at this point becomes $1.02 per cubic foot, and average costs have increased by $0.25 per ton of shape, or more than 0.3 percent above the base. Further utilization of this acid recovery activity allows the plant to carry its discharge reduction on to better than 90 percent (437 ft.³ of sludge discharge) for an increase of $1.40 per ton in average shape cost, which represents a 1.9 percent increase in costs per day and per unit shape output.

To achieve the maximum possible removal level of 99 percent, a complete switchover from sulfuric to hydrochloric acid at the pickling baths is necessary, entailing a marginal removal cost of $8.80 per cubic foot and a 2.3 percent average cost increase above the base. Obviously, if hydrochloric acid costs were to fall relative to sulfuric acid costs, the marginal removal cost to reach this level would also fall.

THE COST OF ATMOSPHERIC DISCHARGE REDUCTION

The pattern observed for waterborne residuals discharge limitation, as we have seen, is generally one of high removal levels attainable for relatively modest cost increases. Now we turn to sulfur dioxide and particulates, where we find a somewhat different situation.

Sulfur Dioxide

In figures 11.6 and 11.7, we show the results of reducing allowed discharges of sulfur dioxide at four of the plant types.[11] One striking feature of figure 11.6 is the similarity of the four plants in their response to the early stages of the restrictions, in the sense that the 50 percent removal level is attainable at every furnace for an emission charge between 8.5 and 10.9 cents per pound. However, the marginal removal cost curves for the predominantly hot metal shops (open hearth, basic oxygen, and constrained capacity duplex) turn sharply upward, at removal levels of respectively 79, 67, and 83 percent,[12] whereas the electric arc plant is able to go beyond 98 percent removal (775 pounds of discharge per day) without an increase in marginal removal cost.

The reason for this divergence lies in the fact that the electric arc plant is able to reduce its sulfur dioxide discharges significantly by switching away from high sulfur fuel oil toward natural gas to meet the heat requirements of its electrical plant and soaking pits. The hot metal shops, on the other hand, rely relatively less heavily on fuel purchase. They have in general, then, more limited opportunities for discharge reduction via low sulfur fuel substitution. In order to reach low discharge levels, they must supplement fuel substitution with desulfurization of internally produced coke oven gas, and, at high removal levels, the altera-

[11] The electric arc plant which purchases electricity from an outside source is not shown because it has almost no way of reducing sulfur dioxide discharges from its low (4,095 pounds per day) bench mark level except by soaking with natural gas instead of fuel oil.

[12] An emission charge of about $1 per pound of sulfur dioxide (not shown in figure 11.9) will produce a 70 percent discharge reduction at the BOF (8,640 pounds of daily discharge), an 80 percent reduction at the OH (5,900 pounds of daily discharge), and an 84 percent reduction at the duplex shop (5,760 pounds of daily discharge).

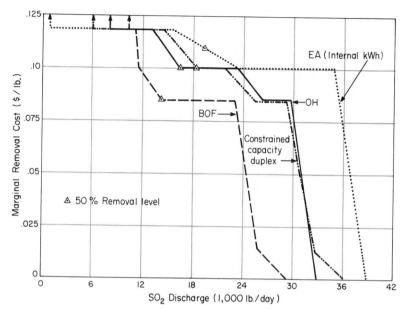

Figure 11.6. SO₂ Discharges and related marginal costs for four plant types.

tion of the blast furnace burden away from sinter toward pellets. This replacement, as previously noted, implies a shift in the location of some of the sulfur dioxide discharge from the mill to the mine.

The hot metal shops are never able to reach the technically feasible minimum discharge level of the electric arc plant regardless of the shadow price on sulfur dioxide because of the irreducible minimum amount of sulfur dioxide discharge associated with the blast furnace slag.[13] In fact, the basic oxygen plant cannot technically go beyond 75 percent removal (7,087 pounds of daily discharge), the open hearth cannot go beyond 86 percent removal (5,903 pounds of daily discharge), and the duplex shop cannot exceed 87 percent removal (4,664 pounds of daily discharge).

Thus, the attainable sulfur dioxide removal levels at the hot metal shops are generally lower, in percentage terms, than those for the waterborne residuals. Furthermore, they involve comparatively high absolute (and percentage) cost increments at all of the plants. For example, reaching the 70 percent removal level involves an 0.6 percent average (and daily) cost increase at the BOF; 1.32 percent at the OH; 1.80 percent at the EA and 1.01 percent at the duplex plant, as shown in figure 11.7.

[13] To a degree this is an artifact of the absence of alternative slag cooling options in the model.

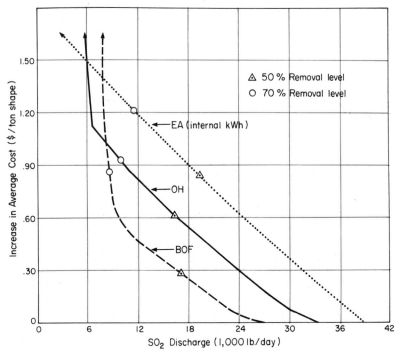

Figure 11.7.   Cost of SO_2 discharge reduction for three plant types.

Particulates

In chapter 8 we set out two particulate removal equipment situations: the bench mark situation in which the steel furnaces are controlled, and the grass roots situation in which they are not. Given the particulate removal requirements elsewhere in the mill, figure 11.8 traces out the marginal removal costs involved in moving from the unconstrained discharge case without any treatment equipment in place at the steel furnaces to the bench mark situation. The marginal costs reflect the capital and operating expense which would be incurred to put steel furnace gas cleaning equipment on line to achieve the (unconstrained) bench mark discharge level. This figure emphasizes that our bench mark particulate discharges reflect substantial reductions below uncontrolled levels.[14] The

---

[14] Because the marginal value of the recovered dust is insufficient to offset the marginal recovery cost at each of the steel plants, it does not pay the producer to recover the steel furnace dust on purely private grounds, given the input price set assumed. See chapter 10 for a more detailed discussion of this issue.

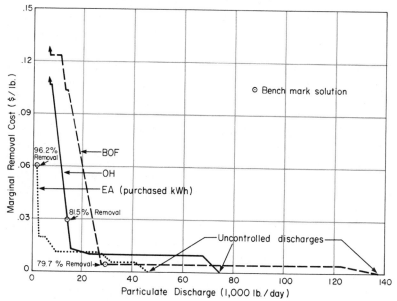

Figure 11.8. Particulate discharges and related marginal costs in the grass roots gas cleaning case.

confusion between generation potential and actual discharges of particulates from the various steel furnaces is pointed up by the following statement from the *New York Times* (January 5, 1975, p. 43), in reference to the agreement between the city of Gary, Indiana and U.S. Steel "to close down its 53 open hearth furnaces gradually and replace them with a *cleaner* [author's italics], more economical method of steelmaking with a [*sic*] basic oxygen process." As figure 11.8 shows, particulate emissions from an uncontrolled BOF plant are almost double those from an uncontrolled open hearth plant; it is not intrinsically a "cleaner" process. The author of the *New York Times* article is mistakenly comparing uncontrolled open hearth discharges and controlled basic oxygen plant discharges.

The required bench mark equipment configuration also involves dissimilar marginal removal costs and discharge levels at the three plant types: a product of discrete linear technologies in terms of equipment type and removal level, disparate dust generation rates at the three steel furnaces, and different grain loadings and gas flow rates which pass through the collectors. That is, because the cost per pound of dust removed in collectors of roughly equivalent efficiencies depends on gas flow rate and grain loading, the bench mark requirement that at least first stage dust removal equipment be operated at the steel furnaces does not imply equal long-run marginal dust removal costs at the several plant types. Furthermore, because most of the dust evolved at the electric arc plant is generated at the steel furnace itself, the first stage application of dust treatment equipment there will reduce mill-wide discharges by a greater percentage than it will at the two hot metal shops, where dust is also discharged from processes related to iron production.

Figure 11.9 demonstrates the correspondence between the model's estimate of marginal particulate removal costs at an EA and the costs reported in a current steel industry publication.[15] The *Steel Facts* costs lie above the model's costs over most of the removal range, in part because they are in current dollars. However, the remaining disparity after these costs are put in constant 1968 dollars[16] is great enough to suggest that something else is going on as well. In fact, the cost difference above 88 percent removal results from a difference in equipment assumptions and the implicit assumption of a very simple example with only one burden used. Thus, their figure for 88 percent removal represents the application of a particular kind of first stage equipment to that burden. To achieve 97 percent removal of dust from the off gases associated with that burden, their simplified mill must install a second stage device. In our model, a higher removal (over 94 percent) is achievable using the first stage equipment, but the marginal costs rise in the 80–90 percent removal range, reflecting the different grain loadings associated with different burdens. However, both of the schedules demonstrate a closely similar pattern of sharply rising marginal removal costs with discharge reduction requirements over about 90 percent.

If we use the uncontrolled steel furnace situation as a starting point, reaching the 70 percent removal level at all three plants is not very expensive, involving only a 0.2 percent increase in average (and daily) cost at the basic oxygen and electric arc shops, and 0.3 percent increase at the open hearth shop. However, reducing discharges below the bench mark level is another matter; here the average cost increment escalates rapidly as discharges are scaled down, even though the marginal removal cost is taken to begin at zero at the bench mark discharge level,

15 "Can We Afford Tomorrow?" *Steel Facts*, Winter 1974, p. 7. The "grass roots-purchased electricity" case from the model is used in order to put the comparison on equal ground with the published cost estimate which neglects particulate removal costs associated with electricity generation. For a more detailed discussion see John E. Barker, "Zero Visible Emissions: What Cost?" Paper presented at the C. C. Furnas Memorial Conference, State University of New York at Buffalo, November 10–11, 1974 (mimeographed).

16 The *Steel Facts* current dollar costs were deflated to a constant 1968 dollar base by application of the Department of Commerce Composite Construction Cost Index.

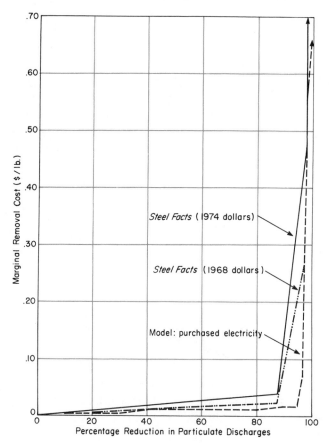

Figure 11.9. Comparison of estimated and reported particulate removal costs for an electric arc shop. (Costs reflect dust removal equipment capital, and operating and maintenance charges.)

because we assume that the steel furnace gas treatment equipment is in place and must be operated. Figure 11.10 displays percentage increases in total daily (and average) steel costs as a function of the absolute discharge level and the percentage reduction in discharges below the bench mark. Observe that for a removal level of about 85 percent, steel production costs at all shops increase about 1.5 percent; this is much above the percentage cost increases for similar levels of water pollution control.

The discharges of particulates for a given effluent charge differ widely among the hot and cold metal shops. Thus, in figure 11.11 we see that for an emission charge of $0.20 per pound, daily emissions are predicted to be about 2,300 pounds at the electric arc plant, 5,700 pounds at the OH, and 6,000 pounds at the BOF. At a charge below this level, the

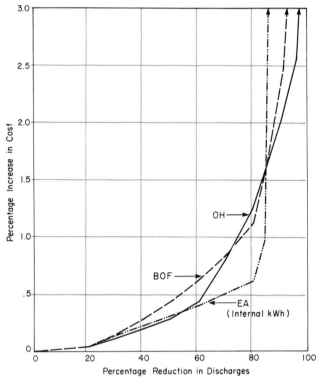

Figure 11.10. Particulate discharge reduction below the bench mark, and related percentage increases in steel cost at three plant types.

disparity widens considerably, both between the hot and cold metal shops and among all three plant types.

Both the extent to which the plants use the coke–sinter–blast furnace combination and the characteristics of the steel furnaces themselves have a large influence on their relative abilities to reduce particulate discharges. Thus, at the BOF plant, very large reductions, in terms of pounds, are possible by installing add-on dust control equipment at the sinter machine, the blast furnace, and the BOF itself. Simultaneously, these treatment process changes are supplemented by alterations in the character of the blast and steel furnace burdens, which lower the particulate generation rate; this means, specifically, the substitution of pellets for sinter at the blast furnace and the replacement of no. 2 bundles with shredded scrap at the steel furnace. These same opportunities exist at the open hearth shop, but they are exhausted more rapidly since the impact of particulate discharge reductions in ironmaking is dampened by the

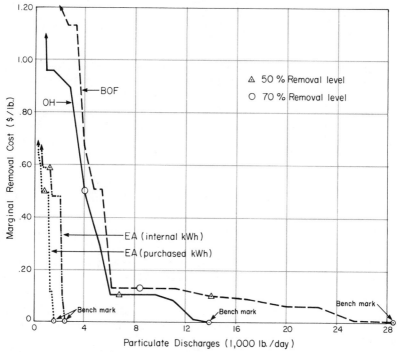

Figure 11.11. Particulate discharges below the bench mark and related marginal costs at four plant types.

use of 50–50 practice at the steel furnace. The electric arc plant, in contrast, has only two places where it can reduce dust emissions: the steel furnaces and the power generating plant. When electricity is purchased, reductions at the latter source are not possible. But discharges in the base case are positively correlated with removal opportunities and are large enough at the basic oxygen and open hearth plants to make these two hot metal shops larger particulate emitters per ton of steel produced than the cold metal shop at all emission charge levels, even though the electric arc plant cannot go much beyond the 84 percent removal level without incurring massive increases in daily cost (figure 11.10).

Thus, in regard to atmospheric discharge reductions from the bench mark levels at the steel plants, we conclude that:

1. The reduction in sulfur dioxide emissions depends heavily on the ability to switch to lower sulfur fuels, and the costs of meeting any particular standards will be very sensitive to fuel prices. At hot metal shops which internally produce sulfur-containing by-product fuels, the possibility for reductions greater than those shown here

may depend, in the future, on the development of better sulfur control in blast furnace slag cooling and the application of flue gas desulfurization processes in sintering.

2. To the extent that a specific plant already operates, for whatever reasons, gas cleaning equipment with efficiencies comparable to those assumed in our base case, very large further reductions in particulate discharges from that plant will be quite expensive. Achieving the bench mark level by installing gas cleaning equipment at the steel furnaces, on the other hand, is rather inexpensive.

SOME PROBLEMS WITH ENVIRONMENTAL POLICY INSTRUMENTS

There is, of course, a whole literature concerned with the choice between discharge standards and effluent charges or subsidies as the instrument for achieving a desired environmental quality policy. We shall not retract our promise to stay off the peculiarly economic ground on which this battle is being fought. Rather, we would simply like to end this chapter with some observations which show that both instruments suffer from potentially serious problems in confronting the real world's tendency to display discontinuities, and to keep changing. First, however, to put the role of the model into perspective in the larger framework of regional environmental management, it is worth considering one of the best-known arguments for charges.

In some recent work, William Baumol and Wallace Oates have argued that since we do not know the marginal removal costs associated with the many residuals and dischargers in a region, it will be essentially impossible to devise a set of standards (discharge allocations) which are efficient, in the sense of meeting a desired set of ambient environmental quality standards at least cost.[17] In this situation, they attempt to prove that only iterative experimentation with a single, region-wide set of effluent charges will ever result in minimum program cost. Thus, that charge at which the standard is just achieved will, in their world, produce this efficient result because the marginal removal costs for all dischargers will have been equated to that charge.

Constant recalculation of the charge level will, of course, raise the program's total cost above the minimum which could be obtained if, given the overall quality standards, the marginal removal cost schedules of all the dischargers were known *a priori*, since production, treatment, and by-product recovery equipment appropriate at one charge may be

---

[17] See William J. Baumol and Wallace E. Oates, "The Use of Standards and Prices for Protection of the Environment," *Swedish Journal of Economics,* vol. 73 (March 1971), pp. 42–54, and William J. Baumol, "On Taxation and the Control of Externalities," *American Economic Review,* vol. 62 (June 1972), pp. 307–322.

inappropriate at the next. Despite this penalty, proponents of achieving environmental goals via effluent charges make the intuitive judgment that such additional costs will not surpass the welfare losses involved in an allocation scheme.[18]

The fundamental problem is not, however, with the iteration procedure. (Although, as we shall note, it is the assumption of ignorance which suggests the particular relevance of models of the type we are discussing.) Rather, the difficulty is with the peculiar version of the natural world assumed by Baumol and Oates. Location does not matter to them, and the marginal contribution of one source to violation of the desired ambient standard is the same as the marginal contribution of every other source. In fact, of course, in nearly every real residuals management context, location does matter, and it is easy to prove that in such cases a single region-wide effluent charge is not the most efficient way of achieving a desired ambient standard.[19]

A trial-and-error technique, without knowledge of the plants' removal cost functions, simply will not work under these circumstances, so the argument for successive rounds of charge setting made on the basis of the procedure's minimal information requirements breaks down. There is no way of knowing whether or not a system of purely arbitrary plant-by-plant discharge quotas will involve a program cost in excess of that involved with the trial-and-error charge scheme.

Moreover, if the cost of simulating the response of industrial plants to proposed ambient standards with a mathematical model lies below the cost of learning through real world trial and error, the argument for transferring the charge- or standard-selection procedure from the world itself to a model of reality becomes compelling.[20] Given a combination

---

[18] This argument is made by Baumol and Oates in "The Use of Standards and Prices." The authors add the caveat that market intervention through the use of acceptability standards implemented by effluent charges should be applied judiciously. Where the existing situation does not seem to imply a high level of external costs, or where no significant damage cost amelioration can be achieved, the status quo should be maintained. They also admit that to make this judgment we must have some notion of the general shape of the schedule relating social welfare to the level of externality generation, which is not an inconsequential requirement.

[19] See, for example, the proof attributed to W. O. Spofford, Jr., and reproduced by Allen V. Kneese in, "Costs of Water Quality Improvement, Transfer Functions and Public Policy," in Henry M. Peskin, ed. *Cost–Benefit Analysis and Water Pollution Policy* (Washington, D.C.: The Urban Institute, 1975). This same assumption, that location does not matter, is made by Freeman and Haveman in A. M. Freeman, III and R. H. Haveman, "Residuals Charges for Pollution Control: A Policy Evaluation," *Science,* vol. 177, pp. 322–329.

[20] Constantly re-evaluating of charge levels in a real world setting, instead of solution of the problem in a modeling context, raises distributional questions as well. In the case of research, the monies will probably come from general tax revenues, whereas in the trial-and-error experimentation case, the question of who pays for the information depends directly on market structure.

of residuals management models of industry and models of the physical world, the policy maker could directly discover an effluent charge structure (or its mirror image, the discharge allocations) which would satisfy the global standard at least cost.[21] Then the choice between a schedule of charges and a schedule of standards could be made purely on the basis of their comparative costs of implementation and enforcement and their robustness in the face of the problems discussed below.

Continuity or Discontinuity

Even if we ignore the error in the Baumol–Oates argument and make no distinction between a unique effluent charge and a locationally differentiated charge schedule, it can be shown that, given a regional quality goal, charges are not invariably a more efficient instrument than standards.

From our experience with the steel industry, we have discovered that the schedules for marginal discharge reduction cost display varying degrees of discontinuity, depending on the particular residual in question and the number of activities available for its removal. Where very few of these alternatives exist, a discharge standard becomes a more precise instrument for the attainment of a specified plant discharge level than an effluent charge. If this happens to be the case for all plants in a region, it is possible that a single effluent charge levied on all dischargers may never satisfy the chosen ambient environmental quality level. (Of course, the aggregated marginal cost-of-reduction curve may be fairly smooth if there are many different dischargers.) Conversely, the wider the range of discharge-reducing activities available to the firm, the more closely the schedule for the marginal cost of reducing the discharges of a residual will approach the continuous version assumed in the usual proofs of the superiority of effluent charges.

Changes in Exogenous Conditions

Let us grant for the moment that the iterative procedure suggested by Baumol and Oates will successfully produce an effluent charge which satisfies the ambient target. Now, without a complete model of the environmental system which can provide the regulator with the true pro-

---

[21] See, for a description of such a model, W. O. Spofford, Jr., C. S. Russell, and R. A. Kelly, "Operational Problems in Large Scale Residuals Management Models," in *Economic Analysis of Environmental Problems*, Edwin S. Mills (ed.) (New York: National Bureau of Economic Research–Resources for the Future, 1975).

gram cost minimum (assuming that the problem of multiple optima does not exist), let us further grant that the iterative process approximates the true minimum better than arbitrary quota setting. However, when fundamental conditions exogenous to the pollution problem change, the reaction of the firm will often involve shifts in production processes, input mix, and so on, which imply very different initial generation rates of residuals and consequently very different discharges for a given effluent charge.[22] Obviously, to get back to the stated ambient quality level, another series of trial charge iterations must be initiated.

From our discussion in chapter 10, we know of many such exogenous influences which may shift the marginal removal cost schedules, at least over some range of discharges. For example, figure 11.12 shows the impact of the introduction of a new technology, continuous casting, on the marginal cost of BOF discharge reduction at the basic oxygen plant. Notice that whatever the original effluent charge level, a lower discharge would be observed after a mill had switched to continuous casting, and some of the differences would be very large indeed. In contrast, figure 11.13 shows what happens to the BOF's marginal particulate removal cost schedule if the pellet price is lowered only 4 percent below the bench mark level. Here, if the original effluent charge were above $0.14 per pound, no change in emissions would be observed, since the marginal cost curve would not be shifted over most of the range.

In the ideal world of perfect and instantaneously acquired knowledge and of costless adjustment, the interaction of direct and indirect influences would not present a serious problem. Since the changing conditions would define a new marginal removal cost curve, and since the regulatory authority would have this information as well as the marginal damage schedule, the new optimum effluent charge would be known. However, we are thinking of conditions in which an effluent charge might be arrived at (perhaps by trial and error) with a view to attaining a desired level of ambient quality in the environment. Nothing is known about damages in dollar terms, but somehow the (political) decision on ambient quality is made and charges are chosen for attaining that level. Unless the quality level is viewed as variable within certain limits, some exogenous influences can cause havoc with the charge scheme if the charges, once determined, are regarded as immutable thereafter. For example, in an integrated (constrained capacity) duplex mill with both basic oxygen and electric arc furnaces, the discharge of sulfur dioxide

---

[22] Discharges will follow initial generation if the reduction observed at the given effluent charge rate is obtained by a treatment process with a particular percentage removal capability, and if that same process is chosen under the new exogenous conditions.

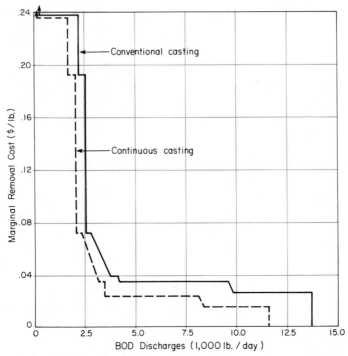

Figure 11.12.   BOD Discharges and related marginal costs at a BOF plant with conventional or continuous casting.

under, say, a $0.12 per pound effluent charge will increase by 42 percent when the ratio of the average scrap steel price to the average hot metal cost doubles.[23]

In this same world, there are problems with standards as well. The decision on ambient quality, however laboriously arrived at, will obviously reflect some balancing of costs against the ambient quality level. To concentrate on the obverse of the difficulty just discussed, we find that the total resource cost of meeting a particular standard can vary widely as the underlying conditions change in the markets in which the firm operates. Although the decision on ambient quality should be reconsidered in these circumstances and readjusted to a new equilibrium where marginal

[23] The effect here is to encourage the firm to charge more hot iron to the BOF steel furnaces, using less purchased steel scrap. The making of more hot iron involves the introduction of more sulfur into the system through the greater quantities of ore and coke required at the blast furnace. Twenty-six percent of this additional sulfur ultimately appears as SO_2 when blast furnace slag is quenched and when by-product fuels are burned. The rest remains in the blast and steel furnace slags.

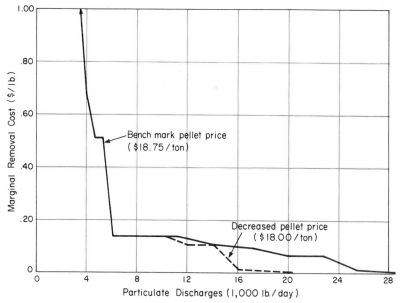

Figure 11.13. Particulate discharges below the bench mark and related marginal costs at a BOF plant given two pellet price levels.

dollar damages equal the marginal cost of program attainment, it is likely that institutional lag will prevent this from happening. Ambient standards, and their associated discharge standards are likely to be difficult to change once they have been arrived at.[24] Thus, rather than producing too much damage, as in the last example of inflexible charges, such discharge standards could result in an overallocation of resources toward residuals removal in the same circumstances. In the case of the duplex steel plant, maintaining the level of sulfur dioxide discharge resulting from a $0.12 effluent charge under base conditions in the face of a doubled scrap–hot metal price relative, rather than accepting an increase in discharges by maintaining a constant effluent charge, implies an average increase in resource cost of $0.84 per ton of semifinished steel shape output (about 1 percent of the base cost).

The choice between charges and standards as a policy instrument is, then, by no means as clear-cut as early discussions couched in theoretical terms would have it. Not only is the world probably characterized by discrete linear technologies, but more important, this world refuses to sit

[24] For example, it has taken the Delaware River Basin Commission more than fourteen years to formulate and implement stream standards, and some industrial critics maintain that the implementation program is bureaucratic and unnecessarily fuzzy. See "Policing an Industrial River," *Environmental Science and Technology,* vol. 5 (October 1971), pp. 996–997.

still and behave consistently with our static models. Since we cannot even predict with certainty how it is going to change, we are driven to analyze decisions under uncertainty if we wish to make the fullest evaluations of the merits of each case in even this relatively simple question. But perhaps even more harrowing for economists is the knowledge that the decision in the case can never be clean; we have to choose between imperfect alternatives, and our choice must depend on the practical importance of the objections we know to exist in principle.

12

POLICY APPLICATIONS AND NEW DIRECTIONS

In chapter 1 we suggested that the formulation and implementation of intelligent environmental policies depend not only on the ability of legislative bodies and executive agencies to collect a vast quantity of data but also on their ability to evaluate the information at hand in order to transform the groundswell of public opinion into sound legislation. Our case for applied linear programming analysis as a useful tool in this regard has partly been made in the preceding chapters, where we attempted to demonstrate what kind of information can be wrung from technical data using a process analysis model. In this final chapter we will complete the line of reasoning begun in the introduction by focusing on two policy issues which have recently received considerable attention: the potentials for increasing the absorption rate of obsolete automobile scrap, and the steel industry discharge guidelines proposed by the U.S. Environmental Protection Agency (EPA) pursuant to the Federal Water Pollution Control Act and Amendments.[1]

We do not pretend to be able to dispel the controversy surrounding either of these issues once and for all. Rather, we hope to show that modeling of important industries can play a useful role in the process of developing policies. Our fundamental contention is that intuition alone is an insufficient tool when applied to complex questions such as how industrial residuals discharge rates and obsolete materials recycling rates may react to a particular confluence of exogenous indirect influences and direct public residuals management actions. What we should expect,

[1] See *Federal Register,* vol. 39 (Tuesday, February 19, 1974), pp. 6485–6505 for a summary of the watercourse discharge guidelines proposed by EPA. These guidelines have since been revised. See *Federal Register,* vol. 39 (Friday, June 28, 1974), pp. 24114–24133.

especially from executive agencies with ample funds at their disposal, is a sensible formulation of the policy problem and the procurement of careful analyses providing results in a format useful for its solution.

THE SCRAP PROBLEM

From an environmental standpoint, the iron and steel scrap problem generally refers to the ability or willingness of steelmakers to absorb postconsumer scrap such as auto hulks and refrigerators offered by scrap processors in the form of no. 2 bundles or shredded scrap.[2] Particular emphasis is most often placed on automotive scrap as representing a major portion of the scrap which historically has accumulated in junkyards or scarred the urban and rural landscape as abandoned hulks. In fact, between 1958 and 1970, the cumulative addition to the backlog of unprocessed vehicles built up in auto wreckers' inventories has been conservatively estimated at 9.9 million units, with an additional 2.9 million abandoned, uncollected automobiles littering the countryside, mostly in rural areas.[3] This buildup in stocks of abandoned automobiles over time may deaccelerate if new processes (such as the scrap shredder) succeed in upgrading the ultimate product and result in lowering the percentage of retired vehicles which are not recycled—currently about 15 percent.[4] However, even if a 100 percent recycling rate for annually retired vehicles is attained in the near future, currently existing stocks will not be drawn down except by natural decay, unless the demand for such scrap becomes sufficient to encourage it. Thus, "the magnitude of the abandoned auto problem appears to be steadily increasing, and some action is indicated both to reduce the abandonment rate and collect the backlog."[5] At the same time there exists a growing concern that we are running down our stocks of nonrenewable resources, such as iron ore, at too fast a rate,

[2] For general information, see Institute of Scrap Iron and Steel, *Landscape 1970: National Conference on the Abandoned Automobile* (Washington, D.C., 1970), and Norward B. Melcher, "Utilization of Ferrous Scrap," *Proceedings of the Symposium on Mineral Waste Utilization* (Chicago: U.S. Bureau of Mines and IIT Research Institute, 1968).

Shredded scrap and no. 2 bundle scrap are produced predominantly from obsolete automotive scrap; of 8.1 million tons produced in 1970, between 5 and 6 million were of automotive origin, according to Booz-Allen, Applied Research, Inc., *An Analysis of the Abandoned Automobile Problem*, PB 221 879 (Springfield, Va.: NTIS, July 1973), pp. 33–34.

[3] Booz-Allen, Applied Research, Inc., *An Analysis of the Abandoned Automobile Problem*, p. 41.

[4] W. J. Regan, R. W. James, and T. J. McLeer, *Identification of Opportunities for Increased Recycling of Ferrous Solid Waste*, PB 213 577 (Springfield, Va.: NTIS, 1972), p. 84.

[5] Booz-Allen, Applied Research, Inc., *An Analysis of the Abandoned Automobile Problem*, p. 82.

leading many persons to advocate the policy position that more recycling of obsolete scrap would be better.

What can the model say about this problem? Well, as we noted in chapter 6, the steel producer faces a dilution problem in making high quality carbon steels from furnace burdens containing purchased steel scrap. Thus, in order for it to be technically feasible for the annual flow of scrapped automobiles of a given design to be absorbed as recycled ferrous inputs in the steel industry, three elements of the system must be in some rough balance.

1. The desired product mix and related specifications for each product.
2. The level of impurity removal undertaken in the scrapping process.
3. The quantity of dilution provided by the steelmaker.

In fact, the intuitively appealing observation that not enough obsolete scrap is being recycled suggests that such a balance is not being produced by the current quasi-private market situation. Some of the factors that may be contributing to the perceived problem follow.

1. The technical frontier defined by the existing types of steel furnace capacity and the level and mix of demand for steels is too restrictive.
2. Market input supply prices for scrap are too high relative to prices of virgin materials from a social standpoint (for example, because of the ore depletion allowance).[6]
3. There is no market mechanism to reflect the external disamenity costs created by the existing auto hulk inventories and the scrap litter dispersed in the countryside.

Our model's particular competence is in the area represented by factor 1. Therefore, we can estimate scrap demand curves under a variety of circumstances, including mixes of proposed policies—and trace the movement of the technical frontier. For example, in figure 12.1 we show the derived demand curves for each of the automobile-derived scraps (no. 2 bundles and shredded) at the constrained-capacity duplex shop under bench mark conditions. Notice that each curve exhibits a severe kink, the location of which is determined by the technological upper limit on scrap use for a given level of output at a given furnace. (The same kink exists for the other furnace types as well.) In general, the upper limit on the use of a specific scrap type will become lower as the scrap's content of residual alloy elements increases. The horizontal distance between the

[6] See Booz-Allen and Hamilton, *An Evaluation of the Impact of Discriminatory Taxation on the Use of Primary and Secondary Raw Materials*, PB 240 988 (Springfield, Va.: NTIS 1975).

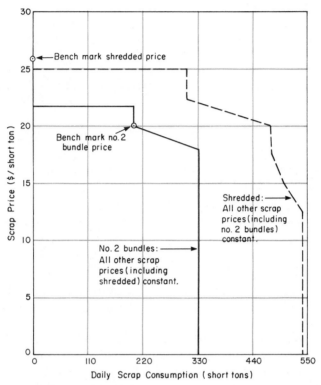

Figure 12.1.   Derived demand curves for no. 2 bundles and shredded scrap (constrained capacity duplex shop).

inelastic portions of the two schedules in figure 12.1 demonstrates this effect.

Since the two scraps are close substitutes, small movements in their price ratio can result in dramatic switches between them as sources of steel mill supply. In the extreme, for a shop of the type assumed for these two demand curves, and given supply functions such that the inelastic portions of the demand curves are relevant, the maximum number of auto hulks recycled daily could be 101 percent higher if shredded scrap were purchased rather than no. 2 bundles. This large change would, of course, result from the combination of the higher upper limit on shredded tonnage used and the lower yield (in tons of scrap per hulk) of the shredding, as opposed to the bundling process.[7] Further increases in hulk consumption at such a plant under these conditions could only be

[7] One ton of no. 2 bundles represents 0.89 auto hulks, and one ton of shredded scrap represents 1.11 auto hulks. (Information provided by James W. Sawyer, Jr. in a personal communication to the authors on July 3, 1974.)

achieved by an increase in output or a shift to steels having higher alloy tolerances.

Because our model provides only partial information on the demand side of the scrap problem, we hesitate to push our conclusions beyond this point. In fact, the steel mill's demand function for scrap is only one component in the steel cycle, and factors 2 and 3 mentioned above, although located elsewhere in the system, have undoubtedly contributed to the situation we face today.

The many submarkets in the system mean that a complex set of economic interactions exist which are difficult to trace when an exogenous shock is imposed, whether it is an engineered policy or an unforeseen development. First, we have three problem areas related to hulk accumulation: the buildup of automobiles abandoned on the countryside, the buildup of scrap yard inventories, and the use of automobile-derived scrap at domestic steel mills. Let us sketch a simple, brief scenario to show how these three components of the system may potentially interact.

Assume that foreign steel producers in resource-poor locations are faced with a rising demand for their products. As a consequence, the demand for U.S. automobile-derived scrap for export goes up. The prices of no. 2 bundle and shredded scrap will be bid up, which, depending on the magnitude of the price rise and the size of the increment to exports, will translate into a decrease of some size in junkyard hulk inventories and into some decrease in the stock of abandoned uncollected hulks. However, given a constant level of domestic output, the rise in the scrap price may imply a decrease in no. 2 bundle and shredded scrap use at domestic mills, which, as we know from chapter 10, means an increase in hot metal requirements per unit output and hence an increase in residuals discharges. In this case there is a tradeoff between the size of the stock of unprocessed automobiles and the level of residuals generation at domestic mills, but this need not always be the case.

In fact, because of the bifurcation of the scrap market, in the sense that a high price offered for scrap may reduce the size of the stock of uncollected, unprocessed automobiles, but discourage consumption at domestic mills, a government policy directed at one part of the system could have undesirable effects on another. In this regard, consider a subsidy on hulk collection. Given the large number of potential scrap collectors, such a policy would provide an incentive to harvest abandoned hulks, and hence have desirable effects on the size of the litter problem. But the operating costs of processing these hulks, the steel mill operating cost, and the level and composition of finished steel demand will determine whether backlogs of automobiles held in junkyards increase by a corresponding amount or whether more obsolete steel is actually recycled. If the former, residuals discharges at steel mills will remain unchanged, while they will decrease in the latter instance.

It is our contention that the scrap problem cannot be fruitfully discussed in terms of the assumption that all scrap prices and quantities supplied and demanded are inexorably tied to observable trends of a single bellwether scrap grade such as no. 1 heavy melting. Attempts to weigh the short-run market impact of environmental policies designed to alter the ratio of scrap consumed per ton of steel produced cannot be made using generalized demand and supply functions for the category "scrap"; this is true not only because these are quite difficult to estimate, but also because the policy itself may be directed toward a particular scrap subcategory, and not scrap taken generally, and therefore may result in substitution between types, perhaps with no impact on total use.[8]

Even when the scrap market is discussed in broad terms, there appears to be considerable confusion in the literature regarding the probable values of the long- and short-run demand elasticity for scrap. In addition, the distinction between these two elasticities is often not clearly presented. For example, one author postulates that "Essentially in the short run (four to eight years) the demand for the factor input, scrap, is inelastic and shifts with adjustments in production, while in the long run the demand curve may have significant elasticity."[9]

Another investigator notes that "a number of environmental analyses of the 'scrap problem' have proceeded on the implicit or explicit assumption of a high price elasticity of short-run demand for scrap and a high responsiveness of total demand to technological changes."[10] However, noting a relatively constant ratio of scrap usage to total raw steel output in the industry, the same author argues that "the total amount of scrap recycled has been a function of industry output, but demand has been very inelastic with respect to price changes and insensitive to the technological changes that one would expect to affect input–output ratios."[11]

This apparent constancy is essentially a long-run phenomenon, partially explained by the fact that the changing pattern of investment in steel-making facilities by furnace type has involved little change in the weighted average hot metal–scrap proportion technically possible within

---

[8] For a critical review of previous efforts to deal quantitatively with the supply side of the ferrous scrap market, see James W. Sawyer, Jr., *Automotive Scrap Recycling* (Baltimore: Johns Hopkins University Press for Resources for the Future, 1974), pp. 92–96.

[9] R. Plater Zyberk, "The Economics of Ferrous Scrap Recycling" (Ph.D. dissertation, Drexel University, 1972), p. 175.

[10] Gerhard Rosegger, "Technological Change and Materials Consumption in U.S. Iron and Steel Manufacturing: An Assessment of Some Environmental Impacts," *Human Ecology*, vol. 2 (January 1974), pp. 25–26.

[11] Ibid., p. 26.

the industry. The crucial question is, of course, why this particular pattern of investment occurred in preference to other alternatives. The fact of its being so does little to explain scrap demand elasticities, nor should it be allowed to impart a mystical constancy to a ratio which is influenced by many factors other than scrap prices. In short, it is unclear whether the long-run scrap demand function truly includes an inelastic price coefficient, or whether shifts in short-run supply and demand schedules have left the scrap input–steel output ratio unchanged over time, leading to the superficial conclusion that long-run scrap demand is price inelastic, *ceteris paribus*. Thus, the blurring of very important distinctions between short- and long-run demand, and scrap demand in general and scrap demand by particular type, both impair our ability to judge the impact of policies designed to encourage the recycling of one or many scrap grades, or even to understand why the market fails to reabsorb a greater portion of scrapped automobiles.

To analyze fully the impact of various policy prescriptions on the rate of absorption of automobile hulks and other types of scrap, a more extended, regionalized model of the steel cycle would be required. The components of such a model, which would provide supply and demand functions for the various scrap types and other intermediate products in the cycle, and hence the market clearing quantities and prices for each scrap type and other products under the various policy situations, are blocked out in figure 12.2. Given a model of this sort, the range of policies which could be tested would include:

    I. Policies affecting the supply of recycled ferrous materials
        1. Subsidy on scrap recycling equipment (shredders) or scrap collection
        2. Inventory tax on accumulated automobiles held by auto wreckers
        3. Disposal fee on deregistered automobiles
        4. Revised scrap transportation rates
        5. Subsidy to scrap exporters
        6. Restrictions on scrap exports
        7. Restrictions on scrap imports
   II. Policies affecting the supply of virgin ferrous materials
        1. Elimination or reduction of the iron ore depletion allowance
        2. Revised iron ore transportation rates
  III. Policies affecting ferrous materials demand
        1. Subsidy on automobile-derived scrap purchases
        2. Subsidy for investment in scrap-intensive steel production technologies (EA, or scrap premelting at BOF facilities)
        3. Regulation of obsolete scrap usage rates

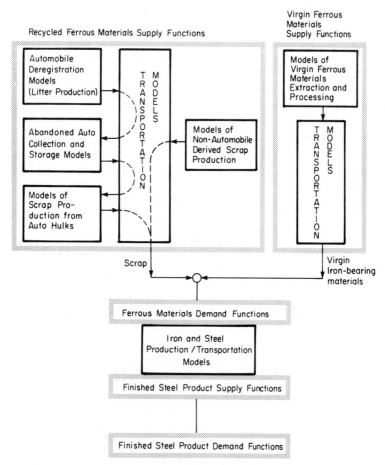

Figure 12.2.   A regionalized model of the steel cycle.

IV. Policies affecting finished steel product demand and design
    1.   Tax on automobile manufacturers for use of copper and other
        key tramps in major components such as wiring, etc.
    2.   Regulation of automobile design standards.

Some of these policy recommendations border on the fatuous (especially III.3), while others are more sound, and have received serious
consideration.[12] However, because the ferrous scrap problem is complex,

[12] For one set of recommendations, see Oscar W. Albrecht and Richard G. McDermott, *Economic and Technological Impediments to Recycling Obsolete Ferrous
Solid Waste,* PB 223 034 (Springfield, Va.: NTIS, 1973), pp. 4–6. For a more sophisticated comparative evaluation of sixteen alternative strategies, see Booz Allen, *An
Analysis of the Abandoned Automobile Problem.* For some specific proposals, see

and because "very little is known about the sensitivity of the steel industry to various kinds of action available to the Federal Government,"[13] it is obvious that further research, if it is to succeed in clarifying the interrelationships between recycled and virgin ferrous materials in the steelmaking cycle, must be couched in more comprehensive terms of the sort outlined above.

NATIONALLY ESTABLISHED INDUSTRIAL RESIDUALS
DISCHARGE GUIDELINES

Under the Federal Water Pollution Control Act Amendments of 1972,[14] the Administrator of the Environmental Protection Agency is required to publish effluent limitations guidelines for use in the formulation of permit effluent limitations restricting the discharge of residuals from industrial and other point sources. The actual effluent limitations (as opposed to effluent limitations guidelines) are established by state or EPA regional officials in connection with the discharge permit program set up by the act.[15] Although the act contains provisions for the imposition of effluent restrictions designed to implement applicable water quality standards, the above-mentioned effluent limitations are related solely to technology. In this regard, the act sets two deadlines for achievement of effluent limitations. By July 1, 1977, industrial sources must achieve effluent limitations which require the application of the "best practicable control technology currently available" (BPCTCA), and by July 1, 1983, they must achieve effluent limitations which require the application of the "best available technology economically achievable" (BATEA).

For the steel industry, EPA has developed its proposed guidelines through privately contracted studies and consultation with industry

---

Hon. Martha W. Griffiths, "Legislation Introduced to Amend Internal Revenue Code to Provide Federal Tax Incentives to Utilize More Recycled Solid Waste Material," *Congressional Record,* June 30, 1972, pp. E 6629–6630.

[13] Albrecht and McDermott, *Economic and Technological Impediments,* p. 6.

[14] See, U.S.C. §1151 *et seq.* as amended Oct. 18, 1972, Public Law No. 92-500, 86 Stat. 816.

[15] The act specifies that the discharge permit granting authority specify effluent limitations for point sources using the suggested guidelines as a bench mark, but the steel industry claims that, in practice, the guidelines proposed by EPA tend to "preempt the function of the permit granting authority by specifying effluent limits which are apparently to be mechanically applied on a nationwide basis." In their view "this egregious approach disregards the provision of section 301 and 304 of the Act and renders superfluous the permit system contemplated in section 402 of the Act." See "Comments of American Iron and Steel Institute on Environmental Protection Agency's Proposed Effluent Limitations Guidelines and Standards: Iron and Steel Point Source Category" (Washington, D.C.: AISI, April 5, 1974), pp. 18–19.

groups, but the process has not gone smoothly. On the contrary, guideline development has been marked by contentiousness. Industry spokesmen have challenged the standards suggested to EPA by its engineering consultant, the NUS Corporation, while EPA, after several unsuccessful informal attempts to elicit information has resorted to formal orders requiring Bethlehem and U.S. Steel to cooperate in the provision of information to help the agency develop its water discharge standards.[16]

It would be naive to expect anything other than an adversary relationship between EPA and the steel industry, especially since the latter could most charitably be described as taciturn when it comes to the release of useful information. However, much of the fault lies with the law itself, which, as written, is clumsy.[17] Unfortunately, the appearance of precision in the guidelines themselves is misleading; they are structured in such a way that any number of daily discharge levels for the mill can result from them. In addition, industry spokesmen have expressed concern over the availability of the suggested technologies and their ability to satisfy the numerical discharge limits.[18]

The first of these problems arises because the guidelines are set by subprocess. That is, each production segment in the steel production chain is allocated its own set of BPCTCA and BATEA guidelines (expressed per unit of intermediate output) for the set of residuals discharged by the mill. For example, the coke plant is allowed to discharge x pounds of suspended solids per ton of coke produced, the sintering plant y pounds per ton of sinter, the blast furnace z pounds per ton of molten iron, and so on.[19]

This technique implies that the final permitted discharges for a specific plant will vary depending on the particular set of assumptions about relative input prices, etc. used in determining the mill configuration, and thus the level of production of coke sinter, and so on. Table 12.1 shows what this means at two plant types, the BOF and OH,

[16] For the industry viewpoint, see "Cleanup Down by the Old Mill Stream," *Environmental Science and Technology*, vol. 8 (April 1974), pp. 314–315; "Seeking Practical Environmental Guidelines," *Steel Facts* (Fall 1973), p. 10; and "Comments of American Iron and Steel Institute." The EPA orders to U.S. Steel and Bethlehem Steel are reported in *Air and Water News* vol. 8, no. 19 (May 13, 1974), p. 4.

[17] Discussions with John Hansen, Visiting Scholar at Resources for the Future 1973–1974.

[18] "Comments of American Iron and Steel Institute," p. 7.

[19] The alternate FWPCA approach calls for states to identify those of their waters for which the above BPCTCA effluent limitations are not stringent enough to implement applicable water quality standards. After identifying these waters, the states are directed to calculate and establish "total maximum daily loads" for those pollutants which cause the violation of the applicable ambient standards. It would appear that allocations of these loads are to be made in the form of more stringent limitations imposed upon those who discharge into these "water quality segments." The lack of specificity in regard to methodology in formulating such allocations makes it difficult to envision how this alternative approach is to be implemented.

when an important indirect influence, the scrap price, changes. In the table, the EPA guidelines shown in column one (expressed in terms of subprocess output) have been multiplied by the daily subprocess operating levels calculated by the model for the open hearth and basic oxygen plants. The sum across each residual category provides the allowable daily millwide discharge of each type of residual under two sets of scrap price levels at each plant type.

From the table we see that the daily allowable residuals discharges at the open hearth plant increase by 23 to 33 percent when scrap prices are doubled above their bench mark levels, while discharges at the basic oxygen plant hardly react at all. So, although the EPA standards give the impression of precision, they are really very imprecise; there is no single way of translating them into allowable daily discharge levels by type of plant, or of calculating the percentage of residuals discharge reduction they imply. Since there are a number of indirect influences which can cause a reshuffling of intermediate input coefficients, as we have shown in chapter 10, and since the proper focus of concern is with aggregate millwide discharge levels per unit time designed to reach a particular ambient standard, the existing legislation and the resulting EPA standards can be said to be badly conceived.

There are at least three problems with the EPA standards other than their imprecision which, when added to these, make the standards seem particulary wrongheaded. First, the standards, being set on a national basis, pay no attention to plant location. As we have already seen in the preceding chapter, locational factors are relevant in the minimum cost attainment of a targeted level of ambient quality. Second, even if we have, say, two or more steel plants adjacent to each other and discharging into the same river reach so that location becomes unimportant, the discharge levels allowed the plants under the EPA guidelines will not in any way reflect the cost-minimizing allocation of discharges among them, as long as the plants have different marginal removal cost schedules. On the contrary, the allowable millwide discharges in the EPA system depend only upon the sum of the subprocess guidelines for a particular residual multiplied by its intermediate output coefficient, as shown in table 12.1. Therefore, there is no guarantee that one plant, in meeting the EPA guidelines on a particular residual, will necessarily be incurring the same marginal removal cost as its neighbors. In this event, discharge restrictions on the lower cost dischargers could be tightened simultaneously with the relaxation of restrictions on the higher cost dischargers until marginal removal costs are equalized, and total removal costs minimized. Finally, the guidelines share a deficiency with our linear programming model; they do not take scale economies in treatment equipment costs into consideration. Hence,

TABLE 12.1 *The Effect of the Scrap Price Level on Daily Plant Discharges Allowed at Two Plant Types by the Proposed EPA BPCTCA Effluent Guidelines*

Mill characteristics and residual	EPA 30-day average BPCTCA guidelines[a]	Open hearth plant daily discharges		Basic oxygen plant daily discharges	
		With basic scrap prices	With doubled scrap prices	With basic scrap prices	With doubled scrap prices
Mill characteristics					
Ton coke per day		1150	1420	1660	1690
Ton sinter per day		1350	2340	3110	3160
Ton molten iron per day		1450	1810	2120	2160
Ton molten steel per day		2770	2770	2770	2770
Watercourse residuals discharges allowed					
Five-day BOD from coke plant	0.219 lb. per ton coke	251	312	363	369
Total five-day BOD		251	312	363	369
Oil from					
coke plant	0.0218 lb. per ton coke	25	31	36	37
sintering	0.0042 lb. per ton sinter	6	10	13	13
Total oil		31	41	49	50
Phenol from					
coke plant	0.003 lb. per ton coke	3	4	5	5
blast furnace	0.0042 lb. per ton iron	6	8	9	9
Total phenols		9	12	14	14

Cyanide from					
coke plant	0.0438 lb. per ton coke	50	62	73	74
blast furnace	0.0156 lb. per ton iron	23	28	33	34
Total cyanide		73	90	106	108
Ammonia from					
coke plant	0.1824 lb. per ton coke	209	260	303	308
blast furnace	0.1302 lb. per ton iron	189	236	276	281
Total ammonia		398	496	579	589
Suspended solids from					
coke plant	0.073 lb. per ton coke	84	104	121	123
sintering	0.0208 lb. per ton sinter	28	49	65	66
blast furnace	0.052 lb. per ton iron	76	94	110	112
OH furnace	0.0208 lb. per ton steel	58	58	n.a.	n.a.
BOF furnace	0 discharge	n.a.	n.a.	0	0
Total suspended solids		246	305	296	301

Note: n.a. indicates not applicable.

a Coverage in the proposed guidelines is limited to the extent that heat discharge limitations are not specified, and no limitations are currently available for the conventional rolling and finishing process subcategory. 30-day Average Guidelines are defined as the maximum average of daily discharge values for any period of 30 consecutive days. See *Federal Register*, Feb. 19, 1974: pp. 6485–6505.

they penalize small plants which have technologies identical to large plants, since the larger plant's discharge guideline is a linear transformation of the small plant's, while its residual reduction costs are not.

The Costs of Attainment

Given the fact that the water-course discharge guidelines and the atmospheric performance standards will be with us for a while, an obvious question is how much it will cost the steel industry to meet them. To date, a number of studies have been undertaken to analyze the economic impact of either one or both of these media standards on the steel industry.[20] Not surprisingly, a wide range of opinion exists about the expected costs of meeting the 1977 and 1983 water standards, as well as the air pollution standards. For example, in the Kearney report we find a low cost calculated from the Cyrus Rice data of $0.88 per ton of finished steel required at existing mills to meet the 1983 watercourse discharge guidelines. Costs calculated by Kearney on a similar basis but from industry data are $4.16 per ton of finished steel above the low estimate.[21] Further, in order to satisfy both the 1983 watercourse discharge guidelines and the atmospheric discharge performance standards, Kearney reports that existing mills may incur costs between a low of $14.91 per ton of finished steel, and a high of $26.62.[22] Much of this disagreement

[20] (1) *Development Document for Effluent Limitations Guidelines and New Source Performance Standards: Iron and Steel Industry*, a draft report by the Cyrus William Rice Division, NUS Corporation for the U.S. Environmental Protection Agency (Washington, D.C., June 1973); (2) *A Study on the Economic Impact on the Steel Industry of the Costs of Meeting Federal Air and Water Pollution Abatement Requirements*, 3 vols. (Springfield, Va.: NTIS, July 27, 1972, PB 211-917, 211-918, 211-919); (3) James S. Cannon, ed., *Environmental Steel* (New York: The Council on Economic Priorities, 1973); (4) Kaoni Takahashi, "The Economic Impact of Water Pollution Abatement: The Blast Furnaces and Steel Mills Industry" SIC 3312, June 20, 1974, The Conference Board, New York City. A study which briefly summarizes the estimates of some of its predecessors is *Economic Analysis of the Proposed Effluent Guidelines for the Integrated Iron and Steel Industry*, a report by the A. T. Kearney Co., Inc., for the Office of Planning and Evaluation, U.S. Environmental Protection Agency EPA-230/1-73-027 (Washington, D.C., Feb. 1974).

[21] A. T. Kearney Co., *Economic Analysis*, p. VI-3.

[22] Ibid., Exhibit VI-4. The cost-calculating methodology in the Kearney report (and in many of the other studies as well) is ill-defined and poorly conceived. For example, although no procedural notes are attached to Exhibit VI-4, it appears that the authors arrived at their cost estimates in the following manner: (1) Estimate total capital costs incurred over the period (1973–83) for air and water pollution control. (2) Multiply total capital costs by 0.33 to determine "annual operating cost." (3) Divide "annual operating cost" by a typical expected annual steel production level to get operating cost per ton of finished steel.

It is hard to have much confidence in the resulting cost estimates, not only because of the disparity between the "low" and "high" capital requirements, but also because the 0.33 rule of thumb may not provide a close approximation of the discounted capital and variable costs incurred to meet the standards. The Kearney

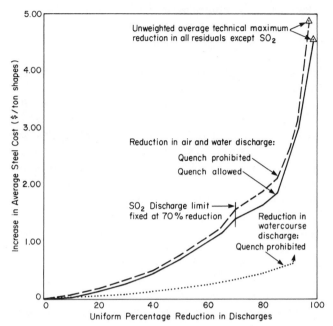

Figure 12.3. The cost of uniform reduction in discharges below the bench mark at the BOF plant.

has probably arisen because there is no consensus of opinion as to what the standards actually imply, beyond the suggested installation of various types of treatment equipment. In fact, the cost-estimating studies are even more vague about the goal which is to be reached than the original NUS document which outlined the tentative subprocess discharge restrictions for EPA.

In light of the *a priori* faults of the federal standards mentioned above, as well as the absence of any standards applicable to the conventional finishing section of the mill,[23] it would be senseless to plunge into the cost estimation debate with the linear model. What we can do is show the effect that uniform percentage reductions in discharges below the bench mark would have on average steel costs. Figure 12.3 shows average cost increases occasioned at the BOF plant by uniform percentage reductions in (1) water-course discharges when quenching is prohibited, (2) atmospheric discharges and water-course discharges when quenching

---

authors are not alone in their use of such shortcut methods. This lack of uniformity in methodology across the cost estimating studies, coupled with the wide range of opinion about costs, almost guarantees confusion and disagreement.

[23] Development of final rolling and finishing standards is underway at EPA, but they were not published at the time of this writing.

is prohibited, and (3) atmospheric discharges and water-course discharges when quenching is subject to the corrosion cost penalty but not prohibited.[24]

The cost-of-uniform-reduction schedules under simultaneous air and water side reductions display a distinct break at the 70 percent level. This break is an artifact of our procedure because, since it is technically infeasible to reduce sulfur dioxide discharge much below the 70 percent level, we have adopted the convention of holding it there as we pass to higher levels for the rest of the residuals. The principal lesson of the schedules is that reductions in both atmospheric and water-course discharges appear to involve costs about 300 percent above reductions in water-course discharges alone over most of the reduction range.[25] This confirms our earlier observation in chapter 11 that the achievement of low discharge levels of atmospheric residuals will tend to cause greater absolute average steel cost increases than the achievement of low discharge levels for most waterborne residuals. Further, percentage steel cost increases associated with the maximum possible air and water discharge reductions at our BOF plant (shown in table 12.2) agree in a rough way with the conclusions reached in an independent 1973 British study.[26] There, after correcting for differences in base years, and numer-

[24] Solids are neglected in all of these parameterizations. The residuals whose discharges are uniformly reduced are BOD, oil, phenols, cyanide, ammonia, suspended solids, sulfide, heat, and where relevant, sulfur dioxide and particulates.

[25] This ceases to be true for watercourse discharge reductions beyond the 90 percent level because, to achieve the maximum technically possible watercourse discharge reduction, the model opts for a solution very similar to that associated with the maximum possible atmospheric *and* watercourse discharge reduction situation. (Specifically, the solution involves the introduction of pellet burdens at the blast furnace.)

[26] I. Codd "Pollution Control and the Iron and Steel Industry," Paper presented at the United Nations Industrial Development Organization's Third Interregional Symposium on the Iron and Steel Industry, Brazilia, Brazil, October 14–21, 1973 (Mimeographed, ID/WG.146/114), p. 41.

Codd's cost figures are in 1973 dollars per long ton of finished product, while ours are in 1968 dollars per short ton of semifinished shapes. The correction factor we use is based on 30 percent inflation over that period and a yield of 87 percent in going from semifinished shape to finished product. In addition, it should be noted that the plant configuration assumed by Codd differs from ours to some extent; and that he makes no attempt to precisely quantify the percentage discharge reductions achieved by his postulated mix of pollution control devices. However, Codd's tables 1 and 2 (pp. 46–47) indicate that recovery levels generally above 90 percent are expected. This latter uncertainty is very likely to outweigh the other problems of comparability because as our figure 12.3 shows, the cost curve is nearly vertical in the region of interest, above 90 percent.

A newer version of the model, reporting costs in 1973 dollars and reflecting some additional operating options and some revisions of specific cost and input estimates is described in Clifford S. Russell, William J. Vaughan, and Harold C. Cochrane, "Government Policies and the Adoption of Innovations in the Integrated Iron and Steel Industry," a report to the National Science Foundation under grant number DA-43748, in preparation at Resources for the Future.

TABLE 12.2 *Maximum Possible Discharge Reductions from the Bench Mark at the BOF Plant in Three Situations*

Costs and residuals	Case I: water only (quenching prohibited)	Case II: air and water (quenching prohibited)	Case III: air and water (quenching allowed)
Total daily cost ($)	177,900	181,500	180,670
Average steel cost ($ per ton shape)	76.0	77.60	77.20
Increase in total daily cost from base ($)	7,800	11,360	10,520
Increase in average steel cost from base ($ per ton shape)	3.33	4.85	4.50
Percentage increase in cost from base	4.57	6.68	6.18
Residuals discharged[a]			
Waterborne			
Five-day BOD lb. per day	316	316	149
% decrease	97.7	97.7	98.9
Oil lb. per day	342	342	331
% decrease	95.5	95.5	95.7
Phenol lb. per day	10.4	10.4	9.2
% decrease	99.4	99.4	99.5
Cyanide lb. per day	3.7	3.7	0
% decrease	92.8	92.8	100
Ammonia lb. per day	52.7	52.7	0
% decrease	98.7	98.7	100
Suspended solids lb. per day	702	702	692
% decrease	94.2	94.2	94.3
Sulfide lb. per day	2.2	2.2	0
% decrease	99.7	99.7	100
Heat 10^6 Btu per day	0	0	0
% decrease	100	100	100
Airborne			
Sulfur dioxide[b] lb. per day	21000	8640	8640
% decrease	27.0	70.0	70.0
Particulates lb. per day	6490	1130	1120
% decrease	77.0	96.0	96.0

[a] Solids not included.
[b] Held at 70 percent in the simultaneous air and water discharge reduction cases.

aires, the cost of "pollution control" was calculated to be less than $3.75 per ton of semifinished shapes. This study concluded that "for an integrated steelworks of standard European design the cost of pollution control, to existing standards in most developed countries, is *very moderate* indeed. The total capital cost of good pollution control equipment is shown to be ~4.5% of the total plant capital cost." For the record, table 12.2 summarizes the cost and discharge data associated with the maximum reductions possible in the BOF version of the model. If the specifics of the federal regulations are ever fully sorted out, solutions of this sort would be helpful in predicting their cost impact.

USE OF THE MODEL IN POLICY FORMULATION: A CASE STUDY

Although the federal standards are too vague and the reported costs of their attainment too gross to warrant any comparison with the model, there are policy makers at various levels of government who are thinking about alternatives to the guidelines, and to illustrate how the model can be of use in such enterprises, we describe here how it has been used to estimate the reaction of a steel mill to effluent charges. Specifically the state of Maryland's Department of Natural Resources asked what the model could reveal about the likely response of the Bethlehem Steel Corporation's Sparrows Point plant to a trial set of effluent charges. The proposed charges were:

Residual	*Charge per Pound*
Waterborne	
BOD	$0.10
Suspended solids	0.06
Heat	0.03
Airborne	
Sulfur dioxide	0.05
Particulates	0.02

In order to tailor the model to represent the Sparrows Point plant, the following steps were taken on the basis of information supplied by the Maryland Environmental Service.

1. A combined basic oxygen–open hearth steel plant was constructed which produces about 90 percent of its raw steel output by the basic oxygen process.
2. The basic oxygen furnaces were equipped with a wet gas cleaning system which must be operated to remove at least 94 percent of particulates generated.
3. A coke oven gas desulfurizing unit was assumed to be in place though it was not being operated. (We saw in chapter 10 that these units are unprofitable given current market prices for sulfur and sulfuric acid.)
4. Scrap prices were doubled from their 1968 levels to reflect the currently high cost of scrap relative to blast furnace iron. All other

input prices and equipment operating and capital costs remain in 1968 dollars.

These adjustments were undertaken to reflect the equipment configuration at Sparrows Point in a rough way, but the Environmental Service was cautioned that the model should not be regarded as a perfect proxy for the Sparrows Point plant for two reasons.

1. The model's coverage of steel rolling and finishing is much less sophisticated than the actual rolling and finishing network at Sparrows Point. We make no provision for electro-zinc plating, electrolytic tin plating, hot-dipped tin plating and wire drawing, which are all processes used at Sparrows Point.
2. Our plant, including its waste treatment facilities, is scaled for capital cost estimating purposes to a much lower operating level than the actual level existing at Sparrows Point. Therefore, where scale economies in treatment equipment capital and operating costs exist, the model is likely to underestimate the level of removal achieved in response to effluent charges.

As a final caveat, we emphasized that the linear programming model is constructed to satisfy a cost minimization criterion, which means that the level of final product output must be specified as an intial condition. Because the level of final output is not a variable, the model cannot represent potential responses to effluent charges which involve the adjustment of final output levels. Further, as the reader knows, the model does not tell us what percentage of the increased costs due to effluent charges will be passed on to customers and what percentage will be borne by the producer, since no final product demand functions are specified.

In addition to the charge set suggested by the Maryland Environmental Service, the model was confronted with three other trial charge sets respectively 0.5, 1.5, and 2.0 times the suggested charges in order to supply broad response coverage.

Effluent Charges	*Charge Set 1*	*Charge Set 2*	*Charge Set 3*	*Charge Set 4*
BOD (cents/lb.)	5.0	10.0	15.0	20.0
Suspended solids (cents/lb.)	3.0	6.0	9.0	12.0
Heat (cents/10^6 Btu)	1.5	3.0	4.5	6.0
Sulfur dioxide (cents/lb.)	2.5	5.0	7.5	10.0
Particulates (cents/lb.)	1.0	2.0	3.0	4.0

These four distinct charge sets were applied in two situations: one in which the plant is free to route its contaminated coke plant liquors to the quenching station where they are evaporated, and one in which it is prohibited from doing so. In the first case, in response to effluent charges

TABLE 12.3   Reaction of the Sparrows Point Model to Four Effluent Charge Sets: Quenching with Raw Liquor Allowed

Response to charges	Charge set 1	Charge set 2 (MES)	Charge set 3	Charge set 4
Plant cost reaction—increases in:				
Total out-of-pocket cost from base of which:[a]	0.64	1.11	1.46	1.74
Total resource cost[b] ($ per ingot ton steel)	$\left\{0.14\right.$	$\left\{0.19\right.$	$\left\{0.61\right.$	$\left\{0.64\right.$
Total effluent tax payment ($ per ingot ton steel)	$\left.0.50\right\}$	$\left.0.92\right\}$	$\left.0.85\right\}$	$\left.1.10\right\}$
Total out-of-pocket cost from base (%)	0.99	1.72	2.24	2.68
Total resource cost from base (%)	0.23	0.30	0.93	0.97
Plant discharge reaction percentage changes				
Watercourse discharges from base				
BOD	−73	−82	−82	−85
Oil	−36	−62	−62	−83
Phenols	−100	−100	−100	−100
Ammonia	−100	−100	−100	−100
Suspended solids	−67	−75	−75	−75
Heat	−45	−45	−46	−46
Atmospheric discharges from base				
Sulfur dioxide	−12	−12	−66	−66
Particulates	−14	−14	−43	−43
Phenol and other vapors[c]	+	+	+	+
Water withdrawals from base				
Water for all uses	−33	−35	−36	−36

[a] The increase in the total out-of-pocket cost above the unpenalized (no charges) solution represents the sum of the additional variable and discounted capital costs occasioned by the charges plus the total tax payment (i.e., the charge on each residual multiplied by its discharge level).

[b] The increase in the total daily resource cost is equal to the increase in variable and discounted capital costs above the (essentially variable) production cost of the "no charges" situation.

[c] A positive increase in gaseous ammonia, phenol, hydrocarbons, sulfur, and cyanide emissions is expected, but is not quantified here.

the plant can reduce water-course BOD, oil, ammonia, phenol, and cyanide discharges by transforming these residuals into atmospheric discharges. It bears an internal corrosion cost penalty (specified in the model) while the public at large suffers some (unknown) damages from the vaporized equivalents of the former water-course discharges. Whether or not there is a net reduction in damages in this instance depends on the respective magnitudes of the damages incurred when the residuals show up in the air instead of the water. When quenching is prohibited, the plant cannot trade off reduced water-course discharges for increased atmospheric discharges of the relevant residuals. Instead, by-product recovery and/or liquid waste treatment equipment must be built in response to effluent charges to reduce water-course BOD, oil, phenol, and ammonia discharges at the coke plant without increasing the discharges of their vaporized equivalents. This distinction, we reiterate, is vital to a proper understanding of the steel mill residuals management problem.

Table 12.3 details the difference in costs and discharges between the no-charges situation and each of the four trial charge sets when quenching is allowed. Notice that water-course discharges of phenol and ammonia can be completely eliminated at the expense of an increase in atmospheric discharges of their gaseous equivalents. Further, notice that because more than one residual is generally present in a waste liquor stream, an effluent charge on one residual, say BOD, brings about a net reduction in the water-course discharges of the other residuals. Finally, the charge set suggested by the Maryland Environmental Service appears likely to bring about large percentage reductions in water-course discharges, but only minor percentage reductions in sulfur dioxide and particulate discharges. It appears that in order to get large reductions on both the air and water sides, the atmospheric charges of set 3 would have to be combined with the water-course charges of set 2.

The increase in total out-of-pocket cost shown in table 12.3 above the initial no charges situation for any charge set is composed of two parts: the increase in resource costs associated with input mix alterations, changes in production process, introduction of waste treatment, and the tax payment the producer must make.

In comparison with table 12.3, table 12.4 shows that when quenching is not allowed, lower percentage reductions in water-course discharges (except heat) are associated with each charge set, while total out-of-pocket costs, in both absolute and percentage terms, are higher. Of course, balancing this is the fact that no increase in gaseous ammonia, phenol, sulfur, and cyanide emissions from the quenching station is observed. It still holds true that the Maryland Environmental Service charge set will not encourage significant percentage reductions in sulfur dioxide and particulates.

The percentage reductions shown in tables 12.3 and 12.4 were applied to the daily Sparrows Point discharge levels reported in *Environmental Steel* to give some idea of what the absolute daily discharge levels might be at Sparrows Point if charges were imposed. The results appear in table 12.5. Also shown is the expected level of tax revenue which would be forthcoming at the various charge levels, not an unimportant piece of information for both the regulatory authority and the taxpayer.

Although we have no way of knowing how accurate or helpful these results actually were, except for a gracious note of thanks from the Mary-

TABLE 12.4 *Reaction of the Sparrows Point Model to Four Effluent Charge Sets: Quenching with Raw Liquor Prohibited*

	Charge set 1	Charge set 2 (MES)	Charge set 3	Charge set 4
Plant cost reaction—increases in:				
Total out-of-pocket cost from base of which:[a]	0.68	1.25	1.62	1.92
Increase in total resource cost[b] ($ per ingot ton steel)	0.07	0.27	0.69	0.72
Total effluent tax payment ($ per ingot ton steel)	0.61	0.98	0.93	1.20
Total out-of-pocket cost from base (%)	1.05	1.93	2.49	2.96
Total resource cost from base (%)	0.11	0.42	1.06	1.10
Plant discharge reaction—changes in:				
Watercourse discharges from base				
BOD (%)	−30	−76	−73	−76
Oil (%)	−30	−62	−58	−79
Phenols (%)	0	−97	−94	−94
Ammonia (%)	0	−98	−93	−93
Suspended solids (%)	−65	−74	−75	−75
Heat (%)	−45	−45	−46	−46
Atmospheric discharges from base				
Sulfur dioxide (%)	−12	−6	−66	−66
Particulates (%)	−14	−14	−43	−43
Phenol and other vapors (%)	0	0	0	0
Water withdrawals from base (%)	−32	−35	−34	−34

[a] The increase in the total out-of-pocket cost above the unpenalized (no charges) solution represents the sum of the additional variable and discounted capital costs occasioned by the charges plus the total tax payment (that is, the charge on each residual multiplied by its discharge level).

[b] The increase in the total daily resource cost is equal to the increase in variable and discounted capital costs above the (essentially variable) production cost of the "no charges" situation.

land Environmental Service, their interest does confirm our belief that models of industrial residuals management can in general be useful in the formulation and implementation of environmental policies.

NEW DIRECTIONS

In this book we have described the characteristics and performance of a linear model designed to facilitate the study of some important questions concerning residuals management in the steel industry. A principal aim kept in mind in the construction of the model has been to permit the exploration of the effects of changes in relative prices, available tech-

TABLE 12.5 *Sparrows Point Daily Discharge Levels (Obtained by Applying the Model's Calculated Percentage Discharge Reductions at Four Effluent Charge Sets to Reported Discharges in the Absence of Charges)*

	CEP Data: No charges[a]	Charge set (Raw liquor quenching allowed)				Charge set (Raw liquor quenching prohibited)			
		1	2 (MES)	3	4	1	2 (MES)	3	4
Daily plant discharges									
Watercourse									
BOD (lb.)	128,706	34,800	23,200	23,200	19,300	90,100	30,900	34,800	30,900
Oil (lb.)	34,400	22,000	13,100	13,100	5,840	24,000	13,000	14,400	7,210
Phenols (lb.)	4,880	0	0	0	0	4,880	146	293	293
Ammonia (lb.)	16,500	0	0	0	0	16,500	329	1,150	1,150
Suspended solids (lb.)	184,000	60,800	46,000	46,000	46,000	64,400	47,900	46,000	46,000
Heat[b] (10^6 Btu)	37,300	20,500	20,500	20,100	20,100	20,500	20,500	20,100	20,100
Atmosphere									
Sulfur dioxide (lb.)	151,000	133,000	133,000	51,400	51,400	133,000	142,000	51,400	51,400
Particulates (lb.)	168,000	144,000	144,000	95,700	95,700	144,000	144,000	95,700	95,700
Phenol and other vapors (lb.)	n.a.	+	+	+	+	0	0	0	0
Water use (10^6 gallons per day)	689	461	448	441	441	468	448	454	454
Approximate daily tax revenue ($)[c]	0	8,640	15,200	15,200	19,600	11,500	16,600	17,000	21,900

[a] Discharge levels obtained from James S. Cannon, ed., *Environmental Steel.*

[b] Average of winter and summer for CEP data (assumes a 4.5° F rise).

[c] Calculated by summing each discharge times its effluent charge,

$$T = \sum_{i=1}^{5} D_i e_i$$

where T = total tax payment at a given charge set, D_i = discharge of residual i, e_i = effluent charge on residual i. The discharge of residual i was calculated from the percentage reductions predicted by the model (tables 12.3 and 12.4) and the CEP data on Sparrows Point's existing effluents.

nology and other influences seemingly unrelated to residuals management. Thus, the model is able to show us several facets of the complex set of issues that is the steel industry's residuals management problem. We have discovered that technological change is not necessarily the bogeyman some would have us believe, since continuous casting appears to be both more profitable for the steel firm and easier on the environment than the conventional process. But we also have found that the solution to one problem may imply greater difficulties elsewhere. For example, decreasing waterborne residuals discharges can imply increased discharges to the air (or land) unless by-product recovery is practiced.

The model as it now stands could surely be improved upon, not only in terms of the coefficients themselves, but in terms of coverage and structure as well. Specifically, the scope of the model could be extended to cover ore extraction and processing, raw material transportation, and other parts of the steel production network currently treated as exogenous. These improvements, although interesting for their own sake, would also widen the potential areas of application for the model. One of these has already been mentioned: the appraisal of the comparative economics of virgin versus recycled ferrous input consumption in the steel industry.

A second area, in which work is currently under way, is the investigation of the various influences upon the future pattern of technological change in the industry, especially government policies which either directly or indirectly influence the adoption of innovation.[27] It is to be hoped that estimates of the future alternative patterns for technological change in the steel industry can be made on the basis of characterizations of new technologies, alternative future relative input price movements, and postulated mixes of government policies, using a redesigned version of the model.

[27] Work on a project funded by the National Science Foundation entitled "Government Policies and the Adoption of Innovations in the Integrated Iron and Steel Industry," has been initiated at Resources for the Future, Inc. by the authors and Hal Cochrane of the Colorado State University Economics Department. (NSF Grant No. DA-43748.)

ABBREVIATIONS

acf	actual cubic feet
acfm	actual cubic feet per minute
AIME	American Institute of Mining, Metallurgical and Petroleum Engineers
AISI	American Iron and Steel Institute
BOF	basic oxygen furnace
BTX	benzene, toluene, and xylene
BATEA	Best Available Technology Economically Achievable
BDSA	Business and Defense Services Administration
BPCTCA	Best Practicable Control Technology Currently Available
Btu	British thermal unit
CQ	commercial quality steel
CCW	Cost of Clean Water
c.i.f.	cost, insurance, and freight
CEP	Council on Economic Priorities
DQ	drawing quality steel
EA	electric arc furnace
ESP	electrostatic precipitator
EPA	Environmental Protection Agency
FWPCA	Federal Water Pollution Control Act
f.o.b.	free on board
GNP	gross national product
HEW	Department of Health, Education and Welfare
ICC	Interstate Commerce Commission
MRI	Midwest Research Institute
NAS	The National Academy of Science
NAS–NAE	National Academy of Science–National Academy of Engineering

NAPCA   National Air Pollution Control Administration
NEPA   National Environmental Policy Act
NPDES   National Pollution Discharge Elimination System
NTIS   National Technical Information Service
OH   open hearth furnace
ppm   parts per million
RFF   Resources for the Future, Inc.
scf   standard cubic feet
S.D.   standard deviation

GLOSSARY OF STEEL-MAKING TERMS

acid   a compound capable of reacting with a base to form a salt.

acid pickling   the removal of scale (rust) from steel using an acid bath. This process produces a smooth surface on steel that is about to be rolled.

base   a compound capable of reacting with an acid to form a salt.

biochemical oxygen demand (BOD)   the weight of oxygen required to change a quantity of organic material to a stabilized (oxidized) form. That is, one pound of BOD is a quantity of organic material which would, under specified conditions of temperature and over a specified time, use up one pound of oxygen from water. The applicable time unit is usually included in the term; thus, five-day BOD is a measure of oxygen used up by oxidation over a five-day period.

blowdown   water which is removed from a recirculating system in order to control the buildup of dissolved and suspended solids.

breeze   coke fines.

burden   the raw materials blend put into a process unit. For example, the blast furnace burden is made up of coke, limestone, and iron-bearing material.

by-product   a product other than the intended product of a manufacturing process which has a price or internal value great enough to justify its recovery.

BTX   (benzene, toluene, and xylene) aromatic hydrocarbons.

carbon adsorption   a treatment method for removal of organic contaminants from wastewater by passing it through a bed of granulated carbon.

charge   see *burden.*

fines   particulate matter small enough to sift through screens used in the production process.

forerunnings   that proportion of crude light oil (2 percent by volume) that distills completely below 311° F in the light oil fractionation still, where progressive distillation separates it from the higher boiling-point compounds, benzene, toluene, and xylene. Forerunnings are composed principally of cyclopentadiene, carbon disulfide, and a mixture of olefin and paraffin hydrocarbons containing five or six carbon atoms.

galvanizing   the coating of steel with a thin film of another metal, usually of the zinc family, for protection against rust.

gangue   worthless rock or vein matter in which valuable metals or minerals occur. In iron ore, gangue consists mostly of silica and alumina, which can be removed from the ore in the blast furnace by use of a flux.

greenfield site   used to denote investment decisions where no equipment of any kind is already in place, i.e., where a new mill is to be planned and built from the ground up. Contrasts with *brownfield site,* which refers to decisions where some part of a mill already exists.

heat   a complete steelmaking cycle, involving the charging, meltdown, refining and tapping of the furnace.

light oil   a clear, yellow-brown oil with a specific gravity of about 0.88. It is a mixture of all those products of coal gas with boiling points ranging from 32° F to 390° F, containing well over 100 constituents. Most of these are present in such low concentrations that their recovery is seldom practicable. The principal usable constituents are benzene (60–85 percent), toluene (6–17 percent), xylene (1–7 percent), and solvent naphtha (0.5–3 percent).

metallurgical coal   low-ash, low-sulfur bituminous coal with a volatile matter content such that the coke made from it has the resistance to crushing required in the blast furnace burden.

mill scale   a coating of iron oxides which forms on the surface of steel that has been worked at temperatures exceeding 800° C.

no. 2 bundles   old black and galvanized steel sheet scrap, hydraulically compressed to charging box size and weighing not less than 75 pounds per cubic foot. May not include tin or lead-coated material or vitreous enameled material.

no. 1 heavy melting steel   wrought iron and/or steel scrap ¼ inch and over in thickness. Individual pieces not over 60 × 24 inches (charging box size) prepared in a manner to ensure compact charging.

no. 1 factory bundle   homogeneous new (prompt) scrap steel with no paint or nonferrous elements present, except those in solid solution in the steel. Factory bundles receive a premium price because they are low in contaminating elements.

phenols   refers both to a specific compound and to a class of similar compounds. Thus phenol has the formula C_6H_5OH and is a hydro-carbon compound with an attached OH radical. The phenols are similar compounds with different numbers of carbon and hydrogen atoms: the cresols (C_7H_7OH) and the xylenols (C_8H_9OH). Within each of these latter groups a number of different atomic arrangements are possible, hence the plural form of the names. Phenols may be toxic to aquatic life and impart an undesirable taste and odor to water even when present in very low concentrations.

practice   the kind and quantity of inputs used for any particular cycle in a given process unit. Thus, a "70–30 practice" indicates the proportions of iron and scrap charged in the chosen blast furnace.

quenching   cooling by direct contact with water, or in some cases, with raw ammonia liquor. The process is used to cool coke after it leaves the ovens in order to prevent it from burning up in the open air.

refractory   material used in the construction of the interior of a furnace, where it must withstand the effects of high temperature, chemical action, and mechanical strains without fusing, fracturing, or eroding excessively. Refractories are classified as acidic, basic, or neutral. The acid materials contain considerable proportions of silica and combine readily with basic oxides. Neutral refractories either lack basic or acidic properties (graphite), or have these properties in an equal balance (chromate). Basic refractories contain mostly lime or magnesia (dolomite).

residual   a process output, the price or internal value of which does not cover the variable costs of its recovery. The identity of the residuals from a particular process depends on relative prices and thus may change over time.

shop size   annual steelmaking capacity.

shredded scrap   homogeneous iron and steel scrap, shredded and magnetically separated, originating from automobiles, unprepared no. 1 and no. 2 steel, miscellaneous baling and sheet scrap.

spent acid   acid that has been used in pickling to the extent that reaction of acid and rust can no longer proceed at reasonable speed. When this condition is reached, there will still be free—that is, unreacted—acid present in the solution.

tailing   a residual product containing little or no useful mineral content, which results from ore-dressing operations designed to reduce the ratio of gangue to valuable mineral.

tarry matter   a by-product of high-temperature coal carbonization consisting of tar acids, neutral oils which are principally aromatic hydrocarbons, and a residual pitch.

thiophenes   a heterocyclic liquid from coal tar, which, along with carbon disulfide, accounts for most of the sulfur found in crude light oil. It can be removed from the oil by washing with sulfuric acid.

top gas   the mixture of gases at the top of the blast furnace.

wash oil   an absorbent oil used to recover light oil from coal gas. Wash oil must have a boiling point above 390° F, low viscosity, high stability, high absorptive capacity, and low specific gravity.

TABLE REFERENCES

American Iron and Steel Institute. Various years. *Annual Statistical Report*. Washington, D.C.: American Iron and Steel Institute.

American Iron Ore Association. 1969. *Iron Ore: 1969*. Cleveland: American Iron Ore Association.

Baldwin, E. H., and I. M. Mathieson. 1960. "Scottish Experience with Fluxed Sinter," *AIME Blast Furnace, Coke Oven and Raw Materials Conference Proceedings*, vol. 18. New York: American Institute of Mining, Metallurgical and Petroleum Engineers.

Barnes, T. M., Albert O. Hoffman, and H. W. Lownie, Jr., January 1970. *Evaluation of Process Alternatives to Improve Control of Air Pollution from Production of Coke*. Report by Battelle Memorial Institute to the U.S. Department of Health, Education and Welfare, National Air Pollution Control Administration, Division of Process Control Engineering. Springfield, Va.: National Technical Information Service PB 189 266.

Barnes, Thomas M., and H. W. Lownie, Jr. 1969. *A Cost Analysis of Air-Pollution Controls in the Integrated Iron and Steel Industry*. Report by Battelle Memorial Institute to the U.S. Department of Health, Education and Welfare, National Air Pollution Control Administration, Division of Economic Effects Research. Springfield, Va.: National Technical Information Service PB 184 576.

Battelle Memorial Institute. 1964. *Technical and Economic Analysis of the Impact of Recent Developments in Steelmaking Practices on the Supplying Industries*. Columbus, Ohio.

Beychock, Milton R. 1967. *Aqueous Wastes from Petroleum and Petrochemical Plants*. New York: John Wiley and Sons.

Black, J. H. 1960. "The Problem of Coke Oven Ammonia Recovery," *AIME Blast Furnace, Coke Oven and Raw Materials Conference Pro-*

ceedings, vol. 18. New York: American Institute of Mining, Metallurgical and Petroleum Engineers.

Blaskowski, H. J., and A. J. Sefick. 1967. "Economics of Gas Cooling and Gas Cleaning Systems Associated with the BOF Furnace," *Iron and Steel Engineer,* vol. 44.

Boylan, Myles G., Jr., "The Economics of Change in the Scale of Production in the U.S. Iron and Steel Industry from 1900 to 1970," Ph.D. dissertation, Case Western Reserve University, December 1973.

Bowman, Ray O. 1959. "Wilputte Centrifugal Extractor Phenol Plant," *AIME Blast Furnace, Coke Oven and Raw Materials Conference Proceedings,* vol. 17. New York: American Institute of Mining, Metallurgical and Petroleum Engineers.

Brough, John R., and Thomas F. Voges. 1970. "Water Supply and Wastewater Disposal for a Steel Mill," *Water and Wastes Engineering,* (January).

Cannon, James S., ed. 1973. *Environmental Steel.* New York: The Council on Economic Priorities.

Chemical Pricing Patterns. 3rd ed. 1971. New York: Schnell Publishing Co.

Cootner, Paul H., and George O. G. Löf. 1965. *Water Demand for Steam Electric Generation.* Baltimore: Johns Hopkins University Press for Resources for the Future.

Cousins, W. G., and A. B. Mindler. 1972. "Tertiary Treatment of Weak Ammonia Liquor," *Journal of the Water Pollution Control Federation,* vol. 44 (April).

Custer, C. C. 1964. "The Quality Aspects of a Cold Metal Practice *vs.* a Hot Metal Practice." Presented at the 47th National Open Hearth and Basic Oxygen Steel Conference. American Institute of Mining, Metallurgical and Petroleum Engineers.

Dancy, T. E., A. T. Sadler, and H. N. Lander. 1962. "Process Analysis of Blast Furnace Operation with Oxygen and Steam," *AIME Blast Furnace, Coke Oven and Raw Materials Conference Proceedings,* vol. 17. New York: American Institute of Mining, Metallurgical and Petroleum Engineers.

Dearden, John. 1962. *Iron and Steel Today.* 2nd ed. London: Oxford University Press.

Derge, Gerhard, ed. 1964. *Basic Open Hearth Steelmaking.* 3rd ed. New York: American Institute of Mining, Metallurgical and Petroleum Engineers.

Dittman, Frank W. 1965. "Oxygen Steelmaking Cost Comparison: Kaldo *vs.* L.D." *Journal of Metals,* vol. 17 (April).

Doi, Y., and K. Kasai. 1960. "The Making of Self Fluxing Sinter and the Blast Furnace Practice with its 100 Percent Sinter Burden," *AIME*

Blast Furnace, Coke Oven and Raw Materials Conference Proceedings, vol. 18. New York: American Institute of Mining, Metallurgical and Petroleum Engineers.

R. L. Duprey. 1968. *Compilation of Air Pollution Emission Factors.* A report for the U.S. Department of Health, Education and Welfare, Public Health Service, Consumer Protection and Environmental Health Service, National Air Pollution Control Administration. Springfield, Va.: National Technical Information Service PB 190 245.

Elliot, A. C., and A. J. Lafreniere. 1963. "Solvent Extraction of Phenolic Compounds from Weak Ammonia Liquor," *Industrial Water Wastes,* vol. 8 (Sept.–Oct.).

Federal Register. February 19, 1974.

―――. June 28, 1974.

Fisher, C. W., B. D. Hepner, and G. B. Tallon. 1970. "Coke Plant Effluent Treatment Investigations," *Blast Furnace and Steel Plant,* vol. 58 (May).

Fogleman, E. L., D. O. Gloven, and H. B. Jensen. 1970. "Operational and Economic Aspects of Prereduced Iron Usage in Electric Arc Furnaces," *Blast Furnace and Steel Plant,* vol. 58 (October).

Graff, Howard M., and Sidney C. Bouwer. 1965. "Economics of Raw Materials Preparation for the Blast Furnace," *Journal of Metals,* vol. 17 (April).

Griffen, John. 1956. "The New High-Grade Iron Ores and Agglomerates and Their Effects on Coke Rates," *AIME Blast Furnace, Coke Oven and Raw Materials Conference Proceedings,* vol. 15. New York: American Institute of Mining, Metallurgical and Petroleum Engineers.

Gurnham, C. Fred. 1965. *Industrial Waste-Water Control.* Vol. 2 in the Massachusetts Institute of Technology Chemical Technology Monograph Series. New York: Academic Press.

Henschen, H. C. 1968. "Wet *vs.* Dry Cleaning in the Steel Industry," *Journal of the Air Pollution Control Association,* vol. 18 (May).

Hill, J. B. and H. Epstein. 1959. "Blast Furnace Results with Pellet and Sinter Burdens," *AIME Blast Furnace, Coke Oven and Raw Materials Conference Proceedings,* vol. 18. New York: American Institute of Mining, Metallurgical and Petroleum Engineers.

Hoff, H. 1961. "Fundamentals of the Treatment of Brown Fumes from the Basic Oxygen Process," *Stahl und Eisen,* vol. 81 (September). Trans. by Henry Brutcher, No. 5159. Altadena, Calif.: Henry Brutcher Technical Translations.

Holowatty, M. O., R. J. Wilson, and A. M. Schwarz. 1963. "Performance Evaluation of a Blast Furnace Burdened with Sized Ore, Sinter and Pellets," *AIME National Open Hearth Committee Proceedings,* vol.

22. New York: American Institute of Mining, Metallurgical and Petroleum Engineers.

Joyce, D., W. P. Dowhaniuk, and B. Marsden. 1956. "Operating Experiences with High Beneficiated Burdens," *AIME Blast Furnace, Coke Oven and Raw Materials Conference Proceedings,* vol. 15. New York: American Institute of Mining, Metallurgical and Petroleum Engineers.

Kik, Frank R. 1960. "Blast Furnace Sinter Related to Burdening and Charging," *AIME Blast Furnace, Coke Oven and Raw Materials Conference Proceedings,* vol. 18. New York: American Institute of Mining, Metallurgical and Petroleum Engineers.

Klein, E. 1958. "Sintering of High Grade Hematite Ore with Special Reference to Time Additions and Reducibility," *AIME Blast Furnace, Coke Oven and Raw Materials Conference Proceedings,* vol. 18. New York: American Institute of Mining, Metallurgical and Petroleum Engineers.

Lowry, H. H. 1963. *Chemistry of Coal Utilization.* New York: John Wiley and Sons.

Maggio, Ralph Anthony. 1966. "A Simulation Model for Open Hearth Steelmaking." Ph.D. dissertation, Ohio State University.

McGannon, Harold E., ed. 1964. *The Making, Shaping and Treating of Steel,* 8th ed. Pittsburgh: United States Steel Corporation.

Nelson, Francis D. 1962. "Relative Economics of Utilizing Roof Lance Oxygen in Open Hearth Furnaces," *AIME Open Hearth Furnace Conference Proceedings,* vol. 45. New York: American Institute of Mining, Metallurgical and Petroleum Engineers.

Nelson, W. L. 1970. *Guide to Refinery Operating Costs.* Tulsa, Okla.: The Petroleum Publishing Company.

Nemerow, Nelson Leonard. 1963. *Theories and Practices of Industrial Waste Treatment.* Reading, Mass.: Addison-Wesley.

Nitchie, C. M. 1964. "Improvements in Blast Furnace Operation," *Iron and Steel Engineer,* vol. 41 (January).

Ohio River Valley Water Sanitation Commission, Steel Industry Action Committee. 1953. *Reducing Phenol Wastes from Coke Plants.* Cincinnati.

———. 1958. *Dust Recovery Practice at Blast Furnaces.* Cincinnati.

Ozolins, Guntis, and Raymond Smith. 1966. *A Rapid Survey Technique for Estimating Community Air Pollution Emissions.* A report to the U.S. Department of Health, Education and Welfare, Division of Air Pollution. Public Health Service Publication No. 999-AP-29. Cincinnati, Ohio.

Patterson, J. W., and R. A. Minear. *Wastewater Treatment Technology.* Report prepared by the Illinois Institute of Technology for the State of Illinois Institute for Environmental Quality. Springfield, Va.: National Technical Information Service PB 204 521.

Pinchbeck, P. H., E. W. Nixon, and C. Riley. 1966. "The Role of Sulfur in Carbonizing and Ironmaking," in *Le Coke en Sidérurgie*. Charleroi, Belgium: European Iron and Steel Community.

Regan, W. J., R. W. James, and T. J. McLeer. 1972. *Identification of Opportunities for Increased Recycling of Ferrous Solid Waste*. Report by the Institute of Scrap Iron and Steel to U.S. Environmental Protection Agency, Office of Solid Waste Management. Springfield, Va.: National Technical Information Service, PB 213 577.

Rowe, A. D., H. K. Jaworski, and B. A. Bassett. 1970. "Waste Gas Cleaning Systems for Large Capacity Basic Oxygen Furnaces," *Iron and Steel Engineer*, vol. 47 (January).

Russell, Clifford S. 1973. *Residuals Management in Industry: A Case Study of Petroleum Refining*. Baltimore: Johns Hopkins University Press for Resources for the Future.

Sawyer, James W., Jr. 1974. *Automotive Scrap Recycling: Processes, Prices and Prospects*. Baltimore: Johns Hopkins University Press for Resources for the Future.

Silver, J., P. J. Koros, and R. L. Schoenberger. 1970. "The Effect of Use of Bundled Auto Scrap on Sheet Steel Quality," *Facts,* 31st ed. Washington, D.C.: Institute of Scrap Iron and Steel.

Speer, Edgar B. 1962. "The Changing Open Hearth." *Iron and Steel Engineer,* vol. 39 (March).

Spofford, Walter O., Jr. 1971. "Solid Residuals Management: Some Economic Considerations." Resources for the Future Reprint No. 98. Washington, D.C.: Resources for the Future.

Stapleton, J. M., N. W. Lindbloom, and D. H. Regilin. 1959. "Ironmaking—Past Achievements, Present Limitations and Future Prospects," *AIME Blast Furnace, Coke Oven and Raw Materials Conference Proceedings,* vol. 17. New York: American Institute of Mining, Metallurgical and Petroleum Engineers.

Steel. December 30, 1968.

Strassberger, J. H. 1958. "Experience at Wierton," *AIME Blast Furnace, Coke Oven and Raw Materials Conference Proceedings,* vol. 17. New York: American Institute of Mining, Metallurgical and Petroleum Engineers.

Trozzo, Charles L. 1966. "The Technical Efficiency of the Location of Integrated Blast Furnace Capacity." Ph.D. dissertation, Harvard University.

University of Minnesota Bulletin: Mining Directory Issue. 1968. Minneapolis, Minnesota.

United Nations, Economic Commission for Europe. 1962. *Comparison of Steelmaking Processes.* ST/ECE/STEEL/14.

———. 1966. *Economic Aspects of Iron Ore Preparation.* ST/ECE/STEEL/14.

———. 1968. *Air Pollution by Coking Plants.* ST/ECE/COAL/26.

U.S. Department of Commerce, Business and Defense Services Administration. 1966. *Iron and Steel Scrap Consumption Problems.* Washington, D.C.: Government Printing Office.

U.S. Department of Health, Education and Welfare, Public Health Service, Division of Air Pollution. 1969. *Mineral Industry Surveys: Coke and Coal Chemicals.* Washington, D.C.

———. Various years. *Minerals Yearbook.*

U.S. Department of the Interior, Federal Water Pollution Control Administration. 1967. *The Cost of Clean Water,* vol. 3: *Industrial Waste Profile No. 1: Blast Furnace and Steel Mills.* Washington, D.C.: Government Printing Office.

Uys, J. M., and J. W. Kirkpatrick. 1963. "The Beneficiation of Raw Materials in the Steel Industry and its Effect on Air Pollution Control," *Journal of the Air Pollution Control Association,* vol. 13 (January).

Varga, J., Jr., and H. W. Lownie, Jr. 1969. *A Systems Analysis Study of the Integrated Iron and Steel Industry.* Report by Battelle Memorial Institute to U.S. Department of Health, Education and Welfare, National Air Pollution Control Administration, Division of Process Control Engineering. Springfield, Va.: National Technical Information Service, PB 184 577.

Vaughan, William J. 1975. "A Residuals Management Model of the Iron and Steel Industry: A Linear Programming Approach." Ph.D. dissertation, Georgetown University.

Wagener, Deitrich. 1968. "Development Trends in European Coke Plant Techniques," *Blast Furnace and Steel Plant,* vol. 56 (October).

Waverman, Leonard. 1973. "Remarks on a Continental Gas Model," in *Energy Modeling,* Milton Searl, ed. Baltimore.: Johns Hopkins University Press for Resources for the Future.

Wilson, Phillip J., Jr. and Joseph H. Wells. 1950. *Coal, Coke and Coal Chemicals.* New York: McGraw-Hill.

Wilson, R. J. 1958. "Blast Furnace Operation with Humidified Blast," *AIME Blast Furnace Proceedings,* vol. 17.

Woods, A. P. and C. R. Taylor. 1946. "A Statistical Method and Results of a Study of Factors Affecting Open Hearth Production Rate," *Blast Furnace and Steel Plant,* vol. 34 (July).

INDEX

Abe, Masatoshi A., 8n

Acids: oil treatment with, 45–46; for pickling process, 140–141, 153–154

Acid sludge, 23, 37, 46; cost of neutralizing, 266–268

Ackerman, Susan Rose, 255n

Adams, W., 8n, 103n

Agarwal, J. C., 91n

Air dispersion model, 9

Air Quality Control Region, inventories, 5n

Alan Wood Steel, 6n

Albrecht, Oscar W., 290n

American Institute of Mining, Metallurgical and Petroleum Engineers, 96n

American Iron and Steel Institute, 154, 208

Ammonia discharges, 9, 19, 24; carbon treatment for, 57; cost of recovery, 246–248; liquor for quenching process, 43, 45; marginal removal cost, 263; recovery of, 36, 37, 38, 51–53; removal of, 36; still for, 51, 52; stripping of, 36, 53, 55

Anderson, David R., 170n

Andreev, V. P., 75n

Annealing, 143

Aquatic ecosystem model, 9

Armco Steel, 145n, 151n, 153n

Atmospheric discharges, 24; bench mark versus actual, 200–201, 202; from finishing process, 191; from ironmaking, 25–26; marginal removal cost for, 268–276; ore prices and, 240; pellet prices and, 222–223; from quenching, 43; from sintering, 24–25. *See also* Dust discharges; Gas; Gas cleaning system; Particulate discharges; Sulfur dioxide discharges

Automotive scrap, 106–107; backlog of, 284, 287; elasticity of demand for, 288–289; policies for increasing absorption rate of, 283, 289–291

Baker, E. C., 93n

Barker, John E., 272n

Barnard, P. G., 84n

Barnes, Thomas M., 8n, 41n, 100n, 129n, 170n, 195n, 231n

Barnhardt, T. F., 154n

Bashforth, George Reginald, 98, 109n

Basic oxygen furnace (BOF), 9; cost of reducing waterborne discharges from, 18–19; description of, 28, 110; dry system for cleaning, 121–122, 171–172; energy use, 13–14; increasing use of, 103; price of hot iron for, 17; residuals discharges, 18–19, 185, 188; response to ore prices,

319

Library of Congress Cataloging in Publication Data

Russell, Clifford S
  Steel production.

  Includes index.
  1. Steel-works—Waste disposal. 2. Steel-works—Environmen-
tal aspects. 3. Steel. I. Vaughan, William J., joint author.
II. Resources for the Future. III. Title.
TD899.S7R87   669'.142   75-36945
ISBN 0-8018-1824-9